D1476735

Confessions of Guilt

From Torture to *Miranda* and Beyond

GEORGE C. THOMAS III

RICHARD A. LEO

OXFORD
UNIVERSITY PRESS

OXFORD
UNIVERSITY PRESS

Oxford University Press, Inc., publishes works that further
Oxford University's objective of excellence
in research, scholarship, and education.

Oxford   New York
Auckland   Cape Town   Dar es Salaam   Hong Kong   Karachi
Kuala Lumpur   Madrid   Melbourne   Mexico City   Nairobi
New Delhi   Shanghai   Taipei   Toronto

With offices in
Argentina   Austria   Brazil   Chile   Czech Republic   France   Greece
Guatemala   Hungary   Italy   Japan   Poland   Portugal   Singapore
South Korea   Switzerland   Thailand   Turkey   Ukraine   Vietnam

Published by Oxford University Press, Inc.
198 Madison Avenue, New York, New York 10016

www.oup.com

Oxford is a registered trademark of Oxford University Press

Library of Congress Cataloging-in-Publication Data
Thomas, George C. (George Conner), 1947–
Confessions of guilt : from torture to Miranda and beyond / George C. Thomas III, Richard A. Leo.
    p.   cm.
Includes bibliographical references.
ISBN 978-0-19-533893-5 (hardcover : alk. paper) 1. Police questioning—History.
2. Confession (Law) 3. Torture. I. Leo, Richard A., 1963– II. Title.
HV8073.3.T46   2012
363.25′4—dc23   2012003725

1 3 5 7 9 8 6 4 2

Printed in the United States of America
on acid-free paper

To Yale Kamisar
For His Inspiration

CONTENTS

PREFACE

In the course of writing this book, we surveyed sources from many eras and in varied databases. Our methodology was, roughly, as follows. For the oldest sources, up to and including the Year Books and the Old Bailey records to the end of the seventeenth century, we tried to include or cite every relevant source that we uncovered. As the records became more plentiful, we included representative samples of the various approaches that we found. In America, cases are scarce until the late nineteenth century, and often the early American cases we included are the only ones of that type that we found. But the early American cases follow the English cases of the period so closely that we believe the American cases we present accurately describe the law of the time.

To minimize footnotes, we did not use multiple citations to the same work if it is easy to find the referenced page from an earlier citation in the same paragraph.

We owe debts to many. Though we will undoubtedly omit some, we would be remiss if we did not name the following: Paul Axel-Lute, Deputy Director & Collection Development Librarian, Rutgers University, Newark, Law Library, for invaluable help locating and understanding many exotic and esoteric documents; Karin Johnsrud, Head of Reference, Fordham Law School Library, for help locating nineteenth-century New York documents; Maureen Cahill, Student Services Librarian at the University of Georgia Law Library, for help researching the origin of an 1861 Georgia statute regulating interrogation; Paul Brand and David Seipp, for help with the Year Book documents; Fabio Arcila, Al Garcia, Adam Gershowitz, Mark Godsey, Peter Honigsberg, David Johnson, Greg Mark, Dan Medwed, Wes Oliver, John Parry, Larry Rosenthal, and Mark Weiner for helpful comments, Jared Eber, Monica Kaul, Rachel Gruenstein, Dan LeCours, and Henry Snee, for research help; and Bill Hilger and Mary Ann Moore for technical help. We would also like to thank Martin Tulic for indexing this book, India Gray for copy-editing and James Cook of Oxford University Press for his editorial guidance throughout the project.

We thank four reviewers appointed by the publisher—Donald Dripps, Mike Seidman, Andrew Taslitz, and an anonymous reviewer—for penetrating and extremely helpful comments. Finally, we thank three scholars and friends who blazed trails for us. Wes Oliver wrote extensively about a New York statute codified in 1829 that is crucial to our argument in chapter 4; while we ultimately disagree with the conclusion that he draws, his analysis helped sharpen ours. Bruce Smith alerted us to possibility that the English Indictable Offences Act of 1848 had the effect of facilitating the introduction of statements made to magistrates as well as informing the accused that he had a right not to answer the magistrate's questions.

And a special thanks to our friend and mentor, Yale Kamisar. He blazed trails for those of us who have sought to understand police interrogation and the law of confessions. No one has been as influential or as wise.

Confessions of Guilt

CHAPTER 1

Introduction

Consider two interrogations separated by the Atlantic Ocean and 170 years. As described by the London *Times*, an English magistrate in 1832 examined a prisoner suspected of a "horrid" murder.[1] Though not yet required by law, the magistrate's clerk warned the prisoner "that he was not bound to say anything to criminate himself." He was also cautioned that anything he had to say "would be taken down in writing, and, if necessary, produced as evidence on his trial." The clerk told the suspect that the magistrates were "ready to hear what he had to say" if "from any motive of unburdening his own conscience, or allaying the intense anxiety of the friends of the deceased, or from the desire of relieving those who might now be labouring under unjust accusation or suspicion."

In 2004, the *New York Times* described, in general terms, the interrogation of the so-called twentieth hijacker in the Guantánamo Bay prison camp.[2] Interrogators at the prison camp "received Pentagon approval to use special, harsher interrogation procedures" on Mohamed al-Kahtani. "A senior Pentagon civilian lawyer said there was 'some urgency' to increasing the pressure on this detainee because he likely 'had information that the people at Guantanamo believed was important, not just about perhaps 9/11, but about future events.'"

The 2004 story did not contain details of the "harsher interrogation procedures" because "they remained classified." A 2002 memo leaked to the press in 2006, however, said that the Justice Department had approved twenty interrogation practices that fell "just short of those that might cause pain comparable to 'organ failure, impairment of bodily function or even death.'"[3] Released by order of President Obama, the 2002 memo to the CIA approved interrogation methods such as cramped confinement, stress positions, sleep deprivation, water-boarding, and the use of insects to terrorize suspects.[4]

When using insects during interrogation, the interrogator tells the suspect that a stinging insect will be placed with him in a small closed box; instead, they put in the box a nonstinging insect, like a caterpillar.[5] The box is so small he is not able to use his hands to resist the insect as it crawls on his skin. Water-boarding, which has received more attention, is described as follows:

3

[T]he individual is bound securely to an inclined bench. . . . The individual's feet are generally elevated. A cloth is placed over the forehead and eyes. Water is then applied to the cloth in a controlled manner. As this is done, the cloth is lowered until it covers both the nose and mouth. Once the cloth is saturated and completely covers the mouth and nose, air flow is slightly restricted for 20 to 40 seconds due to the presence of the cloth. This causes an increase in carbon dioxide level in the individual's blood . . . [that] stimulates increased efforts to breathe. This effort plus the cloth produces the perception of "suffocation and incipient panic," i.e., the perception of drowning. The individual does not breathe any water into his lungs. During those 20 to 40 seconds, water is continuously applied from a height of twelve to twenty-four inches. After this period, the cloth is lifted, and the individual is allowed to breathe unimpeded for three or four full breaths. The sensation of drowning is immediately relieved by the removal of the cloth. The procedure may then be repeated. The water is usually applied from a canteen cup or small watering can with a spout. You have orally informed us that this procedure triggers an automatic physiological sensation of drowning that the individual cannot control even though he may be aware that he is in fact not drowning. You [the CIA] have also informed us [the Department of Justice] that it is likely that this procedure would not last more than 20 minutes in any one application.[6]

Other interrogation techniques observed by the FBI included chaining suspects to the floor, "hand and foot in a fetal position" in rooms either very hot or very cold and then leaving them alone for many hours while they urinated and defecated on themselves.[7] One detainee was found with a "pile of hair next to him. He had apparently been literally pulling his own hair out throughout the night." Moreover, as chapter 10 will show, much evidence exists that terrorism suspects have been sent to other nations by a process called "extraordinary rendition" that allows their intelligence agencies to use interrogation methods, perhaps including torture, that American law prohibits.

What can we learn from these stories? England in 1832 did not have a written constitution with a bill of rights.[8] Yet the magistrate approached a suspect accused of a horrid murder with a tenderness that Wigmore would later condemn as one of the "absurdities [that] have disfigured the law of the admissibility of confessions."[9] Absurdities or not, hundreds of English and American cases for over a century manifested, in Wigmore's words, "nothing but sentimentalism, a false tenderness to criminals, and an unnecessary deviation from principle."[10]

In 2002, the United States, with its written constitution and commitment to due process, was willing to use extremely coercive interrogation techniques, if not outright torture, to obtain statements. In 2003, President George W. Bush appointed Jay Bybee, one of the authors of the 2002 memorandum, to the Ninth Circuit Court of Appeals. In April 2009, the *New York Times* called on Congress to impeach Judge Bybee because he approved the CIA interrogation methods.[11]

What explains the differences in these approaches to justice? We first turn to the themes of this book and then to our terminology and some examples of our thesis to answer this question.

A. Themes

Perhaps the difference in the 1832 English case and the Bush-era interrogation of suspected terrorists is that one occurred during peacetime and the other occurred during what President Bush termed a war. He claimed that prisoners at Guantánamo Bay and other, undisclosed, sites in Europe were "enemy combatants" who did not qualify for protection by the Geneva Conventions, let alone our Bill of Rights.[12] This legalistic account explains less than an alternative, but deeper, story that tracks the legal realism school. Legal realism, which began with Karl Llewellyn and Felix Cohen in the 1930s, holds that abstract legal doctrine is rarely, if ever, determinative of difficult cases.[13] Difficult cases, those where reasonable judges could differ about the result, will be determined by factors other than a legal rule. Therefore, as we will show, the modern rule that a confession has to be voluntary to be admissible tells us almost nothing about which confessions are admissible in close cases.

The legal realist would explain the persistence of harsh interrogation techniques at Guantánamo Bay by noting the deaths of 3,000 Americans on 9/11 and the threat of additional, more damaging attacks hanging palpably in the air in the months that followed. These were threats to our very way of life, threats that appeared greater than any posed by ordinary crime. Indeed, the Council on Foreign Relations agreed with the president that the attacks on 9/11 "constituted acts of war."[14] Thus, the courts would be tempted to allow the executive much more discretion at Guantánamo Bay than they would allow police investigating crimes. Alan Dershowitz, noted civil libertarian and Harvard professor, put himself solidly in the legal realism camp when he appeared on *60 Minutes* on January 20, 2002. He claimed that American law would permit torture warrants to be used to get information from terrorists.[15] He denied making a normative argument; his realist point was that when interrogators believe that torture is the "only way of saving 500 or 1,000 lives, every democratic society would, has, and will use torture."

The realist can make a deeper claim than raw, utilitarian balance. The way courts approach interrogations and confessions depends, in large part, on how the actors in the legal system view themselves and the suspects and defendants who interact with them. Why were English judges of the early nineteenth century so deeply skeptical of confessions? By the 1820s, England was one of the richest, most powerful nations in the world and was almost immune from foreign invasion. Parliament and the monarchy had reached an accommodation that produced a stable government. The philosophy of the Whigs had percolated through the society, influencing the way the upper classes viewed the lower classes. Judges, drawn from the Whig upper class, tended to be benevolent toward lower-class defendants,[16] particularly those who were charged with a relatively trivial theft that was nonetheless considered a capital offense by Parliament.

As Louis Michael Seidman demonstrated, liberal ideology (Whig in the eighteenth and early nineteenth centuries) requires justification when unleashing State power to punish,[17] and that would be particularly true when the punishment is death. What better justifies deploying the awesome power of the State than a confession of guilt? Stalin recognized this, of course, when he held "show trials" in which defendants confessed their guilt; the "choice" these defendants faced was either to die after enduring unbearable pain or (they hoped) to die quickly after confessing.[18] But to Whig judges, a coerced confession was not consent to the State's punishment. Thus was born the notion that a freely willed, voluntary confession could be admitted to show guilt but not one that failed to manifest the will of the confessor.

Our book will explore a realist explanation of the evolution of the law of interrogation and will not involve itself with high constitutional theory or international law. We will not concern ourselves with the Geneva Conventions or whether the due process clause should protect noncitizens. Indeed, our enterprise in the first eight chapters is descriptive rather than normative. We make a realist claim that the perceived threat to America after 9/11 helps explain the resort to harsh interrogation methods and that cultural forces largely explain why English judges were so receptive to claims of involuntary confessions in the nineteenth century. We make no claim about the justification or correctness of either legal artifact or, for that matter, whether the threat perceptions of the relevant legal actors were well grounded.

Outside the law of interrogation, the Alien and Sedition Acts are an example of how law changes to accommodate threats—real or imagined. In 1798, many in America became convinced that Napoleon was loading troops onto ships headed for America. A French émigré wrote in his diary, "People acted as though a French invasion force might land in America at any moment. Everybody was suspicious of everybody else: everywhere one saw murderous glances."[19] The Congress that nine years earlier had sent the Bill of Rights to the states responded by giving the president authority to deport any resident alien considered "dangerous to the peace and safety of the United States."[20] When it became known that Napoleon's troops were headed for Egypt, rather than America, the Alien and Sedition Acts became a major political liability for Adams in the election of 1800.[21] The threat retreated, and America could afford to debate civil liberties rather than reflexively restrict them.

Our book will show the link between the fear of threats and the law of interrogation. The casual reader of Supreme Court cases would come away with the impression that Western culture obtained confessions through torture and inquisitorial practices until the seventeenth century when torture and brutish coercion gradually gave way, in fits and starts, to a modern conception of suspects possessing autonomy and dignity interests that must be respected—finally arriving at the shining accomplishment of *Miranda v. Arizona*.[22] Rather than force a confession from the mouth of a suspect, American police were required to tell the suspect that he had a right to remain silent and a right to counsel before submitting to a single question. Water-boarding is dismissed in the conventional narrative as an aberrant side trip taken by those who do not sufficiently value autonomy and dignity.[23]

We will show that this account is profoundly wrong on three levels. First, as John Parry demonstrated, the notion that torture essentially disappeared at the end of the eighteenth century is a rose-colored view of history. After examining the history of how our police, our military, and our prison officials have used violence as a means to an end, Parry concluded that while we mouth platitudes abhorring torture, we tolerate a lot of it. Indeed, "torture may be compatible with American values in practice and with the legal system we have constructed to serve those values."[24] Parry also concluded that "being a torture nation" in practice "could be as important a part of the U.S. legal and political system as the ban on torture" that is too often ignored.

Second, we will show that the acceptance of harsh interrogation tactics is always rooted at least in part in the changing perceptions of external and internal threats. When these threats appeared high, as the Tudor and Stuart monarchs perceived them to be, torture and extreme forms of coercion were used to get confessions, mostly in treason cases. When threats to the established order appeared low, as they did in the United Kingdom in the early nineteenth century, almost any interrogation was viewed as too harsh. Indeed, British courts developed during this era, and Parliament ultimately embraced, an approach to interrogation strikingly similar to *Miranda*.

Third, the shining achievement of *Miranda* is largely an illusion, one that benefits suspects much less than it appears to do. We will argue that the *Miranda* illusion ultimately puts suspects who seek to suppress their confessions in a net-worse position than they were prior to *Miranda*. As chapter 9 will show, courts sometimes appear to use a *Miranda* waiver as proof that the subsequent confession was voluntary even when police use techniques that could be viewed as coercive.

Rather than a progression from more to less violence in obtaining confessions, the history of Anglo-American interrogation reveals that it has gravitated from one extreme to another four different times. One might think of it as a pendulum rather than a continuum. As chapter 2 makes clear, early law on the Continent routinely permitted torture to obtain confessions; indeed, judges were required to order and supervise torture when needed to obtain confessions.[25] During the reign of the Tudors and the Stuarts in England, torture was used, though not very often, to obtain confessions. As a method of obtaining confessions, torture died out in England in the seventeenth century, although pretty extreme coercive methods were still tolerated.

Things began to change in the mid-seventeenth century, as chapter 3 details. By 1677, we see pleas in the Old Bailey that confessions should not be fully credited by juries, claims that were typically cloaked in a language of fear.[26] It is during this period that confession law makes one of its pendulum loops from one extreme to the other. The sixth edition of Hawkins's *Pleas of the Crown*, published in 1787, had English law forbidding the admission of confessions produced "either by the flattery of hope, or by the impressions of fear, *however slightly the emotions may be implanted* . . . for the law will not suffer a prisoner to be made the deluded instrument of his own conviction."[27] The language about "flattery of hope" and "deluded instrument" was added by the editor of the sixth edition, Thomas Leach. What we will thus call the Hawkins-Leach dictum ruled the confession world for roughly a century. Confessions were suppressed, for example, if produced by an exhortation to tell the truth.[28] Even a warning that the accused need not answer was sometimes held to be an improper inducement.[29] But the Hawkins-Leach dictum began to lose force in the latter half of the nineteenth century, as courts moved toward a more rationalist, utilitarian approach to confessions.

Chapter 4 examines the American law of confessions from colonial days to the publication of Wigmore's second edition of his treatise on evidence in 1923. Unsurprisingly, American law tracked English law closely during most of this time, embracing the Hawkins-Leach dictum and then beginning to move toward a rationalist law of interrogation. Chapter 5 seeks to plumb in more depth the cultural forces that played a role in shaping this turn in interrogation tactics, both in England and in the United States. Some factors were shared by both countries: Cities became larger and denser; handguns became more widely available; criminals became more brazen; fear of crime and violence increased sharply, aided in no small part by sensationalist newspaper coverage. Perhaps equally important, the Whig influence waned, to be replaced by a concern with the collective. And later in the period, the Great Depression robbed Americans of hope.

Chapter 6 examines a particular dimension of the pendulum swing toward an interrogation law dominated by crime-control goals; one that appeared in the

United States but not in England. A brutal method of interrogation, known as "sweating" or the "third degree," appears near the end of the nineteenth century and was tolerated, unofficially, for roughly a half-century. In addition to the cultural factors we shared with England, America experienced mass immigration that created ethnic ghettos in our cities and contributed to the rise of organized crime. Prohibition, a war for America's soul, also benefited organized crime. One response to these cultural forces was the third degree. But it, too, would lose its grip, and confessions law struggled again toward the Hawkins-Leach dictum. Formally, at least, in 1966 we arrived back in the Hawkins-Leach world of 1787 when Chief Justice Earl Warren found five votes to decide in favor of the defendants in *Miranda*.

Chapter 7 sketches the *Miranda* "revolution." We show how American law gradually built toward *Miranda* as other methods of regulating police interrogation were found to be unsatisfying. By 1966, the Court decided that it needed a "wide" rule that would apply to almost all interrogations because its previous attempts to offer guidance on a case-by-case basis had largely failed. But, as chapter 7 demonstrates, a "wide" rule requires a fully theorized Supreme Court opinion with a deep justification. Unlike the Court's right to counsel "revolution," *Miranda* never achieved a deep justification and thus was an easy target for its many critics, including later courts that gave its robust dicta a stinting application in many doctrinal areas.

Thus, as chapter 8 demonstrates, *Miranda*'s "victory" over high-pressure police interrogation was mostly rhetorical. Suspects waive their *Miranda* rights 80% of the time and, once police get a waiver, courts permit intense, lengthy interrogation, including some of the techniques condemned in *Miranda*. The tactical position of suspects who waive *Miranda* is roughly where it was when *Miranda* was decided; the only difference is that, at some level, most suspects know that they do not have to talk to the police. They just do it anyway. This chapter examines whether, routine waiver notwithstanding, *Miranda* has accomplished any of the goals that are explicit or implicit in Chief Justice Warren's opinion.

Whether *Miranda* was a victory for suspects facing custodial interrogation or a retreat from the Court's earlier attempts to regulate police interrogation, it has survived despite a constant barrage of criticism from those who think it offers too much protection from police interrogation. It survived the storms of the late 1960s and 1970s—youth protests, Vietnam, soaring crime rates, civil unrest in the cities, and Richard Nixon. It also survived Ronald Reagan and Edwin Meese, the attorney general whose office of legal policy attacked *Miranda* as a case with "no basis in history or precedent" and founded on "a willful disregard of the authoritative sources of law."[30] According to the Meese Report, *Miranda* was a "decision without a past" and a decision "without a future." Yet *Miranda* still stands, having survived the Meese Commission as well as the Burger and Rehnquist Courts, though some would say that it took some pretty serious hits along the way.

Chapters 9 and 10 reflect a change in our approach, from descriptive to normative. Chapter 9 confronts the problems that *Miranda* has either caused or failed to resolve. Whether the large number of waivers is mostly a result of police pressure or mostly suspects acting to maximize what they perceive as their self-interest is nearly impossible to know. But we do know that vulnerable suspects, particularly juveniles and mentally impaired suspects, are less able to act on the warnings supposed to protect suspects from the coercive atmosphere of police interrogation. We propose approaches to the future law of interrogation that will reveal more about why suspects confess and will help ameliorate the problem of vulnerable suspects.

Chapter 10 seeks to glimpse into the future of the law of interrogation. We believe that the law of interrogation in the United States will fracture between investigation of ordinary domestic crime and investigation of terrorism. Where domestic crimes are concerned, we believe that recording police interrogations will become ubiquitous. Once a recording requirement is in place, bringing light to the black box of police interrogation, legislatures and courts can choose how much to limit interrogation to protect against false confessions and to advance the autonomy interests of suspects.

What the future holds for government interrogations of suspected terrorists is less clear and more ominous. When the Catholic Church in Spain decided that its existence was threatened by nonbelievers, the Spanish Inquisition was the result; the Church and the government turned to torture to get confessions and repentance from those who were viewed as threats.[31] As the Spanish Inquisition makes plain, a culture faced with the perception of its demise— however far-fetched that perception may prove to be—will resort to torture to obtain confessions from those who appear to pose threats. Some will say that Western civilization has evolved since the sixteenth century and that modern decency and humanity will lead us to eschew torture. Others will say, remember Guantánamo Bay.

As long as we are spared another major attack, the use of harsh interrogation tactics against suspected terrorists, particularly ineffective tactics, will likely decline. Indeed, the growing sense of security in our country is one reason Barack Obama was elected president; he has already taken steps to reduce the coerciveness of interrogation and to end extraordinary rendition. Shortly after he became president, Obama signed an executive order prohibiting "the transfer of individuals to other nations to face torture or otherwise for the purpose, or with the effect, of undermining or circumventing the commitments or obligations of the United States to ensure the humane treatment of individuals in its custody or control."[32]

But if the perception of the threat escalates, so too will the pressure to use coercion against suspected terrorists.

B. Terminology and Examples

Here, we clarify our terminology and offer some examples of our thesis. We will use "confession" to mean any statement that the state secures from a suspect or a defendant and then seeks to use to secure a conviction of crime. It would thus even include statements that the speaker intended to be exculpatory. And it includes confessions of guilt in court that today we call "guilty pleas." Moreover, confessions can be, and often are, made to private persons who later testify about them at trial. But we are principally concerned with the process that the State uses to extract incriminating statements. The modern term for this process is "interrogation." Finally, though we begin with Roman law and take a brief tour of the Continent during the Middle Ages, our goal is to trace English interrogation law from the eleventh century until it becomes American law.

The law that regulates interrogations and confessions reflects the institutions that identify threats to the established order. To survive, every culture must identify the conduct that would destroy it either from the inside or the outside. Once that conduct is identified, institutions within the culture will develop tools that seek to uncover those who are threats and render them harmless. Whether a particular tool works efficiently, or at all, to uncover and remedy threats is an empirical question. But that cultures develop tools intended to counteract threats explains, to a large extent, the remarkable "journey" of the law of confessions.

A culture can be destroyed from the inside as well as the outside. According to Hepworth and Turner, the dominant group in a culture seeks to control "the legal and moral apparatus" and "to defend a central core of values against certain peripheral subgroups. Successful degradation of the periphery simultaneously has the effect of legitimising the power of the dominant group as the custodian of moral values."[33] Those who reject those moral values are a threat to the established order, though the perceived degree of threat is the key to understanding the link between threat and the level of interrogation pressure that the legal system will permit. As we will see in chapter 3, "torture warrants" that permitted torture to obtain confessions disappeared in England shortly after Elizabeth's reign ended. In part, this reflected a calmer period for the English monarchy after the stormy years of Henry VIII and Elizabeth.

One effective way of controlling the "legal and moral apparatus" was to hang wrongdoers in public. Public hangings were a popular pastime in England until they were abolished in 1868.[34] For example, the London *Times* reported that the crowd at an 1831 hanging numbered "at least 10,000 persons."[35] The news account of an 1806 hanging noted that "[a]ll the public avenues" near the execution site "were filled with spectators" who began to assemble four hours before the hanging.[36] Part of the ritual was for the condemned prisoner to confess his crime on the scaffold and pray for forgiveness. It was an acknowledgment of the authority, and correctness, of the State's taking a life, as well as an admission that the prisoner was at fault for the harm that he or she caused.

Those who did not confess or who claimed innocence were urged to confess by ministers who counseled the criminals in their cells and by ministers present at the execution. Charles Hussey, convicted of murder, refused to confess prior to his hanging on August 3, 1818, despite entreaties from two ministers.[37] Over the next month, the *Times* published at least three articles about Hussey's meetings with a minister in his cell. An August 10 story claimed that he signed a confession in his cell.[38] An August 22 story was subtitled "Considerable doubts are entertained as to the correctness of Hussey's confession."[39] A September 3 story noted that "the public mind" had "been disquieted by what has falsely been called the Confession of Charles Hussey."[40] The *Times*, and surely the public, was expressing a deep need to have a true, private confession from the man who had been hanged without making a public confession.

Convicted in 1818 of murdering his father, Chennel maintained his innocence to the end.[41] When he insisted that "his life had been sworn away by false testimony," a minister read from Psalms and the book of Job. He still insisted on his innocence. The day of the execution, a minister told him that "however he might conceal the crime from men, he could not elude the all-seeing eye of that God before whom he was in a few hours to appear." Some crimes could be kept private, "but crimes against society should be confessed for the satisfaction of society. It was a duty he owed to his country, friends, and neighborhood . . . and he hazarded his salvation by leaving the world with a lie in his mouth."

The exhortations were in vain. An "immense" crowd gathered to witness the execution. A minister, who had visited his cell, and a jailer, who had transported him from prison, urged him to confess. His accomplice, who stood beside him on the platform, was encouraged to "make disclosures." Neither man replied. An officer asked Chennel "if he was ready to perform his promise and make confession." He again refused and again "protested his innocence." The minister "ascended the platform, and addressed to Heaven in their behalf an excellent and affecting prayer. . . . No appearance of a design to confess being made, the platform was drawn from under them, and they were launched into eternity."

The news account concluded: "The public may perhaps think that we have entered into too minute details on these executions, but they will excuse us when they think of the useful lessons that may be learned from it. The fatal effects of profligacy and depraved habits in the lower classes . . . were never more eminently exemplified; and we shall think no details too minute, and labour misspent, which may impress deeper so important a conviction." The focus on the internal threat to the culture is clear.

What constitutes a threat differs from culture to culture. Fifteenth-century Spain considered Judaism to be a threat to its culture.[42] We will show in chapter 4 that those suspected of being witches were deeply feared in New England in the seventeenth century. The early Roman emperors and Stalinist Russia considered Christianity to be a threat. In the account offered by the Gospels—whether true or not, it reveals cultural views of the perceived threat—the priests and scribes demanded that Jesus confess whether he was the Christ. Pontius Pilate asked him whether he was king of the Jews; the chief priests and elders accused him of being Christ a king.[43] It is clear from the context that a claim to be the Christ or king of the Jews would have been an admission that he posed a threat to Roman rule.

A modern example of how threats vary across cultures is Japan, where crime rates are far lower than in the United States. For example, for each robbery in Tokyo in 1991, New York City had 462 robberies.[44] Thus, one might expect that Japanese interrogation would be less aggressive than here. It turns out, however, that quite abusive interrogation techniques are tolerated in Japan. The explanation, we believe, is twofold. First, the Japanese goal of an orderly society is threatened even by low levels of crime. Second, probably because of the low tolerance for crime, the failure to confess is itself viewed as outside the moral order. Thus, our thesis would predict conduct such as that recorded by David Johnson. In one case, the prosecutor beat two elderly men suspected of corruption.[45] The prosecutor called one a "fucking pig" and beat him so severely it took three weeks for his injuries to heal.[46] The other was beaten for hours, at one point spurting blood onto the furniture and floor. The prosecutor told him: "You asshole. . . . This is the authority of the state at work. Don't you get it?"[47]

Two controls, or brakes, have long existed on the use of coercion and torture to obtain confessions. The more obvious is a concern about false confessions. To be sure, particular cultures will vary in how they implement the false confession brake. Those who implemented the Spanish Inquisition showed no outward concern with false confessions; perhaps they assumed God would not tolerate falsehoods in his name. The Stalinist show trials were in part premised on the belief that enough force could produce both agreement about guilt and consent to the execution.[48] As long as agreement was obtained, a "false confession" was a contradiction in terms under the totalitarian Stalinist ideology. But, as noted earlier, a coerced confession does not signal consent under liberal, Whig ideology. Chapter 6 will make plain that the official American law of interrogation has always required a freely willed confession.

The second control on the use of force to obtain confessions focuses on the individual suspect rather than the justice system. At least since the eighteenth century, Anglo-American suspects have had rights against the State that limit interrogation. These rights have two overlapping foci. One kind of right is an autonomy interest in making up one's mind whether to confess. A suspect's autonomy is diminished when he is subjected to relentless interrogation, trickery, and coercion even if there is a zero risk of a false confession. Imagine a suspect who confesses after a long brutal interrogation but who is later proven guilty by a perfect DNA match. A second interest, more difficult to articulate, may be called a dignity interest. Though it often overlaps with the autonomy interest, one could imagine cases where a suspect is treated in ways that deny her dignity, and yet she still makes up her own mind to confess.

An example in which dignity and autonomy diverge is *Lisenba v. California.*[49] Lisenba was interrogated for at least thirty-two hours without a break; police only stopped because he passed out.[50] He was questioned two weeks later for ten hours and confessed, according to his testimony, after a deputy sheriff threatened him with violence.[51] Yet, he claimed that it was not the threat that caused him to confess because "there were not enough men in the District Attorney's office to make him talk, and if [his accomplice] had not talked he would never have told the story."[52] It appears that Lisenba chose to confess because he wanted to tell his side of the story. While he could argue plausibly that his dignity interest was violated, his testimony that he chose to confess for his own reasons makes it much more difficult to argue an autonomy violation.

At some point, the diminishment of autonomy or dignity is reason enough to forbid particular interrogation techniques without regard to concerns about false confessions. Where to draw that line has been the source of debate for centuries. Yale Kamisar created the theoretical structure for *Miranda* in a monograph that argued, "To the extent the Constitution permits the wealthy and educated to 'defeat justice,' if you will, *why shouldn't* all defendants be given a like opportunity?"[53] Gerald Caplan critiqued the robust autonomy argument as the "sporting theory" of justice: "Fairness, so defined, dictates that neither side should have an undue advantage; the police and the criminal should be on roughly equal footing and the rules of the game should be drawn to avoid favoring one side or the other."[54]

The false confession and autonomy-dignity controls interact in complex ways with the need for a culture to protect itself from threats. This need rises and falls with the perceived vulnerability of the culture. All other factors being equal, the greater the perceived threat, the more coercion a culture will tolerate to root out threats to its existence and control.

To be sure, there *are* other factors that influence the shape of the law regulating the interrogation process, including, as we will see, individual actors who helped shape the law. A factor that deserves its own category is proportionality. It has two dimensions. Along one dimension, the State is unlikely to use brutal methods to extract confessions to minor crimes. Along another dimension, judges are increasingly likely, other factors held even, to suppress confessions as the penalty the defendant faces outweighs the harm he or she is charged with causing. As we will see in chapter 3, English judges in the early nineteenth century often strained to find reasons to suppress confessions of petty theft made by servants who, at least in theory, faced the death penalty. We will demonstrate how the interrogation law variables interact as we present the law's history.

C. "In the Midst of Crises"

Our thesis can be simply stated. A culture's perception of threats to its existence is an important determinant of the level of interrogation pressure that its legal system will tolerate. Implicit in this thesis is that law is, at least in part, a captive of cultural forces. The liberal view that law constrains actors is true within only a narrow range. A good example is 9/11 and the Guantánamo Bay detention facility. Courts looked the other way as the Bush administration claimed the right to hold "enemy combatants" indefinitely and use extreme interrogation methods against them. The response of the American people? We reelected George W. Bush.

Noting the "major error in judgment" the Supreme Court made in 1944 when it permitted the confinement of 110,000 Japanese Americans in detention camps, Peter Honigsberg likens that error to the modern Court's easy acceptance of the term "enemy combatants," which was "designed to circumvent the Geneva Conventions and international human rights laws."[55] Errors like these are clear in hindsight but more difficult to identify, and for the law to prevent, in real time. Recall Dershowitz's claim that if interrogators believe that torture is the "only way of saving 500 or 1,000 lives, every democratic society would, has, and will use torture."

Broadening the point, Morgan Cloud observed, "[H]istory teaches that in the midst of crises—when the future course of events remains unknown—those charged with preserving the nation will resort to drastic tactics unacceptable in more placid and tranquil times."[56] One of Cloud's examples is that the Continental Congress in 1777 "authorized the seizure and lengthy incarceration of Quakers suspected of being British sympathizers precisely because they were Quakers."[57] The rationale? Congress declared that Pennsylvania and Delaware were "threatened with an immediate invasion from a powerful army" and that "the principles of policy and self-preservation require that all persons who may reasonably be suspected of aiding or abetting the cause of the enemy, may be prevented from pursuing measures injurious to the general weal."[58]

To be sure, we are not apologists for unlimited executive discretion during times of crisis and neither is Cloud. After noting the natural inclination to resort to "drastic tactics," Cloud wrote that history "also teaches that opposition to these tactics is essential if democratic values and mechanisms are to survive the crises. . . . [T]he struggle to define and enforce our constitutional norms is an ongoing process, and that process is aided by, and may depend upon, the actions of those who resist expansion of government power at the very time when it seems to be most needed."[59] Indeed, Cloud concluded that the Quakers achieved a "relatively quick release"—unlike the Japanese-American detainees during World War II—in part because of "relentless efforts by the captives and their supporters to persuade political leaders that the seizures violated fundamental rights."[60]

One can only imagine the difficulty in pressing constitutional norms against executive power if terrorists used nuclear weapons against our cities.

PART

THE FIRST REVOLUTION IN INTERROGATION LAW

From Torture to Protecting Autonomy

CHAPTER 2

Early Interrogation Law

As we demonstrated in chapter 1, the law of confessions reflects the institutions that identify, or create, deviance. We also surveyed what we called "brakes" that help control those suspected of crime or deviance. Perhaps the most obvious is the concern about false confessions. Another is the autonomy interest of the suspect, consisting of a dignity interest and an interest in being free to make up one's own mind whether to self-accuse of a crime. And there is a proportionality principle that causes the State to avoid brutal methods to obtain confessions to minor crimes; it also causes judges to draw back from imposing penalties that seem to outweigh the harm a defendant is accused of committing. Most of these brakes, or controls, can be seen as far back as Roman law.

A. Ancient Law Regulating Interrogation

According to German historian Adolf Friedrich Rudroff, torture "was used from time immemorial against slaves, partly to strengthen testimony, partly to extort confessions."[1] The Roman historian Titus Livy in the massive *History of Rome* recounts an examination of slaves in 210 B.C. during which "they all confessed."[2] Indeed, torture was routinely used during the Roman Republic to obtain confessions, but only from slaves.[3]

That torture could be used only against slaves during the Republic is evidence of the autonomy control. As Hepworth and Turner note, the Western law of confessions is premised on the notion of "the self-activated rational individual."[4] Roman citizens fit that category; thus, torture would have been deemed a violation of the right to make a rational decision. A slave, by contrast, "was a thing ... [that] had no rights."[5] Yet even those who had no rights, who were not considered self-activated rational individuals, would be protected by the false confession parameter that was developing in Roman law.

By the early years of the empire, judges were cautioned to observe safeguards thought to prevent false confessions. Caesar Augustus, who ruled Rome from 27

B.C. to 14 A.D., cautioned that the investigation of crime "should not begin with the application of pain, and that reliance should not be placed entirely on torture."[6] The infliction of pain should be used only on those "so close to being proved [guilty] by other evidence" that the confession "appears to be the only thing lacking."[7] Hadrian, emperor from 117 to 138 A.D., embraced the same notion and added the observation that some "have so little endurance that they would rather tell any kind of lie than suffer torture."[8]

During the second century, the Roman Empire's peak, the use of torture was extended to free persons.[9] It is unsurprising that a judicial system ultimately answerable to an emperor would degrade the autonomy of defendants and witnesses. The use of torture not only expanded beyond the class of slaves during the empire, but it also became more frequent. "Judges were always prone to think that torture was a short cut to the truth and to start torturing witnesses and the accused right away; this became all the more common when torture was made applicable to free persons."[10] The emperors "frequently warned [provincial] governors against this tendency, telling them not to start by torturing witnesses but to try to establish a case by argument, and in particular not to torture an accused unless there was a *prima facie* case against him."

All sorts of reasons might explain why torture was first applied to free persons during the empire and invoked more frequently. The empire needed efficient judicial outcomes, and torture was an efficient way to produce confessions. It is also conceivable that judges increasingly used torture as the empire grew larger and accumulated more enemies, which made it more vulnerable. Strachan-Davidson concludes that the Roman law courts in the period 300–500 A.D. "share in the general demoralization of the age" and participated in the "machinery of cruelty and rapacity" of the later empire.[11] The evolution of the law of confessions is consistent with the hypothesis that Roman judges perceived a threat to their way of life that led to the greater use of torture to obtain confessions.

Better proof is available for why European justice turned to torture in the thirteenth century. In 1215, at Pope Innocent III's insistence, the Fourth Lateran Council barred the participation of clerics in the ordeals of hot iron and water.[12] In that era, the ordeals were the principal means of settling disputes when guilt was not made clear through confession or a defendant caught red-handed. Ordeals were explicit invitations for God to reveal which party was telling the truth. In the ordeal of hot iron, for example, if the burned hand was healing after three days, that litigant was telling the truth. Granting the premise that God would reveal the truth-teller, the ordeal was infallible. Clerics were critical to its implementation because they wrapped the burned hand, unwrapped it three days later, and proclaimed whether the burn was healing.

When clerics were forbidden this role, the proof dimension of the ordeal was suddenly lost. Both English and European justice systems cast about for a mechanism that was as infallible as possible. (We defer the English story to section B of this chapter, noting here only that English law never embraced torture to obtain confessions in routine cases.) In a search for a system that would not convict the innocent, thirteenth-century European law required that no conviction could be entered unless there were two eyewitnesses or a voluntary confession.[13] The net effect of this rule of evidence was to make it impossible to convict on circumstantial evidence, no matter the strength of the evidence, unless the defendant confessed. The inability to convict in many cases was a threat to order in Europe. The twin controls—fear of false confessions and value of autonomy—that would normally prevent torture to obtain confessions were not weighty enough at this time in history. As John Langbein puts it, "No society will long tolerate a legal system in which there is no prospect of convicting unrepentant persons who commit clandestine crimes."[14]

The law in Europe thus began to accept torture as a means of obtaining confessions in cases where the circumstantial evidence suggested guilt. Again according to Langbein, "The law of torture grew up to regulate this [European] process of generating confessions."[15] There is no reason to assume that Europeans were simply more tolerant of torture than their English counterparts—indeed, the kings and privy councilors who designed and administered the English justice system were largely descended from the Normans. Thus, the more permissive attitude toward torture on the Continent probably resulted from the greater perceived threat to peace and order created by the rigid European two-witness rule.

England avoided resort to the two-witness rule because of reforms implemented a half-century before the Fourth Lateran Council, in Henry II's 1166 Assize of Clarendon, to which we now turn.

B. Confessions and the Assize of Clarendon

Prior to the Assize of Clarendon, robbery, theft, and murder were resolved by a variety of proof mechanisms. A person caught "red-handed"—i.e. with proof of the crime in his possession—was "brought before some court ([likely] enough it is a court hurriedly summoned for the purpose), and without being allowed to say one word in self-defense, he will be promptly hanged, beheaded, or precipitated from a cliff, and the owner of the stolen goods will perhaps act as an amateur executioner."[16] In the absence of clear evidence of guilt, cases were decided by confession, testimony, the swearing of oaths, and examination of documents. The early English turned to the ordeal "when other ways of discovering the truth were not available."[17]

The ordeals that migrated to England, perhaps as early as the late seventh century and certainly by the tenth century, were developed by the Frankish tribes in Europe.[18] Even if one accepted the premise of the ordeals, it was a deeply unsatisfying method of settling disputes. It was, at least sometimes, corrupt by the reign of England's second king, William II, son of William the Conqueror. He ridiculed the ordeal of hot iron when fifty men accused of taking the king's deer were, in 1098, made to carry the hot iron and then presented themselves three days later with unburnt hands.[19] Perhaps the iron was not so hot.

Another problem with the ordeal was that a specific accusation was "normally decided by battle."[20] Trial by battle, as the name implies, sometimes meant a dawn-to-dusk battle where one party died horribly. Bartlett quotes an account of a trial by battle in which Guy "unhorsed" Herman who then disemboweled Guy's horse.[21] They fought with swords "until both, exhausted by the weight and burden of arms, threw away their shields and hastened to gain victory" by wrestling. Guy seemed to have prevailed but Herman put his hand under Guy's armor, "seized him by the testicles" and "hurled Guy away from him; by this tearing motion all the lower parts of the body were broken so that Guy, now prostrate, gave up, crying out that he was conquered and dying." Needless to say, the prospect of facing trial by battle must have discouraged private parties from making accusations.

Crime was rampant in England during the twelfth century, particularly during the contested reign of Stephen.[22] "The collapse of the machinery of government in Stephen's reign had been almost complete."[23] Powerful lords walled themselves off in castles, "levied payments from the villages" and when all the money was gone, they "plundered and burned all the villages."[24] The tyranny of the castle owners led to an English world, as described by contemporary English monks, where "[i]f two or three men came riding into a village, all the villagers would flee, for they thought they were robbers."[25]

William the Conqueror's great-grandson was crowned King Henry II in 1154.[26] He quickly asserted a kingly authority that Stephen lacked. He recovered all the territories and rights of lordship that had been lost to Scotland, France and Wales during Stephen's reign.[27] To restore order, he destroyed the castles of the barons who opposed him and claimed royal ownership of all lands that had ever been owned by kings of England.[28] Later, he reshaped the administration of justice. To the end of "preserving peace and maintaining justice," the Assize of Clarendon, 1166, consolidated power in the royal courts and gave sheriffs more power to arrest those who served the castle lords.[29]

But by far the most significant change was that justice did not have to await the victim or the victim's family to take action. If a jury of presentment, similar to a modern grand jury, found reason to suspect robbery, theft, or murder, then the defendant was given a chance to prove his innocence by the ordeal of water.[30] The jury of presentment, representing the community, displaced private justice at the hands of victims for the crimes of robbery, theft, and murder. The conceit created by the Assize of Clarendon, which continues to this day, is that crimes harm the State. Today, criminal defendants are prosecuted by a state, by the United States, or by the people of a state, as in *The People v. O. J. Simpson.*

When the ordeals disappeared in 1217, English judges soon took the verdict of the inquest as guilt rather than probable guilt. It was a natural progression. Because juries had been making judgments about probable guilt for a half-century, they could be trusted to determine the ultimate truth about guilt. English law thus never adopted the European rule requiring two eyewitnesses or a voluntary confession.[31] English juries could convict on strong circumstantial evidence, and no reason existed to resort to torture to obtain confessions.

Indeed, the Assize of Clarendon implicitly rejects untrustworthy confessions. Chapter 13 provides that "if any one, in the presence of lawful men or the hundreds, make confession of robbery, murder, theft, or the reception [hiding] of those committing them, and should later wish to deny it, let him not have law."[32] To translate a bit, "let him not have law" denied the confessor the ordeal as a means of vindicating innocence. "[T]he hundreds" is possibly a reference to the hundred man, the head of the district responsible for organizing villagers to catch thieves and robbers.[33] The requirement that the confession be heard by "lawful men" excludes men whose oath was not accepted because they had been convicted of a crime or had otherwise "diminished their lawfulness."[34] In sum, confessions proved by trustworthy men could be accepted as true, and no need existed for the proof of the ordeal. Untrustworthy confessions were not accepted as proof.

The Assize of Clarendon is now almost 850 years old, but it is an uncannily modern treatment of confessions. Both then and now if the confession is trusted to be true, it disposes of the case. Under Henry's law, the case was literally over because the defendant was denied a chance to prove his innocence. The confession amounted to a conviction. Today, the effect of a confession is less formal but dramatic nonetheless. If a judge admits a confession, juries rarely acquit. Defendants have the constitutional right to explain to the jury why the confession is untrue.[35] But the odds of an acquittal are so low that few defendants proceed to trial once the judge rules a confession admissible.

In Henry II's day, the effect of a confession turned on the trust that the legal system could put in the one who heard the confession. While this rule will be amended in various ways over the next 850 years, it remains the core of the law of confessions today. We see this idea in the earliest English confession case we found, discussed in the next section. The process is also much the same today. A grand jury decides whether there is probable cause to believe the defendant guilty and then, as a practical matter, the burden shifts to the defendant to disprove the State's case.[36]

C. From the Assize of Clarendon to the Torture Warrants

We begin with a distinction that will be important for the rest of this chapter and the next. Two very different categories of confessions existed in English law. The most common form in the early period was an admission to judges in court that constituted a conviction. This is the descendant of a confession to "trustworthy men" in the Assize of Clarendon. It was the end of the case. The second type is "mere confessions" that had no formal legal effect. These included statements to the justices of the peace, to coroners during inquests, and to victims and bystanders. The "trustworthy men" category from the Assize of Clarendon had, in effect, been narrowed to judges.

We see examples of both types of confessions in the Year Books, a massive collection of the law reports of medieval England. Our source for the Year Books cases is the website created by Professor David Seipp, who has indexed and translated over 22,000 of these reports that "are our principal source materials for the development of legal doctrines, concepts, and methods from 1290 to 1535, a period during which the common law developed into recognizable form."[37]

The earliest English confession case we found was in 1295, in the twenty-third year of the rule of Edward I. A tall "immensely powerful" man who was a "born soldier," Edward led English armies against Wales and eventually, incorporated Wales into England in 1284.[38] He then turned his attention to Scotland, seeking a diplomatic and political takeover. When that failed, he was the first English king to attempt to conquer Scotland.

On the judicial front, the measures taken by Edward's great-grandfather, Henry II, in the Assize of Clarendon had established a stable legal order. Henry III, Edward's father, had also done much to regularize the legal order. While the local shire courts continued to function, the royal courts heard all cases where the jury of presentment found reason to suspect defendants.[39] The threat from crime, and thus from that form of deviance, was far lower in 1295 than it had been in 1166 when Henry II established the Assize of Clarendon. Thus, our thesis predicts that courts would be more willing in 1295 to take seriously a claim that a confession was given unwillingly or was untrue.

We see this in Robert Butler's case from 1295. While in prison awaiting trial, he confessed to a coroner that he was "a thief, murderer and robber, etc."[40] Coroners functioned as investigating magistrates, gathering evidence in homicide cases and reporting that evidence at the defendant's trial. In Butler's case, the coroner provided the written confession to the royal justices, who called Butler to appear before them to see if he would acknowledge his confession in court, thus in effect pleading guilty. He did, but he claimed that he made the confession to the coroner "because of the rigour and harshness he had sustained in prison, in order to be relieved from his distress."

Notice the procedural posture here. The confession to the coroner was not itself a conviction. To convict him in the king's court, the justices required his appearance before them "to see if he was willing to confess what he had admitted before the coroner."[41] If he had denied the confession, then a jury would determine his guilt or innocence. When he admitted the confession, his first line of defense was to claim that he confessed because of prison conditions.

While little is known about prison conditions in England in the thirteenth century, it is safe to assume that prison was a horrid place. The two major London prisons of the time were Fleet and Newgate, both built in the twelfth century.[42] Newgate was built later than Fleet, and we know more about it.

> Very soon after it had been opened Newgate Gaol had acquired an espe-
> cially terrible reputation for its unwholesome environment, the distresses
> of its prisoners and the cruelties of its staff. . . . The smells of Newgate
> were renowned and for centuries they polluted the whole of the
> surrounding locality. Lack of hygiene and faulty sanitation caused fre-
> quent outbreaks of fever and the annual death-rate was extremely high.[43]

The case report from the Year Books does not explain why Butler thought that the prison conditions should relieve him of the legal effect of his confession. It is possible, we suppose, that he was making a dignity or autonomy claim. Six centuries later, an American defendant named Ernest Miranda would make a similar dignity-autonomy claim—that the rigor and harshness of police interrogation should relieve him of the consequences of confessing. But we are doubtful that, in 1295, autonomy or dignity claims would cause a court to disregard a confession made to a coroner. Indeed, we are skeptical that an English subject, in 1295, would be aware of a right that could require the king to provide decent prison conditions. Thus, the more likely underlying claim is that the rigor and harshness of the prison conditions compelled Butler to confess falsely. A false confession, as the Assize of Clarendon recognized, is of no value to a legal system.

To decide Butler's claim, the justices sent for three prisoners and asked them if the conditions were as Butler described. According to the report: "They say no."[44] Not satisfied, the justices then sent for the "keeper of the prison" and made him swear to tell the truth. Unlike today, in medieval times oaths were taken very seriously. It is fair even to say that an oath created a sacred obligation to comply with the oath or face God's damnation. The jailer testified that Butler's account of the prison conditions "was never true." The justices then asked Butler for a response. He repeated his claim that he confessed because of the "harshness of the prison," but he quickly retreated to a second argument—that he was a clerk and thus had a clerical privilege not to be tried in the royal courts. He lost on that claim, too, for technical reasons that need not concern us.

The significance of Butler's case is the court's response to the argument that the confession should not "count" as a guilty plea because it was induced by prison conditions. One possible response was to deny the legal premise of the claim, to say it did not matter whether you confessed to escape the rigorous conditions. This the court did not do. Apparently accepting the legal premise that a false confession should not be deemed a conviction, the justices went to the trouble to call three fellow prisoners as well as the keeper of the prison before they ruled that the factual premise was false. It appears that, by 1295, English justices accepted the proposition that harsh treatment might compel a defendant to confess falsely. Under the Assize of Clarendon, a confession would not operate as a guilty plea unless it was made to a trustworthy witness. In 1295, English courts continued to recognize that untrue confessions should not be treated as guilty pleas.

To be sure, the crimes Butler faced were capital offenses, and the proportionality principle suggests that judges should tread lightly and not be too eager to accept a confession. But in a way that misses the point. It was the judges' willingness in 1295 to take seriously Butler's argument that a false confession should not be credited that makes his case significant.

A different dimension of the evolving law of confessions can be seen in a case that took place in 1348, the year the Black Death reached its deadly peak in England.[45] The criminal procedure of the time required defendants who had been found probably guilty by the jury of presentment to relate their version of the case to the royal justices. In doing so, defendants would sometimes state facts that admitted guilt. In those cases, the justices treated the defendant's statements as a guilty plea and entered a conviction. The only time the question was submitted to the trial jury was when the defendant's presentation did not admit guilt.

On arraignment for the death of W.C., the defendant, Tailour of S., told the justices that he would "tell the Court the case as it was."[46] He wanted to strike someone else with his knife but "W.C. came between them to settle (appeaser) the fight, and the defendant struck him with his knife, not willing or knowing, so by misadventure [accident]." But this particular claim of accident was, under English law, an admission of the felony of homicide. Justice William de Thorp, Chief Justice of the King's Bench, said that the defendant's explanation was

> cause enough to adjudge him to death, because it was the law that if two persons fought together, and one came between them to settle (appeaser) the contest, and one or the other struck and killed him, he was guilty of this felony, because he began the wrong (le mal), and did it of his own wrong, and not by misadventure.

To his horror, Tailour's defense had collapsed into a guilty plea to a capital crime! But de Thorp said that if the defendant wished to put himself "on the jury" (have a jury decide guilt), the court would ignore his guilty plea and "receive him of grace."[47] The latter likely means that the court was free to accept the guilty plea and sentence him to death but chose, in its discretion, to let the matter be settled by the jury.[48]

We see here a new wrinkle in the English law of confessions. It was not enough that the confession was the truth, as was the issue in Butler's case and in chapter 13 of the Assize of Clarendon. Nothing suggests that Tailour's statement was false. Yet the court permitted him, in effect, to withdraw his confession because it had been made without knowledge that he was pleading guilty. Tailour's case is evidence that English justices weighed whether admissions were made with knowledge of their consequences before entering a conviction. This, of course, is recognition of the defendant's autonomy in a context where the proportionality principle suggests caution in finding the defendant guilty.

Getting to the truth might be the first value served in the law of confessions. But getting to the truth in a way that recognizes the suspect as a free-willed autonomous actor with dignity interests is another value served by the English law of confessions. Perhaps the horror of the Black Death contributed to the creation of autonomous English subjects. It had been "widely known" since 1346 "that a plague of unparalleled fury was raging in the East" and making its way westward.[49] Europe and England succumbed in 1347 and 1348.[50] A natural reaction to watching an agonizing death fall remorselessly on a quarter of the population would be to take the side of a defendant who had unwittingly condemned himself to the gallows.

To understand the next case requires that we explain the doctrine of "approvement," which gave judges discretion to permit a defendant who had confessed his crime to accuse or "approve" others of the crime.[51] If the approved defendants were convicted, the original defendant was banished but would escape the death penalty. We know that approvement was recognized in English law as early as the mid-thirteenth century because Bracton mentioned it in his treatise.[52]

An unnamed defendant in 1411 attempted to approve others to obtain release from jail in a homicide case.[53] Because this was a "gaol release" case and not a trial, the judge who heard the case, Stourton, was not one of the king's justices. Indeed, the court clerk noted that he was not even a serjeant, the highest rank of lawyers. Though the record is far from clear, it appears that the defendant asked Stourton if he could confess his felony in court and then approve others of the crime. Stourton told him that he should have confessed in prison rather than in court. Once he confessed in court, he could not approve others because a confession in court would result in his being "hanged forthwith." The judge then told the defendant that he "ought not to confess the felony in hope of saving his life." The outcome of the case is not given, but no grounds appear to permit his release from jail. He likely was brought to trial later in the king's court.

The case is best read, we think, as evincing Stourton's desire to protect the defendant from confessing his guilt while ignorant of the consequences. To be sure, Stourton's advice that a confession in court would preclude becoming an approver seems to be incorrect.[54] Perhaps this is why the clerk recorded that Stourton was neither a serjeant nor a justice. But if Stourton was sincere, it is another example of a judge seeking to prevent an admission of guilt from someone who did not know the consequences of confessing. It is an example of the evolving autonomy of the English subject.

But the autonomy sword had two very sharp edges in that era. The edge that could hurt defendants was that a guilty plea made without coercion and with knowledge that one was pleading guilty was conclusive proof of guilt. A defendant named Gower had earlier confessed in court that he had "consented to and abetted the death of A."[55] He was convicted and permitted to abjure the realm. In 1345, he was found in the realm, taken before the King's Bench, and asked "why they should not proceed to execution" on the earlier conviction for his failure to stay out of the realm.

Gower's defense was that the earlier conviction was unfounded because he only aided in the death and could not be convicted until the one who committed the killing, the principal, was convicted.[56] As the principal had not been convicted, Gower argued that his earlier conviction was void. While his defense was valid in law, the court ruled that it applied only to defendants who put their case to the jury. It did not protect defendants who confessed. Indeed, the justices made the remarkable statement that even if there had been no murder, "still his confession condemned him."

Executing innocent men who have chosen to confess to a capital crime seems to take autonomy too far. Yet in an eerie parallel, some judges and prosecutors today have argued that a wrongful conviction should stand if the time for appealing or challenging it has passed. Justice Scalia remarked: "There is no basis in text, tradition, or even in contemporary practice (if that were enough) for finding in the Constitution a right to demand judicial consideration of newly discovered evidence of innocence brought forward after conviction."[57] Scalia seems to say that once the legal system has spoken and the time to review the outcome has passed, it becomes a permanent legal fact in the universe, at least as far as the United States Constitution is concerned. That approach to legal finality could justify the court's view in Gower's case that a false confession, willingly made, led to a valid conviction that could not be challenged.

The autonomy of English defendants in that era did not extend to the right not to plead to the charge. Defendants who did not plead their cases could be found mute by malice and hanged. Incentives thus abounded for defendants to talk before the justices and the jury. In a 1406 case, the inquest found the defendant mute by malice and "[a]warded that the felon be hanged," but the justices said it was not necessary to enter judgment on that charge because the defendant had acknowledged the felony in an earlier proceeding.[58]

An alternative to being hanged for refusing to plead was the quaint *peine forte et dure*, or "hard and forceful punishment."[59] According to Matthew Hale, a defendant subjected to *peine forte et dure* was "put into a dark, lower room" in the prison and "laid naked upon the bare ground upon his back . . . his legs and arms drawn and extended with cords to the four corners of the room, and upon his body laid as great a weight of iron, as he can bear, and more." He was given three morsels of bread without drink and afterwards fed nothing and allowed only to drink standing water "next [to] the door of the prison" until he died. It is an odd view of autonomy, to modern eyes, to recognize the right not to be tried until one has entered a plea but then allow the crown to kill the defendant who refuses to plead.

Other sources indicate that if the defendant relented and agreed to plead and to be tried by a jury, the weight would be removed.[60] This description of *peine forte et dure* is consistent with cases we found where the justices pleaded with defendants to enter a plea, explaining what would happen if they did not. In one case from 1492, Justice Fairfax told the defendant to "take good care of yourself, my friend, and think carefully what a great offence it is against God to murder [yourself] voluntarily through obstinacy. . . . In any case, twelve men will perhaps find you not guilty."[61] The defendant pleaded not guilty. Again, we see concern with autonomy.

One way for a defendant to challenge a confession would be to show that it was produced by coercion. We saw a foreshadowing of that argument in Butler's claim that the prison conditions caused his confession. The argument appears, more fully formed, in an early civil case about twenty years after Butler's case. In 1313, a defendant sought to avoid having to pay a bond by claiming "that he executed the bond under coercion of imprisonment."[62]

In 1353, a defendant used the coercion defense successfully in a criminal case, albeit not in a confessions context. Arraigned for stealing two shillings worth of bread, the defendant said that she did it "by the command of the one who was her husband at that time."[63] The judges refused to rule in her favor and allowed the case to go to the jury, which "found that she had done it by the coercion of her husband against her will . . . and thus she went acquitted." The theory here, expressed in modern form, is that the will of the coercer substitutes for the one who is coerced, rendering her guiltless. Implicit in the sketchy case report, of course, is the notion that in the fourteenth century, wives did their husband's bidding without question.

Most of the early confessions cases featured admissions that were both freely given and knowing. About one-third of the confessions cases from this century involved a defendant who confessed freely and then claimed he was a cleric.[64] If he proved he was a cleric, by reading from the Bible, the court would deliver the defendant to the ordinary—the bishop acting in his ecclesiastical capacity—for punishment.[65] About another third of the cases involved a freely given confession and then a request to become an approver of others.[66] The majority of the final third involved a confession that was merely mentioned in passing. For example, in 1492, Archer confessed to the coroner that he killed a man.[67] The issue at trial was whether he would plead to the charge or stand mute.

The argument that a coerced confession was questionable as evidence in a criminal case does not appear in anything like the modern form until we arrive at a period that John Langbein called the "century of torture": 1540–1640.[68] As we will see, even under rulers like Henry VIII, "Bloody Mary," and Elizabeth, torture was sufficiently rare that it was an outlier rather than the norm. Indeed, the challenge for Langbein was to explain why if the English used torture occasionally to obtain evidence, its use did not become routine as it had in European justice.

D. Torture Century: 1540–1640

Following Langbein, our interest in torture is only when used to obtain confessions.[69] Violence was endemic in English society of this time, but its use was almost always to dispatch one's enemies, to force a defendant to submit to a jury (*peine forte et dure*), or to punish defendants convicted of particularly dangerous or loathsome acts. For example, the Year Books contain an account of the Earl of Kent's attempt to overthrow Henry IV in 1399.[70] Though the account has, in modern times, been dismissed as a forgery,[71] it would not have been included in the Year Books if it lacked verisimilitude. In the Year Book account, two of the defeated earls were beheaded on the spot. A third escaped but was later captured and beheaded in front of a large crowd. Then "his head was taken to London and set up on London bridge."

A relatively common form of execution was drawing and quartering. The point to this barbarous practice was to make the condemned man suffer as much as possible prior to death and to desecrate his body. Here, for example, is the sentence pronounced after Sir Walter Raleigh was convicted of treason:

> [You are] to be hanged and cut down alive, and your body shall be opened, your heart and bowels plucked out, and your privy members cut off, and thrown into the fire before your very eyes; then your head to be stricken off from your body, and your body shall be divided into four quarters, to be disposed of at the King's pleasure. And God have mercy upon your soul.[72]

None of these practices involved confessions. But we know, because they kept good records via the Privy Council, that the English did sometimes use torture to produce confessions. An advisory body to monarchs since the Norman kings, by the sixteenth century the Privy Council included judges, barons, king's serjeants, and the king's attorney.[73] Torture to obtain evidence required written authorization by the Privy Council or the monarch, and many of those warrants survived.[74] The warrants spanned the years 1540–1640. There is every reason to believe that the warrants that survived disclose most of the use of torture to obtain evidence. As Langbein puts it: "If there had been any massive use of torture before the records began to evidence it in 1540, or after they cease to disclose it in 1640, or omitted from the records for the intervening century, literary and other sources would alert us."[75]

If the English monarchs were ever to use torture routinely, it would have been in the period from 1540 to 1640—a period that saw three monarchs who were more than willing to use terror and repression to rule England.[76] Henry VIII's often despotic rule is well known. His daughter, Mary I, reinstituted Catholicism as the state religion, which made her the target of the Protestants who had ruled England under her father.[77] She was known as "Bloody Mary" because 300 Protestant "heretics" were burned at the stake during her reign. Elizabeth's reign was calmer than that of her father and sister, but she obviously felt threatened—two-thirds of all surviving torture warrants were issued while she was queen.[78] Indeed, upon Elizabeth's death, torture warrants became very infrequent, sputtering to an end during the reign of Charles I in 1640. Two years later, the English civil war would begin, and yet only one torture warrant was issued in the years leading up to the war.

Thus, while the period from 1540 to 1640 was almost certainly not the totality of English use of torture to obtain confessions, it *was* almost certainly the period of its most frequent occurrence. If we find few torture warrants during this period, it must mean that the English rarely used torture to obtain evidence. And we do find few torture warrants. Langbein records eighty-one Privy Council torture warrants, or an average of fewer than one per year.[79] Even if the records show only one-third of all torture warrants that would be an average of three uses per year of torture to obtain confessions. Langbein concludes: "Relative to the thousands of felony investigations each year, the number of torture cases was minuscule."[80] Blackstone draws an instructive distinction when he concludes that the rack "was occasionally used as engine of state, not of law, more than once in the reign of queen Elizabeth."[81] Torture, then, was not part of the English system of proof.

If torture was not part of the standard proof in England, as it was on the Continent, why was it used at all? Langbein's study of the torture warrants persuades him that it was used principally to protect the state from treason and counterfeiting and, occasionally, when a powerful figure had been the victim of crime.[82] The first two connections fit our thesis that when a State feels threatened, and there are no threats greater than treason or counterfeiting, it will respond with whatever is necessary to ensure its survival. The use of torture when a powerful figure had been the victim of a crime is simply an artifact of political power.

To say that the English did not view torture as a routine method of extracting confessions is not, of course, to say that the English did not use coercive interrogation methods. As we will see in a moment, compulsion, force, and violence were standard interrogation methods, at least by 1547 in treason cases. We are back to the question asked at the end of the last section: Why would a legal culture that permitted convicted defendants to be drawn and quartered not routinely permit torture to obtain evidence, as was done on the Continent? Langbein's answer is that the English legal system obtained a sufficient number of convictions in jury trials at which much evidence was admissible, while on the Continent, the two-witness rule made convictions difficult to obtain.[83] Thus, by 1628, torture to obtain evidence in England "was falling into desuetude," an "English experiment" that "left no traces."[84]

Langbein's account seems right, as far as it goes, but still leaves the bigger question unanswered. If the English viewed torture as simply another tool to uncover truth, it would have been used routinely. There must have been a suspicion that torture did not produce truth, a belief that can be traced back to Roman law. A manifestation of the reluctance to rely on tortured confessions appeared early in the "torture century." In 1547, Parliament sought to cleanse treason prosecutions of torture when it forbade an indictment or conviction of treason unless the defendant "be accused by two sufficient and lawful witnesses, or shall willingly without violence confess the same."[85]

The 1547 Treason Act can be explained, of course, as a limit on the power of the monarch to bring down his enemies. That Parliament enacted it only months after the death of Henry VIII manifests this motive. It seems likely, though, that Parliament was also acknowledging the unreliability of confessions produced by violence. Staundford's treatise, published in 1557, noted that when a defendant is charged with a felony, confessions to the judge at arraignment are "the best and surest answer that be in our law for quieting the conscience of the judge and for making a good and firm condemnation" as long as the confession "did not proceed from fear, menace, or duress."[86] This concern seems pretty clearly directed at the unreliability problem. Thus, Staundford's principle and the motivation behind the 1547 Treason Act probably come from a common source. Unfortunately, that source is lost in what we call the "missing century." But first a brief detour to the Star Chamber.

E. Star Chamber

When interrogation methods are the issue, the Star Chamber is perhaps the most well-known English institution. Leonard Levy wrote about it extensively in *Origins of the Fifth Amendment*, which won a Pulitzer Prize in history.[87] Levy's thesis is that the reaction to the Star Chamber helped develop the English principle against self-accusation.[88] In 1638, John Lilburn refused to take an oath to tell the truth to the Star Chamber, which sought to question him about his unlicensed publishing activities. As we will see in chapter 7, the Court in its famous *Miranda* case relied heavily on Lilburn's persecution by the Star Chamber to expand the privilege to cover custodial police interrogation.

Yet, despite the fascination of this mostly secret court, it is largely beside the point for our enterprise, with one exception that we note in the next section. First, this history has been thoroughly, perhaps obsessively, documented. We have little to add, though we would remind readers that John Lilburn's fight against the Star Chamber was not about its substantive power to compel confessions but, rather, the procedural rule that those who appeared before the Star Chamber could be compelled to swear an oath to tell the truth. Lilburn, and many others, argued that the crown lacked the power to compel anyone to swear an oath to tell the truth. As noted earlier, oaths at the time created a solemn obligation to tell the truth. Thus, if someone could be compelled to take an oath to tell the truth, then he was forced to be his own accuser. But it was self-accusation that critics of the Star Chamber condemned, not involuntary confessions. Thus, the fight over the Star Chamber has nothing to say substantively about whether a confession is admissible.

Second, its mostly secret nature means that historians lack the kind of records that are available in the Year Books and the records of the Old Bailey. Third, as an arm of the crown that did not have to follow the common law,[89] its machinations tell us nothing about the common law of confessions. As Bentham put it, "In the common law courts, these [Star Chamber] enormities could not be committed."[90] Indeed, defendants were not permitted to testify under oath in common law courts, and no issue of refusing to take an oath could ever arise in these courts.

Finally, whatever value the Star Chamber adds to the English confession story, that court was abolished by the Long Parliament in 1641.[91] Most of the movement toward the modern law of confessions occurred after 1641. This is the story to which we now turn.

F. The "Missing Century": 1535–1674

The "missing century" is actually a century and one-third of another (but that does not make a very good title). The Year Books ceased in 1535, and the Old Bailey trial records do not begin until 1674. There are, to be sure, individual case reports in various volumes published by the Selden Society for the period from 1535 to 1674, but these are scattered and difficult to search. We found several statements of concern about how confessions were obtained in this period, two of which we have already noted. The earlier is the Treason Act of 1547 that required two witnesses unless the defendant "shall willingly without violence confess" the treason. The second, ten years later, is Staundford's treatise, which broadened and deepened the principle. Staundford noted the value of confessions of felonies to the judge, as long as they "did not proceed from fear, menace, or duress." Compared to the Treason Act, Staundford's principle is broader because it applies to all felonies and not just to treason. It is deeper because it cannot be fully explained as an attempt to limit the power of the king.

Another early mention of concern about confessions appears in the November 20, 1606 Articles, Instructions, and Orders contained in the 1606 Charter from James I that established the two Virginia colonies. In setting out the right to a jury trial by twelve "honest and indifferent persons," the document continues: "and that all and ever person or persons, which shall voluntarily confesse any of the said offenses" shall be convicted as if found guilty by a jury.[92] This is the earliest use of the "voluntary" terminology that we found in English law. The same locution shows up in a 1662 Virginia statute that criminalized certain religious observations.[93]

We found another reference to voluntary confessions in a treatise about the Star Chamber. William Hudson wrote, in 1635 or earlier, that when "dangerous persons" acted in ways that "may be very likely to endanger the very fabric of government, these persons [could be] apprehended by a pursuivant or messenger, and privately examined [before the Star Chamber], without oath, or any compulsory means, concerning the fact."[94] If the person denied the accusation, then the Star Chamber had to proceed by written evidence. "But if he confesses the offence freely and voluntarily, without constraint, then may he be brought to the bar" and examined orally. Like the Treason Act of 1547, the Star Chamber procedures recognized an exception to the formal means of proof—two witnesses testifying to treason or the requirement of proceeding by written evidence only—when the accused confessed the act "willingly without violence" or "freely and voluntarily."

Coke's *Third Institutes of the Law of England*, published in 1644, also contained a reference to voluntary confession. After a felon took sanctuary in a church, his "voluntary and particular confession of the felony before the coroner" justified a judgment that the felon abjure the realm.[95] Here, of course, "confession" is used as a plea of guilty. The reference to voluntary confessions in sanctuary cases is oddly narrow. Coke speaks more than once in his *Third Institutes* of "confession" as a plea,[96] but the only other reference we found to a "voluntary" confession was when Coke was paraphrasing the Treason Act of 1547.[97] Perhaps the hallowed place of sanctuary in English law, drawing on God's protection, required more of confessions given while in sanctuary. More likely is that, by 1644, Coke just assumed that pleas to judges had to be voluntary. That was, after all, Staundford's view almost a century earlier.

To be sure, Coke was the king's prosecutor in the Gunpowder Plot cases as well as in Sir Walter Raleigh's prosecution, to which we shall turn shortly, and both featured torture to obtain a confession. The Gunpowder Plot was a plan to blow up the House of Lords.[98] Guy Fawkes was found guarding thirty-six barrels of gunpowder on November 5, 1605. He admitted that he had "been at the bottom" of the plot and "that there were fellow-conspirators whom he refused to name." In seeking more details about the conspiracy, King James I ordered by letter that, if necessary, Fawkes be tortured into confessing: "'If he will not otherwise confess' . . . 'the gentler tortures are to be first used unto him, *et sic per gradus ad ima tenditur*' [and thus by steps extended to greater ones]."[99]

Coke was one of the commissioners to whom the king's letter was directed. It is doubtful that he personally inflicted the torture that Fawkes suffered, but he certainly knew it had been authorized. But what should we make of Coke's involvement in an examination that included torture? First, the Gunpowder Plot trials occurred almost forty years prior to the publication of his *Third Institutes*. Moreover, Coke did not authorize torture of Fawkes and, as far as we know, might have thought it wrong. Finally, the thesis of this book holds that a government or a prosecutor could approve torture in a case where the State's existence is threatened, as in the Gunpowder Plot, and still believe that a confession in an ordinary criminal case had to be voluntary before a judicial officer could accept it. As for the threat to the crown posed by the Gunpowder Plot, Gardiner's account, published in 1897, offered a partial excuse for the torture given the very real possibility of a general Catholic uprising. "We cannot deny that, at that particular moment, they had real cause for alarm."[100]

Notice, however, that Staundford's principle is limited to confessions to the judge, Hudson's rule to confessions before the Star Chamber, and Coke's rule to confessions to a coroner. None would apply to "mere confessions" made outside a formal setting. Whether the Treason Act of 1547 prohibited the use of out-of-court confessions turned out to be controversial. Because confessions were used in lieu of two witnesses who otherwise would testify in court, the Act appears to make witnesses unnecessary only when a defendant confessed in court. But political realities being what they are, within a few years of Henry's VIII's death, English courts felt pressure to relax the treason rule so that confessions made prior to trial could be used instead of two witnesses. Coke was a particularly adept proponent of this interpretation, as we shall shortly see. Parliament would later, in 1695, make clear that the confession to treason, given "willingly without violence," had to be in open court to avoid the two-witness rule.[101]

Thus, the best reading of Staundford, Hudson, Coke, the 1606 Virginia Charter, and the Treason Act of 1547 is that these expressions of concern with confessions produced by violence were not limited to confessions made in formal proceedings. The "mere confessions" that had no formal legal effect were beginning to be viewed skeptically during this period. Larry Herman uncovered three cases from this period evincing concern about the voluntariness of confessions made outside of the trial itself.[102] In the 1551 treason prosecution of the Duke of Somerset, the prosecutor asked witnesses about out-of court confessions that the crown assured the jury "were true" because "what was sworn was without any kind of compulsion, force, or envy, or displeasure."[103] When the Bishop of Ross accused the Duke of Norfolk of treason in 1571, he was examined in the Tower of London; the crown assured the jury that the bishop was "examined freely, and without any compulsion."[104] In 1600, Sir Christopher Blunt and four other defendants were accused of raising an army to demand concessions from Queen Elizabeth.[105] Three of the defendants had confessed to treason, and the queen's counsel argued that additional proof was unnecessary because the confession "came voluntarily from every man examined, no man being racked or tormented."[106]

Three years later, the crown used a confession from the alleged co-conspirator of Sir Walter Raleigh made to the Privy Council to prove Raleigh guilty of treason. Coke was the crown's lead prosecutor. Raleigh demanded, unsuccessfully, that his accuser be produced in court to repeat the confession. Raleigh claimed that his accuser had been held "close prisoner" for eighteen weeks and "was offered the rack to make him confess."[107] The judges denied that the threat occurred, thus signaling that the argument would have had force if it had been true.

Raleigh's claim is now understood as the right to confront one's accusers, a right enshrined in our Sixth Amendment. But at the heart of the claim is the notion that an involuntary confession is not good evidence because it is untrustworthy. The reason he wanted to confront his accuser in court was to obtain a noncoerced and thus more trustworthy version of events. By the time we arrive at Hawkins's *Pleas of the Crown*, a little more than a century later, the common law had evolved a crude method to deal with out-of-court confessions of accomplices. They were simply inadmissible. Indeed, the only rule that Hawkins states in connection with out-of-court confessions is that they were admissible only against the maker.[108] This solved the problem of the unavailable accomplice confessor because his confession was not admissible in the trial of the principal.

If Raleigh had been able to persuade the judges that the confession was not made voluntarily or willingly, the legal effect during most of this early period was not the modern remedy of suppression but, rather, was for the judge to instruct the jury that it should consider that the confession had been produced by coercion or out of fear and thus might not be reliable. (We will cover this in chapter 5.) If that was the appropriate remedy in 1603, it would not have done Raleigh much good even if the justices agreed that the confession of the alleged accomplice was coerced. Coke told the jury that the king's safety required a conviction.[109] Protecting the king from those who might be plotting his death was probably a higher-order value than giving defendants the right to prove their innocence.[110] The jury deliberated a mere fifteen minutes before finding Raleigh guilty of high treason.[111]

Outside of treason cases, we found few out-of-court confessions during this period. The confessions that appeared in early English case law were mostly admissions made in court when defendants told their side of the events, claimed benefit of clergy, or sought to approve (accuse) others of the crime. Part of the explanation for the lack of out-of-court confessions in the run of the mill cases was that no law enforcement mechanism, in the modern sense, existed in this period. Police did not exist. Sheriffs and constables could make arrests in fresh pursuit but did not investigate "stale" crimes. Grand juries were not as aggressive as Henry II contemplated in the Assize of Clarendon, and it generally fell to the victim or the victim's family to prosecute crimes.

Another reason for the lack of confessions in the modern sense is that juries of the period were "self-informing" juries: men chosen from the neighborhood precisely because neighbors would know the character of the parties and might even know something of the crime. Thus, the juries served as witnesses as well as triers of fact, and there was little need for other evidence. Langbein notes that "[a]s late as Fortescue (1460s), it was being boasted that the English jury merged witnesses and triers."[112]

Although the notion of self-informing juries persisted beyond the fifteenth century,[113] the transition to juries as impartial fact-finders was well underway by the turn of the sixteenth century. Impartial fact-finders require evidence, which would include out-of-court statements. If self-informing juries were in decline by the sixteenth century, we should see evidence of evidence-gathering taking place before trial.

And we do. By the terms of the Marian bail and committal statutes of 1554 and 1555, justices of the peace were required to transcribe in writing the statements of the accuser and other witnesses, under oath, and the accused, not under oath, before deciding whether to admit the accused to bail.[114] "The JP's job was to help the accuser build the prosecution case, rather than to serve as a neutral investigator seeking all the evidence, inculpating and exculpating."[115] The statements were used by the victim of the crime, often in consultation with a court clerk, to frame an indictment.[116] The unsworn examination of the accused was "routinely read in evidence at his trial."[117]

By 1555, the justice of the peace had become the focal point for gathering evidence of crimes. Confessions were now a routine part of the crown's case. Yet the lack of organized case reports during this period makes it difficult to assess what kinds of arguments were offered when those statements were introduced at trial. We see at least the beginning of a claim that "mere confessions" must be voluntary to be fully credited in Raleigh's trial and in the sixteenth century cases that Herman uncovered.[118] Seventy years after Raleigh's trial, similar claims would begin to appear in English trials held in the Old Bailey. The records of trials in the Old Bailey, available online, are a rich repository of evidence about English criminal trials. This is the story to which we turn in chapter 3.

CHAPTER 3

English Interrogation Law
from 1674–1848

London's Great Fire of 1666 began in the shop of Charles II's baker on Pudding Lane.[1] By the time it died out three days later, it had burned 436 acres, 15 of 26 wards, 13,200 homes, 400 streets, 89 churches, and many schools, hospitals, libraries, and other public structures.[2] A monument marks the spot where the fire stopped. The inscription notes that the fire began at Pudding Lane and ended at Pye Corner, evidence, according to a "non-conformist preacher," that the fire manifested God's wrath on London for the sin of gluttony.[3]

The Great Fire destroyed London's medieval courthouse.[4] A replacement, Justice Hall, was completed in 1674 but quickly became known by the street on which it was located. Old Bailey Street followed the lines of the original fortified wall that was called a "bailey." The three-story, Italian-style brick building was conveniently located close to Newgate Prison, still standing (and polluting the air) five centuries after its construction. In front of the courthouse was the Sessions House Yard, where litigants, witnesses, and court personnel could gather. The area inside the wall, where prisoners awaited trial, was called the bail dock. It was separated from the street by a brick wall with spikes on top to keep prisoners from escaping.

The ground floor had no walls, allowing fresh air to circulate and decrease the risk that "gaol fever"—typhus—would spread from the prisoners to others in the courtroom.[5] While that was probably a good idea, imagine the Old Bailey in the winter months when rain, cold, fog, sooty air, and the fetid smell of Newgate Prison would attend the proceedings. The accused stood at "the bar" facing the witness box; the jurors were seated on both sides of the accused. The judges were on the other side of the courtroom.

The great value of the Old Bailey to historians is that, from the beginning, records were kept of the trials. The earlier records are sparse, but a sparse record is better than none.

A. A Revolution Begins in Interrogation Law: 1677–1787

Langbein claims that the English rule about involuntary confessions "pops out" in July 1740.[6] John Beattie similarly concluded from his review of the Surrey records that there was not "much concern being expressed in court before the 1730s about the way that confessions had been obtained."[7] Both claims, of course, are about out-of-court confessions rather than confessions to judges that were guilty pleas. Whether there was "much" or "not much" concern is a question of semantics, but we found prior to 1740 several expressions of concern that confessions should not be obtained by promises or from fear.

We discussed in chapter 2 the 1295 argument that prison conditions compelled the defendant to confess falsely. The earliest confession case we found in the Old Bailey records—from July 11, 1677—was sparse indeed. We reprint it here in full:

> There succeeded a long and remarkable Tryal of a young Girl for murdering her own Mother by poyson. The Prosecution was grounded wholly upon her own voluntary Confession, and several worthy persons proved that she had acknowledged it to them; and also that she for several times had endeavoured to poyson a Lady with whom she lived, though through mercy she had recovered and was in health again: but that not immediately concerning the present Case, the Girl denying the poisoning of her Mother now at the Bar, as likewise for that it did not appear that her Mother was at all poisoned, or any suspitio [sic] raised thereon, she was brought in not Guilty.[8]

Though the key to the case was that the crown failed to prove that the defendant's mother was poisoned, the clerk thought it important to note that the defendant's confession was "voluntary" and had been repeated to "several worthy persons." This probably signals an awareness that confessions are less valuable as evidence if involuntary. We found another murder case from 1677 where the clerk recorded that the confession was voluntary.[9] These cases suggest that judicial concern about out-of-court confessions arose many years earlier than Langbein and Beattie conclude.

A modern form of a coercion argument appears in 1686. Ames Spencer, a maid, was charged with grand larceny for stealing a guinea from her master.[10] The master initially blamed his wife, and she then blamed the maid. "[C]arrying her before the Justice [of the peace], she confessed she had it, and took it to satisfie a Man whose debt she had run during her being out of Service." But she denied the theft in court, and because her "Confession" to the justice was "look'd upon as the effects of Fear, she was Acquitted." The sketchy report does not indicate what caused her fear, but the concern with "the effects of Fear" on confessions is plain.

Concern with confessions induced by fear appears in a 1688 shoplifting case. A store owner seized a suspect who had been "hankering around his Shop the Night the Robbery was committed."[11] When he confronted her with his suspicions, she was "not . . . confident enough . . . to deny the Fact at that time, though in Court, she, as well as her Companion, disowned it." The report concludes: "The Jury weighing the Circumstance, that the first Confession might proceed from Fear, they Acquitted them of the Felony."

We found four other cases from the period 1688–1712 involving claims that the confession should not count against the defendant. Though the defendant lost each case, the existence of the claim shows that the law was beginning to recognize its validity. In 1688, an apprentice was accused of stealing from his master.[12] When his confession was introduced in court he said, "That what he had confessed was through Fear and Constraint, by reason his Master had struck him, and dealt roughly with him, to extort an Acknowledgment." But other witnesses testified that his confession appeared to be "rather frankly, than by compulsion."

A defendant accused of counterfeiting in 1694 used a "fear" claim—that "what he acknowledged" to the justice of the peace "was out of fear."[13] The report concludes that "all this was no Evidence for him," and he was convicted of high treason and sentenced to death. A servant accused of stealing a silver cup disavowed her confession to the magistrate because "she did not know what it was she said, for that at that time she was in great fear."[14] The jury convicted her. A defendant accused of stealing a horse confessed it before the justice of the peace. At trial, there was evidence that "he had been a very honest Man, and he said he was frightened into a Confession." But the jury did not "believe him innocent," and he was sentenced to death.[15]

These cases signal that English law was beginning to turn. We remind the reader of the distinction between "mere confessions," those made outside of trial and thus without any formal consequence, and those made to a judge or coroner. The Old Bailey cases we have seen, unlike the earlier Year Book cases, involve "mere confessions." Despite the indications in the Old Bailey cases from as early as 1676 that "mere confessions" produced by fear or threats should somehow be discounted, we see no evidence of any concern about these confessions in the leading treatise of the early part of the eighteenth century, William Hawkins's *Treatise of the Pleas of the Crown*. As we saw in chapter 2, the 1721 edition of his treatise provided that confessions made out of court, not under oath, including those taken by justices of the peace are "allowed to be given in Evidence against the Party confessing, but not against others."[16]

Hawkins's Chapter 46 treatment of "mere confessions" can be usefully compared to his more elaborate statement about confessions given in court. We also see here the proportionality principle at work. After first noting that a confession to a crime in court "carries with it so strong a Presumption of guilt" that it "estops" a not guilty plea, Chapter 31 provides that in capital cases courts should be "very tender in going upon Presumptions." Thus,

> where a Person upon his Arraignment actually confesses himself Guilty, or unadvisedly discloses the Special Manner of the Fact, supposing that it does not amount to Felony, where it doth, yet the Judges, upon probable Circumstances, that such Confession may proceed from Fear, Menace, or Duress, or from Weakness or Ignorance, may refuse to record such Confession, and suffer the Party to plead Not Guilty.[17]

To modern eyes, it is positively perverse that confessions made in court were subject to concerns about fear, menace, duress, weakness, or ignorance, but Hawkins expressed no similar concerns about confessions made out of court. Obviously, coercion would be easier to hide if conducted in private. For an explanation, recall the 1348 case in chapter 2 where Justice William de Thorp permitted the defendant to withdraw his confession so that the jury could decide his fate.[18] The confession made to the court was, unless excused by grace, a final conviction. The confession made to the justice of the peace or the victim of the theft, on the other hand, was merely a piece of evidence.

As evidence law became more sophisticated, the distinction between confession as a guilty plea and confession as evidence became more difficult to maintain. Indeed, an awareness of the effect of fear on out-of-court confessions appears in Matthew Hale's *The History of the Pleas of the Crown*, published in 1736. The examination of the prisoner required by the Marian statutes was often a critical part of the crown's case.[19] Hale cautions justices of the peace to testify that the prisoner confessed to them "freely and without any menace, or undue terror imposed upon him."[20] That Hale's *History of the Pleas of the Crown* was not published until fifty years after his death in 1676 raises a nice question about when that passage was written. The passage says that Hale saw cases where acquittals were obtained by defendants disavowing their confessions, suggesting that he wrote it. The editor, Sollom Emlyn, claims on the title page that the treatise was "published from his Lordship's Original Manuscript. . . . To which is added A Table of Principal Matters."[21] The implication is that Emlyn added nothing of substance. The earliest Old Bailey case we found questioning "mere confessions" was in 1677, but there is no reason to think that it was the first one. Hale could have seen, from his time as a judge, acquittals resulting from challenges to confessions made to justices of the peace.

Of course, it is also possible that the passage about unfree confessions was added by Emlyn before publication in 1736. That seems unlikely to us because Emlyn used footnotes to update Hale's work. For example, one note states that the practice described in the text had been changed by statute.[22] Elsewhere, a note states, "These words are not in the MS but they or others to the like effect are manifestly wanted to supply the sense."[23] An editor who was this scrupulous about small changes was unlikely to add entire sections of text without acknowledging that he was doing so.[24] If Hale wrote the passage urging magistrates to testify that the prisoner "freely confessed," then the concern about voluntariness was manifest more than half a century earlier than Langbein and Beattie claim.

In any event, the publication of Hale's *History of the Pleas of the Crown* in 1736 gave voice to the concerns we saw in the scattered Old Bailey cases about unfree confessions made out of court. Hawkins seemed to have sensed the dissonance between his in-court and out-of-court confession principles,[25] though the distinction persisted in the subsequent editions of his treatise until the seventh, published in 1786. To say that unfree out-of-court confessions are suspect does not, however, dictate what should be done if a confession is found to be unfree. The concern in Hale's *History of the Pleas of the Crown* about unfree confessions does not appear to entail a rule of suppression. The passage concludes, "for I have often known the prisoner disown his confession upon examination, and hath sometimes been acquitted against such his confession."[26] To be acquitted "against" a confession implies that the jury heard and rejected the confession because of doubts about its credibility.

In all the cases we saw up to 1740, it appears that the jury heard the confession that was challenged as unfree and then decided whether, or how much, to "discount" it. In the 1600 case where the prosecutor assured the court that the defendants' confessions "came voluntarily . . . no man being racked or tormented," the prosecutor said that the confessions "would be credited in the world."[27] The implication is that the jury should credit the confession. In the 1688 case of *Smith and Simmons*, the reporter wrote, "The Jury weighing the Circumstances, that the first Confession might proceed from Fear, they Acquitted them of the Felony."[28] This report is clear that the jury heard the confession and then discounted it because it "proceed[ed] from Fear." One might wonder how the reporter would know what influenced the jury. Most likely, the answer is that the reporter simply drew an inference from the testimony and the verdict.[29]

But the remedy for a confession induced by fear would change, beginning with the 1740 case *Tobias and Rachael Isaacs*;[30] the case Langbein cites as the beginning of the voluntariness rule. Rachel Isaacs and her husband were charged with theft from her master, who testified that "when I taxed her with taking [his goods], she deny'd it with Earnestness for 2 Hours, but upon my promising to be a Friend to her, and that I would not hurt [her], she confessed." The case report continued:

> The Prosecutor was not allowed to proceed; and another Witness afterwards offering to give an Account of what she had confessed to him, was likewise stopped; because a Confession obtained on a Promise of

Friendship, or by false Insinuations . . . ought not to be given in Evidence against a Prisoner.

On the substance, the *Isaacs* court held it unfair to obtain a confession from a servant by a promise of leniency. The master told her that he was her friend and he would not hurt her, and she presumably relied on that promise. To hold her confession unfree is thus consistent with the seventeenth-century cases we saw earlier. But the radical change in *Isaacs* is the remedy. Rather than advising a jury to consider the circumstances in which the confession was made, or simply trusting the jury's common sense, *Tobias and Isaacs* held that a confession obtained by a promise of friendship "ought not to be given in Evidence against" the defendant. This states a rule of suppression. The jury could not hear the offending confession.

A year later, in the *Trial of Charles White*, the defense lawyer objected to the admission of the magistrate's pretrial examination on the ground that the crown had not demonstrated that the defendant's confession was "voluntarily made."[31] If not voluntarily made, the argument went, "it ought not to be read." Not reading the confession, of course, is a form of suppression. The judge ruled the objection improper, because it was not timely made, but conceded that otherwise "it would have been proper for us to enquire by what means the confession was procured."

For much of the period prior to 1740, judges "appear to have left it to the jury to assign what weight they would to confessions," but *Tobias and Isaacs* ushered in an era of instability in the English approach to confessions prompted by threats or promises.[32] Some judges followed the old rule and made no comment on the confession. Some judges followed *Tobias and Isaacs* and would not let the jury hear the confession. A third approach was to tell the jury that it should "consider" when weighing the confession whether the defendant had "any promises of Indulgence before he confessed."[33] In a 1742 case where that question was raised, but not answered (at least in the Old Bailey records), the jury acquitted.[34]

As early as 1755, the justice of the peace manuals began to require that the statement to the justice be voluntary—a synonym for a confession freely given—and to imply a rule of suppression if it was not voluntary. The first edition of Richard Burn's 1755 manual contained quite detailed prescriptions about taking the examination mandated by the Marian statutes. One sentence provided, "Which examination, being voluntary, and sworn by the justice or his clerk to be truly taken, may be given in evidence against the party confessing, but not against others."[35] Burn cites Hawkins and Hale for this proposition, but neither cited passage is good authority. The Hawkins passage in the edition that was current in 1755 (the third, published in 1739) does not use the term "voluntary" but merely repeats the rule from the 1721 edition that out-of-court confessions are admissible only against the maker.[36]

The passage that Burn cited from Hale's *History of the Pleas of the Crown* requires "the justice or his clerk" to swear to the accuracy of the statement and to certify it to the criminal court to be "given in evidence against the offender," but nowhere requires the statement to be voluntary.[37] We saw earlier that a different section in Hale's *History of the Pleas of the Crown* (indeed, in a different volume) does caution the magistrate to testify that the statement to him was made "freely and without any menace, or undue terror."[38] That advice is roughly like cautioning the magistrate to testify that the statement was voluntary, and it is odd that Burn does not cite this passage in Hale.

Burn probably drew the rule that confessions to the justice of the peace had to be voluntary from *Tobias and Rachel Isaacs* and other Old Bailey cases that we described. He then threw in an oddball citation of Hawkins and Hale—then, as now, writers probably figured that they could not go wrong citing Hawkins or Hale. A rule of suppression is probably entailed in Burn's notion that the voluntary confession of the defendant *"may be given in evidence."*[39] A contrary rule seems likely when the confession was not voluntary. The Burn approach, both to remedy and to voluntariness of out-of-court confessions, is a radical change from the 1721 Hawkins rule that permitted all out-of-court confessions to be admitted against the maker, but the change happened without comment that we could find.

As for the reason that English law developed along the Burn line, Lord Chief Baron Gilbert grounded the rule in the concern with reliability. His treatise on evidence, published in 1756, includes a section dealing with interested witnesses. That section notes that the "voluntary Confession of the Party in Interest is reckoned the best Evidence" because it is against the interest of the speaker.[40] Gilbert goes on to caution that "this Confession must be voluntary and without Compulsion."[41] In this, he writes, "we do certainly follow the Law of Nature, which commands every Man to endeavor his own Preservation; and therefore Pain and Force may compel Men to confess what is not the Truth of Facts." As to remedy, Gilbert is unclear. He merely says that "such extorted Confessions are not to be depended on." That is consistent either with not letting the jury hear the coerced confession or the judge warning the jury not to depend too heavily on the confession.

Langbein argues that, by the 1760s, departures from the rule of suppression "cease to be reported" because "practice had become law."[42] It is not as clear to us as it is to Langbein that this was the settled rule. Michael Foster's 1762 *Crown Cases* mentions no such rule, though he does express a concern about the reliability of out-of-court confessions in treason cases. In a passage that would influence Blackstone, Foster noted that in treason cases, "hasty Confessions made to Persons having no Authority to examine, are the Weakest and most Suspicious of All Evidence. Proof may be too easily procured, Words are often Mis-reported, whether through Ignorance, Inattention, or Malice, it mattereth not the Defendant."[43] To call confessions weak and suspicious evidence, however, is more consistent with admitting the confession, and cautioning the jury, than suppressing it.

Langbein's first examples fail to make the point that suppression was the rule by the 1760s because each simply notes that the confession was prompted by a promise or a threat and then reports that the defendant was acquitted.[44] It is entirely possible that the jury heard the confession and decided that the defendant should not be convicted based on that kind of evidence. To take one example, a wigmaker in 1764 accused one of his employees, Benjamin March, of stealing four guineas.[45] March confessed after his employer said, "deliver [the guineas] up, and no creature shall know of it." The jury acquitted March. The case report contains no language indicating that the judge refused to let the jury hear the confession. Langbein attempts to finesse the lack of evidence of suppression by noting that there was no doubt that the defendant was guilty and, therefore, "the acquittal could not have resulted from a rule of weight or credit."[46]

But this reading imposes modern logic on an eighteenth-century jury and also assumes that reliability was the only value served by the early English law of confessions. As we have seen, principles of autonomy, fairness, and proportionality also manifest themselves in the evolving voluntariness rule. The jury could easily have thought March guilty but that it was unfair for the employer to break his promise. Indeed, the March case is a particularly weak piece of evidence for Langbein's argument because, as he notes himself, the employer did not want to prosecute and begged the justice of the peace not to send the case to trial.[47] All of this the jury heard. The theft of four guineas was a capital offense. It is quite likely that the jury heard the confession but decided to enforce the promise that the employer made to March rather than send him to the gallows.

Langbein's 1769 example, *Balfe and Kirk*, hits the nail on the head. Justice Gould stated from the bench that "when evidence is giving to the court upon the confession of the prisoner, the rule of law is this, That no confession ought to be produced but what is spontaneous, and not such that the party is drawn into by collusion."[48] With a rhetorical flourish, Gould concluded that "it is against the very genius of the law of England [for such confession] to be given in evidence." To be sure, the remark about remedy is dicta because Justice Gould admitted the defendant's statement in response to a question that invited the defendant "to boast of more than he had done." The defense argued that the question "was a natural encouragement" for him to give an exaggerated and thus somewhat untrue confession. Justice Gould rejected the argument, but defense counsel's willingness to object to such slight encouragement shows how quickly English law was evolving on this point. Not quite twenty years later, Hawkins's treatise would condemn confessions motivated "by the flattery of hope, or by the impressions of fear, *however slightly* the emotions may be implanted."[49] *Balfe and Kirk* demonstrate that this notion was already bubbling up from the defense bar in 1769.

But *Balfe and Kirk* hardly settled the English law of confessions. Indeed, Sir William Blackstone expressed no concern about confessions in the first seven editions of his monumental treatise, through 1775, other than referencing the statutory requirement that confessions to treason had to be made willingly and without violence. The seventh edition appeared six years after Justice Gould's bold pronouncement in *Balfe and Kirk* that no confession should be admissible unless it was spontaneous. *Balfe and Kirk* had probably not come to Blackstone's attention because it was not reported by Thomas Leach in his *Cases in Crown Law*.

In Blackstone's 1778 edition, the last that he prepared personally, an insertion in the section about treason expressed profound skepticism about confessions in general. Importantly, while his 1778 edition tracked Foster's 1762 language, Blackstone broadened the concern beyond treason cases:

> In the construction of [the treason] act it hath been holden, that a confession of the prisoner, taken out of court, before a magistrate or person having competent authority to take it, and proved by two witnesses, is sufficient to convict him of treason. But hasty unguarded confessions, made to persons having no such authority, ought not to be admitted as evidence under this statute. And indeed, even in cases of felony at the common law, they are the weakest and most suspicious of all testimony; ever liable to be obtained by artifice, false hopes, promises of favour, or menaces; seldom remembered accurately, or reported with due precision; and incapable in their nature of being disproved by other negative evidence.[50]

Something seems to have happened between the seventh and eighth editions that caught Blackstone's attention, but he cites no authority. That delicious mystery is beyond the scope of our work. The important point is that by 1778, the most widely read English treatise writer had officially condemned confessions as "the weakest and most suspicious of all testimony." To be sure, Blackstone's 1778 expression is unclear whether the remedy is one of suppression or merely a suggestion that judges warn juries about its weakness.

The law on the suppression point was, however, beginning to settle by 1783. In *Rex v. Thompson*, the officer told the suspect that he would take him before a magistrate "unless you give me a more satisfactory account" of the events.[51] Even though the judges conceded that the official's statement "scarcely amounts to a threat," it was nonetheless a "strong invitation to him to confess." The court noted that it "is almost impossible to be too careful upon this subject" because "[t]he prisoner was hardly a free agent at the time" he responded to the official's statement. The opinion cautioned that "[t]oo great a chastity cannot be preserved on this subject." The confession "ought not to be received." *Thompson* is clear that a slight threat is sufficient to render a confession objectionable and that the proper remedy is suppression. Leach did include *Thompson* in *Cases in Crown Law*, though not until the 1800 edition.

In 1784, Justice Gould, the author of *Balfe and Kirk*, followed *Thompson* and ruled "that the slightest hopes of mercy held out to a prisoner to induce him to disclose that fact [of his guilt], was sufficient to invalidate a confession."[52] Three years later, Thomas Leach added a paragraph to the 1787 edition of Hawkins's *Treatise of the Pleas of the Crown* (Hawkins died in 1746 but his treatise lived on) that tracked Gould's "slightest hope" formulation and, like *Thompson*, made plain that the proper remedy was suppression:

> The human mind, under the pressure of calamity is easily seduced, and is liable, in the alarm of danger, to acknowledge indiscriminately a falsehood or a truth, as different agitations may prevail. A confession, therefore, whether made upon an official examination or in discourse with private persons, which is obtained from a defendant, either by the flattery of hope, or by the impressions of fear, however slightly the emotions may be implanted, is not admissible evidence; for the law will not suffer a prisoner to be made the deluded instrument of his own conviction.[53]

Leach's language tracks language in *The King v. Warickshall*, an Old Bailey case four years earlier where the court said that "a confession forced from the mind by the flattery of hope, or by the torture of fear, comes in so questionable a shape when it is to be considered as the evidence of guilt, that no credit ought to be given to it."[54] It is not surprising that Leach drew from *Warickshall*. We know that he had a copy of the manuscript of the case because he included it in the first edition of his *Cases in Crown Law* in 1789.[55]

The law of confessions was now settled in a very different mold than a half-century earlier. In 1721, Hawkins stated that all out-of-court confessions were "allowed to be given in Evidence against the Party confessing, but not against others." In 1787, Leach stated a rule of suppression in the Hawkins treatise based on slight influences that might cause hope or fear. We will refer to this as the Hawkins-Leach dictum. This is perhaps unfair to Blackstone, who articulated a similar skeptical view nine years earlier, or even to Staundford and Foster. But Blackstone and Leach were the first two treatise writers to make clear that skepticism about confessions applied to all cases of felony, and the Leach statement of skepticism is more profound than Blackstone's. The latter speaks generally of confessions being weak and suspicious while the former emphasizes that the slightest influence is too much. Moreover, the metaphor of a confessing suspect being made the "deluded instrument of his own conviction" is irresistible. So Hawkins-Leach dictum it is. And this is perhaps unfair to Leach, who actually wrote the words, but we'll stop with the attempt to achieve perfect fairness.

And what was happening on the Continent at this time? As of the date *Rex v. Thompson* said that "[t]oo great a chastity cannot be preserved" when deciding whether a confession is improperly influenced, judicial torture was still being used in Belgium—it would not be abolished until France conquered Belgium in 1794.[56] Judicial torture had been abolished in France, but only three years before *Thompson*. It had been abolished in Austria in 1776, and the last judicial torture in Germany was authorized in 1752.

The Western world was moving away from using confessions produced by coercion pretty much in tandem, although the English were pressing the point the most forcefully. It is no exaggeration to say that the English confessions world turned upside down between 1721 and 1787. What caused this radical shift in the law of confessions?

B. Causes of Skepticism About Confessions

Wigmore's explanation for the skeptical attitude of English judges, in part, was based on their view of the class structure. Confessions might typically result from "a subordination, a submission, half-respectful and half-stupid, on the part of the 'lower classes' toward those in authority."[57] John Langbein rejects this explanation because "[s]ocial stratification was centuries old" when the voluntariness rule appears "and the further back the more striking."[58] Langbein argues that the exquisite concern with voluntariness "was grounded in precisely those concerns about the potential unreliability of prosecution evidence that had motivated" other changes in English criminal procedure of the period, including the decision to permit counsel to represent felony defendants at trial.[59]

Wigmore is closer to the mark than Langbein. Though Langbein is right that English criminal procedure was moving toward a greater emphasis on reliability, the extent of the shift in confessions law from Hawkins in 1721 to the skepticism expressed by Blackstone in 1778 and Thomas Leach in 1787 simply cannot be explained by reliability concerns. By the 1800s, English courts were suppressing confessions made when suspects were encouraged to tell the truth or were cautioned that they did not have to answer questions—hardly a manifestation of a reliability norm. Something in addition to a concern with reliability was going on in English confessions law of this period.

Along with the trappings of modernity, the century prior to 1787 brought a dramatic change in how human actors were perceived. The Glorious Revolution that swept James II from power in 1688 swept into power those with a Whig philosophy. The Whigs rejected the absolute power of the monarch and insisted that governance be shared with the people through Parliament. John Locke identified a law of nature that makes humans "all equal and independent"; there-fore, "no one ought to harm another in his life, health, liberty, or possessions."[60] In Locke's state of nature, "men are not bound to submit to the unjust will of another."[61] Even Thomas Hobbes, a royalist who believed in a strong monarchy, claimed a right to disobey the sovereign when it commanded the subject to do an act that would injure or destroy him.[62]

And the monarchy had changed. After the Oliver Cromwell experiment in republican government ended in 1660, Charles II reclaimed a weakened monar-chy. In 1688, the Glorious Revolution "concentrated power in the hands of an oligarchy of Whig nobles and virtually ended interference with the local justices [of the peace], even by [royal] judges."[63] As historian Alan Harding put it, the "gentry entered an age of prosperity in which the J.P.s could afford to treat pop-ular disorder with comparative leniency." While Harding's point is limited to the justices of the peace, it applies equally well to the trial judges who sat in the Old Bailey. One aspect of the weakened monarchy was that the royal judges were no longer supervised by the crown. Judges had more power to dispense mercy or justice to fit the individual case.

Langbein is thus wrong to dismiss a class explanation of skepticism about confessions on the ground that social stratification was "centuries old." What is important, in our explanation if not in Wigmore's, is the Whig philosophy in the eighteenth century. Whig judges looked at the lower classes through a different lens than judges would have used in the sixteenth and seventeenth centuries.

Still, one must account for the fact that Whig judges were in power roughly a century before the appearance of Blackstone's skepticism and the Hawkins-Leach dictum. What explains the robust embrace of confession-skepticism in the late eighteenth century? Part of the explanation is that England was, by 1787, a world power, both by force of her navy and her dominant position as the most important trading partner with the world.[64] England was at peace and thus faced no imminent external threats.

Internal threats are probably more important than external ones in judging a culture's tolerance for harsh interrogation tactics, and fear of crime is an impor-tant internal threat. By the mid-eighteenth century, English criminal procedure was ill-suited to deal with urban crime. Without police, justice largely depended on victims to institute prosecutions, aided by the grand jury that Henry II had instituted. While that system was probably adequate for crime in villages and small cities, where the identity of the malefactor was usually known or easily ascertained, it did not prove adequate for a city like London, which, by 1760, had a population of roughly 750,000.[65] Robberies were a particularly severe problem. The robber could appear from a dark alley, commit the crime, and then disappear into London's crowded streets. "The inadequacy of medieval machinery to cope with the problems of a modern metropolis is . . . shown most clearly by the outbreak and long continuance of a severe epidemic of street robbery" in the early eighteenth century.[66] The epidemic persisted for decades. Henry Fielding, the novelist and magistrate, in 1751 published a pamphlet entitled *An Enquiry into the Causes of the late Increase of Robbery*.[67]

In 1754, John Fielding succeeded his half-brother, Henry, "as the leading magistrate in Westminster . . . in the midst of a crime wave in London."[68] In response to the crime wave, Sir John Fielding effected changes in criminal procedure that made confessions easier to obtain and admit. He recognized that English criminal procedure lacked an effective mechanism to investigate and solve these street crimes before they were tried in the Old Bailey. That was where the magistrate's examinations became critical. To help produce evidence, Fielding created a clearing house to gather and store information about crimes and suspects and also released that information to the London press.[69]

More relevant to our project, he organized a small group of proto-detectives, called the Bow Street runners, who were available "to investigate offenses, apprehend suspects, and in general support the efforts of victims of crime to bring perpetrators to be examined and prosecuted."[70] At Bow Street, Fielding enlarged the magistrate's role so that stronger cases could be sent to the Old Bailey. One innovation was that "on every Wednesday three or more Justices sit there [at Bow Street] from Ten to Three, in Order to re-examine all such Prisoners as have been committed in the preceding Week."[71] Though Fielding claimed that the purpose was to allow the accused to "shew their Innocence," Beattie concludes that the real motive was to give victims an opportunity to identify "those they accused and to sign a deposition to that effect."[72] This "identity parade" would put pressure on suspects to make a statement. Police still use that technique today.

Fielding persuaded Parliament to expand the number of magistrates who sat at Bow Street and, in 1768, he announced that the Bow Street office would be open "daily . . . from Ten to Two, and from Five to Nine."[73] His reputation as "an active and knowledgeable magistrate" attracted victims from other parts of London, willing to travel long distances for a better chance to prosecute those who had wronged them.[74] In sum, by the 1760s, what had once been a fairly level playing field at the magistrate's examination—a victim prosecuting the case against an accused before a magistrate who was mostly passive—had turned into a more intense experience.

Fielding's heightened pressure on suspects did not escape attention. A 1773 letter to John Fielding, published as a pamphlet, said that those who had heard Fielding's "improper questions and authoritative manner of asking them, have very justly compared you to an inquisitor general, instead of a British magistrate."[75]

The writer asked how Fielding could justify "demanding of the unhappy prisoners what they have to urge in their defence" when the laws "suppose every man innocent till he is convicted by the unanimous determination of his peers."[76] In language that portends Blackstone's skepticism and the Hawkins-Leach dictum, the writer urged Fielding, "View him, Sir, in all that pertubation of mind common to distress, and answer me, how you can extort from him a confession that finally destroys every hope of justice and mercy on this side [of] the grave."[77]

The Fielding innovation in magisterial examinations, more than any other development, explains why judges at the Old Bailey became increasingly skeptical of confessions. As we move into the nineteenth century, other changes reinforced the tendency to be skeptical of confessions and lenient toward offenders. It appears that London was becoming less violent by the late eighteenth century,[78] perhaps partly as a result of Fielding's changes in procedure. A guidebook published in 1802 claimed "that no city in proportion to its trade and luxury is more free from danger to those who pass the streets at all hours, or from other depredations, open or concealed, on property" than London.[79] A late nineteenth-century English political scientist noted that the eighteenth and nineteenth centuries brought a "change in the attitude toward social questions which was the outcome of the new spirit of humanity, the new command of material resources, and the new belief in environment rather than Providence as the cause of many human ills."[80] Humans mattered. They could act on the universe to make it better, fairer, and more just.

Moreover, as the power of the monarch receded, a new mechanism of social control was necessary. From 1689 to 1800, Parliament quadrupled the number of capital offenses—to over 200—as a way of maintaining order,[81] but that created an unintended backlash. Wealthy judges were reluctant to hang a young offender who had, for example, stolen a piece of silverware from her master. When Parliament removed the option of a lesser penalty, prosecutors, magistrates, judges, and juries "were tempted to strain the law to avoid the risk of what was felt to be an unjust penalty."[82]

A news account from 1818 shows the emotional difficulty of imposing the death penalty on so many offenders. The story recounts the sentencing of three defendants—one was convicted, essentially, of stealing five pounds; one for stealing property greater than forty shillings from a dwelling; and the third, Mary Smith, of passing a forged note. The judge "condemned" all three to death. He noted the possibility that the sovereign might extend mercy to the first two but "with respect to the last, it was very doubtful. . . . The three seemed much affected; Mary Smith wept aloud."[83]

Though *in terrorem* mechanisms have been for millennia at the core of Western social control, governance is more effective if it does not depend solely on terror. "If authority was to be respected, then power had to be exercised in ways that commanded respect and elicited consent."[84] To charge a servant with a capital offense, and then suppress her confession and spare her life, was likely a remarkably effective way both to command respect and elicit consent to be governed. It also reinforced the *in terrorem* power of the law. She and other servants would likely think twice before stealing the master's silver in the future.

Religion played a role in the attitude of English judges of the period. The Christian religion, with its emphasis on mercy and forgiveness, was part of the fabric of English life during this era in a way that probably cannot be grasped today. Speaking of eighteenth-century England, O'Gorman wrote, "In theory, at least, landowners were expected to treat their tenants with generosity and kindness and to behave with Christian mercy towards them, especially during emergencies or in times of want and difficulty."[85] Judges were empowered to grant Christian mercy when the tenants and servants were foolish enough to confess to capital crimes in response to an inducement. Indeed, in explaining how the English law of confessions had developed its tenderness toward suspects, Justice Parke in 1852 said, "We all know how it occurred. Every Judge decided by himself upon the admissibility of the confession, and he did not like to press against the prisoner, and took a merciful view of it."[86]

While the Whig philosophy that humans mattered, and that mercy was often appropriate, was important in the development of the Hawkins-Leach dictum, English courts and commentators settled on reliability as the formal rationale for suppressing confessions. Earlier in this chapter, we quoted the sixth edition of Hawkins on the influence of "flattery of hope" and "impressions of fear" on suspects who are being questioned. That quote captures the Whig concern with human autonomy. But the rest of the quote makes plain that for Leach more was at stake than autonomy or dignity. After saying that "the law will not suffer a prisoner to be made the deluded instrument of his own conviction," the passage continues:

> But if any facts arise in consequence of even such a confession, they may be given in evidence; because they must ever be immutably the same, whether the confession that disclosed them be true or false; and justice cannot suffer by their admission. The truth of these contingent facts, however, must be proved independently of, and not coupled with, or explained by the conversation or confession from which they are derived.[87]

This passage makes two points. First, if a confession leads to other evidence, that derivative evidence is admissible whether or not the confession was taken in compliance with rules designed to protect the suspect's autonomy.[88] Second, judges must be careful not to allow a possibly false confession to be used to prove derivative evidence. But as long as a court was assured that the evidence was not proved by a confession that might be false, even the exquisite Hawkins-Leach concern with autonomy did not move Whig judges to suppress reliable evidence of guilt.

For many decades, English courts followed the Hawkins-Leach dictum and applied what amounted to a presumption of inadmissibility in cases where suspects were subject to influences that might move them to confess. It is, as we will see, a rebuttable presumption, but if the prosecution could not point to some factor that erased the influence, English courts usually held the confession inadmissible. Indeed, in some cases, courts accepted the argument that the process of being questioned was itself an improper influence! We will turn to the doctrine that limited questioning after sketching the roles of the relevant legal actors in the investigation of crime in England during this period.

C. Justices of the Peace, Coroners, Mayors, and Police

Justices of the peace—also called magistrates—were the principal investigators of crime from the sixteenth century until organized police forces gradually began to handle that function in the nineteenth century. To be sure, investigation of crime was only one part of the very broad function of the Quarter Sessions, where the justices sat. Following the Restoration, the Quarter Sessions had "become the most important organ of local government as well as the chief seat of local jurisdiction."[89]

Our focus, of course, is on the criminal investigative role, which largely consisted of examining the complainant, the suspect, and witnesses that either party offered. The examinations of all but the suspect were under oath. The Marian committal statutes required the examinations to be taken down in writing and certified to the criminal trial court.[90] For example, in an 1819 trial for the theft of beer, the last item of evidence was the magistrate's clerk who "produced the examination and confession of the prisoners, which he had voluntarily signed."[91] These examinations could be conducted by other officials, including mayors.[92]

The examinations were not directed solely at determining who committed the crime but also at locating any property that had been stolen. An 1816 news account reports that two young women were given "another long examination" by the magistrate who was investigating the theft of thirty pounds and a gold watch.[93] The suspects had already confessed to the theft, and the "long examination" was to find what the suspects had done with the stolen property.

The Bobbies, then known as the Peelers, were created as an organized police force in 1829 under Home Secretary Sir Robert Peel.[94] To be sure, some police functions had been discharged for centuries by constables, sheriffs, and night watchmen. A search of the London *Times* from 1800 to 1811 for "watch house" produced 551 news stories, and almost all of them were describing police watch-houses. For example, in 1802:

> A poor woman was apprehended on Thursday, as disorderly, and taken to the watch-house at St. Margaret's. On being searched, 38 [pounds] in gold was found on her, besides some silver. On being brought before the Magistrate, at Queens-square, on Friday, a warrant was issued to search her lodgings, where . . . [a] great deal of property, of various kinds, was also found.[95]

In 1807, the victim of a pickpocket brought the young female suspect to the watch-house, where a search turned up nothing.[96] As she denied the crime "in the most solemn manner," the victim consented to her discharge. The patrol officer then took it upon himself to follow the suspect home. "As soon as he entered her room she fell a crying, and offered him five guineas of what she had got. . . . She afterwards confessed to the whole."

Prior to 1829, the watch-houses, the constables, and the magistrates worked together to maintain order by removing crime suspects from the streets. What changed in 1829 with the creation of the Bobbies was that their explicit goal was to solve crimes rather than just maintain order. Police headquarters became known for its public entrance, Scotland Yard, which became world famous for its ability to solve crimes. Naturally, as police sought to solve crimes, they began to question suspects after they were arrested and before they were brought before the magistrate. News accounts in the 1830s begin to feature sustained police questioning, often conducted by the police superintendent. In an 1831 case, a nineteen year old who worked at an auction house was suspected of stealing 500 pounds from the house.[97] The suspect "was closely questioned" by the superintendent of police and a security guard of the store until he made a "full confession of his participation" in the crime and "disclosed the names of his accomplices." A news account from 1833 had the magistrate's clerk calling the superintendent of police to restrain a suspect who was trying to flee.[98] After detaining the suspect, the superintendent "took down his confession in writing."

Coroners were required to conduct inquests upon "notice of a violent death" from a "peace officer" of the place "where the body lies dead."[99] They would issue a "warrant to summon a jury . . . to inquire, when, how, and by what means the deceased came by his death." The duty of the coroner was to conduct an "inquisition" of those who might be guilty and "put in writing" the material evidence presented.[100] If the coroner found individuals "culpable by inquisition . . . they shall be taken and delivered to the sheriff, and shall be committed to the gaol."[101] Though there were technical differences between the inquest and the examination by the justice of the peace, they are unimportant for our purposes. Like the justice of the peace examinations, the coroner's examination was made available at the defendant's trial.

An 1830 news account provides a useful summary of the criminal procedure of the time.[102] On the morning of January 7, the body of John Connell was found near the "low water mark" on the shore opposite the island of Valentia, off the coast of Ireland. A police captain reported this fact to the nearest magistrate, who sent a police officer to bring Mrs. Connell before the justice. After the magistrate completed his examination, she was released, presumably for lack of evidence. But the next morning "in consequence of some circumstances which came to light in the interval," the police captain again went to the magistrate "who agreed with him that there were grounds for arresting" Mrs. Connell and a man named M'Carthy Lawney. The magistrate issued a warrant for their arrests. The police arrested Mrs. Connell that night and obtained a "voluntary confession [from Mrs. Connell] of being accessory to the murder of her husband."

Lawney, however, had escaped to the "cliffs on the west end of the island."[103] The police called in the Coast Guard to prevent escape by water and succeeded in capturing him when he tried to escape by road. A coroner's inquest found a verdict against Lawney for "[w]ilful murder by strangulation" and against Mrs. Connell for aiding and assisting Lawney. The next step should have been trial in the Old Bailey, but we found no records of it having occurred.

The 1830s were a transition period in which English magistrates continued the formal questioning of witnesses and of the accused, while the police began to assist in various ways. One form of police assistance was informal questioning of witnesses before the magistrate's examination. Another form, as was plain in the Lawney case, was to investigate the facts surrounding the crime. We now turn to the law that regulated questioning of suspects during this period.

D. The "Deluded Instrument" Era in the English Law of Interrogation

One question we faced was when to end this chapter's coverage of the British law of confessions. Because our ultimate goal is to explain the development of the American law of confessions, we could have ended with the Hawkins edition that added the "deluded instrument" footnote or *Thompson* with its remark that "too great a chastity cannot be preserved" on the issue of suspect autonomy. *Thompson* was decided the year Britain lost the American War of Independence.

To end there would have missed two important developments. First, the case law that developed from *Thompson* and the Hawkins-Leach dictum is fascinating and better developed in English law than in American law. Second,

Parliament's reaction to judicial excesses is an important part of the confessions story. Parliament intervened in 1848 and, four years later, a panel of distinguished English justices rejected the line of cases holding that the mere giving of a caution made a confession involuntary. Thus, we decided to end our English journey in 1852, though we will broaden the focus in chapter 7 when we seek to understand how and why English and American judges threw off the "deluded instrument" vision of suspects.

1. WARNINGS

In 1755, the justice of the peace manuals began advising magistrates that the prisoner's statements had to be voluntary before they were admissible at trial. Classifying statements as voluntary is a contingent legal conclusion that can vary enormously depending on the judge. Bruce Smith has shown that as trial judges found more and more statements involuntary, magistrates reacted by beginning to warn suspects that they did not have to answer questions.[104]

The earliest case Smith cites is the 1796 trial of Robert Davidson.[105] In answer to the question of whether he had apprised "the prisoner of the consequences of making any confession," the magistrate responded, "I have the minute [of the examination] in my book in these words." At that point, he was interrupted by defense counsel and never answered the question. Thus, we do not know precisely how the magistrate warned Davidson, but we do know that magistrates began a self-help program to increase the utility of their examinations. The motive for this development is obvious. The magistrates of that period viewed their task as helping solve crimes and convict guilty suspects. When statements were rejected, guilty defendants were more likely to walk free, an outcome to be avoided if possible.

By 1813, seventeen years after Davidson's trial, a prominent treatise by William Dickinson found a "duty of the magistrate to apprise the prisoner that his examination may be produced on his trial, and to give him a reasonable caution, that he is not required to criminate himself."[106] According to Dickinson, the origin of this requirement was "[t]he excessive mildness usual in exercise of the English jurisprudence." This characterization suggests that the suppression of reliable statements had, in Dickinson's opinion, become too frequent.

A news account from 1815 showed a magistrate advising a suspect "not to expect any thing in consequence of making such a confession."[107] In an 1832 case, a magistrate testified that he told the suspects "to say any thing or nothing, as they pleased; he held out no inducement, nor held out any threat to make them confess, but rather the contrary. He told them what they said would be taken down in writing, and it would be given in evidence against them."[108] In 1838, Chief Justice Denman sought to correct a "prevalent error" in how the warnings were given. The magistrate should "entirely . . . get rid of any impression that may have before been on the prisoner's mind, that the statement may be used for his benefit; and the prisoner ought also to be told that what he thinks fit to say will be taken down, and may be used against him on his trial."[109]

As coroners discharged judicial functions roughly like that of the magistrates, it should not be surprising that we found cases where the coroner warned the suspect before questioning him. The earliest that we found was an 1817 murder case, where the coroner informed the suspect "that any confession he might make on that occasion would be produced in evidence against him on his trial, and would probably lead to his conviction."[110] Then the coroner said that if the suspect wanted anything "he had to say taken down, the Coroner would readily accede to all his wishes." The suspect confessed to a brutal murder.

Police were gradually taking over the role of questioning suspects prior to trial, and they might have warned suspects just as the magistrates had been doing for many years. The evidence here is less clear. The news accounts discussed earlier where the police superintendent questioned suspects make no mention of warnings. An 1836 case seemed to assume that if the constable had cautioned the witness, it would have removed the taint of an inducement made by an innkeeper in the presence of the constable.[111]

An 1837 case admitted a confession made to a police officer who testified that he did not caution the suspect.[112] The judge said, "I should not myself, if placed in such a situation, put a question to a prisoner without cautioning her," but he found that the officer's failure to do so was not "improper." In 1843, however, a constable took it upon himself to warn the suspect "you must be very careful in making any statement to me or anybody else, that may tend to injure you."[113] Not that it did the crown any good. Justice Coleridge held that the warning itself was enough "to make an impression on the prisoner's mind, tending to make him state a falsehood." The critical point, for Coleridge, was that the "prisoner's mind must be left entirely free." We will return to this point in the next subsection.

In 1852, a police constable gave essentially the same caution that magistrates were required to give, and the confession was held admissible.[114] The point to the warnings, of course, was to avoid the Hawkins-Leach dictum about inducements. We turn now to that development.

2. INDUCEMENTS TO CONFESS

The Hawkins-Leach dictum forbade the use of "flattery of hope" and "impressions of fear" to obtain confessions. That approach proved popular with English judges in the period, roughly from 1783 to 1852. Here is Chitty's description, in his 1816 treatise, of the Hawkins rule:

[N]o improper influence, either by threat, promise, or misrepresentation, ought to be employed [by the magistrate]; for however slight the
inducement may have been, a confession so obtained cannot be received
in evidence, on account of the uncertainty and doubt whether it was
not made from a motive of fear or interest than from a sense of guilt.[115]

Chitty broadened the Hawkins concern with "flattery of hope" and "impressions of fear" to include all "improper influence[s], either by threat, promise, or
misrepresentation." A year after Chitty's 1816 edition, *Rex v. Wilson* suggested
that the very examination itself could be an improper inducement.[116] This, of
course, was the United States Supreme Court's theory in *Miranda v. Arizona*—
that the process of questioning itself put pressure on the suspect to talk. The case
report in *Wilson* does not indicate whether the magistrate cautioned the suspect
that he need not answer, but the magistrate testified that he offered no inducement while examining him "at a considerable extent, in the same manner as he
was accustomed to examine a witness." The King's Bench held the suspect's
statements inadmissible because an "examination of itself imposes an obligation
to speak the truth. If the prisoner will confess, let him do so voluntarily. Ask him
what he has to say?"

Wigmore claims, quite correctly, that *Wilson* is an outlier.[117] In *The King
v. Lambe*, The Twelve Judges of England considered in 1791 the question of
whether statements made to a magistrate were admissible even though the examination was not signed by the accused or the magistrate as required by the Marian
acts.[118] All twelve agreed that a transcription of what the accused said during an
examination was admissible at the common law and that nothing in the Marian
acts changed that result.[119] That should have been the end of the matter, at least
based on modern notions of precedent, because The Twelve Judges was a "sacred
institution" consisting of the four judges who presided over each of the three
royal courts—the King's Bench, the Common Pleas, and Exchequer.[120] "When a
point of difficulty arose that a trial judge was reluctant to decide on his own,
especially when capital sanctions were involved and the convict would otherwise
be promptly executed, the judge could defer sentencing and refer the question to
[The Twelve Judges]."[121] Their decision "would clarify future practice."[122]

Thus, *Wilson* should not have suppressed the statement made in response to
the magistrate's examination. In 1826, *Rex v. Ellis* explicitly declined to follow
Wilson.[123] But even here, we see profound respect for the suspect's autonomy. He
had "claimed the right of his attorney's attendance and assistance" during the
magistrate's examination. The magistrate refused. When this fact was noted at
trial, the King's Bench "suggested, that as the prisoner had been refused profes-
sional assistance, the case should not be further pressed: this was assented to by
the counsel for the prosecution, and the prisoner was acquitted."

The next move in the chess game of interrogation law was the defense claim that the mere giving of a caution could be an improper inducement. In *Regina v. Drew*, the clerk "told [the prisoner] not to say anything to prejudice himself [during the examination], as what he said I should take down, and it would be used for him or against him at trial."[124] This is a pretty robust warning of the right to remain silence. But it would not suffice in England at this time. Justice Coleridge's entire opinion follows:

> This is an inducement, and it was held out by a person in authority. I am of opinion that the prisoner's statement cannot be given in evidence. I cannot conceive a more direct inducement to a man to make a confession, than telling him that what he says may be used in his favour at the trial.

Drew can be usefully contrasted with *Regina v. Holmes*, decided a year earlier.[125] After the magistrate had completed his examination of the complainant's witnesses, the suspect began to tell his side of the story. The magistrate stopped him: "'Be sure you say nothing but the truth, or it will be taken against you, and may be given in evidence against you at your trial.'" Queen's counsel argued that the "only proper question is, whether the words said to the prisoner had any tendency to induce him to make a false statement" and that, here, the prisoner was "cautioned not to state anything that is false." The Queen's Bench agreed and allowed the statement into evidence.

But it was *Drew*, and not *Holmes*, that proved influential in the 1840s. *The Queen v. Harris*, involved the theft of oats in Wales in 1844.[126] The magistrate's clerk, probably trying to avoid *Drew*, told Harris that "he was at liberty to make any statement, but 'that whatever he said would be taken down and used against him.'" Note that the caution was that what he said would be used against him rather than, in *Drew*, for *or* against him. Here is the remarkable exchange at trial between Justice Maule and the queen's counsel on the issue of admissibility:

Maule, J.—That will not do.

E.V. Williams.—I submit, my lord, that it is perfectly regular; it is not like the case of *The King* [sic] *v. Drew*, where the prisoner was told that whatever he said would be used for or against him; here the prisoner was expressly told that whatever he said would be used against him.

Maule, J.—The prisoner was told that *whatever* he said would be taken down and used against him. I cannot say that that did not induce him to say something which he thought might be favourable to him. I shall reject the statement.

Wigmore condemned cases like *Wilson, Drew,* and *Harris* as a "perversion of normal reasoning."[127]

English courts also worried about the effect on suspects who were urged, by a magistrate or someone else, to tell the truth or face the music. Most cases held that this, too, was an improper inducement. In 1830, a confession was held inadmissible when made after a doctor said to the suspect "'you are under suspicion of this, and you had better tell all you know.'"[128] In 1839, the Queen's Bench rejected a confession given in response to "'[y]ou had better tell how you did it.'"[129]

Promises of favor would also taint confessions. In an 1818 case, the victim of a theft admitted promising "to be lenient if the prisoner confessed."[130] In *Rex v. Cooper and Wicks*, the magistrate told Cooper that if he made "a disclosure, he [the magistrate] would do all that he could for him."[131] Both confessions were rejected. In 1742, a question was raised—by the judge, probably—whether the defendant "had any promises of Indulgence before he confessed; for the Jury will consider that."[132] The question is not answered in the Old Bailey report, but the jury acquitted.

Boswell, a murder suspect in 1841, asked to see the handbill offering a reward for the capture of the murderer.[133] The handbill stated that a pardon would be recommended for an accomplice who turned in the "person who actually committed the murder." The authorities showed Boswell the handbill and, three days later, he confessed and claimed to be only an accomplice. The *Boswell* trial judge initially suggested that the confession was admissible, probably because of the three-day interval between reading about the pardon and the confession.[134] But later in the trial, evidence was received that Boswell told a policeman "that he saw no reason why he should suffer for the crime of another, and that as the government had offered a free pardon to anyone concerned who had not struck the blow, he would tell all he knew about the matter." Once that evidence was admitted, the trial judge concluded: "It now appears with sufficient clearness that the prisoner in making the statements ascribed to him was influenced by the hope of pardon held out by authorized parties." The court ordered the confession stricken from evidence. Boswell was found not guilty.

The inducement probably had to be given by someone with authority to deliver on the promise, though an 1837 case disclosed a "difference of opinion among the Judges" whether the lack of authority made the confession "receivable."[135] Cases decided in 1833 and 1834 refused to allow confessions made in response to inducements by individuals without legal authority; in one, the inducement was a stranger advising the suspect at the scene of the crime that he should "split" and not suffer for his co-felons.[136] The issue of authority was not discussed in either case.

But even if authority was required, it was often present in England of that era. Most crimes, except homicide, were prosecuted by the victim. When the victim-prosecutor promised not to prosecute in exchange for a confession, this was an inducement every bit as powerful as a similar offer from a magistrate. We found many cases holding that inducements made by victims tainted confessions. In a typical case, the victim of the theft told the suspect that if she returned the property "I would proceed no further with her."[137] The entire defense was, "I leave myself to the mercy of the court; the prosecutor promised that if I would own to it, he would not hurt me." The jury acquitted.

Given the prominence of victims in prosecuting crime in this era, it is not surprising that we found few cases holding confessions admissible because of a lack of authority in the one making the inducement. An 1809 court held a confession admissible when induced by a plea "to tell the truth" from neighbors, "who had nothing to do with the apprehension, prosecution or examination of the prisoner."[138] Similarly, in *Rex v. Wild*, neighbors induced a confession to murder by telling the thirteen-year-old suspect to kneel down and give a truthful answer in the presence of the Almighty.[139] The judges unanimously held the confession "strictly admissible," without stating their theory.[140]

A proper caution could end the effect of the improper influence. In *Rex v. Clewes*, a magistrate, who was also a clergyman, met with Clewes after his arrest and told him that if he was not the one who struck the fatal blow, the magistrate "would use all his endeavors and influence to prevent any ill consequences from falling on him."[141] Later, Clewes sent for the coroner, apparently prepared to make a confession. The coroner cautioned Clewes that any confession or admission "would be produced against him at the next Assize" on a trial for murder, "and that no hope or promise of pardon could be held out to him, either by his Majesty's government or anybody else."[142] The King's Bench held that the caution given just prior to the confession "must be taken to have completely put an end to all hopes that had been held out."[143]

Gilham was arrested for the murder of a female servant who, apparently, caught him stealing goods belonging to her master.[144] In jail, he appeared distraught, and the jailer advised him what passages to read in the prayer book that he brought with him. Gilham asked to speak to the chaplain of the jail who explained "what he considered to be the nature of true repentance."[145] Part of "true repentance" was to "repair" the injury "he had done [to] his fellow creatures" as well as "any injury done to the laws of his country."

After the chaplain left, Gilham told the jailer that he was prepared to confess. The jailer cautioned him: "'Don't tell me any thing but what you would wish the mayor and magistrates to know; for whatever you tell me I must inform them of.'"[146] The prisoner confessed the murder and said he also wanted to confess it to the mayor. When the mayor arrived, he too cautioned Gilham, very much in the way the United States Supreme Court would later require in *Miranda*:

Before you say any thing, I think it necessary to apprize you . . . that it will probably be given in evidence against you. You are therefore to exercise your own discretion, and say little or nothing, as you may think best, and if you have changed your mind since you sent [for] me, and do not choose to say anything, I will retire, and shall not feel at all angry with you for having brought me down [here] unnecessarily.[147]

Gilham repeated his confession to the mayor, whose clerk took down the confession. When Gilham read it over, his hand shook so badly he could not sign his name. But he said "it was all true."

Given the solicitude shown by the mayor, the Assize Court could easily have held, as in *Clewes*, that the caution broke the causal chain back to the chaplain. But the court did not rely on lack of causation to hold the confession admissible, focusing instead on the kind of inducement being offered. The court drew a distinction between inducements based on religion and the hereafter and inducements made by those who have legal authority over the prisoner.[148] Looking at it from the twenty-first century, it would seem that if the person making the inducement has no authority to deliver on the promise, then the pressure put on the suspect by the human actor would be decidedly less. Looking at it from the 1829 perspective, confessing to obtain "repentance" does not justify concluding "that the confessions given under such motives are untrue."[149] In 1829 England, one did not lie to God. In 1853, the advice "[d]on't run your soul into more sin, but tell the truth" was held not to be an improper inducement.[150]

At the height of the English embrace of the Hawkins-Leach dictum, many confessions to capital crimes were rejected largely on the ground that the autonomy of the suspect had been overridden. Here, again, we note the proportionality principle. When faced with a death sentence or a finding that the confession was not freely given, courts rarely insisted that the inducement cast substantial doubt on the confession's reliability. Outside of the religious context, courts rarely cited lack of authority of the inducer as a reason to admit a confession. But times were changing.

3. COUNTERCURRENTS IN ENGLISH LAW

Even at the height of English solicitude toward suspects who confessed their crimes, some judges were unwilling to give a robust embrace to the Hawkins-Leach dictum. As we noted earlier, *Warickshall* held in 1783 that stolen property discovered by means of an inadmissible confession was nonetheless admissible as long as it could be identified as the stolen property without using the confession.[151] In 1784, Justice Buller went so far as to suggest that the confession itself should be admissible because "the reason of rejecting extorted confessions is the apprehension that the prisoner may have been thereby induced to say what

is false; but the fact discovered shews that so much of the confession as immediately relates to it is true."[152] And the court said in *Warickshall* that "the consequences to public justice would be dangerous indeed" if the jury did not learn
that the accused knew where the stolen property was found.[153] To suppress that
fact "would be holding out an opportunity to compound felonies."

Later in the period, judges began to caution magistrates not to go too far in
discouraging confessions. The King's Bench in 1832 said that magistrates should
not tell suspects not to confess.[154] The magistrate should instead caution the
suspect that he should expect no favor from confessing. After that, "it ought to be
left entirely to himself whether he will make any statement or not: but he ought
not to be dissuaded from making a perfectly voluntary confession, because that
is shutting up one of the sources of justice."

In 1836, the King's Bench refused to suppress a statement made in response
to a forgery victim's exhortation "to be sure to tell the truth."[155] Unmoved by the
argument that this plea creates "an intimation that it will be better for him if he
confesses the charge," Justice Littledale instead indulged a reliability rationale.
He read the cases "to exclude all confessions which may have been procured by
the prisoner being led to suppose that it is better for him to admit himself to be
guilty of an offense which he never really committed." But it "can hardly be said
that telling a man to be sure to tell the truth, is advising him to confess what he is
really not guilty of."

Some threats and inducements were rejected as insufficient to cause a confession. A threat to call for a constable the next morning did not taint a confession
made to the constable because the inducement was "at an end" when the suspect
was put in the hands of the constable.[156] The offer to let a suspect see his wife if
he told where the stolen property was located was not a sufficient inducement
to render the confession inadmissible.[157]

As for examinations by magistrates, these continued under the authority of the
Marian acts as amended by later acts. Given the strictness of the Hawkins-Leach
dictum, one could expect that the statutory regime would be strictly applied, but it
was not. Two requirements added later were that the prisoner sign his statement
and that the magistrate furnish him a copy of the statement. Even if the magistrate
failed to do these required acts, courts by the 1830s admitted the statements.
"What a prisoner says [to the magistrate] is evidence against himself, whether the
officer was right or wrong in not returning the statement, or furnishing a copy of it
to the prisoner. That is quite a collateral inquiry."[158] Moreover, oral statements the
accused made that were not transcribed were nonetheless admissible by testimony
of the magistrate or his clerk.[159]

Even at the height of the power of the Hawkins-Leach dictum, it was limited
to threats and inducements. The very same Lord Coleridge who, in 1837, would
find the giving of a caution to be an impermissible inducement held in 1835 that

a statement made to a constable when the accused was drunk was admissible, and this was true even if the constable had plied the accused with liquor hoping he would incriminate himself.[160] "[T]o rendered a confession inadmissible," Coleridge wrote, "it must either be obtained by hope or fear."

But the strongest blow to the robust application of the Hawkins-Leach dictum was delivered by Parliament in 1848 in the Sir John Jervis Indictable Offences Act, which standardized the duties of justices of the peace in serious criminal cases.[161] Section 18 of Chapter 42 of the act required magistrates to read to the accused the depositions taken from other witnesses and then to say to the suspect: "Having heard the Evidence, do you wish to say anything in answer to the Charge? You are not obliged to say anything unless you desire to do so, but whatever you say will be taken down in Writing, and may be given in Evidence against you upon your Trial."

One who comes upon this provision without knowing the history might think that it resulted from wanting to protect suspects from overbearing examinations.[162] That, after all, was one of the motives that prompted *Miranda v. Arizona*. But this was probably not Parliament's goal in the 1848 act, as Bruce Smith recognized.[163] Context is critical.

Statements made by the accused pursuant to Section 18 were transmitted to the criminal court and "may, if necessary, be given in Evidence against him, without further Proof thereof." This is probably the key component of the act. Section 18 also required the magistrate

> give [the accused] clearly to understand, that he has nothing to hope from any Promises of Favour, and nothing to fear from any Threat which may have been holden out to him to induce him to make any Admission or Confession of his Guilt, but that whatever he shall then say may be given in Evidence against him upon his Trial, notwithstanding such Promise or Threat.

While this might be intended to relieve the accused of the pressure of prior threats or promises, it also prevented the accused from arguing that a threat or promise caused him to confess. It is, in effect, a legal rule that cleanses the statement of any prior influence and thus avoids the Hawkins-Leach dictum.

Moreover, the English courts quickly reduced the significance of this second required caution. In *Regina v. Sansome*, the magistrate gave the general warning that the accused was not required to say anything but failed to give the warning that he should have nothing to hope from any promise or to fear from any threat.[164] Sansome's counsel argued that without both warnings, the statement to the magistrate should be inadmissible, that the second caution was a "condition precedent" to admissibility.[165] That was certainly a permissive reading of Section

18, and a trial court opinion had agreed, in dicta, with the "condition precedent" reading.[166] But the Queen's Bench held unanimously that the second caution was not required.[167] "It is always wise to give the second caution," Justice Alderson wrote, because if an inducement or threat had been made earlier, then Section 18 would not save the confession.[168] But "[a]s there was no evidence of any promise or threat, there was no necessity for showing that the second caution had been given."[169]

To be sure, Section 18 might have reduced the coerciveness of the magistrate's examination. It directed the magistrate to ask only "do you wish to say anything in answer to the Charge." If this replaced the more extensive examination that magistrates sometimes conducted, it would have greatly lessened the pressure of the examination. Even if Parliament did not intend to limit the magistrate, that would likely be the practical effect. Why engage in a detailed examination when Parliament has offered an easier path? Moreover, by 1848, London police were beginning to assume the role of examining suspects, and magistrates were probably only too happy to relinquish that task.

Parliament's ultimate goal in Section 18 seems to have been more convictions. As magistrates had been cautioning suspects for decades by 1848, there was no reason to require cautions. The innovation in Section 18 was to make statements admissible if the magistrate complied with the requirements set out there. Section 18 was probably more the friend of the crown and its prosecutors than the accused.

We defer until chapter 5 our theories about why Parliament might have wanted to make confessions easier to admit as well as the developments that followed enactment of the Section 18 of the Indictable Offences Act. But it seems relatively clear that the attitude toward interrogation and confessions was beginning to change in England. We will next trace a similar evolution of the law in America.

CHAPTER 4

Early American Interrogation Law

Reported criminal cases were rare during the colonial period. Case reports in general were scarce and criminal cases even scarcer. But the Salem witch trials provide an example of how the colonists were, at least by the late seventeenth century, drawing back from the use of torture to obtain confessions. The 1641 Massachusetts Body of Liberties provided, "No man shall be forced by Torture to confesse any Crime against himselfe," though it permitted torture when it was "very apparent" that one convicted of a capital crime had "other conspiratours, or confederates."[1] "Barbarous and inhumane" torture, however, could not be used in any event. The threat posed by confederates in a capital crime who might otherwise not be identified was thought sufficient to warrant "humane" torture, whatever that meant.

The Salem witch hunt fits neatly with our theme that harsh interrogation methods are rooted in perceptions of threat to the established order from internal and external threats. The Massachusetts colony of the period faced many threats to its survival but not internal ones. The colony was a homogenous society that imposed order in large part by a belief in a vengeful God who "directly caused or allowed everything that happened in daily life."[2] Witches would be about the greatest threat that Massachusetts Puritans could imagine. Nor would Puritans think that witches had autonomy worth respecting. Witches were, after all, doing the work of the devil.

The year 1641 was at the end of what Langbein calls the Torture Century in England,[3] and it is not surprising that torture was both permitted and tightly regulated in the Body of Liberties. But the witch trials did not occur until 1692 when torture as a means to obtain evidence had apparently disappeared in England and was rapidly declining on the Continent. Thus, its use in the Salem witch trials should have proved controversial and of limited frequency. Both turn out to be true. Despite the popular conception that confessions were routinely tortured from witches, the evidence suggests that most confessed to obtain leniency rather than as a response to torture.

John Proctor wrote a letter from prison claiming that his son was tied "Neck and Heels till the Blood gushed out of his nose" when he was being questioned by magistrates.[4] Lawrence Friedman claims, without citing an authority, that "fifty or so were tortured or terrified into confessions."[5] "Terrified" covers a lot of ground that would not include torture as it was understood in the seventeenth century. The evidence suggests that far fewer than fifty were tortured. One historian notes that the proportion of confessions among the accused "remained disappointingly low" until the Salem magistrates, in a decision "virtually without legal precedent for capital offenders," began "to exempt confessors from execution."[6] Torture is remarkably effective in producing confessions. Thus, a low confession rate early in the investigation suggests that the incidence of torture was low.

Putting to one side the number of suspects tortured in Salem aside, the trials provide the only evidence of torture used in Massachusetts to obtain confessions that we found. Moreover, we found no evidence of torture being authorized, or used, to obtain confessions in the other colonies. By the time of the Salem witch trials, the torture moment in the Western world had passed. Cotton Mather, instrumental in the prosecution of the witches, acknowledged that torture was against English principles when he encouraged magistrates to use aggressive methods to obtain confessions, but to stop short of the "un-English method of torture."[7] The Vermont Supreme Court in 1803 declared that "the practice of torture to extort confessions" was "certainly never sanctioned by the common or statute law of our *English* ancestors."[8] That torture was used at all in Salem, despite Mather's admonition, demonstrates the power of the deviance of witchcraft.

Beyond the witch trials, what we know about colonial criminal procedure comes principally from treatises and justice of the peace manuals. As in England, justices of the peace were central to American crime investigations in the days before organized police forces came into existence. The colonial courts were bound by the Marian pretrial commitment statutes that required the justice of the peace to examine the complainant and the accused prior to trial. The records of the New Jersey Oyer and Terminer Court from 1749–1757 reflect the introduction into evidence of a pretrial examination in about 10% of the cases.[9] Defendants who confessed to the justice of the peace were probably more likely to plead guilty—many guilty pleas appear in the Oyer and Terminer records— and thus the 10% figure probably understates the frequency of pretrial examinations. Goebel and Naughton found records of "numerous examinations" of justices of the peace in colonial New York.[10]

We found no evidence that American judges began to be skeptical of confessions in the period 1760–1790 as did their English counterparts. To the extent that this phenomenon is real, and not merely an artifact of the relative lack of records in the colonies, the cause is probably a different culture. While the colonies were largely populated by the English, American culture was different from English culture in ways that made skepticism about confessions less likely to arise spontaneously here. The Hawkins-Leach dictum is likely a byproduct of a settled, hierarchical culture, not one struggling to invent itself roughly along egalitarian grounds with a passion for equality.[11]

But, as we will demonstrate in the next section whether or not the Hawkins-Leach skepticism arose here, American culture proved to be a hospitable place for its growth.

A. America's Place in the World

Though the Treaty of Paris would not be signed for two more years, the War of American Independence was over, and won, when General Cornwallis surrendered his army at Yorktown, Virginia in October, 1781. America would face many perils over the next half-century, including the weak central government created by the Articles of Confederation and fear of invasion from France. One peril young America would not face was the threat of internal upheaval. American Indians and slaves posed profound problems that were managed for centuries by dehumanizing both groups, but within the governing white population, there was no similar internal threat. The population that did not emigrate to Canada or Europe after the revolution was united by a belief in the grand American experiment in democracy, however much they disagreed over the proper role of the new federal government.[12] By comparison with England, America had no large cities and thus no large urban underclass. London in 1815 had a population of over 1.4 million.[13] New York in 1810 had a population of 93,000 while America's fourth-largest city, Boston town, had only 33,000.[14]

The America that is revealed in the pages of the founding documents—however flawed the execution—is a robust embodiment of the Whig principles that contributed to the Hawkins-Leach dictum. The Declaration of Independence was premised on "self-evident" truths "that all Men are created equal, that they are endowed by their Creator with certain unalienable Rights," and that governments "deriv[e] their Just powers from the Consent of the Governed."[15] Our Constitution begins with "We the People" and then creates a template for a government that would "secure the Blessings of Liberty to ourselves and our Posterity."[16] The Bill of Rights created a series of rights vested in "the People" against the government and concludes by proclaiming that all rights not dealt with in the Constitution are "reserved to the States," or "to the people."[17] Judges who subscribed to these principles would likely follow, if not develop, a skepticism about confessions made by vulnerable suspects to those in power.

We present early American cases in two periods, from independence to the 1920s. The 1920s are a key decade because of John Henry Wigmore's hugely influential treatise on evidence, published in 1904 and 1923. The first edition attacked the cases that followed the Hawkins-Leach dictum as essentially irrational. The second edition marshaled an impressive list of cases that had rejected the Hawkins-Leach dictum in favor of something roughly like Wigmore's rationalist approach.

B. American Confessions Cases to 1923

1. EARLY CASES, STATUTES, AND EXAMINATIONS

After the political separation from England, American courts continued to follow the common law, often relying on English treatises and precedents. For example, 1847 saw the publication of the first American edition of Lord Hale's *History of the Pleas of the Crown*, more than thirty years after the end of the War of 1812.[18] To be sure, that edition had been "Americanized" to some extent because the cover page claims that it has notes and references to later cases, added by two lawyers of the Philadelphia bar. But the critical point is that American lawyers and judges of the day believed that they "owned" common law just as much as the English courts where it was developed. Nothing was at all unnatural about taking Hale's treatise, written in England sometime before 1677, and adapting it for American courts and lawyers in 1847 by adding notes to later cases.

Blackstone had an even longer shelf life, a new edition last appearing in the United States in 1916.[19] As we saw in chapter 3, Blackstone's 1778 statement of the rule about confessions was roughly as solicitous of the autonomy of suspects as the Hawkins-Leach dictum. In a locution that did not change from 1778 to 1916, Blackstone's *Commentaries* cautioned that "hasty, unguarded confessions" to felonies "are the weakest and most suspicious of all testimony; ever liable to be obtained by artifice, false hopes, promises of favor or menaces; seldom remembered accurately, or reported with due precision; and incapable in their nature of being disproved by other negative evidence."[20]

The Pennsylvania General Assembly in 1777 manifested deep skepticism about confessions when it refused to permit treason to be proved by confession, thus rejecting the English approach in the Treason Act of 1547.[21] Ohio and Virginia followed the English law, permitting a conviction of treason upon a "voluntary confession."[22] The United States Constitution also permits treason to be proved by a "Confession in open Court."[23]

Many, but not all, states continued to follow the Marian committal statutes either by assuming they were still in effect in the United States or by codifying them.[24] MacNally's 1804 treatise, published in Philadelphia for an American audience, noted that a "confession of the defendant himself" taken pursuant to the Marian statutes "is legal evidence against the party confessing."[25] South Carolina decreed in 1715 that the Marian statutes were in effect and did not repeal that edict after the Revolution.[26] Some states made material changes in the Marian statutes. Virginia repealed the Marian statutes in 1792 and enacted a state law successor that authorized examination of the complainant and witnesses in support of the complaint but not the accused.[27] A Georgia justice of the peace manual cautioned in 1835 that "though the statutes . . . authorize an examination, they are not compulsory on the prisoner to accuse himself."[28] One option the Georgia manual noted was for the accused to remain silent. We see here the beginning of the notion that statutes could not deprive the accused of his right against compelled self-incrimination.

As for how the examination took place, American law manifested the same concern as English law about influences on the suspect. The burden to prove that any statements made to the magistrate were not unduly influenced was on the State. An 1803 Delaware case held that the recorded examination could not be received in evidence at trial unless the magistrate appeared to "prove the circumstances, whether by menacing, hope, etc."[29] The justice of the peace manuals drew heavily from Hawkins-Leach when they gave advice about how to examine suspects to protect against confessions that courts might find to be unfree. Some examples include the *New Virginia Justice* (1820), *The Alabama Justice of the Peace* (1822), the *Pennsylvania Justice of the Peace* (1839), and *The Massachusetts Justice* (1847).[30] A representative sample appears in the *Pennsylvania Justice of the Peace*: "A confession forced from the mind by the flattery of hope or the torture of fear, comes in so questionable a shape, where it is to be considered the evidence of guilt, that no credit ought to be given to it, and therefore it is to be rejected."[31]

It is unclear whether the same forces that led English magistrates to begin warning suspects were also felt by American magistrates. The New York legislature viewed the magistrate's role in bail and committal as critical, enacting a statute in 1787 that required magistrates to examine the accused.[32] By the time we get to 1813 in England, William Dickinson's handbook proclaimed "the duty of the magistrate to apprise the prisoner that his examination may be produced at trial, and to give him a reasonable caution, that he is not required to criminate himself."[33] But an 1815 manual published for New York justices of the peace, while insisting that confessions made during the examination had to be taken without "any promise of favour, menace, or undue terror," makes no mention of warnings.[34] An 1819 edition of *Conductor Generalis*, published in New York, had the same flat rule that Hawkins introduced in 1721: "that the confession of the defendant, taken upon an examination before justices of the peace, or in discourse with private persons, may be given in evidence against the party confessing, but not against others."[35]

Greenleaf's 1842 treatise did not mention warnings, though he stressed that the "*manner of the examination* should be particularly regarded; and if it appears, that the prisoner has not been left wholly free, and did not consider himself to be so, in what he was called upon to say, or did not feel himself at liberty wholly to decline any explanation or declaration whatever, the examination is not held to have been voluntary." [36] This is consistent with the practice of warning suspects that they need not answer. But it is not the same as requiring warnings.

By 1842 at least three states—Arkansas, Missouri, and New York—had committal statutes that required magistrates to warn the accused of his right not to answer questions and his right to consult with counsel.[37] Greenleaf does not mention this development, suggesting that it was not widespread. Oddly, he cites the New York statute as adopting "the principles" of the Marian acts without mentioning the broad New York right to be warned of the right not to answer and the right to consult with counsel.[38]

The concerns reflected in the Hawkins-Leach dictum were thus making themselves felt in the United States by 1848 when Parliament required magistrates to warn the accused before questioning him. The concerns about promises of favor, menaces, and "undue terror" (one wonders what level of terror was thought to be "due") were in part concerns about false confessions and notions of proportionality. We now turn to that thread in early American law.

2. CONCERN ABOUT FALSE CONFESSIONS
AND PROPORTIONALITY

Concern about false confessions explains an early arson case from Pennsylvania. Dillon, twelve years old, was arrested on December 18, 1791,[39] three days after the Bill of Rights went into effect when Virginia became the eleventh state to ratify it. This was eight years after the English *Thompson* case, four years after the Hawkins treatise first warned about the "flattery of hope" and the "impressions of fear," and five years before the first evidence appears of English magistrates warning suspects (*Davidson*). Initially examined by the mayor of Philadelphia— who was conducting the pretrial examination—Dillon "made no confession." Later

> he was visited and interrogated, by several respectable citizens, who represented to him the enormity of the crime; urged a free, open, and candid, confession, which would so excite public compassion as, probably, to be the means of obtaining a pardon; while a contrary course of conduct would leave him, in case of a conviction, without hope: and

they added, that they would themselves stand his friends, if he would confess. The inspectors of the prison endeavoured, likewise, to obtain from him a discovery of his offences, and of his accomplices. They carried him into the dungeon; they displayed it in all its gloom and horror; they said that he would be confined in it, dark, cold, and hungry, unless he made a full disclosure; but if he did make a disclosure, he should be well accommodated with room, fire, and victuals, and might expect pity and favour.[40]

Dillon acknowledged his guilt and repeated his confession the next morning in a statement "which was formally, and to all appearance, voluntarily, made before the mayor." As the pressures on the young suspect prior to his confession were profound, the judges were understandably skeptical about the confession. Charging the jury, the judges admitted that circumstantial evidence supported the confession and that Dillon had "expressed no wish to retract the statement."[41] Yet the "true point for consideration is, whether the prisoner has falsely declared himself guilty of a capital offense? If there is ground even to suspect, that he has done so, God forbid, that his life should be sacrifice!" Their final words to the jury were, "Though it is [your] province to administer justice, and not to bestow mercy; and though it is better not to err at all; yet, in a doubtful case, an error on the side of mercy is safer, is more venial, than error on the side of rigid justice." The jury acquitted.

A concern with false confessions also underlies the corroboration rule that developed very early in this country. A 1794 Delaware trial court held that confessions are admissible if corroborated, noting generally that a confession "is certainly the best and highest evidence."[42] The court conceded that some cases were skeptical of confessions but concluded that "they only apply to cases which are unsupported by any evidence from circumstances in aid of the confession." To reject confessions, "would free almost every criminal from the fears and the dangers of a prosecution. Our courts of criminal jurisdiction might as well be closed at once." But an early Tennessee case rejected the corroboration exception to the Hawkins-Leach rule of inadmissibility on the ground that "the exception will destroy the rule. Few cases, indeed, occur without facts to which part of the confession will apply."[43]

A North Carolina trial court in 1797 held that corroboration could made a confession admissible even if it was "extorted by violence," though the jury "should be very cautious . . . and examine every circumstance with the most critical nicety before they [find the prisoner guilty]."[44] The same year, in *State v. Long*, another North Carolina trial court held that even a voluntary confession could not be admitted without corroboration.[45] The defendant had "confessed to the owner he had taken the horse, and begged forgiveness." At trial, Long's confession was the only evidence offered. Following the Hawkins-Leach dictum, the North Carolina court stressed that a "confession from the very nature of the thing, is a very doubtful species of evidence, and to be received with great caution." While a confession can corroborate itself, as when it "relates circumstances which are proven to have actually existed," if the confession is "naked unattended with [corroborating] circumstances," it is not sufficient by itself to convict.

Faced with a "naked confession," the trial judge in *Long* instructed the jury to acquit: "As there are no confirmatory circumstances in the present case, it is better to acquit the prisoner." Lacking corroboration, the Hawkins-Leach skepticism prevailed.

> It is hardly to be supposed that a man perfectly possessed of himself, would make a confession to take away his own life. It must generally proceed from a promise or hope of favour, or from a dread of punishment, and in such situations the mind is agitated—the man may be easily tempted to go further than the truth. Besides, the witness respecting the confession, may have mistaken his meaning. How easy is it to understand the speaker differently from what he meant? and the smallest mistake in this particular might prove fatal.

We see here the two strands of Blackstone's skeptical view of confessions.[46] First, they may proceed from influences that can interfere with a suspect's rational calculus. Second, they might not be reported accurately. *Long* adds a dimension to the second concern. Even if the words are accurately reported, the speaker's meaning is contextual and could be misunderstood. The corroboration principle is a part of the requirement that the State prove the *corpus delicti*, or "body of the crime."

Long cites no authority for the corroboration principle. An 1816 New York case said that the corroboration rule was "established in the criminal courts in England," but gave no citation, and we found no English case on point.[47] To be sure, Hale's *History of the Pleas of the Crown* contains a sort of aspirational statement along those lines: "I would never convict any person of murder or manslaughter, unless the fact were proved to be done, or at least the body found dead."[48] Hale cites two cases where a defendant was convicted, without proof of a body, only to have the putative victim show up alive after the defendant was executed. These cases are a *reason* to have a *corpus delicti* rule but are not *evidence* of the rule. Wigmore found English law on this point "in an unfortunate state of obscurity, subject to much difference of opinion."[49] In 2003, David Moran concluded that the *corpus delicti* rule "never actually became a part of the English common law."[50] Richard Leo and his co-authors agree.[51]

In the 1816 New York *corpus delicti* case, the only witness to a larceny had "gone to sea, and was supposed to be drowned."[52] When the prosecutor offered to read the magistrate's examination to the jury, the court sustained the objection of the defense lawyer, Dr. John A. Graham, and held that "the mere confession of the prisoner, out of court, will not be sufficient to produce a conviction." Without the confession, the jury acquitted the defendant, whose last name was Hope. After the verdict, Graham put his hand on his breast and said, "Hope springs eternal in the human breast." He then turned to the defendant and, with a flourish, said: "Now you can go." We will return in a moment to the charismatic John Graham, Doctor of Laws.

While the proportionality principle might in part explain *Hope*—the crime charged was only larceny—an early New Jersey case must be based solely on concerns about false confessions. In 1818, a ten-year-old slave confessed to murder after he was "taken apart by one or more of the jurors" of the inquest "and told that *he had better confess* the whole truth."[53] The trial court admitted the confession, the jury convicted, and the ten-year-old boy was sentenced to die. The New Jersey Supreme Court vacated the conviction. Quoting the Hawkins-Leach "deluded instrument" passage, Chief Justice Kirkpatrick concluded that the confession "was not lawful evidence against him."[54] The age of the suspect was important to the court's decision but equally important was the lack of corroborating evidence. The court noted that the only evidence against the defendant was "a simple naked confession, *disclosing no fact, pregnant with no circumstances to give it authority, or in any way to corroborate it.*"[55]

American states embraced the *corpus delicti* rule. David Moran's 2003 survey concludes that the rule is today followed in thirty-nine states, though the rationalist move in the last century has undermined its efficacy. Moran finds that some states "have substantially weakened its impact by finding the requirement satisfied by the most minimal independent evidence."[56]

What emerges from the early American cases is that voluntary, credible confessions were admissible. As demonstrated, corroboration was one way to demonstrate credibility. Another was penitential. An 1818 Massachusetts case admitted a confession made to members of the defendant's church, stressing that there "was no compulsion," the confession was "purely voluntary," and "[a]s it was penitential, it must be believed to be sincere, and therefore credible."[57] Indeed, "[t]hose who heard it were bound, as good citizens, to make it known to the appointed guardians of the public morals." Even in the absence of positive evidence of credibility, some early American courts were less skeptical than their English counterparts. A Delaware court in 1808 held that telling the suspect "that it 'would be better for him to confess'" did not bring the case under the English "authorities" cited by the defendant. [58]

3. AUTONOMY CONCERNS

False confessions were a major concern of early American law. But American courts, like English courts, were also motivated by the Whig principle that humans should not be induced to harm themselves. The Hawkins-Leach dictum that "the law will not suffer a prisoner to be made the deluded instrument of his own conviction" supported the rationale of many American cases of this period. In suppressing a statement made by a suspect who expressed hope of favor if he confessed, an 1839 Vermont case quoted *Starkie on Evidence*: "A confession must never be received in evidence, where the defendant has been influenced by *any* threat or promise."[59] If there was a possibility that a defendant acted "under the expectation of favor," the court thought "it safest to err on the side of humanity and exclude such confessions."

Perhaps the most solicitous American statement of the autonomy-based norm that lurks in the law of confessions appears in an 1823 Tennessee appellate case. After first commenting that confessions are "liable to a thousand abuses," the court wrote:

> Confessions are made by persons for whom humanity can not but feel; in distress, in want of advisers, deserted by the world, in chains and degradation, their spirits sunk, fear predominant, hope fluttering around, purposes and views momentarily changing, a thousand plans alternating, a soul tortured with anguish, and difficulties gathering into a multitude. How uncertain must be the things which are uttered in such a storm of the passions! And this is not all; how easy is it for the hearer to take one word for another, or to take a word in a sense not affixed to it by the speaker! And for want of an exact representation of the tone of voice, emphasis, countenance, eye, manner, and action of the one who made the confession, how almost impossible is it to make third persons understand the exact state of the mind and meaning of the one who made the confession. For these reasons, evidence of confession, though admissible, is yet received with great distrust, and under the superintendence of very solicitous apprehensions for the wrong it may do. The admissibility is made to depend on its being free from all suspicion of having been obtained by any threats of severity or promise of favor, and of every influence, even the minutest, having been exercised over the mind of the person in order to induce a disclosure.[60]

If courts rigorously applied the solicitous norms articulated here, few confessions would be admissible. What confession is free from "every influence, even the minutest, having been exercised over the mind"?

Ultimately, one cannot separate concerns with autonomy from those about false confessions. In an 1845 Delaware case, a "servant girl," twelve years of age, was charged with arson that caused the death of two children.[61] She confessed to her mistress who told her that the case against her was very strong and that she would not be punished if she confessed. In rejecting the confession, the majority relied on Hawkins-Leach: "However slight the promise or threat may have been, the confession cannot be received."[62] One judge dissented, noting that the rationale of the "no inducement" rule was not whether the influence "induced the confession, (for that would exclude every confession that was asked for)." Instead, the "danger is that this hope, thus held out to an agitated mind, might possibly induce an *untrue* confession."[63] That standard was not met, the dissenting judge concluded.

Greenleaf's evidence treatise, probably the most influential American evidence treatise of the nineteenth century,[64] prefaces its discussion of confessions with a variation of the Hawkins-Leach dictum:

> [T]he evidence of verbal confessions of guilt is to be *received with great caution*. For, besides the danger of mistake, from the misapprehension of witnesses, the misuse of words, the failure of the party to express his own meaning, and the infirmity of memory, it should be recollected that the mind of the prisoner himself is oppressed by the calamity of his situation, and that he is often influenced by motives of hope or fear, to make an untrue confession.[65]

Greenleaf then adds a new concern, reflecting the beginning of organized police. He noted the "zeal" that "so generally prevails, to detect offenders, especially in cases of aggravated guilt, and the strong disposition, in the persons engaged in pursuit of evidence, to rely on slight grounds of suspicion, which are exaggerated into sufficient proof." This is a remarkably modern formulation of concern with "tunnel vision"—police and prosecutors focusing on a suspect based on weak evidence while excluding other suspects.[66]

Yet on the next page, Greenleaf reminds the reader: Subject to these cautions, it is generally agreed, that *deliberate confessions of guilt* are among the most effectual proofs in the law."[67] He noted that if the confession is deliberate and voluntary, the jury is entitled to assume "that a rational being will not make admissions prejudicial to his interest and safety, unless when urged by the promptings of truth and conscience." Statements were admissible if "induced by *spiritual exhortations*, whether of a clergyman, or of any other person."[68] They were admissible if made because the prisoner was drunk or "by a promise of some *collateral benefit or boon*." Perhaps most significantly, Greenleaf read English doctrine to permit a confession to be admitted if secured by deception or by a "false representation made to him for that purpose, provided there is no reason to suppose that the inducement held out was calculated to produce any untrue confession, which is the main point to be considered." Indeed, Greenleaf goes so far as to say that in "all these cases the evidence may be laid before the jury, however little it may weigh, under the circumstances, and however reprehensible may be the mode in which, in some of them, it was obtained."

To this point, we have demonstrated that early American courts were generally receptive to the Hawkins-Leach dictum, both on the ground of preserving autonomy and that of avoiding false confessions. Yet the corroboration exception in the early cases and Greenleaf's 1842 description is evidence of a countercurrent in the direction of admitting confessions if the false confession concern can be assuaged. One development that balances convicting the guilty with concerns about autonomy and false confessions was New York's requirement that magistrates must warn suspects before questioning them. We turn to that requirement in the next subsection and focus on New York City, both because New York was the first jurisdiction to require warnings and because a more coherent story can be told by keeping the focus narrow. We then expand the scope of the inquiry to other states.

4. NEW YORK REQUIRES WARNINGS

In 1828, the New York legislature required that magistrates tell the suspect that "he is at liberty to refuse to answer any question that may be put to him."[69] No other state required warnings at the time, and Parliament would not require warnings for almost twenty years. The New York statute was similar to the English treatises of the time—e.g., Dickinson, 1813 and Chitty, 1816—in requiring the magistrate to inform the suspect of his right not to answer questions.[70]

But the New York legislature went further than the English treatises and further than Parliament would go in 1848. It required the magistrate to tell the suspect that he had a right to counsel and to allow the suspect "a reasonable time to send for and advise with counsel."[71] Moreover, again unlike anything that had come before or that Parliament would do, New York gave suspects the right to have counsel present during the examinations of all witnesses. The Revised Statutes of Missouri, 1835, and Arkansas, 1838, closely followed New York's language requiring warnings and permitting defense counsel during the examination.[72]

In effect, the New York legislature anticipated *Miranda* by more than a century and a quarter. What motivated this radical move? Wesley Oliver is, we think, the first to write comprehensively about the New York innovation.[73] He argued that the practice of giving warnings developed in America for the same reason as in England—to avoid having confessions excluded because of judicial concern about the pressure of being examined by the magistrate.[74] Oliver cites no New York cases prior to the 1828 act expressing concern about the pressure of the magistrate's examination. We found no mention of that issue in that period despite devising several computer searches.

Oliver offers an 1845 case where a trial judge rejected a confession from a person who was not able to appreciate "in her mental agony" the "force and effect" of what she "might utter."[75] The confession was given to an alderman, who was presumably questioning her in place of a justice of the peace, and he warned her "that she was not obliged to answer any questions that would criminate herself."[76] The court held it would be "proper to apply Lord Denman's rule" (probably from *Regina v. Arnold*, decided in 1838[77]) "and exclude the evidence, because she had not been warned that what she might say would be used in evidence against her."[78] We would give this case less weight in explaining the 1828 act than Oliver does because it is a trial court opinion and the trial judge said, "Such a caution may not *always* be necessary to warrant evidence of a prisoner's statements."[79] More importantly, it occurs sixteen years *after* the legislature acted to require warnings.

Of course, the New York legislature might have been aware of the concern in England, most vividly expressed in 1817 in *Rex v. Wilson*, that the pressure of the examination might be too much to bear.[80] And the New York legislature *had* raced to codify the Marian acts in 1787, even before ratifying the United States Constitution, suggesting a felt need to have examinations and the evidence that they produced admitted at trial. But having seen no New York cases like *Wilson*, it seems unlikely to us that the state legislature would have been motivated by fear of losing confessions. Moreover, the cases that precipitated Section 18 of the English Indictable Offenses Act of 1848 seem to have been *Drew* and *Harris* with their "excessive[ly] mild[]" holding that the giving of warnings caused statements to be inadmissible,[81] and these cases had yet to occur when the New York legislature required that magistrates warn the accused of the right counsel and the right not to answer the magistrate.

Oliver's argument that the 1828 act was mostly about ensuring the admissibility of confessions is also called into question by the New York legislature's creation of a right to counsel during the magistrate's examination. There was a reason that, for centuries, English law allowed felony defendants to use lawyers only to argue points of law.[82] Lawyers were perceived to be impediments to getting to the truth about the case. English law did not permit lawyers to argue facts on behalf of felony defendants until 1836.[83] The New York legislature must have known of the potential impediment that lawyers would pose during the examination. Indeed, a former state attorney general, said in comments published in 1823 "that considerable inconveniences and injurious delays might well result from [lawyers] being habitually present at the examination."[84]

The decision of the New York legislature to permit the accused to consult with counsel before being examined by magistrates *and* to have counsel present during the examination was one of great import and cannot, in our view, be explained by equating what New York did in 1828 with Parliament's purpose in enacting the Indictable Offenses Act in 1848. We think that John A. Graham is the reason the New York legislature acted in 1828. This is the same John Graham who represented Charles Hope in the 1816 *corpus delicti* case discussed previously. He made, in 1823, an argument that foreshadowed *Miranda* with amazing precision. We offer some details about the lawyer who invented *Miranda* 143 years before the United States Supreme Court would discover it in the Fifth Amendment.

Graham's grandfather, an Edinburgh clergyman, emigrated to the colonies in 1718; Graham's father was a prominent surgeon in Connecticut.[85] Graham read for the law in a Connecticut law office and was admitted to the bar there in 1785. He was admitted to the New York bar in 1805 "and practised chiefly in the criminal courts."

Graham was in love with his own voice. A reporter of a case noted that he "addressed the court in an elegant and flowery harangue of some length."[86] In 1812, he published a book of his arguments to the jury or judge in twenty-three cases, a sort of early *Advertisements for Myself.*[87] The flyleaf of the book featured a drawing of Graham that shows him to be handsome and dashing. The cases ranged from bigamy and adultery to grand larceny, rape, and arson. One might have thought he would have included only cases he won but, in fact, of the twenty-three cases, he lost fifteen. Obviously, he thought his arguments worth preserving in any event.

In one case, he maintained that his client was not guilty of assault and battery because the victim had been working on the Sabbath and thus was "literally and truly in the service of the devil."[88] Left unstated, but implied, was the principle that it was justifiable to beat those who do not obey the Sabbath. The argument failed to persuade the jury. He defended a slave against a charge of bigamy.[89] Graham conceded that the man had two wives but claimed that a slave, who had no right to make "any civil contract," could not validly marry and thus could not be guilty of marrying twice.[90] In response to an argument that permitting bigamy among slaves "will sap the foundation of all morality," Graham proposed that instead of cutting "off a twig or a limb of a tree," that government "should lay the axe to the root [of slavery]." Slavery is the evil, Graham said: "*Make the slave free—there is the remedy.*"[91] He was, of course, correct on the larger point. But the jury convicted on the bigamy charge.

He defended a husband against his wife's assault and battery charges by claiming that the wife possessed "all the virtues of the *witch of Endor.*"[92] He promised that he would prove to the satisfaction of the jury that the wife "is the most fiery, masculine, and blood-thirsty, of any woman this court or jury ever saw: in short, she is a disgrace to her sex." This transparent appeal to sexism worked. The jury acquitted.[93]

Perhaps his most amazing argument was in support of a motion to vacate a conviction for stealing a turkey.[94] He contended that the indictment was flawed because trial revealed that, when the defendant took the turkey, the poor bird was dead, its head, wings, and feet removed. Thus, "instead of its being a *turkey*, it was only the *skeleton* or *dead body* of a *turkey*. This I take to be sound *logic*; since it could not fly, having no wings; and having no head, it could not see; and having no toes, it could not walk. . . . *Ergo*, it cannot be a *turkey*, as charged in the indictment, but must be considered *a dead carcass*."[95] His motion for a new trial was overruled.

From these cases, the reader can see that Graham was willing to test the boundaries of accepted legal thought. Now we move to 1823. His client, Hiram Maxwell, was charged was grand larceny, "stealing a Horse and Gig, value $350."[96] When the prosecutor offered the defendant's examination before the magistrate, Graham objected on the ground that the defendant had not been warned of his rights.[97] To understand the argument requires a bit of history. New York's initial 1777 constitution had a right to counsel but no explicit right against compelled self-incrimination.[98] A state bill of rights, ratified in 1787, also failed to specify a right against compelled self-incrimination.[99] But the constitution of 1821 included, in article VII, section 7, a right to counsel and a right not to "be compelled, in any criminal case, to be a witness against himself."[100] Graham argued that by pairing the right against compelled self-incrimination with the right to counsel, the new constitution created a right not to be questioned by a magistrate without knowing that one had both access to counsel and the right not to answer questions.

Graham's argument consumed sixteen pages in a report of the Maxwell case he published later in 1823, albeit with generous margins. "There is evil in the city.—Evil did I say? Yes! an evil greatly to be deprecated. I allude to the mode and manner practised in taking the examinations of persons charged with crime."[101] Part of Graham's rationale was autonomy and fairness. He worried about an accused being struck "with *horror*" as he faces the examination, while the clerk records "whatever perchance may fall from the lips of this half-distracted prisoner, who, with stammering accents, and eyes staring wild afright, begins as he is commanded, to *confess*."[102] But he mixes in a concern with false confessions: "Thus ignorant, blind, and frightened, as it were, out of his senses, the prisoner often signs or acknowledges to matters and things contained in the examination, which, in fact and in truth, he is perfectly innocent and ignorant of."[103]

To put flesh on the bones of his argument about false confessions, Graham cited a case where his client, Henry M'Fall, was convicted on the basis of an uncorroborated confession.[104] Graham claimed that M'Fall was *"since proved innocent* of the *crime, and pardoned by the executive."* M'Fall's case goes "fully to prove the incalculable mischiefs and injustice these confessions produce in our land of liberty."

After noting the "mischief" in M'Fall's case, Graham returned to his "evil" theme. He compared the magistrate's examination to the inquisitions in Spain, Portugal, and Italy, though he conceded that he gave "a decided preference in favour of our New-York police over an Italian or Spanish inquisition."[105] He also compared the "unconstitutional and *illegal"* examinations with a "corroding cancer" to which he offered "the amputating knife, which shall cut up by the roots its spreading *malignancy."*[106]

Claiming that a "new era has commenced," Graham read to the court section 7 of article VII, with its right to counsel and right not to be compelled to be a witness.[107] From these rights, he deduced that magistrates should "give to every prisoner brought before them, charged with crime, the following information, to wit:"

> 1st. Prisoner, you are entitled to counsel.
> 2nd. Your confession must be free and voluntary, without fear, threats, or promises.
> 3rd. You are not bound to answer any question which may tend to criminate yourself.
> 4th. Whatever you confess against yourself, may be made use of on your trial in aid of your conviction.[108]

Without this warning, Graham argued, "the examination becomes a mere nullity—*void in law—void in conscience,* and cannot be read in evidence against the prisoner on his trial."

But Graham was ahead of himself in 1823. The judge said that he "agrees with Doctor Graham, in most of his points," but he found that the statement to the magistrate "appears to have been voluntarily made by the prisoner" and allowed it to be read to the jury.[109] The jury "found the prisoner guilty, without leaving the box," which suggests why Graham worked so hard to keep the statement from the jury.[110] Presumably, many suspects were in the same situation.

Four months later, July 4, 1823, Graham spoke at City Hall in New York City as part of the celebration of the forty-seventh year of American independence.[111] He began by noting the "approbation with which many of the greatest and wisest Philosophers, Civilians, Orators and Statesmen in our country have been pleased to favour my speech in the case of Hiram Maxwell agreeing with me in the doctrine I there had the honour to advance and advocate."[112] He said he was republishing his argument, "together with the letters and opinions" he had been "honoured in receiving from these great lovers of liberty, humanity, and justice." The letter writers included John Adams and Thomas Jefferson as well as John Marshall, John Jay, three former governors of New York, and Andrew Jackson, who would be nominated for president in 1824 and would win election in 1828.[113]

John Adams, who had defended clients against British persecution, was very much in favor of Graham's argument.[114] To Adams, the only justification for a "personal examination" of an accused "before a magistrate" was to provide "an opportunity of being witness for himself in his own favour." But "no insidious questioning ought to be put to him, by which he may be betrayed into any confession of any fact that may discover his guilt, if he is guilty. His examination ought to be public, and he ought to be allowed counsel, if he can have it." John Marshall noted that, as we saw earlier, Virginia had no law permitting magistrates to examine the accused, but Marshall said, in italics, that "where the contrary practice prevails, it would seem proper that it be regulated by principles you lay down."[115]

At the Fourth of July celebration in 1823, Graham called for the New York law to be "corrected and amended by the legislature as to put it wholly out of the power of an *ignorant* or *captious* magistrate from taking a confession of a prisoner charged with crime, without first informing him of his legal rights."[116] Many of the letters he had received came from prominent, powerful New Yorkers. Ambrose Spencer, a former chief justice of New York, noted that "great abuses have taken place in the examination of prisoners" and expressed hope that Graham's remarks "may have the effect to produce a re-examination of the law on this subject."[117] Thomas Emmet, a former attorney general, disagreed that counsel should be present, but nonetheless agreed that Graham had "pointed out abuses which I have long been convinced exist to a great degree," abuses that are "repugnant to humanity and oppressive to the accused."[118] Without warnings, "the examination is a trap for the terrified and unwary, and calculated to cheat him out of his acknowledged privilege that he is not bound to criminate himself."[119] Another letter referred to "the examinations in our Police Office" that "are as frequently the means of entrapping the innocent, as they are of detecting the guilty."[120]

Another former attorney general of New York, Josiah Hoffman, conceded that remedial legislation "may be necessary to correct the evil" but maintained that "existing law, if rightly administered," would make new statutes unnecessary.[121] *"Let the courts reject every examination where the accused has not been fairly cautioned, and duly advised as to his situation, and the examining magistrates will soon be taught their duty."*[122] This, of course, is what happened in England, with the result that justice of the peace manuals as early as 1813 recommended warnings prior to examination. Hoffman's letter suggests that New York courts were not following their English counterparts. If New York trial judges were suppressing statements on Hawkins-Leach grounds, magistrates would probably have responded as in England by warning suspects.

Pierre Van Wyck, a former district attorney of New York City and County, characterized the magistrate's examination of the accused without warnings as "an instance of inquisitorial subtlety and tyrannical energy at the very threshold of every criminal proceeding."[123] He also made the point Yale Kamisar would make in 1965: Counsel at trial is rendered largely moot if the accused has "all his hopes of life swept away by a dash of the magistrate's pen—a record made in five minutes which seals his ruin and insures his conviction as a felon."[124] Graham's speech "ought not to be lost sight of until a reform is effected in the practice of the Police."[125]

The New York code of 1813 authorized examinations by magistrates but did not require them to provide any kind of warnings.[126] The New York legislature added elaborate procedures to warn the accused in 1828. Something happened between 1813 and the act of 1828, and we believe that it was the influence of John A. Graham. To be sure, the evidence is circumstantial. We have the letters written in 1823 from men in power in New York and across the young nation. Several letters insisted that the practice of examining suspects needed radical reform. Moreover, there is no similar development in treatises of the period or in other states. Finally, Graham's 1823 argument tracks the 1828 statutory regime quite closely.[127]

"1st. Prisoner, you are entitled to counsel." Section 14: "[T]he prisoner shall be allowed a reasonable time to send for and advise with counsel. If desired by the person arrested, his counsel may be present during the examination of the complainant and the witnesses on the part of the prosecution, and during the examination of the prisoner."

"2d. Your confession must be free and voluntary, without fear, threats, or promises. 3d. "You are not bound to answer any question which may tend to criminate yourself." Section 15: "At the commencement of the examination, the prisoner shall be informed by the magistrate, that he is at liberty to refuse to answer any question that may be put to him."

"4th. Whatever you confess against yourself, may be made use of on your trial in aid of your conviction." There is no direct analog to Graham's "4th" in the New York act, though being told that one does not have to answer and that one has the right to consult with counsel before answering strongly implies that the statements might be used in aid of a conviction.

Oddly, the act does not specify what use will be made of these examinations, though the 1830 Edwards treatise on New York law discusses the new statute and concludes, "It is important that these examinations should be correctly taken, for in certain cases they may, if regularly taken, be received in evidence on the trial against the prisoner."[128] While the limitation to "certain cases" is not explained, Edwards seems to say that following the statute permits use of the examinations. If the reason the legislature required warnings was to ensure admissibility of confessions, it would be an oversight of major proportions not to specify, as Parliament did, that "whatever you say will be taken down in Writing, and may be given in Evidence against you upon your Trial." Thus, we conclude, contrary to Oliver, that the New York legislature was not trying to ease the admission of confessions but, instead, was giving voice to concerns raised by John Graham.

By 1830, the New York rules governing arrest and examination by magistrates were clear. The arresting officer had a duty to bring the suspect before the magistrate, whose duty it was to examine any witnesses, warn the suspect of his rights, examine the suspect, and then to bail, release, or commit the suspect.[129] It was a remarkably "clean" procedure. But organized police were on the horizon and they would gradually usurp the magistrate's role in questioning suspects. The 1828 commitment procedure appeared just as the colonial system of law enforcement was breaking down in New York City. The system left from colonial days was based primarily on constables, marshals, the night watch, and justices of the peace. For example: "An ordinance of 1801 required the high constable to enforce all state laws affecting the peace of the city and all corporation ordinances."[130] Around 1800, there were sixteen constables and seventy-two watchmen.[131] Vagrants, thieves, and those who violated the public order were arrested by constables or marshals and brought before the justices of the peace.

This system was, by 1828, giving way. "By the late 1820's more and more observers thought the watch incompetent and inadequate, but as yet there was no strong movement for radical re-organization" of New York's law enforcement.[132] "The beginnings of industrialization, large-scale immigration, slums, religious, racial, and ethnic rivalries, and the growth of machine politics all complicated the city's police problem."[133] But there is no contradiction between rising social unease and the legislature's decision to reform magistrate examinations. It is easy to look back now and identify the mid- to late-1820s as the beginning of a more complicated police problem, but the legislature was living in real time. The use of constables, the night watch, and justices of the peace to control crime and deviance had been the norm in New York City for two centuries. Any perceived failures in that venerable system could be fixed, contemporary politicians would have thought, by simply expanding the watch and the number of constables and marshals. The number of watchmen, for example, increased from 72 in 1800 to 400 in 1826.[134] The number of marshals grew from 40 in 1800 to 100 in 1832.[135]

Moreover, the brunt of the increase in crime and violence occurred in the 1830s and 1840s, after the protective examination rules were in place. Richardson identifies the period 1830–1845 as reflecting a "marked upsurge in crime, vice, and disorder."[136] There were two riots in 1834 that required militia to put down, and a great fire of 1835 led to "looting so widespread that the mayor again had to call in troops."[137] Immigration into the United States from 1820 to 1831 was only 175,000. It would grow to over one million in the period from 1832 to 1846.[138] The number of watchmen in New York City by 1845 was 1096, compared to 72 in 1800.[139] In sum, the New York legislature in 1828 would not have perceived New York City as about to fall off a cliff of crime and unrest and could, therefore, afford to create Graham-inspired rights for those accused of crime and being examined by the justices of the peace.

Responding to the rapid increase in population, crime, and deviance, the first New York City police force that we would recognize as "police" was established in 1845.[140] By the 1850s, it was clear in New York City "that police interrogations were regularly occurring."[141] As magistrates were required to warn the suspect of his or her right not to answer, it would make sense for the police to give warnings when they engaged in the same form of investigation. Little evidence suggests that they gave warnings.

In part this is because New York courts by the middle of the nineteenth century were moving toward a less skeptical view of confessions.[142] The legislature of this era seemed more concerned with crime control.[143] As our theory predicts, a rising concern with crime and social unrest reduces the importance of the autonomy rights identified by Graham in 1823. The Commissioners on Practice and Pleading presented to the legislature in 1855 a report recommending changes to the New York code of criminal procedure.[144] A note about the law surrounding confessions of defendants said, "The law has been too tender in this respect. It should be its policy, as the Commissioners conceive, to let in all the light possible, trusting to the discretion of juries to distinguish between the false and the true."[145] The concern here is with false confessions rather than with autonomy.

By 1875, the police were brazen about their crime control goals. Testifying before the police commission, the police superintendent said he ignored the requirement that those arrested be promptly brought before a magistrate because "I believed it to be my duty to detain the prisoners until I could procure the witnesses necessary to secure a conviction."[146] He testified that he "refused to allow the relatives to see the prisoners to prevent any communication between them that would defeat the ends of justice and that would interfere with the conviction of the prisoners and the return of the property." He hewed to the letter of the law, correctly claiming that "there is no statute that makes it the duty of the Police" to give the warnings required of magistrates.

During this period, magistrates had adopted the practice of ending the examination if the suspect indicated that she did not want to be questioned.[147] This practice is consistent with, if not compelled by, the 1828 statute that gave the prisoner the "liberty to refuse to answer any question that may be put to him."[148] But the committee read the provision differently, insisting that a suspect "should have no right of waiving examination, although, of course, he could not be constrained to answer. . . . [I]t was the duty of the magistrate to examine [the suspect] rigorously as to the circumstances of the case; and, beyond all doubt, were this law complied with, a very great benefit to the administration of justice would be obtained."[149]

The committee that issued this report was aptly named "The Select Committee Appointed by the Assembly of 1875 to Investigate the Causes of the Increase of Crime in the City of New York." Something fundamental had changed. The New York legislature in 1828 required warnings regarding the rights to silence and to counsel before a magistrate could examine a suspect. By 1876, the legislature was willing to let police question without warnings and was urging magistrates to pressure suspects to answer questions. Whatever interest in the rights of suspects that John Graham had helped create had largely disappeared.

Then, oddly enough, in 1881 the New York legislature rewrote the 1828 provisions to radically restrict the scope of the magistrate's examination of the accused.[150] Magistrates were no longer required to tell the accused that he was at liberty to refuse to answer questions, but the scope of the examination was severely restricted. In effect, the right to be warned that the accused could refuse to answer was replaced by a procedural mechanism that prevented the accused from being "sharply and closely interrogated, improper answers extorted, apparent contradictions emphatically noted, and the whole served up with a too destructive ingenuity, and handed over to the public prosecutor," as one of Graham's correspondents described the magistrate's examination.[151] Perhaps those legislators concerned with crime control saw eliminating the warning of the right to silence as a fair trade for limiting the scope of the examination, and vice versa for those who valued autonomy interests of the accused.

In any event, the magistrate's examination had long since ceased to be the principal means of obtaining incriminating responses from suspects. The police had taken the lead, and the only protection against police questioning was against obtaining involuntary statements—and giving a caution did not seem necessary to prove a statement voluntary.[152] Policing on the ground had adjusted to crime control concerns. Friedman observes that in the dense cities of this era, the "policeman's force was the only kind of law that ever penetrated that [urban] jungle."[153] His example is New York City police officer Alexander S. Williams who became "famous in the 1870s because he 'invoked the gospel of the nightstick' and organized 'a strong arm squad.' Patrolling the Gas House District, Williams 'clubbed the thugs with or without provocation,'" claiming "that 'there is more law in the end of a policeman's nightstick than in a decision of the Supreme Court.'" In 1894, the *New York Times* referred to a "Clubbers Brigade" within the police force, an informal coalition of officers whose purpose was "to show that the New-York police force is superior to the law and can club citizens with impunity, without fear of dismissal or criminal prosecution."[154]

How times had changed since Dr. John A. Graham climbed the steps of the City Hall of New York City and made his Fourth of July speech in 1823.

5. THE INFLUENCE OF JOHN HENRY WIGMORE

Dean of the Northwestern University School of Law for many years, Wigmore continues to influence evidence law more than a century after publication of his treatise on the law of evidence in 1904. He condemned and ridiculed the cases that followed the Hawkins-Leach dictum. He called them "absurdities [that] have disfigured the law of the admissibility of confessions."[155] Wigmore was influenced by Jeremy Bentham's critique of the common law privilege against compelled self-incrimination.[156] As we pointed out in chapter 3, and as Wigmore demonstrated in his treatise, the privilege has a distinct historical origin and role from the common law confessions doctrine.[157] Yet, both can shield the guilty from prosecution. Thus, Bentham's critique of the privilege undoubtedly influenced Wigmore's view of the Hawkins-Leach dictum.

Bentham, with characteristic flair (if not overstatement), condemned the privilege as it had been applied in English law as "not a mere impropriety, but a sophism, a fraud."[158] He saw the privilege as protecting against forced self-accusation of crime. But, to Bentham, that was different from permitting those already accused of a crime the right to refuse to answer questions. The latter practice had the effect of "[c]onfounding interrogation with torture: with the application of physical suffering."[159] As currently practiced, the privilege against compelled self-incrimination benefited the "evil-doers of all sorts and sizes" and harmed the community.[160]

In his 1904 treatise, Wigmore accused judges of "excessive caution in listening" to arguments based on the Hawkins-Leach dictum when deciding the admissibility of confessions, a caution that has "given an appearance of sentimental irrationality to the law and has obstructed the administration of justice."[161] He described "almost incredible" results—confessions excluded because the prisoner was shown a handbill offering a reward or was told that what he said could be used against him.[162] Another case excluded a confession made on a promise to give a glass of gin.[163]

These cases were "absurdities" to Wigmore because they exalted autonomy over the goal of preventing false confessions while convicting guilty defendants. To Wigmore, the only defensible principle for suppressing a confession was that "under certain circumstances it becomes untrustworthy as testimony."[164] This principle explains the development of much criminal procedure doctrine in the nineteenth century,[165] and Wigmore's theory thus unified and rationalized the law of confessions. The test that he fashioned for his trustworthiness principle was a product of rational, Enlightenment thinking:

> Human nature being what it is, *were the prospects attending confession* (involving the equalization or averaging of the benefit of realizing the promise or the benefit of escaping from the threat, against the drawbacks moral and legal of furnishing damaging evidence), *as weighed at the time against the prospects attending non-confession* (involving a similar averaging), *such as to have created, in any considerable degree, a risk that a false confession would be made?* Putting it more briefly and roughly, Was the inducement such that there was any fair risk of a false confession?[166]

Wigmore recognized that courts did not explicitly apply the test that he espoused. He argued, though, that in many cases courts were applying something like his trustworthiness test and simply naming the result either "voluntary" or "involuntary." Wigmore argued that, when applied to statements, the voluntariness test was "practically colorless and unserviceable."[167] Wigmore's famous example of the "unserviceable" nature of the voluntariness test is that "[a]s between the rack and a false confession, the latter would usually be considered the less disagreeable; but it is nonetheless voluntarily chosen."[168] All conscious choices are, in some sense, voluntary.

Philosophers from Aristotle to Alan Wertheimer have made the same point. When the bank robber displays a weapon and says to the teller "your money or your life," handing over the money is, after all, a choice on the part of the teller.[169] Famous for being a tightwad, Jack Benny hesitated when faced with the choice of his money or his life. The robber waved his gun insistently and Benny finally replied: "I'm thinking, *I'm thinking.*"[170] One might call the choice involuntary because the teller and Benny should not have been forced to make that choice. But the parameter that does the work here has nothing to do with voluntariness, as Wertheimer demonstrated, and everything to do with a normative theory about whether the choice the robber offered was a reasonable one.[171] That theory, of course, must ultimately draw from moral philosophy and not a mechanical notion of voluntariness. We will return to the normative dimension of the law of interrogation in chapter 10.

The Wertheimer view of voluntariness fits comfortably with the analysis in chapter 3. Whig philosophy, the relatively low level of crime, and British world dominance led to a view that it was immoral to force lower-class suspects to choose between silence and answering the accusations of their employer or of the magistrate. By the time we get to Wigmore, however, many courts and observers no longer thought it immoral to pressure a suspect to choose whether to remain silent or to answer questions about a crime.

As Wigmore recognized, however, confessions law was unsettled in 1903. Some cases continued to cling to the early nineteenth-century worldview that he considered a "perversion of normal reasoning"[172] while others, and sometimes in the same state, were much less skeptical toward the admissibility of confessions. We will turn to the state cases in a moment. First, we examine the Supreme Court's early confessions cases.

6. EARLY SUPREME COURT LAW OF CONFESSIONS

Perhaps the best example of the continuing power of the Hawkins-Leach dictum, over a century after it was first published, is the 1897 Supreme Court case of *Bram v. United States*.[173] Precisely how *Bram* came to embrace the Hawkins-Leach dictum is bit of a mystery. Four earlier Supreme Court cases had analyzed the confessions issue in a rationalist way. In the Court's first confession case, *Hopt v. Utah*, the defendant confessed after his arrest at a train depot where a large crowd had gathered and the father of the murder victim "was much excited, and may have made a motion to draw a revolver on the defendant."[174] The detective who made the arrest sent Hopt to jail in the company of a police officer. The detective joined them in two or three minutes "and immediately the accused commenced making a confession."

The police officer who took Hopt to jail did not testify. Because the detective could not testify to what the officer said in his absence, and given the state of English law, the Court acknowledged it was plausible to argue that the prosecution bore the burden of proving lack of inducement and, thus, the failure to have the officer testify was fatal to the State's case.[175] But John Marshall Harlan, a giant in the history of the Court, was having none of the Hawkins-Leach solicitude. "While some of the adjudged cases indicate distrust of confessions," Harlan wrote, "the rule against their admissibility has been sometimes carried too far, and in its application justice and common sense have too frequently been sacrificed at the shrine of mercy."[176] The proper test to use was not whether *any* threat or promise had been made but, rather, whether the threat or promise was sufficient to deprive a suspect "of that freedom of will or self-control essential to make his confession voluntary within the meaning of the law."[177] Lacking evidence of "inducements, threats, or promises," a unanimous Court affirmed the conviction.

In 1895, in another opinion by Harlan, the Court refused to follow the English cases that found an improper inducement in being urged to tell the truth: "[T]elling a man to be sure to tell the truth is not advising him to confess anything of which he is really not guilty."[178] A year later, a defendant's lawyer "insist[ed] that there cannot be a voluntary statement, a free, open confession, while a defendant is confined and in irons, under an accusation of having committed a capital offense."[179] The Court rejected the argument.

While confinement "bears upon the inquiry whether the confession was voluntarily made, or was extorted by threats or violence, or made under the influence of fear," confinement "is not in itself sufficient to justify the exclusion of a confession, if it appears to have been voluntary and was not obtained by putting the prisoner in fear or by promises."

Also in 1896, *Wilson v. United States*[180] found no due process violation when a magistrate examined Wilson in a courtroom filled with a crowd that earlier had "gathered around him, and threatened to mob him."[181] Wilson argued that his statements were not voluntary because he was not "warned that the statement might be used against him, or advised that he need not answer."[182] This, of course, is the argument that prevailed in *Miranda*. *Wilson* held that the lack of warnings "went to the weight or credibility of what he said," but did not "require his answers to be excluded on the ground of being involuntary, as matter of law."

At the end of 1896, the Court's view was that confessions were an important class of evidence as long as they were reliable and voluntary—whatever the latter term meant. The Court had yet to find an inducement or threat sufficient to render a confession inadmissible. The "voluntariness" issues had been decided by unanimous Courts.[183]

Along came *Bram* a year later. Unlike earlier opinions, a divided Court embraced Hawkins-Leach, now emphasizing autonomy rather than reliability. The same nine men who decided the previous three cases were still on the Court. The justices who wrote opinions in two of the prior confessions cases, Justice Brown and Justice Fuller, dissented in *Bram*. Oddly, the Court changed doctrinal "horses" in *Bram*. The earlier confessions cases had relied on the common law of confessions, while *Bram* explicitly relied on the Fifth Amendment privilege not to be compelled in a criminal case to be a witness against oneself. Why the Court turned to the Constitution rather than continue to rely on the common law rule is another mystery. The mystery deepens because the Court relied on common law authorities to give meaning to the Fifth Amendment privilege. Why not just rely on the common law directly, as the earlier cases had? The only explanation we have is that, as the country moved into its second century, it might have seemed a good idea to house the common law confessions rule in the Constitution to give it more stability.

Yet one wonders: Why not due process of law? It makes more sense to house a common law rule of evidence in the due process clause, which guarantees a fair judicial process, than in a privilege that began as a right not to take an oath before the Star Chamber. As Wigmore argued, the privilege historically covered only statements made "under process as a witness."[184] Larry Herman concluded that Wigmore was wrong on this point,[185] but Herman also concluded that *Bram*'s choice of the privilege made no difference because for seven decades *Bram* "fell into disuse as a restriction on police interrogation."[186] During this period, the Court used the due process clause to decide state confessions cases and various doctrines to decide federal cases, but rarely mentioned *Bram* or the Fifth Amendment privilege.[187]

In *Bram*, a triple murder occurred on an American sailing vessel when it was at sea. After the vessel was towed to Halifax, a Canadian detective first questioned Brown, the second mate.[188] Then he sent for Bram, the ship's first officer. He stripped Bram and searched his clothes. The opinion does not indicate whether Bram was permitted to dress before the questioning began, though the Court seems to assume that he was either questioned while being stripped or was nude when questioned. The customs official testified:

> When Mr. Bram came into my office, I said to him: "Bram, we are trying to unravel this horrible mystery." I said: "Your position is rather an awkward one. I have had Brown in this office, and he made a statement that he saw you do the murder." He [Bram] said: "He could not have seen me. Where was he?" I said: "He states he was at the wheel." "Well," he said, "he could not see me from there."[189]

Though Bram's responses were not a confession in the robust sense of the word, the government introduced them for the inculpatory inference that could be drawn. In an exhaustive opinion that relies heavily on English cases and commentators—including Hale, Hawkins, and Gilbert—the Court ruled that Bram's admissions were inadmissible because they were involuntary. What is striking about the opinion is the change in the Court's attitude. Earlier cases stressed the value of confessions and rejected a range of factors as not requiring suppression. But *Bram* gives a bear-hug embrace to the Hawkins-Leach dictum, suggesting that almost any influence can taint a confession. The Court quoted approvingly the following passage from *Russell on Crimes* that was obviously drawn from the Hawkins-Leach dictum:

> But a confession, in order to be admissible, must be free and voluntary; that is, must not be extracted by any sort of threats or violence, nor obtained by any direct or implied promises, however slight, nor by the exertion of any improper influence.... A confession can never be received in evidence where the prisoner has been influenced by any threat or promise; for the law cannot measure the force of the influence used, or decide upon its effect upon the mind of the prisoner, and therefore excludes the declaration if any degree of influence has been exerted.[190]

One hundred and ten years after Thomas Leach added the "deluded instrument" footnote to Hawkins, its influence was still powerful. Wigmore was, of course, highly critical of *Bram*, characterizing the Court's argument as "labored" and concluding that "it is enough to say that the ruling takes its place among those which have reached the highest pitch of irrationality in this subject, and have done most to reduce the law of evidence to a mass of medieval scholasticism and to put it in a condition to favor criminals."[191]

Justice Harlan, who wrote the Court's first two confessions opinions stressing the value of confessions, did not dissent in *Bram*. On the assumption that Justice Harlan had not taken leave of his senses, one must attempt to reconcile these holdings. The trick is that Bram was told, in so many words, that he was likely to be arrested and prosecuted unless he persuaded the interrogator of his innocence. The temptation to tell an exculpatory story, true or false, is probably greater when a suspect thinks he might escape arrest than when he is already in irons or is being questioned by a magistrate after arrest. Thus, *Bram* is best viewed as an inducement case, while Wilson's mob argument is rooted in threat. A justice could take the view that an inducement to tell an exculpatory story to avoid being charged is more powerful than a vague threat from being questioned in court in front of an angry crowd. Courtrooms are presumably safe venues.

One can thus reconcile *Bram* with earlier holdings, but one cannot reconcile the language and theoretical premises of *Bram* with the Court's earlier confessions cases. *Bram* is one of the quickest turns in doctrine in the history of the law of confessions. The state courts were also going back and forth between a rationalist view of confessions and the Hawkins-Leach dictum.

7. STATE CONFESSIONS CASES: 1876–1925

We will focus on state cases that decided whether an admonition to tell the truth rendered a confession inadmissible. This issue nicely illustrates the divide between the rational and what Wigmore found delusional. Only a judge committed to Whig principles of autonomy could think that being urged to tell the truth somehow forced a suspect to confess. Moreover, as long as courts took seriously the Hawkins-Leach dictum, police were not likely to use threats or trickery to get confessions; a detective who knows he is not allowed to tell the suspect to tell the truth is not likely to use physical coercion or even trickery. We will show that in the evolution from Hawkins-Leach to Wigmore, *Bram* was only a temporary detour on the road.

In 1890, the Michigan Supreme Court held that telling the suspect "he had better tell the truth about it" was an improper inducement.[192] Drawing from Hawkins-Leach, the court said that confessions "must be voluntary, and without *any* influence being exerted by the officer, either of threats, promise, artifice, or duress."[193] By 1910, however, the Michigan court distanced itself from the Hawkins-Leach language in the 1890 case, calling it "broader than was required for the determination of the case there under consideration, and we think, taken baldly and without explanation or qualification, it does not accurately state the law."[194] In the 1910 case, the police had used trickery to obtain a confession. The court said that the law did not condemn the police use of "trick" or "artifice" in the abstract but only when "by use of the trick or artifice, an untrue confession had been secured." The movement from Hawkins-Leach to Wigmore could not be clearer.

In 1874, the California Supreme Court suppressed a confession made in response to an inducement that said in effect, "It will be better for you to make a full disclosure."[195] The court wrote, "The rule is without exception that such a promise made by one in authority will exclude a confession. Public policy absolutely requires the rejection of confessions obtained by means of inducements held out by such persons." The state court reaffirmed that rule in 1890 when a sheriff obtained a confession prompted by "I told him that I didn't think the truth would hurt anybody. It would be better for him to come out and tell all he knew about it if he felt that way."[196]

Eighteen years later, a California court found a confession admissible, and affirmed a death sentence, despite substantial pressure that police put on the suspect.[197] The officer read the confession of a co-participant that incriminated the suspect. The suspect "stated that he preferred to consult a lawyer before making any statement."[198] The officer ignored the request and, instead, turned to the co-participant and asked him if his confession was true. "Yes, it is true," he said and, looking at the suspect, said, "Jack, you know it is true." The suspect "hesitated for a few seconds, and finally said, 'Well, that is the goods, that is true.'"

That the earlier California cases are irreconcilable, in spirit if not precisely on the facts, with the 1908 case is undeniable. How did the court deal with the awkward precedent? It lamely said that trial judges had "a considerable measure of discretion" in deciding the voluntariness issue.[199] But this analytical move is dishonest because the earlier cases had *reversed* trial court decisions to admit confessions. A more honest explanation is that times had changed, and the court was adjusting its confessions doctrine to reflect a new emphasis on crime control and the perceived ability of suspects to make difficult decisions even when facing pressure to talk.

A good case study for the "tell the truth" cases is Georgia. Like many jurisdictions, Georgia lurched back and forth on how much effect to give the Hawkins-Leach dictum. What makes the instability of Georgia law unusual is an 1861 statute that closely tracks the Hawkins-Leach dictum: "To make a confession admissible, it must have been made voluntarily without being induced by another, by the slightest hope of benefit or remotest fear of injury."[200] The statute first appears in a code drafted largely by Thomas Cobb, considered a "brilliant legal scholar."[201] It was the first American codification of all law—the common law, equity principles, and statutes. We lack direct evidence of the origin of the confessions statute because Cobb and the other drafters did not include margin notes giving their sources. According to one historian, the drafters "did not want the legislature to really know how much *new law* they had written into the first code."[202]

We do know that Cobb "took Littleton, Coke and Blackstone" as his sources.[203] It also appears that he knew Hawkins. Compare the statute—"being induced by another, by the slightest hope of benefit or remotest fear of injury"—with the Hawkins-Leach language—"which is obtained from a defendant, either by the flattery of hope, or by the impressions of fear, however slightly the emotions may be implanted."

The eighth and last edition of the Hawkins treatise appeared in 1824, with language identical to that added by Leach in 1787.[204] If Cobb did not have Hawkins open in front of him when he drafted the statute, perhaps he relied on *Stephen v. State*,[205] an 1852 case where the Georgia Supreme Court tracked the Hawkins-Leach dictum:

> It has been forcibly and truly urged that the human mind, under the pressure of calamity, is easily seduced, and is liable, in the alarm of danger, to acknowledge indiscriminately a falsehood or a truth, as different agitations may prevail; and hence the humane rule of evidence, that a confession, whether made upon an official examination or in discourse with private persons, which is obtained from a defendant, either by the flattery of hope or by the impressions of fear, *however slightly the emotion may be implanted*, IS NOT ADMISSIBLE EVIDENCE. For the law will not suffer a prisoner to be made the deluded instrument of his own conviction.[206]

Though the Georgia court did not cite any authority for this robust principle, the language is almost identical to that of the Hawkins-Leach dictum.

The confession at issue was not made to someone in authority, but the *Stephen* court did not seem to think that mattered. The 1861 statute applied to all inducements, not just to those made by persons with authority over the suspect. The state supreme court had earlier expressed that principle in a colorful way, noting that it did not matter for purposes of the confessions rule whether the inducement "came from a talking ass, or a talking snake, a stock, a stone or a stump, man, beast or reptile, animate or inanimate object."[207]

The first "tell the truth" case following enactment of the Cobb statute was *Stafford v. State* in 1876.[208] The murder suspect's cell mate "read the bible to him, and psalms" and told him that "he had better confess and seek his God . . . or God damn it; don't profess to be a religious man."[209] The suspect asked the cell-mate what to do and he "'said if he was guilty of it, it would be better for him to acknowledge it. The state supreme court majority ignored the confessions statute and held the confession admissible. The chief justice took note of the statute and would have suppressed the confession because the "advice" of the cell mate created "the *slightest* hope of benefit or the *remotest* fear of injury."[210] But "[t]he majority of the court" found the confession admissible.[211]

In 1891, the Georgia Supreme Court lurched back toward Hawkins-Leach. *Green v. State* held a confession involuntary because it was precipitated by the comment: "Edmund, if you know anything, it may be best for you to tell it."[212] Justice Lumpkin claimed that his "careful and laborious examination" of books and cases persuaded him that the "tendency of modern judicial opinion is to refuse to admit [confessions] when there is any reasonable ground to believe that they were induced by hope or fear."[213] Indeed, "the slightest hope of benefit, or the remotest fear of injury" would make a confession inadmissible. The court relied mostly on the common law, which, at this stage, was still heavily influenced by Hawkins-Leach.

Three years after *Green*, the state supreme court moved back the other way, admitting a confession prompted when a cell mate "said, 'he better tell the truth; the white folks were going to break somebody's neck'"[214] The court based its holding on the lack of authority of the person who induced the confession, concluding that a remark would be a greater inducement when made by a person in authority.[215] This, of course, ignores the provision in the statute that "the slightest hope of benefit or remotest fear of injury" is enough to make a confession inadmissible.

Citing *Green* but not the statute, the state court moved back toward Hawkins-Leach in 1901, holding a confession inadmissible when the suspect was prompted by the officer's remark "that if she knew anything she had better tell it."[216] In 1906, the state supreme court held inadmissible a confession prompted by an officer saying that "the best thing to do was to go and plead guilty, if he was guilty" and "it would be lighter on him."[217] The court did not cite *Green* but did quote the confessions statute.

In *Wilson v. State*, a detective obtained a confession after telling "the accused that 'it would be better for him to tell the truth about the case.'"[218] The court of appeals began its analysis by noting that "[p]ractically all the authorities agree that the only proper question is whether the inducement held out to the prisoner tended to make his confession an untrue one."[219] This is Wigmore's position, and the court cited him. But it decidedly was not the view of "[p]ractically all of the authorities" in 1917 when *Wilson* was decided. More important, there was, of course, the statute that embraced the Hawkins-Leach dictum and the state supreme court authority of *Green*.

The court of appeals did not ignore or misrepresent the statute as had some earlier Georgia cases. Instead, it used a vivid metaphor to argue that the statute had to be construed to be consistent with the common law:

> This statute, however, is not a fresh particle dropped into the thereto-fore existing body of the law, but it is to be regarded as a rule deducible from the common law, and from many decisions of the courts since the beginning of our jurisprudence. . . . While the test laid down in our Code is a rigid one, it must not be interpreted without regard to the fundamental principles and primary considerations impelling it. As a particle in the great ocean of law, it is to be considered in connection with the currents and tides of that ocean, and as modified and con-trolled thereby.[220]

The court cited no authority for its view that statutes had to yield to the common law. Under that view, what would be the point of enacting statutes in areas covered by the common law? They would either embody the existing common law, and add nothing, or be reformed by courts to reflect the common law, and add nothing. But having changed the standard to Wigmore's "fair risk" parameter, the court was surely right that "[t]elling a prisoner that it will be better for him to tell the truth can hardly, by any process of right reasoning, be interpreted as an invitation to him to make an untrue confession. Advice to tell the truth ought not to be interpreted as an invitation to tell a lie."[221]

In 1924, the Georgia Court of Appeals returned to Hawkins-Leach and *Green*, without mentioning the confessions statute or *Wilson*. *Morris v. State* rejected a confession prompted by a deputy sheriff telling a suspect that "it would be the best for him to tell truth, that all he wanted was truth, and wanted the goods back, and he wanted the defendant to come clean."[222] It is odd that *Morris* ignored *Wilson* because Judge Luke sat on both cases, albeit without writing either opinion.[223]

In sum, the Georgia courts had no coherent approach to confessions prompted by the inducement to tell the truth. Courts sometimes relied on the confessions statute, sometimes ignored it, sometimes noted it without quoting from it, sometimes suppressed the confession, and sometimes admitted it. Courts sometimes said the lack of authority made a confession admissible but more often that it did not. One case even adopted Wigmore's "fair risk" test, which is plainly contradictory to the confession statute. The state of the Georgia confessions law, in 1924, is what one would expect when the law is about to un-dergo a massive change. And change it did.

Wigmore in his 1923 edition cites dozens of cases where confessions were made in response to whippings, threats of whippings, sweat boxes, or the presence of a mob outside the jail.[224] While most of these confessions were suppressed, our point is that while some American courts were having a mostly pointless conversation about inducements to tell the truth, the police were moving to a much more coercive type of interrogation. The next chapter seeks to explain why English and American confessions law moved from Hawkins-Leach to a crime control focus.

THE SECOND REVOLUTION IN INTERROGATION LAW

The Rational Approach Comes of Age

CHAPTER 5

The Rise of Rationality in Interrogation Law

Our goal in this chapter is to sketch the evolution of the law of confessions toward Wigmore's rationalism and away from the Hawkins-Leach dictum that gripped the law of confessions in the nineteenth century. Part of the reaction to crime and threats at the turn of the twentieth century was the third degree used by police when they thought the suspect was guilty and he did not oblige with a confession. We will treat the third degree separately in chapter 6 because, long hidden, it had little effect on legal doctrine. Moreover, the third degree was not in any way a triumph of rationality. As we will see, it was the antithesis of rationality based on the blindly held belief of police that they could determine which suspects were guilty. Without that assumption, the third degree was not only immoral but also illegitimate and irrational. Given enough torture, almost every innocent suspect will say whatever his torturer demands.

To sketch the rise of rationalism, we begin in England, returning to the years when the Hawkins-Leach dictum ruled the confessions world.

A. Confessions and British Interrogation: 1837–1901

Setting off cultural movements with dates is imprecise at best. Though it over-laps a few years with our coverage in chapter 3, we will focus on the reign of Queen Victoria, 1837 to 1901, to continue our study of the connection between cultural changes and the English law of confessions. Victoria died a year into a new century that, three years later, would see the publication of Wigmore's supremely rational treatment of confessions. She became queen three years after Parliament made it a crime to disobey the rules of a Poor Law Commissioner, a regulatory body created for "management of the poor"[1] Problems besetting the densely packed English cities of the time, particularly London, included barely adequate food supplies; the proliferation of debtor's prisons; and urban pockets "notoriously blighted by crime, pollution, and disease."[2]

The Victorian era was marked by a belief that progress could be made on multiple fronts, including that crime could be suppressed.[3] There is a reason that Arthur Conan Doyle's Sherlock Holmes books and stories were so popular during this period. The emergence of the Peelers (London police) in the mid-nineteenth century and the rise of Scotland Yard contributed to the belief that the crime problem was solvable. Because crime, and particularly street crime, was an area where progress was thought necessary by middle-class Londoners, Whig judges now had a countervailing reason not to show too much mercy to prisoners who confessed. And to the extent that the criminal who confessed had committed a crime against the public order, rather than stealing from a master in secret, he was a less sympathetic subject.

We saw in chapter 3 that John Fielding helped turn the magistrate's examination into a crime-fighting tool in response to a crime wave in the mid-eighteenth century. Crime rates in London stabilized in the latter half of the century, only to increase rather dramatically in the nineteenth century as "generation after generation of youngsters flooded to the growing towns, and in many cases joined the ranks of the criminals."[4] Historian J. J. Tobias claims that, while definitive proof is difficult to come by, crime probably flourished in the period 1815–1850.[5] Theft offenses, in particular, posed a much more serious problem as London became larger and less homogenous. Convictions for burglary in England and Wales more than doubled between 1834 and 1844 and increased by another 50% by 1856.[6] From 1800 to 1850, London's population doubled to 2,362,000; it would gain almost another million by 1860.[7] By the mid-nineteenth century, London was home to an increasing number of immigrants—principally Irish, but also French, Italian, German, Spanish, Chinese, Indian, and African.[8]

The absolute crime rate is less important than the public perception of crime. *Oliver Twist* with its shocking images of poverty and crime was serialized in 1837 and 1838 and widely read.[9] One of the novel's central themes is the recruitment of young children to become pickpockets and to work in street gangs. Whatever the official crime rates, the perception was that "hordes of criminal youngsters" roamed the streets in the early 1800s.[10] In 1828, in Bath, 60% of the boys were thought to be criminals.[11]

Chapter 3 details one of Parliament's reactions to the increased concern about crime—the 1848 Sir John Jervis Act that required warnings by magistrates and then made the results of the examinations admissible "without further Proof thereof."[12] We do not claim that a crude causal link exists between changes in English society and the changing judicial attitude toward questioning suspects. But social problems were the target of many reform measures in this era, and street crime would have been seen by judges as a problem that could potentially be solved. One partial solution would be not to release the criminals that the new police had arrested. Allowing the jury to hear their confessions was a natural step in that direction.

In 1852, the Court of Criminal Appeal in *Regina v. Baldry* referred to the 1848 Jervis Act requirement that magistrates caution the accused,[13] and then repudiated the reasoning of earlier decisions that had found a caution to be an improper influence. The opinion is noteworthy for its length—eight pages in an era when many opinions were less than one page. It is also noteworthy that each judge on the panel wrote to express disapproval of the existing law that held a caution itself was an improper influence.

When Baldry was arrested, the constable cautioned that "he need not say anything to criminate himself [but] 'what he did say would be taken down, and used as evidence against him.'"[14] His lawyer quoted the Hawkins-Leach dictum from *Russell on Crimes* and argued that any inducement, even "of the slightest description" created a presumption that the confession was untrue.[15] Sir Jonathan Frederick Pollock, a baron (judge) on the Court of Exchequer who was sitting with the Court of Criminal Appeal, rejected the notion of a presumption. Instead, he said, inducements created a question about whether the statement was true. Notice that both the defendant and the court saw the issue as whether the confession was untrue rather than whether Baldry's will was overborne.

Later in the opinion, Pollock referred to two opinions written by Justice Coleridge, concluding that "with the greatest respect to my Brother Coleridge, I do not approve of the decision in the former or of the arguments made . . . in the latter."[16] The "former" case was *Regina v. Drew*, a case influenced by Hawkins-Leach that we discussed at length in chapter 3. In the other case, *Regina v. Morton*,[17] Justice Coleridge held inadmissible a statement made in response to a warning by the constable. After advising Morton to "be very careful in making any statement to me or anybody else that may tend to injure you," the constable said "but anything you can say in your defence we shall be ready to hear, or send to assist you." Coleridge "upon reflection" adhered to his opinion in *Regina v. Drew* and then reasoned that the use of the word "defence" necessarily conveyed "to the prisoner's mind that what he said would be for his benefit,—the hope is created and remains."

Every judge in *Baldry* made clear that Coleridge's position should be repudiated. Baron Parke wrote, "I have the most unfeigned respect for Coleridge, J. and Maule, J. [who also had held that a caution could be an improper inducement[18]] . . . but I cannot concur in their judgment. I have reflected on *Reg. v. Drew* and *Reg. v. Morton*, and I have never been able to make out that any benefit was held out to the prisoner by the caution employed in those cases."[19] More generally, Parke said, "I think there has been too much tenderness towards prisoners in this matter. I confess that I cannot look at the decisions without some shame."[20] Justice Erle agreed, concluding that in some of the confessions cases "justice and common sense have been sacrificed, not at the shrine of mercy, but at the shrine of guilt."[21]

Justice Williams said that he was "entirely of the same opinion," and that "it is an over-refinement to say that a statement made after such a caution was inadmissible."[22] The judge who presided at trial, Lord Campbell, was part of the review panel. He agreed with the other justices, saying that he was "very glad to find that all this Court concur in the view which I took at the trial, that the evidence was admissible."[23] Wigmore naturally admired *Baldry* because it put "some check . . . to the extravagant policy of exclusion."[24]

Despite *Baldry*'s rational "blast" of logic blended with crime control in 1852, the Hawkins-Leach dictum had remarkable staying power. It moved English judges to suppress confessions for another half-century, as it did in the United States as well. *Bram v. United States*, 1897, is only the most famous example of the staying power of the Hawkins-Leach dictum in the United States.[25] The post-*Baldry* cases make clear that all the Court of Criminal Appeal was rejecting in 1852 was the view that a caution could be an inducement. The heart of the Hawkins-Leach dictum, that even the slightest inducement caused a confession to be inadmissible, was left intact. Two months after *Baldry*, the Court of Criminal Appeal suggested that telling a suspect "she had better speak the truth" was an improper inducement.[26] Justice Erle said, "As a universal rule an exhortation to speak the truth ought not to exclude a confession."[27] Baron Parke said that "cases on this subject have gone quite far enough and ought not to be extended," but conceded that the court was bound to follow the rule "that if the threat or inducement is held out . . . by a person in authority, [the statement] cannot be received, however slight the threat or inducement."[28] *Regina v. Cheverton* reiterated that view ten years later, holding that a statement was inadmissible when made in response to "[y]ou had better tell me all about it; it will save trouble."[29]

Another incremental change in the direction of rationality surfaced in an 1872 trial of a defendant with the appropriate name of "Reason."[30] A police officer had a "conversation" with Sarah Reason about a child who was found drowned in a canal.[31] In the course of the conversation, the officer said, "I must know more about it." Reason then admitted that she had done away with the child in the canal. Justice Keating acknowledged, "In my time," the law had held that a "mere caution by a person in authority would exclude an admission, but since then there has been a return to doctrines more in accordance with the common sense view."[32] Keating found the proper inquiry to be the one that Wigmore would embrace in the first edition of his evidence treatise in 1904. To Keating: "The real question is whether there has been any threat or promise of such a nature that the prisoner would be likely to tell an untruth from fear of the threat, or hope of profit from the promise."[33]

But even in *Reason*, the fractured nature of the law of confessions is apparent. The confession was admitted, but only because Reason had not been in custody when questioned. The "learned judge" summed up by observing that once a suspect was in custody, the police were not permitted to ask questions: "It is the duty of the police-constable to hear what the prisoners has voluntarily to say, but after the prisoner is taken into custody it is not the duty of the police-constable to ask questions."[34]

The same distinction can be seen in an 1885 case, *Regina v. Gavin & Others.*[35] Though Gavin initially denied knowing anything about the theft of two barrels of oysters, he subsequently confessed, apparently as a result of being questioned by police when he was in custody. The court would not admit Gavin's statements and, along the way, the judge gave quite a lecture about the impropriety of police questioning suspects:

> When a prisoner is in custody the police have no right to ask him questions. Reading a statement over, and then saying to him "What have you got to say?" is cross-examining the prisoner, and therefore I shut it out. A prisoner's mouth is closed after he is once given in charge [charged with a crime], and he ought not to be asked anything. A constable has no more right to ask a question that a judge to cross-examine.[36]

The reporter of the decision appended a note suggesting that the decision "seems to conflict with the rule as laid down in the text-books" that required an inducement beyond mere questioning.[37] The reporter acknowledged, however, that the law was unsettled and the rule "can hardly be said to have been free from doubt." There is little wonder that Wigmore spoke of "inconsistent precedents" in the English law of confessions in this era.[38]

During this period, Ireland was part of the United Kingdom of Great Britain and Ireland. In 1822, all the Irish judges participated in a case holding that a statement made to a constable without a caution was admissible if there had been no threat or inducement.[39] By 1839, however, individual judges began to follow English law and suppress statements made to officers who did not caution the suspect.[40] In *The Queen v. Johnston* in 1864, a panel of eleven judges clarified the law, holding a statement admissible that was made to a police officer who told Mary Johnston that she was suspected of stealing boots and then questioned her without a caution.[41] The opinion is an extraordinarily long seventy-five pages and, according to Wigmore, "finally settled" for Irish courts that police failure to caution did not, by itself, require exclusion of statements made in response to questioning.[42]

Wigmore overreaches here. *Johnston's* narrow holding is that when a prisoner is not in custody, the officer's failure to caution does not make her statements inadmissible. Two of the opinions make explicit that the critical fact was whether Johnston was in custody. As Judge Hayes put it, if the defendant "felt herself to be in custody on the criminal charge, then her statements, in answer to the questions, would not have been receivable, unless prefaced by a caution."[43] The principle at work here is that "[u]ntil the criminal feels himself amenable to justice he ought . . . to be dealt with as one at full liberty to act and speak as he may think right" even when speaking with an officer.[44] Thus, *Johnston* is in accord with the English *Reason* case, decided eight years later.

To be sure, the focus in *Johnston* is on the suspect's free will, an inquiry that the judges said should be conducted on a case-by-case basis rather than governed by a rule about whether a caution was given. Judge Hayes commented that a caution might be "the better to insure a voluntary confession, but not as in all cases essential to it."[45] This is a different tone from the early English cases embracing the Hawkins-Leach dictum but consistent with *Baldry*, decided twelve years before *Johnston*. Indeed, *Johnston* relies on *Baldry* as "a strong authority for the admission of such evidence as that here objected to."[46] In sum, *Johnston* and *Baldry* were cut from the same cloth and were harbingers of radical changes to come in the law of interrogation.

While the English cases involving police questions were moving in a direction that Wigmore would later approve, the inducement rule from Hawkins-Leach was still robust. Indeed, in 1881, Justice John Duke Coleridge, the son of the Justice John Taylor Coleridge who wrote *Drew* and other cases embracing a robust Hawkins-Leach dictum, said that his father's position about inducements was settled law. In *Regina v. Fennell*, the victim of the theft said to the suspect that the police inspector, who was present, "tells me you are making housebreaking implements; if that is so, you had better tell the truth, it may be better for you."[47] Fennell made incriminating admissions in response. The trial court held that the admissions could be received in evidence because words addressed to Fennell "did not 'import a threat of evil or promise of good.'"[48] The Queen's Bench, in an opinion by Coleridge, held, "It is well established by the authorities, which all bear in one direction, that this confession was inadmissible after an inducement such as that held out by the prosecutor."[49]

As late as 1898, an English appeals court held a confession inadmissible because the suspect had been asked by the victim of the theft to "speak the truth." In *Regina v. Rose*, the court observed that the rule "is very old" but "is stated just as clearly in the old as in the modern authorities."[50] Indeed, Blackstone's skepticism about confessions, which we quoted in chapter 3, was still present in the 1898 edition of his *Commentaries*.[51] And the editor, George Sharswood, added a footnote that reinforced the skeptical view from over a century earlier. Acknowledging that a voluntary confession is "strong evidence," Sharswood cautioned that a promise or threat, "however slight," renders the confession inadmissible.[52]

That the law was shifting can be seen in the Indian Evidence Act of 1872, largely the work of Sir James Fitzjames Stephen.[53] The heart of the Hawkins-Leach dictum appears in the provision that an admission is not "relevant" if made in response to an "inducement, threat or promise" made by someone in authority.[54] The act also forbids admission of a statement made while in custody of a police officer unless made in the presence of a magistrate.[55] But it permits use of evidence found as a result of a confession that cannot itself be used, and it permits use of a confession if made after the improper influence has "been fully removed."[56] Most notably, the act does not require that the magistrate caution the accused and even specifies that confessions that are otherwise admissible are not made inadmissible because they are "made under a promise of secrecy, or in consequence of a deception practised on the accused person . . . or when he was drunk . . . or because he was not warned that he was not bound to make such confession, and that evidence of it might be given against him."[57]

We do not wish to press the point harder than it will bear. Designing a criminal code for India is obviously different from dealing with domestic interrogation. Moreover, the Indian Evidence Act was the product of the Indian legislative council, not Parliament.[58] Still, we think it instructive that, when English lawyers and judges designed a procedure from scratch in 1872, they did not think it necessary to require that the magistrate caution the accused, and they removed some of the barriers to the evidence-gathering process that the common law had embedded via the Hawkins-Leach dictum.

As Victoria's reign neared an end, most courts still followed the Hawkins-Leach dictum, but thoughtful judges had become quite critical of its underlying premises. We leave the British story at this point because we intend the twentieth century story to be an American one.

B. Confessions and American Interrogation: The Tide Shifts

One theme of our book is that cultures vary in how they view or, perhaps, constitute human actors in the legal system. Monarchical societies consist of "paternal and dependent relationships."[59] We saw both paternalism and dependency in chapter 2 when judges took pity on the poor subjects of the crown who convicted themselves of capital crimes while offering an excuse or explanation for the harm that they caused. In chapter 3, we saw that English judges developed doctrines that permitted the acquittal of servants and other lower-class defendants who confessed to the theft of property of relatively trivial value. If humans were viewed as the pawns of a deity whose will was poorly understood, the relatively harmless errors of particular powerless humans could be counted as "forced errors"—not the fault of the human actor.

But as the eighteenth-century monarchical society disintegrated, the Western world saw "the emergence of the liberal, democratic, capitalistic world of the early nineteenth century."[60] Man was no longer the victim of a cold, cruel world run by a distant God whose will was hidden. The Protestant religion that enjoyed a surge of popularity in the eighteenth and nineteenth centuries was based on the revolutionary notion that humans could speak to God directly. But if man was an agent who acted on the world, rather than its victim, then it made sense to hold defendants responsible for their confessions. Compare the solicitude of Hawkins-Leach that suspects not be made a "deluded instrument of [their] own conviction" with the Alabama Supreme Court's description in 1931 of suspects who had "the bold independence of the fearless and well advised, who challenge every move and demand every privilege of constitutional freedom."[61] Even though the police threatened to arrest the suspect's mother if he did not confess, the Alabama court admitted his confession.

A second theme of our book is that there is a connection, however imperfect, between a culture's fear of deviance and the level of coercion permitted during interrogation. The same social forces that drove police to use the third degree worked on judicial attitudes toward suspects who confessed. As we will see in chapter 6, crime posed a much greater threat in the early twentieth century than in the late eighteenth century. If protecting suspects from the foolish or fated acts of confession was the watchword of the law of confessions from the late eighteenth to the late nineteenth centuries, judges soon recognized the utility of admitting evidence of guilt. That humans were viewed during this period as more like Ayn Rand's heroes than Dostoevsky's Raskolnikov only added to the "price" society was willing to pay for protection from crime and deviance.

By the time John Henry Wigmore revised Greenleaf's treatise in 1899 to reflect a more rationalist approach to confessions,[62] American courts were already moving in that direction. In 1885, for example, the Supreme Judicial Court of Massachusetts held that merely asking a suspect to tell the truth was not an impermissible inducement.[63] In 1891, the Alabama Supreme Court held that a confession was admissible even though the sheriff told the suspect "that it was always best for him, or any one else, to tell the truth about anything."[64] In Wigmore's first edition of his treatise on evidence law, published in 1904, he cited cases from ten states that admitted confessions induced by the exhortation to tell the truth.[65] It is fair to say that Wigmore manifested, and probably contributed, to the sea change in the attitude of courts that was occurring in that era. We searched all state and federal cases for references to Wigmore's trustworthiness test and discovered that it was explicitly adopted by seven states, one federal court of appeals, three federal district courts, and two military courts.[66]

The Montana Supreme Court adopted Wigmore's test in a 1907 opinion that shows the ascendancy of Wigmore's theory that confessions should be suppressed only when there is a fair risk that the interrogation might produce a false confession.[67] Echoing Wigmore, who gets a general citation at the end of the paragraph, the Montana court wrote:

In their desire to get away from the ancient doctrine that a confession by the accused would be received even though procured by torture, many of the courts have gone to the opposite extreme, and have held that any threat or promise made, any fear engendered in the mind of the accused, or any hope of bettering his condition held out to him, however slight, would exclude a confession made in consequence thereof, irrespective of the question whether in fact such threat, promise, fear, or hope could, or in all human probability did, influence the accused to make a false confession. And so we find many instances wherein courts have simply sacrificed justice and common sense upon the altar of mere sentimentality.[68]

Wigmore's test of whether the questioning created a "fair risk" of a false confession is not easy for defendants to satisfy, thus making it a valuable tool for courts that put a higher value on crime solving than suspect autonomy. Adopting Wigmore's test and explicitly rejecting the premises of the Hawkins-Leach dictum, an Oregon court in 1929 noted that "society is at war with crime."[69] Given that rhetoric, the court naturally came down on the side of solving crime, noting that it was "not disposed to allow the niceties of the law unduly to hamper officers in ferreting out crime. Justice must not be sacrificed for technicalities, archaic forms, or maudlin sentimentalism. It is important that those guilty of crime should be made to realize the certainty and celerity of punishment."[70]

In 1934, in the midst of the Great Depression, the Wisconsin Supreme Court stressed the interests of society when considering whether to admit confessions:

The apprehension and conviction of criminals is not a sporting event, and as such to be conducted according to certain ideals as to what constitutes good sportsmanship. There is a tendency to manifest sympathy for an accused criminal, prompted by a feeling that he is the underdog because he must contend against society single-handed. . . . A good deal of the sympathy lavished upon criminals might much better be expended upon their victims and their families. While every defendant is entitled to, and should be assured, a fair and impartial trial, the threat of organized and even sporadic crime against social security, both as respects person and property, is such as to require a firm as well as a just administration of the criminal law.[71]

In the case before it, the Wisconsin court conceded that the investigation of the murder of a fellow police officer was "vigorous and persistent" but stressed that the confessions "bear internal evidence that those who made them had a very high degree of self-possession" and thus were not produced by threats or coercion.[72]

The court held that the confessions were admissible even though motivated by a visit from a minister "called in to pray" with one suspect and a priest "called in to administer spiritual aid" to another suspect.[73] The court boasted of its vigilance in condemning "the subjection of defendants to inquisition by the third degree so-called." But it drew a clear line between mistreatment and taking advantage of a suspect's feelings of "remorse and repentance" that lead him "to confess[] his wrongdoing." Moreover, the court cast a bad light on suspects, rather than police, when it noted that in trying to avoid their "natural" confessions, suspects will make up "stories out of whole cloth."[74]

In 1924, the Illinois Supreme Court put the rationale of the confessions rule this way: "Involuntary confessions are rejected not because of the illegal or deceitful methods employed in securing them but because of their unreliability."[75] The Illinois court elaborated on that rationale two years later:

> The object of every legal investigation being to ascertain the truth, the underlying principle on which confession evidence is, under certain circumstances, rejected is its testimonial worthlessness. If the court could know in a given case that a confession was true, it is clear that the evidence thereof should not be rejected. The wrong done, however reprehensible, in inducing the accused to make a confession could never, rightly considered, require a rejection of the confession, if the court could know as a fact that the confession was true.[76]

A federal court held in 1926 that confronting a suspect with confessions of his confederates that implicated him was neither an "inducement" nor "coercion."[77] The North Dakota Supreme Court held in 1924 that "the employment of falsehood" or "any artifice, deception or fraud" did not require exclusion if "the artifice or fraud employed was not calculated to procure an untrue statement."[78] The Massachusetts Supreme Judicial Court held in 1939 that it was not an improper influence to use a "pretended telegram from a chief of police" to deceive the suspect into thinking that his confederate had accused him.[79] In 1939, the Pennsylvania Supreme Court held that tricking the suspect into believing that the lie detector was infallible did not make the resulting confession inadmissible.[80]

The inducement to "tell the truth" was fast losing its power as a basis to exclude a confession. Other than in Georgia, with its Hawkins-Leach statute, we found no cases after 1903 holding that an exhortation to tell the truth rendered a confession inadmissible. *State v. Dixson* is a good example of the twentieth-century approach.[81] Dixson confessed after the chief of police told him that "if a person told the truth, as a rule, he got out of it a whole lot easier than he would by telling a lot of lies."[82] Acknowledging that there were cases to the contrary, the Montana court held the confession admissible. Citing twenty or so cases, the court claimed that by 1927 the cases to the contrary were "in the minority."[83]

Wigmore's influence was manifest in *Dixson*; the court quoted and applied his fair risk rationale for the law of confessions.[84] By the time of Wigmore's second edition, 1923, he was able to cite over fifty American cases holding that the exhortation to tell the truth did not render a confession inadmissible.[85] By far, the larger number of cases Wigmore cited were decided after 1880, suggesting that as a new century approached, the country and the law were changing. Though it took the Supreme Court almost a century, it expressly repudiated *Bram* in 1991, stating that *Bram* "does not state the standard for determining the voluntariness of a confession."[86]

It is fair to conclude that, by 1941, the Anglo-American confessions world had twice turned upside down—once between 1721 and the Blackstone and Hawkins-Leach editions in 1778 and 1787, and again between roughly 1880 and Wigmore's second edition. We now investigate one of the partly hidden manifestations of the turn toward crime control—the third degree.

CHAPTER 6

The "American Method"—The Third Degree

American police, but not English police, developed the interrogation method known as the "third degree"—the use of intense coercion on suspects to produce confessions. Jerome Frank wrote in 1949, "To our shame be it said that the English, who do not tolerate the 'third degree,' call it the 'American method.'"[1] Many of the same cultural forces operating in England also operated in the United States. One of our tasks in this chapter is to seek differences that explain why our police were willing to use physical force to obtain confessions, while the English police were not.

A. The Culture That Produced the Third Degree

Like other social phenomena, harsh police interrogation tactics did not arise in a vacuum. The early years of America's existence were tumultuous: the War of Independence, fear of foreign invasion, molding the states into a nation, the War of 1812, and the westward expansion into the frontier. But one explanation for the third degree that we must reject is the violent, frontier nature of early American culture. If that were a factor, the American cases would have diverged from the English cases in the early 1800s. They did not. As we saw in chapter 4, one of the most robust expressions of the Hawkins-Leach dictum came from the frontier state of Tennessee in 1823.[2]

The Treaty of Ghent in 1814 ended the War of 1812, as well as our long-standing belligerence with England. Peace ushered in an era of great prosperity for the United States. Prior to 1850, Lawrence Friedman notes that American "opinion exuberantly believed in growth, believed that resources were virtually unlimited. . . . The theme of American law before 1850 was the release of energy, in Willard Hurst's phrase."[3] Between 1850 and 1900, however, Friedman concludes that America changed in fundamental ways. "By 1900, if one can speak about so slippery a thing as dominant public opinion, that opinion saw a narrowing sky, a dead frontier, life as a struggle for position, competition as a zero-sum game, the economy as a pie to be divided, not a ladder stretching out beyond the horizon."

Unlike England, America did not have major cities until the late nineteenth century. When Georgia adopted a statute that embraced the Hawkins-Leach dictum in 1861, the largest city in the state, Atlanta, had fewer than 10,000 residents.[4] Only nine American cities had populations greater than 100,000 on the eve of the Civil War. Chicago at 112,000 was the ninth largest. When the Georgia Court of Appeals staged a full-stage retreat from Hawkins-Leach in 1917,[5] Atlanta's population had grown to 200,000. From 1850 to 1920, New York City grew from 515,000 to 5,620,000, while Chicago grew from 30,000 to 2,700,000, and Cleveland from 17,000 to 800,000. In 1851, London already had a population of 2,600,000.[6]

Another difference between England and the United States during this period was immigration. Though England had an increase in immigration during the nineteenth century, it was but a trickle compared to immigration to the United States.[7] From 1894 to 1914, 1.2 million immigrants entered the United States,[8] and the character of the immigrant population changed dramatically. Prior to 1881, almost 86% of total immigrants arrived from northwest Europe, primarily from Great Britain, Ireland, Germany, and Scandinavia. Beginning in 1881, a major shift occurred in favor of immigrants from southern, central, and eastern Europe. The number of Italians, for example, living in England and Wales in 1911 was 20,389 while over 1.3 million Italians lived in the United States in 1910.[9]

It is conventional wisdom, and correct we believe, that it is far easier to mistreat those who are viewed as the "other." That, of course, is why governments use propaganda during wars to make the enemy seem alien and demonic. It is why the Third Reich portrayed Jews as arrogant Shylocks. It is why slave owners in the American South clung to theories that blacks were subhuman and thus needed to be enslaved. A geography book published in Georgia in 1862, for example, said that members of the "African race" had been brought to North America and "humanely reduced to the proper normal condition of slavery."[10]

Moreover, there was a coarsening of the American character during the latter two-thirds of the nineteenth century. Industrialization, which made humans into moving parts, probably played a part. The decline in religious fervor perhaps played a part. Once again, both of these factors were present in England as well. But a largely neglected, and unique, cause of the coarsening of the American character was the sectional strife that eventually produced the disastrous Civil War and the long nightmare of Reconstruction.

The war itself was unlike any war in history. Its scale was immense. A total of three million men "took up arms between 1861 and 1865. In the South, three out of four white men of military age became soldiers."[11] And the nature of war had changed. "With its large volunteer armies, its longer-range weapons, and its looser military formations, the Civil War thus placed more inexperienced soldiers, with more firepower and with more individualized responsibility for the decision to kill, into more intimate, face-to-face battle settings than perhaps any other war in history."[12] The scope of the carnage was devastating. "The Civil War's rate of death, its incidence in comparison with the size of the American population, was six times that of World War II. A similar rate, about 2%, in the United States today would mean six million fatalities."[13]

But numbers tell only part of the story. Observers "estimated stretches of a mile or more at Antietam or Shiloh where every step had to be planted on a dead body."[14] The tide of the three-day battle at Gettysburg shifted so often that neither side could bury its dead. "So many bodies lay unburied that a surgeon described the atmosphere as almost intolerable. Residents of the surrounding area complained of a 'stench' that persisted from the time of the battle in July until the coming of frost in October."[15] The toll on the human psyche was almost unimaginable. "Killing produced transformations that were not readily revers- ible," changing "the survivors into different men . . . men required to deny, to numb basic human feelings at costs they may have paid for decades after the war ended." Many of the survivors "were never quite the same again after seeing fields of slaughtered bodies destroyed by men just like themselves."[16]

The Reconstruction that followed bitterly divided the country for decades. Unlike wars between nation-states, a failed war of secession leaves deep scars within the unified country. The North deeply resented the horrible costs of the war. The president who had (barely) held together the North during the agonizing long war years was dead: the victim of a Southern assassin.

The South would not easily surrender its view of the former slaves as being inferior to whites. So-called Black Codes sprang up in an attempt to reduce freed blacks to second-class status.[17] Mississippi's 1865 Black Code made it a crime for blacks to give seditious speeches or preach the Gospel without a license from a "regularly organized church."[18] The Ku Klux Klan would for a century be the illegal and violent enforcer of white supremacy.[19] Lawlessness ran, like water, through the streets of the Southern towns. A congressman reported, "Every mail . . . [adds] to the records of injustice and outrage."[20] The policy of the rebels was "to render it so uncomfortable and hazardous for loyal men to live among them as to compel them to leave. . . . Others have been murdered in cold blood as a warning to all northern men who should attempt to settle in the South"[21]

Though the nation gradually re-knit, the wounds were deep and the scars visible for decades. Thirty-five years after the end of the war, the flying of a "cherished relic of the Confederacy"—the battle flag—at a residence in Dover, New Jersey caused "[l]oud-voiced threats" and an effort to tear the flag from its flagstaff.[22] A "hasty retreat" occurred when what appeared to be the barrel of a rifle could be seen in a window. Though the "offensive banner" was lowered that day, the owner flew it on July 4 when all other houses were flying the American flag: "Bitter indeed was the feeling then. The people ran from house to house in a whirl of patriotic anger and gathered in turbulent knots . . . and chafed and fretted themselves into a colonial revolutionary mood, ready and eager for the fray." Cooler heads prevailed and, the *New York Times* reported, "The [rebel] flag still flies."

In 1894, a retired Union naval officer recounted a Civil War battle to 2,000 school children in Brooklyn. At the end of his presentation, he unfurled a "rebel flag" that he had captured during the battle.[23] The children started to applaud, thinking it was the American flag, "but as soon as the stars and bars on a field of red were revealed, the applause turned to hisses and other expressions of hatred." That children born decades after the Civil War knew to hate the Confederate battle flag reveals much about how Southerners had been cast in the role of the "other."

We offer one last story about the lingering, bitter residue of the Civil War, though hundreds could be culled from the *New York Times* archives. In 1881, a statue to Confederate General Stonewall Jackson was unveiled in New Orleans.[24] The *Boston Traveler* was critical of the erection of monuments to "rebel chiefs," a practice that "would not be permitted in any other country." Jackson was, after all, "an able soldier in the service of a party that sought the destruction of the Union, and the preservation of slavery." The paper noted one "good" that would come from the statue: "It will help keep alive the conviction that the Southrons [*sic*] can't be trusted, and that we must insist upon continued defeat of that party which sympathizes with the South" —at the time, the Democratic Party.

England and the United States shared a common tradition of industrialization and urbanization during the late nineteenth century. But the sectional strife that produced the Civil War and the long nightmare of Reconstruction were factors present here but not in England. To be sure, England endured a series of civil wars, from 1625 to 1649 when Charles I was beheaded and Oliver Cromwell began his commonwealth experiment.[25] We suspect that the effects of these civil wars were not as profound as the American Civil War. Certainly, the loss of life was far less and England did not suffer destruction of vast swathes of the country. Moreover, whatever the effects, they would have largely dissipated by the time the Hawkins-Leach dictum appears almost 150 years later. The third degree begins to appear within a decade after the end of the American Civil War.

The coarsening of the American character can be seen in the reaction to crime and deviance in the period after the Civil War. The crime rate in the nineteenth century is a "vexed and difficult subject."[26] But once again, the numbers matter less than the impression. As Friedman notes, "Violent crime, particularly in the cities, becomes less tolerable in an interdependent, industrial society."[27] Partly because of urbanization, partly because of immigration, partly because of industrialization, Americans in this period were fearful. The nation was torn apart by racial prejudice, its law-and-order fabric dangerously fraying. The immigrants, particularly those who could not speak English and who frequented saloons, were perceived as the "other." Some Italian immigrants brought with them organized crime, which became widespread in the early twentieth century. The freed slaves were perceived, in many states, as the "other." The stereotypes of blacks critical to their enslavement did not magically disappear.

Consider the news coverage about the alleged rape of two white women by nine black youths in the Scottsboro, Alabama case, as described by historian James Goodman:

> Writers and editors all over the region agreed that it was . . . a "heinous and unspeakable crime" that "savored of the jungle, the way back dark ages of meanest African corruption." They were revolted by the story, but not surprised. Or if surprised, surprised only by the magnitude of the crime. They expected black men to rape white women. Blacks were savages, more savage, many argued (with scientific theories to support them), than they had been as slaves. Savages with an irrepressible sex drive and an appetite for white women. They were born rapists, rapists by instinct; given the chance, they struck.[28]

Goodman found this news coverage in Southern newspapers, but to infer that these attitudes stayed below the Tennessee or Virginia borders is to engage in fancy. Newspapers in the North and Midwest were not as overt in their racism but plenty of it appears. It was fairly common for "human interest" stories in the North to cast blacks in a negative light. For example, an Indiana newspaper in 1866 published a story entitled "Playing Poker with a Nigger."[29] It quoted a black man using an uneducated dialect, e.g., "wid" for "with" and "dis" for "this." We searched the NewspaperArchive national database for "nigger" for the years 1866, 1867, and 1868 and found 1,561 results. While we did not count the number of stories in Northern newspapers, there were many of them. Deep-seated beliefs about race die very slowly.

Searching the *New York Times* archives for the word "mob" in the headline for September 18, 1900, to September 17, 1901, produced a window into what was a horrific time in America.

November 16, 1900: "Boy Burned at the Stake in Colorado."[30]

December 16, 1900: "Indiana Negroes Lynched; Two Murderers Hanged in Jail Yard by Mob of 1,000 Men."[31]

February 25, 1901: "Attempted Lynching at Matawan, N.J.; Charles Herbert Strung Up Twice by a Mob."[32]

May 31, 1901: "Lynched For Stealing [Hay] Forks: Old Man, His Three Sons, and Another Man Hanged to a Bridge by California Mob."[33]

June 19, 1901: "New Jersey Boy Repels Mob of Masked Men; It Had Assembled to Tar and Feather His Sister's Fiancé."[34]

December 17, 1900: "More Indiana Lynch Law: Third Negro of Gang Which Killed a Barber Hanged By Mob."[35]

July 8, 1901: "Mob Attacks [Major League Baseball] Umpire O'Day."[36]

March 2, 1901: "Prayer Precedes a Lynching: Offered by a Member of the Mob Which Hanged a Negro in Wisconsin."[37]

August 1, 1901: "Two Women Lynched By Mississippi Mob; Mother, Son, and Daughter Put to Death."[38]

August 22, 1901: "Mob Kills An Italian: International Complications May Arise from a Demonstration Against Foreign Labor in Arkansas."[39]

We present a few examples of three archetypes that involve mob violence directed at perceived threats in the culture. One archetype is mob violence triggered by some event other than a crime—typically union activities such as a picket line. In "the United States, volcanic eruptions of labor unrest terrorized the cities in the late nineteenth century."[40] Because that story is well known, we chose stories that involved mob violence not associated with labor unrest.

On May 12, 1901, in a "big tenement house" in "the densely settled portion of the east side" of Manhattan, "an Italian barger" killed a janitor by shooting him five times, twice in the head, once in the neck, and twice in the back.[41] The cause was the janitor telling the man that the latchkey he had requested was going to cost twenty-five cents. After the shooting, "[a]n immense mob gathered, and a riot of the Italians, excited by the shooting, seemed imminent." The dead man had contusions and lacerations consistent with being trampled by the "struggling crowd." This story connects to our themes in two ways. First, it shows how angry and violent some parts of the country had become. Second, the writer manifested a view of Italians as different from others in his comment that "a riot of the Italians, excited by the shooting, seemed imminent."

The second example is actually a cluster of stories from January and February 1901 about Carrie Nation. We were surprised at the depth of feeling, on both sides of the temperance dispute, which was already making itself felt around the turn of the twentieth century. Nation, with her trusted hatchet and usually accompanied by female allies, "smashed" saloons in Topeka,

Wichita, and Enterprise, Kansas and in St. Louis, Chicago, and Des Moines, Iowa. Here is the *Times* account of Nation's second "smashing" of Wichita saloons:

> With hatchets concealed under their cloaks the women entered the saloon . . . and did not leave a complete piece of glass or a working slot machine in the place. All showcases, both for liquors and cigars, as well as the plate-glass windows and doors were broken into smithereens. Next they ran to [another] saloon and had everything in the front of the room, including the plate glass windows broken when [the owner] appeared with a revolver and placed it at Mrs. Nation's head and said that he would blow out her brains if she did not desist. She yielded before the pointed revolver.[42]

The temperance mob moved to another saloon where it was met by police who subdued the women, though not before Nation hit a detective in the face with a poker. When the women promised not to wreck another saloon before noon the next day, the chief of police released them. Nation gave a "street lecture" to the crowd that had gathered outside the city building. "Shaking her fist at the crowd, she said: 'Men of Wichita, this is the right hand of God and I am destined to wreck every saloon in your city.'"

Three days later, a group of women attacked Nation and her followers in the streets of Enterprise, Kansas.[43] As cries of "Kill her! Kill her!" were heard, "a woman, heavily veiled, rained blow after blow upon Mrs. Nation with a horsewhip. Male spectators offered no aid to either side, and quiet was restored only when the police interfered. Mrs. Nation was badly bruised." The assailant was arrested for assault, though Nation said she would forgive her if she "begged her pardon." But the suspect refused, whereupon "Mrs. Nation said she would send her to the penitentiary." Two days later, in Topeka, Kansas, the wife of a saloon proprietor "rained blow after blow on [Nation's] head with a broomstick" while the proprietor "stood by and encouraged the effort."[44]

Other groups in Kansas emulated Carrie Nation. One "completely wrecked the fixtures" in four saloons in Anthony, Kansas.[45] When the proprietor of one of the saloons "attempted to stop" the smashing, the husband of one of the women hit him in the head with a beer bottle, knocking him out, and causing his blood to mix "with liquor which flowed in streams over the floor." A second group, heavily armed "saloon raiders," shot and killed the wife of a bartender in Millwood, Kansas.[46] In 1907, Nation "called at the Executive offices of the White House" and was denied admission."[47] Teddy Roosevelt was president.

The second archetype is killing, without benefit of trial, someone thought guilty of a crime. We warn readers that these stories are gruesome and upsetting. In Florida in 1901, a black man named Rochelle was apparently seen killing a "well known and respectable white woman."[48] Less than ten minutes after he had been put in a jail cell, a mob broke into the jail, took Rochelle, and dragged him to the scene of the crime on a riverbank. "Scream after scream broke from the wretch's quivering lips, followed by groans and prayers for mercy."

"By common consent, burning was to be the penalty. There were no ropes, no plans for lynching by hanging. The stake was the only suggestion as to the proper expiation of the crime." Rochelle was chained to a stake on the spot where the victim had been murdered. "He pleaded for mercy, but in the great crowd around him silence was the only response." Kerosene was poured on Rochelle until his clothes were "well saturated." It was six o'clock and "[t]he crowd was growing, and business in the city had been practically suspended."

> When the match was applied the blaze quickly leaped skyward. The burning body could be seen only as a dark object in the circle of a roaring flame. Then the fire slackened and the writhing body came back in full view, but already the groans had ceased, and the only evidence of life was in the contortions of the muscles of the limbs. For fifteen minutes the body burned, and in a half hour from the application of the match only the charred bones were left as a reminder of the negro's crime and his fate. The crowd dispersed as orderly as it had gathered and at 8:30 to-night the city is quiet.

The "city is quiet," of course, because for that one night a perceived threat had been identified and removed from the community. The *New York Times'* comment that "only the charred bones were left as a reminder of the negro's crime and his fate" comes dangerously close to approving the mob violence. And if the *Times* was quietly approving, imagine the attitude of newspapers in other regions of the country.

The third archetype is killing someone where the evidence is not clear. We present three examples. One involved another burning at the stake. What makes this even more ghastly than Rochelle's case is that Fred Alexander protested his innocence to the end.[49] The mob insisted that he confess. He replied, "I am innocent. . . . I am dying for what another man did. I see lots of my friends here; they know I did not do it." Just before the mob took him to the scene of the murder, they gave him "another chance to confess." He responded, "My God, men! . . . I have told you that I am innocent. I can't tell you any more. I didn't do it."

Alexander "raised his shackled hands and began to speak. 'You are going to kill me whatever I say,' he said; 'but you men are wrong. I want to tell you right now that you've got the wrong man. I did not do that, and some day you men here will run up against the man who did. I know it ain't any use to me to say so, for you're going to kill me; but I didn't do it.'"

The mob's response was to tie him to the stake. "Before the match was applied," the father of the murdered girl asked Alexander if he was guilty. He insisted that "you have the wrong man" and "[y]ou're burning an innocent man." He asked for his mother but she was not in the crowd. While kerosene was poured all over Alexander and the wood at his feet, "he called to acquaintances in the crowd and said good-bye to them." The murdered girl's father lit the fire and, for the last time, "Alexander was asked to make a confession, but he replied that he had nothing to say."

> Men kept piling wood on until about 7 o'clock when the flames were allowed to die down. From 6 to 8 o'clock there was a continuous stream of people going to the scene of the burning. These were persons who had been unable to get away from their work in the afternoon and who were determined not to miss seeing the awful spectacle.

When the fire had cooled sufficiently, "there was a wild scramble to obtain relics. Bits of charred flesh, pieces of chain, scraps of wood—everything that could possibly serve as a souvenir—was seized." This reaction is what one would expect of the victors in a religious crusade. It was as if the onlookers demanded souvenirs of the victory over deviance.

Two days later, the police chief was asked whether "any effort would be made to arrest the leaders of the mob which burned the negro Alexander at the stake."[50] He responded, "No I think not. I know of no movement to arrest any one. I do not approve of the burning of Alexander, but he should have been hanged." A judge said, "The burning part is too bad; it hurts the community. It was intended to give an object lesson, but hanging would have been better." When the mayor was asked if he would take any steps, he said, "It is a State case. I have nothing to do with it." The story concludes with the casual remark that the victim denied that she had identified Alexander as the assailant. She said "that Alexander looked like the man, but she was not positive about it."

The next two accounts are chilling because of the matter-of-fact nature of the reporting. The implication is that it is just not that big a deal when a mob decides to hang someone suspected of a crime even when he denies it. On March 1, 1901, a miner named Dewey Smith killed another miner during a quarrel.[51] Smith claimed it was self-defense, but he never lived long enough to prove it. A mob took him from the hotel where he was being held by the sheriff to the mine where the shooting occurred. The entire account of the lynching in the *Times* follows: "A halt was called under a tree. One of the crowd offered a short prayer, a rope was quickly placed around the negro's neck, and he was hauled up."

Ike Fitzgerald, a black man, was charged with assaulting a nineteen-year-old white girl.[52] On March 16, 1901, a jury was discharged after it could not reach a verdict. The rest of the *Times* story follows: "A different verdict had been expected, and a mob seized the prisoner before the Sheriff could hurry him from the courtroom and hanged him to a tree." The *Times* lodged no criticism of the mob's action.

We wish not to be misunderstood. We note the lack of objection to lawless conduct not because we condemn the writers. Quite the contrary. We take the lack of objection to be an artifact of the coarsened American character in the later part of the nineteenth century. One reader complained that we mistook objectivity for tacit acquiescence. But the *Times* of this era did not hesitate to criticize outrages in other straight news stories. For example, a 1902 story about the third degree said that "the law gives police officers no right whatever to practice such indignities upon prisoners who fall into their hands."[53] The title of a 1908 story about organized crime was "Must Stop Outrages by the Black Hand."[54] What about the outrages of lynching suspects without a trial and who might be innocent? The *Times* had nothing to say.

To be sure, as one reader pointed out, these news accounts do not prove that America was more violent in 1900 than it was in 1860. But the stories do demonstrate that America was angry and violent in 1900. Deviance was perceived everywhere—in saloons, in union activities, in the flood of immigrants, in freed blacks, and in Southern whites who refused to accept the outcome of the Civil War. England had no similar temperance war, no freed slaves, many fewer immigrants, and relatively little labor strife. Thus, it came to be that the third degree became an acceptable form of American, but not English, police interrogation.

We turn now to (mainly) news accounts of the rise and fall of the American third degree.

B. American Police Turn to the Third Degree

Our plan is to present the history of the third degree, including its likely causes and various permutations, and then explain how and why it declined. It was eventually recognized as its own form of deviance and was replaced by an emphasis on police professionalism. The model for police professionalism became an FBI that was radically expanded and molded by J. Edgar Hoover, appointed to run the bureau in 1924.[55]

It is widely believed that the term "third degree" was borrowed from the Masons, for whom the "third degree" is the highest order with the "most grueling initiation rites" that are secret and can never be revealed.[56] But the term also had a procedural definition. According to a 1901 *New York Times* story, the first degree of police interrogation was the examination by officers in the precinct house.[57] The second degree was a suspect's "examination by a detective from headquarters, at the police court." While the examination at the "police court" is not described, it was probably the examination before the magistrate. Those examinations normally took place at what was called the "Police Office" and were recorded by someone called a "police clerk."[58] The *New York Times* article suggests that by 1901 detectives were conducting some or all of those examinations as the "second degree" police interrogation.

The third degree was "the big examination given to [the suspect] at Headquarters by the chief of the Detective Bureau and whatever subordinates he may employ in the operation when the case warrants it." To be sure, the 1901 article makes clear that the questioning often took on a more intense character at the third degree stage, and it was this added intensity that eventually gave the term the meaning that we associate with it today. A similar procedural definition appears in the proceedings of the 17th Annual Meeting of the International Association of Chiefs of Police in 1910.[59]

As Carolyn Ramsey demonstrated, the third degree was not limited to those officially charged with crime.[60] Material witnesses in homicide cases were often held in custody and sometimes put in the "sweat box" in an attempt to elicit evidence. In some cases, of course, a material witness became a defendant. As Ramsey put it, there was a "blurred line" during this period between witnesses and suspects.[61] But in many cases, the witness was held for lengthy periods of time only to be released.

The third degree has been given quite a few scholarly treatments. One of our favorites, because it was written by one of us, is in Richard Leo's recent book, *Police Interrogation and American Justice.*[62] These treatments draw mostly on police biographies, accounts of police reporters, and the voluminous material collected through interviews and fieldwork by the Wickersham Commission in its investigation of law enforcement in the 1929–1931 period.[63]

Instead of revisiting those sources, we relied largely on two sources that were only recently easy to search—case law that can be searched for words and searchable newspaper archives. We chose the *Chicago Tribune* and the *New York Times*, because they were published in the largest cities of the period, and both cities had high crime rates and problems with organized crime. We chose the *Atlanta Constitution* and the *Los Angeles Times* for regional balance. There is, of course, no doubt that cases and news accounts are only the tip of the iceberg, that they dramatically under-count the abuse and brutality that was happening inside police interrogation rooms. Despite the under-counting, news articles and cases are good tools to illustrate our theme that police responded with the third degree when they perceived that they were losing the "war" against crime, particularly in the large cities, and that police turned away from the third degree when the public began to perceive their conduct as deviant.

Searching the case law and newspaper archives allowed us to correct some errors in the conventional wisdom about the third degree. It did not, for example, take the Wickersham Commission's 1931 report to alert Americans to the existence of the third degree. We found dozens of stories in newspaper archives in the period 1880–1930 on harsh police interrogation methods, often called "sweating" the prisoner. Anti-sweating bills were introduced in state legislatures as early as 1906 (Illinois) and enacted as early as 1912 (Kentucky).[64] In 1910 and 1911, a committee of the United States Senate conducted an investigation into the "practice of administering what is known as the 'third degree' ordeal by [federal] officers of the law for purposes of extorting statements and confessions."[65] The California Supreme Court in 1910 condemned a "close examination, characterized by . . . [defendants] as a . . . a relentless sweating process."[66]

At a meeting of the Women's Political League in 1927, a Los Angeles policeman was asked if the third degree was a "habit" at the city jail. His reply: "Lady, if you get locked up there—it's too bad."[67] At least one national magazine recognized the problem by 1926, when the *Saturday Evening Post* described several third-degree techniques and surmised that not all the third-degree stories "can be utterly false and baseless."[68] Thus, the *Post* concluded that the third degree had been used "many times" against suspects "who were still in the eyes of the law, innocent men." The disgrace is that the "public does not concern itself with these unofficial invasions of constitutional rights."

Given the public attention we uncovered, it might seem puzzling that the third degree persisted as long as it did, but the attention was not always negative. In 1901, the *New York Times* described the third degree as "mystical" and then explained that it consisted of police "clear[ing] up the mystery" by getting the suspect to "tell about it by hook or crook."[69] Should the reader feel bad that suspects were tricked, the writer conveniently let the police off the moral hook by positing the guilt of the suspects. The 1926 *Saturday Evening Post* story stated that the "public admires the cleverness of the detective who secures an admission of guilt, regardless of the methods used."[70] Even the use of force was regarded as "[r]aw work, but they had to do it."

As long as the police were viewed as clever stalkers of guilty, dangerous criminals, the third degree could be seen as a necessary strategy to protect Americans from crime and deviance: "Raw work, but they had to do it." And that is how it gained traction in police departments across America.

1. THE BLACK HAND

In section A, we sketched the general outline of the frayed American social order in the late nineteenth and early twentieth centuries. The murder rate tripled between 1904 and 1907, and then gradually escalated another 50% by 1919.[71] It stayed at a rate of seven or eight times the 1904 rate until the advent of World War II. In this subsection, we focus on the particular challenge to police posed by the beginnings of organized crime. In the early days of the twentieth century, organized crime in parts of this country (and in Europe) was generally known as the Black Hand Society. Though we found reports of Black Hand activity in Ohio, Pennsylvania, West Virginia, Indiana, Illinois, Maryland, Toronto, New Orleans, and Atlanta,[72] we will focus principally on its activity around New York. We do not claim that organized crime directly caused police to use the third degree. But the story of police fighting organized crime in the early 1900s illustrates how difficult the task of policing America's large cities had become and how tempting it must have been to "cut corners" by using the third degree to get confessions when the police believed that the suspect was guilty.

One of the early Black Hand techniques was to extort money by sending letters threatening violence and then offering protection for money. A 1904 *New York Times* story told of an attack on a priest who had "been active in efforts to stamp out the 'black hand' letter writers and blackmailers."[73] The attacker said, "I want $35 or your life." The priest responded, "I haven't $35 . . . but I suppose you can have my life." The priest "jumped" for the "highwayman" who struck the priest over the head and "knocked him unconscious." The assailant continued to rain blows on the head of the unconscious man. "Two Italians then happened along and they chased the priest's assailant into the woods, where he escaped."

Also in 1904, a baker in Westchester County, New York, received a letter from the "President [of the] Black Hand Society" that demanded one hundred dollars within ten days or "we will do you to death."[74] The letter promised that if he paid the money, "you will be protected all your life." The news story reported that the same gang had obtained "by threats" more than $1,000 from Italians employed in the area. The same year, a man in New Rochelle, New York, was killed with a stiletto to his heart in a quarrel.[75] Police believed that the quarrel was started as an excuse to kill him because he had refused to pay a "tribute" to the Black Hand.

The last two cases demonstrate not only the threat posed by the Black Hand, but also the problem that police faced in solving these crimes. The police arrested the assailant in the knifing case, but the paper reported that "he refuse[d] to make any statement." The letter to the baker closed with "[y]ou can tell all the policemen of the world we don't fear them. They can't catch us." The baker knew the "young Italian [man]" who delivered the letter but would not divulge his identity because he "fears to have [him] arrested."

Four articles of Black Hand bombs appeared in 1907. A grocery store in Williamsburg, Brooklyn, and a home in Philadelphia were bombed when the owners refused to pay the Black Hand the money that it demanded.[76] A Black Hand agent put a bomb in a stove in an apartment in Mount Vernon, New York, and the explosion blew an arm off the owner's mother and badly burned his wife and ten-year-old daughter.[77] He had refused to pay the $500 demanded in a letter. A powerful bomb set off three days before Christmas 1907 damaged every apartment in a five-story tenement on First Avenue in Manhattan.[78]

The New York detective bureau had a special squad of Italian-speaking officers whose only responsibility was to investigate murders of Italians.[79] The head of that squad, Detective Sergeant Petrosino, told the *New York Times* that there were "at least 10,000 criminals associated more or less closely [as part of the Black Hand] for purposes of intimidation and violence."[80] The *Times* asserted that there were more than 300 Black Hand murders nationwide during the "past few years," and that every day "not less than four Black Hand cases are reported to the police [in New York City], and some days as many as thirty-five."

The title of a 1908 article undoubtedly summed up the feelings of New Yorkers: "Must Stop Outrages by the Black Hand."[81] Sergeant Petrosino's superiors told him that "he could have all the Italian detectives he thought necessary to catch the criminals who have committed the recent bomb outrages in the city and to suppress Black Hand manifestations." There had been six Black Hand bombings of buildings in the prior three weeks.

Six months later, the *New York Times* published the story of Salvatore Spinella under the title "Police Have Failed to Stop Black Hand."[82] He went from a prosperous contractor-painter to a financially ruined man. In his own words:

The Black Hand come and demand $7,000. I tell them to go to hell. They try to blow up my house. I go to the police and fight them as well as I can. They set off another bomb; two, three, four, five bombs. My business is ruined. . . . My family live in terror day and night. There is a policeman in front of my house, but what does he do?

Spinella provided the *New York Times* reporter "evidence to back his story. A file of twenty letters signed 'Mano Nera'—the Black Hand—some of them smudged with blood lay on the table in front of him as he talked." A part of one letter will stand for the rest:

Piece of Carrion: Don't you think you'd better bring us the money? Pig of God, you think that we have forgotten you? No, assassin of God, dog of a God, we will forget you when we have destroyed you and your whole family and all your houses. . . . Now we will see [whether] you have the audacity to bring this letter to the police, and, carrion that you are, if you do that then we will fix you, pig of the Virgin Mary. . . . We swear to you upon the honor of our sworn society that you will shed tears of blood.

The pressure that police felt to respond to the Black Hand and other lawless elements must have been immense. Then there was the police frustration with the judicial process. A 1907 story contained a firsthand account of how the Black Hand manipulated the court system. Sergeant Petrosino was off duty and beginning his vacation when he witnessed a nonfatal shooting on the streets of New York City.[83] He chased the assailant and caught him. The man "handed over the [smoking] pistol, coolly saying that it had just been handed to him by another Italian." Once in jail, "he exhibited plenty of money, and soon had a lawyer at work for him." The case was adjourned several times awaiting the release of the badly injured victim, Rossi, from the hospital.

The defense lawyer then changed strategies from delay to demanding an examination by the magistrate, but by then Rossi had disappeared. It seems likely that the defense lawyer was aware of that fact. The magistrate threatened to dismiss charges unless Petrosino produced Rossi in court the next morning. Petrosino said it took twenty-four hours to find Rossi, whom he brought to court. Now the defense lawyer asked for a postponement, rather than an examination, and the magistrate agreed to postpone taking evidence in the case. Petrosino asked the magistrate to detain the victim "as I knew the witnesses in Black Hand cases usually disappeared." The magistrate accepted Rossi's promise to reappear. Petrosino told the judge that the suspect, Lardiero, "was a bad man who would simply go out and commit murder if allowed to get away with this case, as he had the reputation of having many scalps at his girdle."

Petrosino told the reporter the rest of the story:

On the day set for the examination Rossi sailed for Italy, and when the case was called Lardiero was discharged from custody.

Two weeks ago he shot and killed Dombera, the banker. If the Magistrate had acted properly at the time Lardiero shot Rossi, Lardiero would now be in Sing Sing serving a ten years' sentence and Dombera the banker would be alive.

For his zeal, dedication, and candor, Petrosino would pay with his life, murdered in Palermo, Sicily, in 1909 while on "a secret mission to that country in connection with the Black Hand Society."[84] The next year, Senator Augusto Pierantoni, professor of International Law at the University of Rome, visited New York City to attend a conference. He told the press that "Americans need not be alarmed by the stories of an organized Black Hand Society" emanating from Italy because it had "ceased to exist years ago. It has almost come to be forgotten by all save historians."[85] He scoffed at "the idea that Lieut. Guiseppi Petrosino was murdered at Palermo last year by order of any recognized leader of the Black Hand or Camorra." The notion that the Black Hand had "ceased to exist" is, of course, belied by the fact that the Camorra to this day are one of the organized crime groups that operate both in Italy and the United States.[86]

Petrosino's murder never resulted in a trial, but the *New York Times* reported in January 1910 that the Secret Service had identified the killer.[87] He was, no surprise here, the head of the Black Hand Society in the United States. According to the news story, "a week before Petrosino sailed for Italy there was a meeting" of the Black Hand Society in New York City, and it "was decided that Petrosino had to be killed." The head of the Black Hand was not identified in the story because the Secret Service could not persuade anyone to identify him.

In March 1910, Petrosino's widow unveiled a monument in his honor during a ceremony attended by 200 policemen.[88] Lieutenant Richard Enright told the crowd that the murder of Petrosino was "but a shallow victory" for his killers because his death "has aroused two nations who are resolved that law and order shall prevail." The "forces of light, law, and order" will prevail, he predicted over "the forces of darkness, anarchy, and riot."

And it was not just the Black Hand that was troubling the New York City police. The report of the 1875 legislative committee investigating "the Increase of Crime in the City of New York" noted the "extreme demoralization that has crept all over the [New York City] police force."[89] The committee concluded, "It is undoubtedly, to a great extent, a corrupt force." But whatever demoralization and corruption existed in 1875, it was made worse by the Black Hand.

Here is the Black Hand situation as the New York City police perceived it in the first decade of the twentieth century. Most Black Hand crimes were not reported. When they were reported, witnesses usually disappeared, and Black Hand lawyers navigated their way effortlessly through the court system. How could police make progress against the Black Hand? By obtaining confessions, of course. And how could they best obtain them? Police frustration, meet the third degree.

2. THE BEGINNING OF THE AMERICAN THIRD DEGREE

A 1901 *New York Times* article claims that the origin of the term "third degree" to describe police interrogation was in "police parlance" in the early 1860s.[90] The earliest reference we found to harsh interrogation, involving the "sweat box," was a Reconstruction case from Georgia in 1868.[91] According to an affidavit given by John Strapler, he was arrested, taken to an army base, and interrogated about a murder. When he kept insisting on his innocence, the government detective showed him what amounted to a coffin and said he would spend thirty days in that "sweatbox" if he did not tell what he knew. He continued to claim that he was innocent and was put in the box for thirty-three hours, at which point an army captain took him out of the box. The detective complained that the officer had taken him out too soon.

General George Meade, who had defeated Lee at Gettysburg and now commanded Union occupation forces in Georgia (as well as in Alabama and Florida), dismissed the sweatbox claim as false.[92] In Meade's account, Georgians spread a lie to arouse resentment against the occupying troops. Whether or not Strapler's account was true—the Atlanta newspaper *did* seize on the story to prove Union mistreatment of innocent Southerners[93]—the point is that the "sweat box" was recognized as a form of harsh police interrogation as early as 1868.

Several variations on a "sweat box" are described in the 1901 *New York Times* article that sketched the history and current practice of the third degree.[94] The earliest occurred when a suspect named Brunt was arrested in the early 1860s "purely on suspicion" that he "had stolen a lot of valuable bonds." It was mid-August and "quite warm enough for any one, even in the cool shadows of the old jail." According to the *Times*, the police captain had a stove placed in Brunt's cell where a fire was kept white hot. After several days of temperatures over 100 degrees, the captain visited the cell and told Brunt that the cell "would be kept at about that degree until he decided to confess."

"Brunt held out for three weeks, in which time he had lost about twenty-two pounds, largely as a result of perspiration. When he reached the stage of exhaustion where he felt that death was about to move in and become his cellmate, he weakened and told all." The newspaper writer described the use of the stove as the "third degree."

A *New York Times* article in 1902, "To Abolish the Third Degree," began with statements by lawyers in opposition to the third degree.[95] Then it described variations of the third degree. A Chicago variation included placing biting red ants in the sweatbox and blowing red pepper into the box, causing the suspect to cough and choke. A Memphis variation was to cause scalding hot water to rise in the box as high as necessary to get a confession. A New York variation was a "dark cell" in the Tombs made of iron and stone. The article said that though the cell permitted enough air for breathing, "[a]fter fifteen minutes in this cell one experiences a sensation as of actual suffocation" and "even the boldest of the bad prisoners are as meek as lambs, bleating to get out." Then there is the old standard, beating a suspect with a rubber hose. A seventeen-year-old suspect claimed in 1932 that two Los Angeles police officers took him to the City Hall garage and beat him with a rubber hose until he confessed.[96]

An Arizona variation, which didn't work out for the officers, involved hanging three suspects to force them to reveal the whereabouts of a missing woman.[97] Two died and the third was at the point of death when the news story was published. The officers initially claimed that they had shot the three suspects, about as unlikely a cover story for strangulation as one can imagine. The officers told the truth when they were arrested and were charged with murder. A similar event occurred in Long Beach, California, in 1924 with the added twist that the suspects were black and two of the police officers wore Ku Klux Klan robes while stringing the suspects to a tree by their necks.[98]

Less horrific examples included extended questioning, often without allowing the suspect to sleep.[99] An odd Los Angeles variation consisted of "rubbing the skin of the ears until it peels off, and in rubbing the scalp until the hair drops out."[100] A simple, direct threat, attributed to the chief of police in San Diego, was to "blow your brains out if you don't come clean."[101] That threat led to a lawsuit against the San Diego police department and offending officers.

3. AMERICAN AMBIVALENCE ABOUT THE THIRD DEGREE

Whether the third degree was accomplished by threats, the sweatbox, hanging the suspect, or merely coercive questioning, the American people were ambivalent about its use in the late nineteenth and early twentieth centuries. Many news stories were either noncommittal about the third degree or essentially endorsed it. Of the four newspapers in our database, only the Los Angeles Times did not run at least one or two stories explicitly approving the third degree. If crime rates were lower and crime less violent in Los Angeles than in our other subject cities, that could explain why the Los Angeles Times did not approve of the third degree. One marker of crime rates would be population and population density. In 1920, the population densities of the cities in our sample, per square mile, were New York City, 18,796; Chicago, 14,103; Atlanta, 7,657; and Los Angeles, 1,577.[102] Moreover, our review of the news archives persuades us that the Black Hand Society was limited to the Northeast, Midwest, and South. Much violence attended the grand experiment of Prohibition, and news accounts suggest that it, too, was largely confined to the big cities.

The most remarkable story we found in favor of the third degree appeared in the New York Times in 1877.[103] It described a murder that could not be solved because the victim's wife maintained that midnight burglars had killed him and beaten her. The story then condemned the

> absurd laws which prevent the employment of the rack and the thumb-screw as aids for the discovering of crime. . . . Does any one suppose that, if Mrs. Gunser had been placed on the rack, she would have hesitated

to admit her guilt after the first two or three turns of the windless—especially as her bruises would have rendered her exceptionally open to the influence of the machine?

The story regretted that the police could not have "slowly extracted" her fingernails "with pincers." It mourned the passing of "the skilled engineers who formerly worked the rack and the thumb-screw and the red-hot pincers." We suppose that this could be Swiftian satire because the writer said, "There is not an able detective living who will not promise to make Mrs. Gunser confess every crime in the calendar, provided he is furnished with a good, trustworthy rack and an assortment of other machines modeled upon those used with such excellent results in the Spanish Inquisition." Surely no one could think that getting a confession to "every crime in the calendar" was a good outcome or that the Spanish Inquisition should be emulated. Whether satire or not, we find the story remarkable.

At a more mundane level, several stories from this period seemed to find the third degree necessary or at least understandable. In 1888, the *Chicago Daily Tribune* reported that a female murder suspect was put in the sweatbox "but she obstinately refused to talk," implying that she had some undefined duty to respond to the third degree.[104] An 1896 plot to assassinate the Chicago chief of police was uncovered by putting a suspect in the "sweat box."[105] Also in 1896, a story entitled "Rounding Up the Thugs" reported that the Chicago chief of police "carried on a vigorous war ... against the thugs and robbers who infest[ed] the city."[106] One of the suspects, Red Sullivan, "had to undergo the pumping process in the sweat box in the forenoon and afternoon."

A 1908 *Chicago Daily Tribune* story recounted the murder of two police officers and one holdup victim in a single week in a downtown Chicago neighborhood.[107] The police responded by "putting to rout the army of suspicious characters infesting Chicago." Calling it a "crusade," the news story reported without criticism the arrest of over one hundred men, over thirty of whom were "put through the 'third degree' to learn whether they knew anything of the numerous robberies, street holdups, and saloon 'stick-ups' which are almost daily occurrences" in two precincts in downtown Chicago.

In 1895, the *New York Times* reported that "a self-confessed insurance swindler" admitted killing ten victims and burying their bodies around his property.[108] Because police believed that the suspect's wife "knows much more of the crimes of her husband than she cares to tell," police put her "in the 'sweat box' for three hours." The writer voiced no objection.

In 1905, a woman's head was found in a satchel and the rest of her dismembered body was discovered in two suitcases in the Boston Harbor.[109] The *New York Times* reported approvingly that the New York police solved the "Boston suit case mystery" by putting the suspect "through the third degree," after which "he broke down and said he would confess." A 1907 *New York Times* story recounted a "remarkable confession" of how a gang used ether to render occupants unconscious while "robbing their houses at leisure."[110] The confession was obtained by putting the suspect "through the 'third degree' for a couple of hours." In 1910, the *Atlanta Constitution* characterized as "shrewd detective work" the use of the third degree to force a confession from a black man.[111]

But there were also critical articles. In 1890, the *Chicago Daily Tribune* carried a story titled, "The Police 'Sweat-Box' Exposed," with a subtitle, "Denver Detectives Indicted for Brutal Attempts to Extort Confessions."[112] In 1902, the *Tribune* wrote that the "administration of the 'third degree,' whether by kicking and beating a prisoner or by depriving him of sleep, is as illegal and as immoral as the 'water cure.'"[113] The "water cure" is not described, but it consisted of pouring gallons of water down the throat of a suspect, "until the body becomes an 'object frightful to contemplate.'"[114] "One or two such treatments and the prisoner either talks or dies." The *Chicago Daily Tribune* article concluded that police who use illegal methods to obtain confessions are "law breakers."[115]

In 1897, the *New York Times* was critical of the third degree used on Augusta Nack, a middle-class woman accused of helping her lover murder one of his enemies.[116] The *Times* described the detective bureau's standard operating procedure as one that "sets up a little inquisition of its own and attempts by threats and cajolery and all the other arts at its command to extort a confession of guilt" before bringing the prisoner to the magistrate. In Nack's case, the magistrate "properly and indignantly rebuked the detectives for their procedure," but the police nonetheless "asked that the culprit be remanded to their custody, in order that they might work the inquisition still further."[117] Calling the police inquisition "unfair," the writer speculated that if Mrs. Nack had been "a nervous and high-strung person, she would have collapsed under the ordeal and said anything whatever that promised to bring it to an end." Ironically, she would later confess in open court to assisting in the murder.[118]

If the third degree was inappropriate when directed at a middle-class woman, imagine the outrage when a New York City grammar school principal put two female students "through the 'third degree' to induce confession" to the theft of an umbrella[119] In 1902, the principal was brought before a magistrate by the Society for the Prevention of Cruelty to Children. The magistrate "sharply rebuked" the principal, telling her that this "is not the way to educate girls."

Two *New York Times* stories in 1902—drawn from conversations with lawyers and speeches by judges—were harshly critical of the third degree. The article quoting the judges was more explicit in the reasons for condemning the third degree. It spoke of "bogus confessions" given by "prisoners preferring to plead guilty to some crime they never committed to submitting to such tortures." The article also discussed the impairment of the autonomy interests of suspects. Justice Henry A. Childs "denounced the 'third degree' and the isolation of accused persons as wholly unwarranted by law and as an invasion of the rights of personal liberty and said it was the duty of every lawyer to protest against the continuation of the system." Referring to the third degree in a speech in 1902, Justice Truman C. White said, "Much has been done and much is being done to deprive men of personal liberty, and it ought not to be done."[120]

A 1907 story about a murder in Queens, New York recounted a confession by a twenty-two year old.[121] "It was not until after he had been put through the 'third degree' several times that Becker made a confession and then he started in to confess to any and every body who happened to ask him about the crime. He also confessed to imaginary crimes." Then he turned to the officers: "Now I told what you wanted me to, are you going to let me go now?" Public opinion in the neighborhood where the murder took place viewed Becker "as a victim and not as the culprit," and the grand jury refused to indict.[122]

A 1909 letter to the *New York Times* said the third degree was "torture with the deliberate purpose of destroying the victim's mental poise and forcing a 'confession' in accord with the suspicions of the inquisitors."[123] The writer concluded "that the 'confession' so obtained is wholly unreliable. It proves nothing but the brutality of the method." In 1910, a defendant on trial for murder "caused a sensation" in a New York courtroom when he testified that he was "mauled and beaten" by police until he "could hardly stand. . . . I was told I would escape with a light sentence if I confessed. I did so, as I was only too glad to end the torture."[124]

Also in 1910, a New York trial judge ruled that the defendant's confession "had been wrung from him by threats, rough handling, starvation, and the assurance by the police that conviction would lead to only a few weeks' imprisonment."[125] The judge "believed the prisoner's account of the torture inflicted upon him, and indignantly commented upon it. . . . 'There is no language I could use which would be strong enough to express my abhorrence or condemnation of it.'" In his view, a "heightened respect for the administration of justice" would outweigh the loss of a few convictions.

A 1910 *Los Angeles Times* story quoted a trial judge that a statement "wrung from the accused" by the third degree was "not 'free and voluntary' as contemplated by the [California] statutes."[126] The confession was "secured by methods that would have a better place in the days of the Spanish Inquisition than in the twentieth century." A week later, the *Los Angeles Times* ran a story in which the Washington Supreme Court said that "the methods of the Spanish Inquisition have no place in modern life."[127] The court also said that "an attempt to revive the dungeon, the bludgeon and the like, even in a mild form, ought to call forth the execration of the people."

A 1917 *Los Angeles Times* story noted that a safe-cracking suspect had confessed but "because it appeared the police had used threats in securing [the confession], it was held that it could not be admitted into evidence."[128] The California Court of Appeals in 1925 noted that "the iniquity known as the third degree is stalking rampant throughout the land in flagrant violation of human rights which are supposed to be secured by American constitutions, both State and national."[129] In 1928, the Los Angeles police chief issued a warning in the "Police Bulletin" that "[s]ecuring statements or confessions by the use of threat of force or violence is . . . forbidden."[130] Officers found guilty of using unauthorized "force or violence upon a prisoner" would face "drastic action."

A 1907 *Chicago Tribune* story reported an attempted suicide by a woman, ironically named Nightingale, because of a "grueling third degree or 'sweating' to which she had been subjected."[131] The police "questioned her severely in a vain hope of getting some tangible clew to the murder" of a police officer. "That she withstood the severe inquisition so long, in view of her frail constitution and nervous temperament, [her friends] declare to be a marvel, when robust men have been known to break down and become physical wrecks."

Her friends also said that her case "should hasten the passage of the anti-sweating bill, which came before the last legislature and was tabled in the senate." Not surprisingly, the Chicago police chief was "bitterly opposed" to the anti-sweating bill "on the grounds that it deprived the police of power to secure proof against criminals." More negative publicity about the Chicago police attended the 1913 interrogation of a suspect named Haas who was "so badly beaten" that he was afraid to demand an investigation.[132] That role fell to a real estate salesman named Kirk who was in the police station at the same time as Haas. He saw Haas "hustled" into a police lieutenant's office. After a pause, Kirk "heard a few thuds, then a series of agonized screams." The other officers in the station ignored the sounds. When the beatings continued for seven or eight minutes, Kirk turned to an officer and "demanded to know what was going on."

The officer shook his head but then opened the door to the lieutenant's office and said, "Take that man to a cell if you want to do any beating. . . . Get him out of here. This is no place for a trimming." Kirk could see into the office. "Two big brutes . . . were standing over poor Haas, who was on his hands and knees. These men had even taken off their coats, and they looked like demons from the pit. . . . Haas had no chance. They were kicking him mercilessly and there he was looking up into their faces and pleading for mercy."

In a story published five days later, Hass's cell mate verified Kirk's story. He said that when he first saw Hass, "He looked as if he had been struck by a cyclone or had tried to stop an automobile . . . blood was running down his face. . . . His clothing was almost all torn off . . . I never saw a man so scared in my life."[133]

The police treatment of Haas was outrageous even if he had been guilty. But the *Tribune* reported that he had been mistaken for someone else, someone whom he did not "resemble" even "remotely."[134] Kirk told the *Tribune* that "his blood boiled" at what he saw and that "[t]he sooner the police department is rid of such fellows the better off Chicago will be." An alderman responded to this story by proposing "a thorough investigation of the affair be made . . . at the next meeting of the city council."[135]

In 1913, a lawsuit against the Chicago police chief and state's attorney alleged the third degree in another mistaken identity case.[136] The police arrested a man named Mullen because they thought he was Eddie Waite. He was held for four days without charges filed or any record entered in the police records. During some of this time, members of the district attorney's office subjected him to the third degree. When friends forced his release by a writ of habeas corpus, the district attorney made the first official entry in the police station book. "It was simply this, in red ink: 'Error.'" Mullen's suit asked for $50,000 in damages; we found no follow-up story.

In 1909, the *Atlanta Constitution* ran a story critical of the third degree, concluding: "As likely as not statements wrung forth by terror, fatigue, threats and duplicity will not come within hailing distance of the truth."[137] A year later, the *Constitution* reported that a man who was put through the third degree by Chicago police hanged himself later in his cell, using his handkerchief.[138] The subhead read, *Police Ordeal Proved Too Much for Alleged Murderer*, an "ordeal" that helped "arouse[] much comment about police methods in this city." In the same month, the Atlanta paper described the third degree as "blended about equally of terrorism, barbarity and torture."[139]

But the public continued to be ambivalent about the third degree. The Illinois anti-sweating legislation was tabled in 1906. While it passed both houses in 1917, it was still "strongly opposed" by the Chicago police chief and was vetoed by the governor.[140] In 1923, another anti-sweating bill died in the Illinois senate.[141] In words eerily similar to those of presidential candidate Richard Nixon in 1968, one senator said, "There is too much sentiment for those accused of crime. . . . It is time we are paying attention to the law-abiding citizens." To be sure, the 1922 Illinois Supreme Court made clear that confessions extorted by force were inadmissible,[142] but the anti-sweating bill would have gone beyond outlawing use of force by police. It would have punished police by fine or up to thirty days in jail for seeking confessions by means of "any cruelty, trickery, deception, or by use of what is commonly known as the 'sweat-box' or 'third degree' or 'water cure' or by beating, striking, assaulting or threatening such person, or by depriving such person of food, drink, sleep or other necessities of life."[143]

A 1908 Ohio case demonstrates the ambivalence of the era. The suspect was "beaten over the head with a revolver by one officer, struck with the fist by another, knocked to the ground and in such fear that he befouled himself and cried out 'Kill me, me no care,'" before being dragged in front of a "great crowd" where he gave incriminating answers.[144] The court of appeals reversed the conviction on another ground but wondered aloud about the process that produced the statements:

> While the officers of the law must be diligent in detecting crime and in bringing the guilty to justice and for this purpose the 'third degree' may sometimes be administered in the sweat box, so that clews may be obtained from which conviction may follow, should confessions or admissions obtained under such circumstances be considered voluntary and be used against the accused at his subsequent trial?

After suggesting that the statement might not be admissible, Judge Winch wrote that "we are in doubt upon this matter and a majority of the court is unable to say that reversible error was committed by admitting this evidence."

What explains this ambivalence? It is the old story of balancing the need to keep the cities safe, against the concerns about false confessions and denial of suspect autonomy. The story of New York detective Thomas Byrnes makes this point. An article written by Edward Marshall about Byrnes appeared in the *Atlanta Constitution* in 1894.[145] Byrnes made his "greatest mark . . . when he relieved the money district of New York from fear of robbery." The Wall Street district "constantly contains a greater value in securities, gold and silver coin than any other equal area in the world." The article claims that in the ten years before Byrnes was assigned the district, "thefts amounting in all to $11,000,000 had occurred in this district." That amount would be worth over $200 million today.[146] While that seems exaggerated, it must have been true that thieves saw Wall Street not only as a rich but also as an easy target.

Byrnes said he lay awake for five hours the night he was assigned to the money district before a solution dawned on him, and then "he rolled over to what he says was one of the most pleasant sleeps of his life."[147] First, he ordered an admittedly illegal roundup of known criminals. About 500 men, women, and children were taken in squads into Byrnes's office where he delivered a "brief but impressive lecture." All those who had not already been photographed by police had their pictures taken before they were permitted to leave. Byrnes informed them that four plainclothes detectives would be on every corner in the district, prepared to arrest any of the group who ventured into the Wall Street district, however innocent their intentions might be.

According to the story, nearly one hundred of those who had been warned were later found in the Wall Street district. "So far as is known, without an exception, every one of them was locked up." The author expressed doubt that the arrests were legal but noted that "the crooks" did not take Byrnes to court. Byrnes became a "very rich man" because of tips from Wall Street "stockholders and gold men" that made him "the only man in New York city who can speculate in stocks without the least possible *risk of losing*."[148]

If driving robbers from the Wall Street district was Byrnes's "greatest mark," he also left a mark in the annals of the third degree. A thief locked up and awaiting trial said that he would rather "face the gates of hell itself than to meet Tom Byrnes's eyes when he is angry or wanted to make me think he was angry."[149] A pickpocket said no man should try to lie to Byrnes. "I tried it . . . and he smashed me across the teeth with a pair of handcuffs. Then I told the truth, you bet, for I didn't know but he'd break me in two . . . the next time I lied to him."

The story soothingly assures the reader that it is "not likely . . . that Byrnes often finds it necessary to use physical force, and it is certain that he never attempts it unless he is very sure of the kind of man he is dealing with." Indeed, despite occasionally questioning the legality of Byrnes's methods, Marshall's tone is approving, almost adoring. Byrnes "stands pre-eminent among the detectives and police managers of the world." There "is no one man now living who has built up such a reputation for himself among the law-abiding, or who has created such a wholesome fear among the criminal classes. . . . Scores of criminals avoid New York as they would avoid a pestilential city for no other reason than that he is in it."

The Black Hand Society was but a microcosm in a much larger web of thieves and robbers that made America's large cities fearful and the populace willing to tolerate harsh policing, as long as it was directed at the "criminal classes" and not middle-class women and young female students. Despite the occasionally critical press accounts, the prevailing opinion prior to the Wickersham Commission report might best be captured by the 1913 American Bar Association meeting. The committee on jurisprudence and law reform issued a report that found "in substance that the third degree as depicted in many newspapers does not exist."[150] A minority report, endorsed by a single member of the committee, proposed a resolution charging that police in "many cites disregarded the rights of prisoners." "The majority of the committee rejected this resolution on the ground that the present law regarding the admissibility of confessions was sufficient protection to defendants."

Police denied use of the third degree even after publication of the 1931 Wickersham report entitled "Lawlessness in Law Enforcement." Officials in Buffalo, Cleveland, Detroit, Chicago, Little Rock, Newark, Seattle, San Francisco, Richmond, the Bronx, Queens, Brooklyn, New York County, Trenton, and Camden denied the charges in the report.[151] The director of public safety in Newark said, "Every man under my command knows I will not tolerate the 'third degree.'"

Why did it take the Wickersham Commission to create legal accountability for violent police methods? One might have imagined a flurry of lawsuits like the ones filed by the Wilkes plaintiffs in England over a century earlier. We found only a handful of news reports about suits or criminal charges against police. To be sure, during this period, municipalities could not be sued for violating federal civil rights,[152] but tort suits in state court could have been brought. We saw earlier the Chicago alderman's condemnation of police third degree tactics in 1913 and the subsequent $50,000 lawsuit against the police chief and state's attorney.[153] Oddly enough, another suit against the same defendants was filed three days earlier, seeking $25,000.[154] We could find no connection between the suits nor evidence of other lawsuits against the Chicago police and prosecutors. The ultimate outcome of the suits did not appear in the *Chicago Daily Tribune*.

But if lawsuits were not filed very often, there were real-world consequences for some who practiced the third degree. We saw that the Arizona officers who hanged three suspects were charged with murder.[155] In 1918, a Chicago lawyer was appointed by a magistrate to hear charges that a police officer and the secretary to the state's attorney had abused a suspect during questioning.[156] The lawyer recommended that a grand jury investigate whether assault charges should be lodged against the two. The news account also suggested that the state bar association might "conduct an inquiry into the state's attorney's office" about the use of the third degree. We found no evidence of assault charges being brought or a bar association inquiry, but the grand jury did investigate the state attorney's office and recommended that the office be censured.[157] Five months later, three assistant state attorneys and the secretary resigned. The four were described in the news account as aides who "have frequently been intrusted with the most important cases in the office."[158]

In 1920, a New York City police detective was convicted of assault because of his third degree interrogation of a truck driver.[159] But the charge was made only after a lawyer for the Citizen's Union complained to the mayor and affidavits from a hospital were filed to show the extent of the injuries. Even then, the district attorney apparently dragged his feet on bringing the case to trial, and the detective was not dismissed from the force.[160]

Warrants charging assault and battery were issued by a Chicago judge in 1921 based on allegations of the third degree used in a robbery case.[161] In 1929, a New York City suspect was removed from police custody and turned over to the sheriff's office.[162] According to the news account, the suspect appeared in court for his arraignment "so badly beaten about the face and body that he could scarcely talk or move." If it took that much third degree to merit removal of a suspect from police custody, then removal probably did not happen very often.

Yet the third degree largely disappeared from the American interrogation room, much like the Hawkins-Leach dictum lost its power to shape judicial outcomes in the late nineteenth century. The criticism of the third degree in Illinois led one prosecutor to claim that the "fourth degree"—"employing kindness instead of force"—was a "more efficacious" form of interrogation.[163] An Arkansas judge in 1929 ordered an "electric chair" used to shock suspects into confessing "brought into court and after it had been examined, declared its use was an 'uncivilized' one," adding "'If these people are going to be mobbed before coming up here, there is no use of having a court.'"[164]

The transparency and condemnation of the Wickersham Commission played a critical role in the decline of the third degree. As noted, police departments denied the charges but were stung nonetheless by the depictions of police as corrupt thugs. More important, the police chiefs and prosecutors feared a political backlash that might limit their ability to conduct interrogations.[165] One commentator even suggested taking the interrogation function away from the police and giving it to magistrates, as was the practice in England and the United States for centuries and is still the practice in Europe.[166] At the same time, science was advancing in ways that offered "magic" methods of police interrogation, the most obvious of which was the polygraph or so-called "lie detector."

In 1932, the *Chicago Daily Tribune* quoted the man said to be the "inventor" of the lie detector that the "real merit of the machine lies in 'getting at the truth' without resorting to 'third degree' methods."[167] He said that in eleven years of using the lie detector, only seven persons "lied without being detected." In 1933, the *Los Angeles Times* ran a story with the headline "A Machine That Makes Criminals Confess!" that contained many examples of how the "lie detector" was instrumental not only in "proving guilt" but also in "establishing innocence."[168] The story said that 75% of those who failed the two-stage polygraph interview confessed on the spot. In light of the Wickersham Commission report, which is not mentioned, it is telling that the reporter wrote: "The only torture involved in such a test is self-induced, through fear of being caught and that fear exists whether the man is being cross-examined in the usual way or on a blood-pressure apparatus."

By 1940, the first police interrogation manual, written by police lieutenant W. R. Kidd from Berkeley, California, noted that lie detectors "are an often-useful aid to interrogation" and will "probably continue" to improve as machines and "the technique of operating them" improved.[169] The foreword to Kidd's book was written by August Vollmer,[170] who was "perhaps the leading proponent of scientific policing" in the 1920s and 1930s.[171] He urged police to "replace 'trial and error' methods of criminal investigation with 'more efficient scientific techniques and crime laboratories'"[172] Indeed, one book on police reform has the subtitle: *The Era of August Vollmer, 1905–1932.*[173]

The poster child for the rise of police professionalism was J. Edgar Hoover's Federal Bureau of Investigation. "Reform-oriented police such as Hoover and Vollmer sought to remake police interrogation in the image of scientific crime detection not only to raise the social status of police . . . but also to improve criminal investigation."[174] As for the polygraph, "police reformers hoped it would replace the third degree as a means of investigating suspects and eliciting confessions."

What the police began to learn in the 1930s, if not the 1920s, was that while the third degree might be necessary in Black Hand cases, it was not necessary in ordinary run-of-the-mill cases. Police Lieutenant W. R. Kidd advised in 1940 that the third degree "never be used by police because" it "does not produce the truth," it causes confessions to be suppressed, and "[p]ublic confidence in the police is shattered if knowledge of such methods is publicized."[175] "Perhaps the greatest harm done by the third degree methods lies in the eventual harm to the department" in lost convictions because "[j]udges and juries are ready to believe the defense contention that third degree methods were used."[176] In sum, "If you resort to torture, you admit your victim is the better man. When you 'break' a man by torture, he will hate you. If you break him by your intelligence, he will always fear and respect you."[177]

As befits our thesis, we believe that the lumpy but slowly improving American economy in the 1930s along with a falling crime rate[178] also contributed to the decline of the third degree. By 1940, the evils of fascism were making themselves evident, a trend that probably also reduced use of the third degree. Thus, the third degree largely disappears because it was finally viewed by the police as unnecessary and harmful to the police image.

To say that the third degree largely disappeared is not to say that echoes have not remained at least into the 1990s. Susan Bandes documented two systemic examples from the late twentieth century—the Rampart scandal in Los Angeles and the Area Two Violent Crimes Unit on Chicago's South Side.[179] In 1999, Bandes chronicled specific types of torture in Chicago,[180] most of which were later proven by a team of special prosecutors who spent four years investigating the Area Two Unit. The team's 292-page report, based on more than 700 interviews, concluded in 2006 that "scores of criminal suspects were routinely brutalized by police officers on the South Side of Chicago in the 1970's and 1980's."[181] The report identified three cases of torture that could be proved "beyond a reasonable doubt in court" along with "credible evidence of abuse in about half the 148 complaints they thoroughly investigated." While "most were abused with milder weapons like the fist, the feet, the telephone books," a few "had cattle prods placed against their genitals, guns shoved into their mouths or plastic typewriter covers held over their heads until they passed out,"—just as Bandes documented in 1999.

One of the victims of this police abuse said, "After the third torture session, I understood that these guys weren't going to let me out of there alive if I didn't say what they wanted."[182] He ultimately confessed to a crime that, he says, he did not commit. Because the statute of limitations had expired on the various aggravated assault crimes uncovered by the investigation, federal prosecutors charged Jon Burge, the then-commander of the Area Two Unit, with obstruction of justice and perjury arising from a civil suit.[183] Prosecutors alleged that Burge participated in the torture that included mock executions. He was convicted and sentenced to four and one-half years.[184] A reporter who wrote about the sentence noted a 1929 report about crime, stating that "Chicago was an ethical sinkhole and the Police Department and courts were totally in on the fix." So how much had changed?

Bandes concluded that the Chicago and Los Angeles scandals were evidence "of a much broader systemic dysfunction," one that manifested a "deeply in grained resistance to systemic reform."[185] We are not as pessimistic—heartened by the federal prosecution of Burge, the prosecution of Los Angeles officers connected to the Rampart scandal, and an independent report commissioned by the Los Angeles Police Commission. More fundamentally, we believe that the third degree is isolated because police have learned to get confessions by using gentler and more effective methods of interrogation.

We turn now from the third degree to the Supreme Court doctrines that limited routine interrogation practices in twentieth-century America. Forty years after the Wickersham Commission, we arrive at the shining hill of *Miranda*. Or was it a mirage?

THE THIRD REVOLUTION IN INTERROGATION LAW

Miranda's Volcano—Fiery, Brief, and Dormant

CHAPTER 7

The *Miranda* "Revolution"

We have shown that, over the centuries, the confessions pendulum swung from permitting extreme coercion, or even torture, to the Hawkins-Leach dictum, and then to a rationalist model. Part of the fallout from the move to rationalism was the American third degree. We turn now to the United States Supreme Court doctrine that, with remarkable speed, moved back to a robust embrace of the Hawkins-Leach dictum, at least rhetorically. We saw the Court's early confessions cases in chapter 4. Those were federal cases, where the Court could apply the common law rules or the Fifth Amendment privilege against compelled self-incrimination.

The Fourteenth Amendment requires states to provide "due process of law" before they "deprive any person of life, liberty, or property."[1] A state defendant can appeal to the United States Supreme Court claiming that his confession was admitted in error, thus denying him "due process of law." But the Court was loathe to intervene in state criminal processes, as can be seen in its initial foray into the world of state court confessions cases. In 1907, the Court refused to review a claim that a confession was involuntary because it was made "while in the 'sweat box' of the St. Louis police department."[2] To be sure, the defendant's lawyer did not properly preserve the federal claim, but the Court stated its holding in a way that seemed to preclude relief even to a properly pleaded claim: "[I]f, as decided, the admission of this testimony did not violate the rights of the plaintiff in error under the Constitution and laws of the state of Missouri, the record affords no basis for holding that he was not awarded due process of law."[3]

The implication here, startling though it may be to modern readers, is that the Fourteenth Amendment due process clause did not regulate the admission of confessions but only required that state law be fairly applied. Viewed through a 1907 lens, this is not as odd as it might seem. For over a century in England, as we have demonstrated, the admission of confessions was regulated by common law evidence rules. The Court in 1907 likely thought that common law was the vehicle for regulating interrogations that were not included within the ambit of the Fifth Amendment privilege against compelled self-incrimination, which the Court had not yet applied to the states. Indeed, a year later the Court explicitly held that the self-incrimination clause was not part of the Fourteenth Amendment due process clause.[4] If the common law and state constitutions were the only mechanisms regulating the admission of confessions, then the Supreme Court in 1907 could have believed that state involuntary confessions claims presented no federal issue.

It is difficult to know how long that extreme deference to state power would have lasted but for a series of horrific cases that came from the South. George Thomas has written about the Court's failure in the early twentieth century to save defendants from Southern juries trapped in racist and anti-Semitic cultures.[5] In 1932, the Court did save from execution nine young black men falsely accused of rape in Alabama.[6] And in 1936, the infamous *Brown v. Mississippi* case came to the Court.[7] The road to *Miranda v. Arizona*[8] began in Kemper County, Mississippi on March 30, 1934, when a white man was discovered dead, killed by blows from an axe.[9]

A. The March to *Miranda*

Exactly one week after the March 30, 1934, murder in Mississippi, three black men had been arrested, indicted, convicted, and sentenced to hang.[10] Their confessions were virtually the only evidence presented by the prosecution,[11] and the defense established that the confessions were tortured from the defendants by a mob that included a deputy sheriff. The suspects were subjected to persistent whippings and hangings while being told repeatedly that the torture would continue until they confessed in the very words that the torturers demanded. In one episode, two of the suspects

> were made to strip and they were laid over chairs and their backs were
> cut to pieces with a leather strap with buckles on it, and they were like-
> wise made by the said deputy definitely to understand that the whip-
> ping would be continued unless and until they confessed, and not only
> confessed, but confessed in every matter of detail as demanded by those
> present; and in this manner the defendants confessed the crime, and, as
> the whippings progressed and were repeated, they changed or adjusted
> their confession in all particulars of detail so as to conform to the
> demands of their torturers.[12]

The deputy who had participated in the torture was asked on the witness stand how severely one of the defendants had been whipped in his presence. He responded: "Not too much for a negro; not as much as I would have done if it were left to me."[13] As one of the dissenters in the state supreme court put it:

> The facts are not only undisputed, they are admitted, and admitted to have been done by officers of the state, in conjunction with other par-ticipants, and all this was definitely well known to everybody connected with the trial, and during the trial, including the state's prosecuting attorney and the trial judge presiding.[14]

One mystery is why the state supreme court affirmed a conviction based on a confession obtained by torture. Nine years earlier, in two cases also involving black defendants charged with murder, a unanimous Mississippi Supreme Court embraced the common law rule forbidding confessions taken by force or threat.[15] In one of the cases, *Fisher v. State*, the court waxed eloquently about the need to protect against coerced confessions: "Coercing the supposed state's criminals into confessions and using such confessions so coerced from them against them in trials has been the curse of all countries. It was the chief iniquity, the crowning infamy of the Star Chamber, and the inquisition, and other similar institutions."[16]

But in *Brown*, a majority of the state supreme court looked the other way when the State admitted torture far worse than what justified reversal in the earlier cases. The justice who wrote the dissent in *Brown* was consistent; he wrote the opinion in one of the 1926 cases. The *Brown* majority sought to hide behind the bizarre decision of defense counsel to move to exclude the testimony about the torture. Presumably, defense counsel thought that the added details about the murder were more harmful than the testimony about the torture was helpful. The state supreme court took this procedural turn as a waiver of the right to object later to the admissibility of the confes-sion. But *Fisher* had said that "while it is true that ordinarily the competency of a confession must be raised when the evidence is introduced, there are exceptions to that rule."[17] Certainly, the torture in *Brown* cried out for an exception to any waiver rule.

That was the position of the United States Supreme Court. The state's waiver argument "is a contention which proceeds upon a misconception of the nature of petitioners' complaint. That complaint is not of the commission of mere error, but of a wrong so fundamental that it made the whole proceeding a mere pre-tense of a trial and rendered the conviction and sentence wholly void."[18] Why a majority of the Mississippi Supreme Court did not take that position, given the extreme torture and state precedents that permitted the court to ignore proce-dural errors, remains a mystery. Perhaps the statewide reaction to the murder was more intense in the *Brown* case than in the earlier cases, but we found nothing in our research to support that hypothesis.

Despite the horrific torture and the failure of the Mississippi Supreme Court to follow its own precedents, we are not making a claim that *Brown* should be understood as "the South was evil." Indeed, Thomas has written about the heroism displayed by white Mississippians in *Brown*.[19] The victim was killed by repeated blows from an axe, and it would have been easy for everyone to look the other way when the authorities tried the defendants. But the defendants received able counsel at trial and on appeal from white Mississippi lawyers, including a former governor of the state, and two members of the state supreme court did dissent. Moreover, the authorities prevented lynch mobs from taking matters into their own hands, both before trial and following the reversal by the United States Supreme Court. Neither Ed Johnson nor Leo Frank was so fortunate when convicted of capital crimes in Chattanooga, Tennessee in 1906 and Atlanta in 1915.[20]

Cases like *Brown* showed that it took horrific state conduct to persuade the Court to intervene in state criminal processes. While *Brown* was an easy case to justify federal intervention, it was the beginning of a long, largely unsuccessful doctrinal grind seeking to regulate police interrogation. In Craig Bradley's memorable words, "Having opened the Pandora's box of police interrogation procedures [in *Brown*], the Court was to find that it could never close it."[21]

There are epistemological problems of the first order at the heart of the common law voluntariness doctrine. Courts have used different terms to describe inadmissible confessions without indicating whether they identify different problems. An involuntary confession given because of mental illness seems different from one that is coerced by police interrogators.[22] A confession tricked from a suspect might be viewed as compelled but seems unlikely to be thought coerced. At a more fundamental level, all three terms assume that a court can isolate the will of the suspect and determine whether that will has been overborne. But, as Louis Michael Seidman has noted, "[S]ophisticated lawyers in the 1930s had read and assimilated determinist theories that made the very concept of free will problematic."[23] Following the determinists, "virtually all human conduct was coerced. Choice was always embedded in an external context that made one alternative more attractive than the other; context could always be said to coerce the more attractive choice." Following Wigmore, "Even a person with a gun to his head retained the choice to refuse the demands of the gunman and suffer the consequences."

Not long after *Brown*, the United States Supreme Court decided three state cases that lacked an admission of State violence. As we will see, these cases tested the notion of "voluntary" confessions along with other formalisms that marked nineteenth-century doctrine. As Seidman observed, the New Deal justices whom Roosevelt put on the Court were deeply skeptical of formalism—the most famous example of which was *Lochner v. New York*.[24] In *Lochner*, the Court held in 1905 that freedom of contract was implicit in the due process clause. The "freedom of contract" formalism gave employees the "right" to decide how many hours to work and thus invalidated the New York statute limiting the hours that bakers could work. But in 1937, shortly after President Roosevelt introduced a plan to expand the size of the Court, Justice Owen Roberts changed his voting pattern and the Court upheld, 5 to 4, a state restriction of liberty of contract when necessary to protect the community.[25] Thus ended the formalist notion that freedom of contract had a privileged status somehow "outside" the normal balancing of harm and benefit that attends legislating and judging.

The formalist category that concerns us is the idea that there is such a thing as an involuntary confession. [A]s "soon as the Court moved away from this polar case [of *Brown*,] the difficulties . . . that played so prominently in the New Deal critique of the *Lochner* era re-emerged."[26] As Robert Weisberg puts it, "What image of the autonomous human being do we believe in? The irony is that once modern . . . law eliminated the worst abuses of police interrogation, it finessed the question of the choice-making process of human beings regarding their willingness to submit to state authority or to moral authority. We have had no coherent analysis of what it means to be autonomous in the face of the law, and we are left instead with shallow rationalizations about the psychology of volition."[27]

In the first of the post-*Brown* confession cases, *Chambers v. Florida*, an elderly white man was robbed and murdered. The crime produced "an enraged community."[28] The local sheriff responded by rounding up twenty-five to forty black men. He took several to a jail in a different county because he feared a lynch mob. Some of the prisoners "underwent persistent and repeated questioning" over five days.[29] The defendants claimed that they "were continually threatened and physically mistreated until finally, in hopeless desperation and fear of their lives, they confessed on Sunday morning just after daylight."[30] The State, perhaps learning a lesson from *Brown*, denied that the defendants were mistreated. Justice Black, writing for a unanimous Court, archly noted: "Be that as it may, it is certain that by Saturday, May 20th, five days of continued questioning had elicited no confession." The implication is that something changed to make the defendants confess on Sunday and that "something" might have been an escalation in violence or threats.

In the Court's view, however, it did not matter whether the authorities used violence or even threats of violence. This is where the New Deal skepticism manifests itself. It was enough that the State engaged in "drag net methods of arrest on suspicion without warrant" and then "protracted questioning and cross questioning of these ignorant young colored tenant farmers by State officers and other white citizens . . . where as prisoners they were without friends, advisers or counselors, and under circumstances calculated to break the strongest nerves and the stoutest resistance."[31] The "undisputed facts," the Court unanimously held, "showed that compulsion was applied."[32] Notice the renewed vitality of the Hawkins-Leach dictum and the shift in focus. The critical inquiry was not whether compulsion *moved the suspect to confess*, as it surely did in *Brown*, but merely whether "compulsion was applied."

We do not believe that the shift from confessions "procured by coercion" in *Brown*[33] to whether "compulsion was applied" in *Chambers* was merely a change in locution. Justice Black would have understood that the constructed category of coerced confessions is indeterminate, and that it is difficult, if not impossible, to construct a category of cases where coercion has truly displaced the will of the suspect. It is much easier to decide whether the authorities were attempting to compel a confession.

Black sets the stage for his "compulsion was applied" standard by reminding the reader that due process developed in part from "[t]he rack, the thumbscrew, the wheel, solitary confinement, protracted questioning and cross-questioning, and other ingenious forms of entrapment of the helpless or unpopular who had left their wake of mutilated bodies and shattered minds along the way to the cross, the guillotine, the stake, and the hangman's noose."[34] Notice that "protracted questioning" takes a place along with the rack and screw. Black "closes the deal" by reminding the reader of what was going on in the world in 1940:

> Today, as in ages past, we are not without tragic proof that the exalted power of some governments to punish manufactured crime dictatorially is the handmaid of tyranny. Under our constitutional system, courts stand against any winds that blow as havens of refuge for those who might otherwise suffer because they are helpless, weak, outnumbered, or because they are non-conforming victims of prejudice and public excitement. Due process of law, preserved for all by our Constitution, commands that no such practice as that disclosed by this record shall send any accused to his death. No higher duty, no more solemn responsibility, rests upon this Court, than that of translating into living law and maintaining this constitutional shield deliberately planned and inscribed for the benefit of every human being subject to our Constitution—of whatever race, creed or persuasion.[35]

Three months later, the Court applied the same methodology to *White v. Texas*[36] in a unanimous opinion, again written by Justice Black. White was one of fifteen or sixteen young black men rounded up without warrants or the filing of charges. He claimed that "armed Texas Rangers on several successive nights took him handcuffed from the jail 'up in the woods somewhere,' whipped him, asked him each time about a confession and warned him not to speak to any one about the nightly trips to the woods."[37] As in *Chambers*, the State denied using violence, but one of the Texas Rangers did admit taking White into the woods to interrogate him. The Court offered no analysis beyond quoting *Chambers*: "'Due process of law, preserved for all by our Constitution, commands that no such practice as that disclosed by this record shall send any accused to his death.'"[38]

The Court's concern about confessions made by young black men to white officers in the South can be seen most clearly in *Canty v. Alabama*, where there is (almost) no evidence of abusive interrogation.[39] Canty apparently did not testify, and the only evidence about the interrogation in the state court opinion comes from the prosecution witnesses. One witness testified that Canty had a scratch on the back of his head. Suggested by cross-examination, but denied, was that the officers cursed Canty, told him that they were going to see where his grave was being dug, and subjected him to unmentioned "rough treatment" and "abuse."[40] But there was no direct evidence of any of that treatment. Remarkably, the United States Supreme Court reversed and remanded in a unanimous per curiam opinion that we quote in its entirety: "The motion for leave to proceed in forma pauperis is granted. The petition for writ of certiorari is also granted and the judgment is reversed. *Chambers v. Florida*, 309 U.S. 227, 60 S.Ct. 472, 84 L.Ed. 716, decided February 12, 1940."

Given this solicitousness toward suspects, the next Supreme Court confession case, *Lisenba v. California*, is an outlier.[41] Lisenba planned to kill his wife, Mary, to collect on a double indemnity insurance policy he took out a few months before her death.[42] He enlisted the aid of Charles Hope. They blindfolded Mary, tied her to a table, and forced her foot into a box containing rattlesnakes. She suffered snake bites that made her left leg "greatly swollen and almost black." They left her tied to the table all night, waiting for her to die. But in the morning, she was still alive. Lisenba and Hope then dragged her into the backyard and put her "face down at the edge of a fish pond with the head and shoulders in the water." She drowned. Although Lisenba was an obvious suspect, the police initially closed their investigation without arresting anyone.

In a delicious irony, Lisenba would have escaped the executioner had he not demanded the insurance proceeds. The insurance company checked Lisenba's records and discovered that three years earlier Lisenba had collected a double indemnity insurance policy on his previous wife, which was taken out mere months before she was murdered. The insurance company, smelling a rat, refused to pay, and the police reopened their investigation.

The police account of the interrogation varied from Lisenba's. He said that they beat him black-and-blue, impaired his hearing, and caused a hernia.[43] The police admitted that they subjected him to a grueling interrogation by relays of officers for forty-eight consecutive hours on one occasion; the session ended only when he fell asleep. The state court dissent said that he fell asleep from "fatigue and exhaustion" several times.[44] Despite the grueling first stage of the interrogation, he said nothing that would justify charging him with his wife's murder.

Two weeks later, Hope confessed to the grisly murder, claiming that it was Lisenba's idea to kill Mary and that he had merely assisted. When the prosecutor reinitiated questioning, Lisenba requested counsel. His lawyer was out of town, and his request for different counsel was not granted.[45] The prosecutor turned the interrogation over to the police. After ten hours of interrogation, according to police, Lisenba told a deputy sheriff, "'Why can't we go out and get something to eat; if we do I'll tell you the story.'"[46] After dinner at a café and cigars, Lisenba narrated a story that attempted to shift most of the blame onto Hope. Lisenba said at trial that his confession was false, that he was simply attempting to "retell the tale Hope had told, which had been constantly dinned into his ears."[47]

The California Supreme Court clothed the trial court with "considerable discretion" in confessions cases because admissibility "largely depends upon the special circumstances connected with the confession."[48] Thus, "it is difficult, if not impossible, to formulate a rule that will comprehend all cases." Looking at the facts of the case, the state court found it "not . . . improper" that Lisenba "was questioned for many hours . . . particularly when, as testified, he freely responded thereto."[49] The court stressed that "no promises, immunities, threats or forms of violence were employed to overcome the free will of the defendant."

Two state justices dissented in a lengthy opinion that characterized the majority opinion as "deficient in its statement of the facts."[50] Beyond the dispute about the facts, the dissent also complained about the majority's failure "to adhere to the age old rules and maxims of criminal jurisprudence, which are cherished next only to the Magna Charta as safeguards of life and liberty."[51] To the dissent, the confession should have been held inadmissible because it "followed a long course of deprivation and physical mistreatment of a prisoner held incommunicado."[52]

The United States Supreme Court affirmed, returning by a vote of 7-2 to its earlier view that it should rarely intervene in the criminal process of a "quasi-sovereign" jurisdiction.[53] The outlier status of Lisenba is, we think, explained by five facts: (1) He was not a young black man in the South; (2) he did not confess after the first and by far the longer interrogation; (3) according to the police, the interrogation contained no threats or promises; (4) he confessed only after being told that his accomplice had implicated him; and (5) he later said "that there were not enough men in the District Attorney's office to make him talk, and if Hope [his accomplice] had not talked he would never have told the story."[54] These facts gave seven members of the Court enough ammunition to refuse to disturb the voluntariness findings of the trial judge, the jury, and the California Supreme Court.

But the deference to state courts would not last. The Court had already shown solicitude toward black suspects questioned by white officers in the South. What remained was to extend that attitude to all suspects. The process would begin in earnest in 1944.

Ashcraft v. Tennessee,[55] also authored by Justice Black, does not receive the credit it deserves in the march toward *Miranda.* Though the *Miranda* opinion claimed it was relying on *Bram v. United States,* that truly odd nineteenth-century case cannot bear the weight that the Court placed on it (more about *Bram* later).[56] It is *Ashcraft,* not *Bram,* that is the true ancestor of *Miranda.*[57] Justice Black forges an opinion in *Ashcraft* that required only a small additional step to reach *Miranda.* Justice Jackson, dissenting in *Ashcraft,* saw where the Court was heading and accused the Court of using "the due process clause to disable the states in protection of society from crime," which was a "dangerous and delicate . . . use of federal judicial power."[58] Justice Jackson was joined in dissent by Justice Roberts, who wrote the Court's opinion in *Lisenba,* and Justice Frankfurter, who would later try to salvage confessions law from *Ashcraft*'s analytical structure.

Unlike the defendants in *Brown, Chambers, White,* and *Canty,* Ashcraft was not a poor black man who would expect rough treatment from the police. Ever the advocate, Justice Black sought to turn Ashcraft's stature in the community in favor of reversing his conviction of murdering his wife. He was "a citizen of excellent reputation."[59] A ten-day investigation "had revealed nothing whatever against Ashcraft. Inquiries among his neighbors and business associates likewise had failed to unearth one single tangible clue pointing to his guilt." The point here is that the interrogation was a "fishing expedition" that lacked a foundation. While this charge was leveled against the Star Chamber in seventeenth-century England, and appears in *Chambers* and *White,* the Court had yet to hold that an arrest without probable cause could cause a confession to be suppressed.[60]

Nor was that the holding in *Ashcraft.* Instead, the Court held that the confession was involuntary. Because Ashcraft was interrogated for thirty-six hours "without sleep or rest" by "relays of officers, experienced investigators, and highly trained lawyers," the police conduct bordered on the third degree, and the holding is unexceptional.[61] It is the analytical structure that is pathbreaking. The Court analogized the situation of a suspect to that of a criminal defendant on the witness stand, an analogy that Yale Kamisar would recreate in vivid fashion in 1965. Before we get to Kamisar, here's Justice Black's 1944 version:

> It is inconceivable that any court of justice in the land, conducted as our courts are, open to the public, would permit prosecutors serving in relays to keep a defendant witness under continuous cross examination

for thirty-six hours without rest or sleep in an effort to extract a
"voluntary" confession. Nor can we, consistently with Constitutional
due process of law, hold voluntary a confession where prosecutors do
the same thing away from the restraining influences of a public trial in
an open court room.[62]

Of course, the courtroom analogy would find almost any extended police
questioning to be coercive. The *Ashcraft* Court comes close to saying that when
it observed, "We think a situation such as that here shown by uncontradicted
evidence is so inherently coercive that its very existence is irreconcilable with
the possession of mental freedom by a lone suspect against whom its full coercive force is brought to bear."[63] Though the Court was careful to limit its holding
to the "situation such as that here shown," Justice Jackson was not fooled. In his
dissent, Jackson asks the hard question: "If thirty-six hours is more than is permissible, what about 24? or 12? or 6? or 1? All are 'inherently coercive.'"[64]

Jackson sees the game here. Going down the *Ashcraft* road will relieve future
Courts from having to identify the external force that overbore the suspect's
will. It will be enough to conclude that pressure was applied. The latter is obviously far easier for the defendant to show than the former. To be sure, the Court
began developing this due process analytical framework in *Chambers* when it
said that whether or not violence was done or threatened, the "'undisputed
facts showed that compulsion was applied.'"[65] But *Ashcraft* moves the analytical
ball toward the Hawkins-Leach dictum in three important ways. First, Ashcraft
was not a young, poor, black suspect who might be less able to resist the official
interrogation than someone who was a fixture in the community. Second, the
courtroom analogy in *Ashcraft* raised the specter that any police questioning of
a suspect in custody might be coercive. Third, the Court begins to view routine
police interrogation as potentially deviant. Unlike *Chambers* and *White*, there
were no dragnet arrests and detention of many suspects in *Ashcraft*. Unlike
Brown, there was no torture.

If the police are to be believed, Ashcraft faced an intense, lengthy police interrogation, from which he emerged "cool, calm, collected, normal," with "eyes
not bloodshot," and with "no outward signs of being tired or sleepy."[66] Yet without rejecting the police account, the Court describes what Ashcraft endured as
an example of "secret inquisitorial practices."[67] The Court cautioned that defendants have difficulty contesting "the inner details of secret inquisitions . . . , particularly where, as here, he is charged with a brutal crime, or where, as in many
other cases, his supposed offense bears relation to an unpopular economic, political, or religious cause."[68] Then, the coup de grace for 1944. Noting that the
American Constitution protects against conviction "by means of a coerced
confession," the Court wrote:

There have been, and are now, certain foreign nations with governments dedicated to an opposite policy: governments which convict individuals with testimony obtained by police organizations possessed of an unrestrained power to seize persons suspected of crimes against the state, hold them in secret custody, and wring from them confessions by physical or mental torture. So long as the Constitution remains the basic law of our Republic, America will not have that kind of government.[69]

To use a movie analogy, this is Rick in *Casablanca* persuading Ilsa to go with Victor by telling her: "It doesn't take much to see that the problems of three little people don't amount to a hill of beans in this crazy world." The *Ashcraft* Court is asking the state courts, what's the trouble of a few unsolved murders if the alternative is a regime like Nazi Germany?

As to the doctrine that *Ashcraft* announces, Jackson sees the future. "Arrest itself is inherently coercive, and so is detention. When not justified, infliction of such indignities upon the person is actionable as a tort. Of course such acts put pressure upon the prisoner to answer questions, to answer them truthfully, and to confess if guilty."[70] To Jackson, the majority's holding portends: "A confession is wholly and incontestably voluntary only if a guilty person gives himself up to the law and becomes his own accuser." While *Miranda* will not go quite that far, it will hold that a single question asked of a suspect who is under arrest is too much pressure. That idea was first planted in *Chambers*, applied in *White* and *Canty*, and then expanded to almost *Miranda* size in *Ashcraft*. After *Ashcraft*, all that remained was for the Court to recognize the logical implications of its assumption that custodial police interrogation is inherently coercive. But it took more than two decades of stumbling through the voluntariness fog to get to *Miranda*.

Spano v. New York, offers another example of what the Court considered deviant police interrogation.[71] Spano faced "skillful" questioning by a prosecutor and was, over eight hours, "subjected to questioning not by a few men, but by many."[72] The questioning about a murder "continued into the night" as the authorities ignored Spano's "repeated refusals to answer" on advice of counsel and "his reasonable requests" to speak to his lawyer.[73] Three times the police sought "to extract sympathy" from Spano by telling him that he had gotten his childhood friend, a rookie police officer, in trouble by calling him for advice.[74] Spano could get his friend, who had a pregnant wife and three children, out of trouble only by confessing. The Court held that Spano's "will was overborne by official pressure, fatigue and sympathy falsely aroused."[75] The latitude given police interrogators is shrinking fast. An eight-hour interrogation, persistent to be sure but far less persistent than in *Ashcraft*, is now viewed as "abhorren[t]" and "illegal":

The abhorrence of society to the use of involuntary confessions does not turn alone on their inherent untrustworthiness. It also turns on the deep-rooted feeling that the police must obey the law while enforcing the law; that in the end life and liberty can be as much endangered from illegal methods used to convict those thought to be criminals as from the actual criminals themselves.[76]

The Court's tolerance for persistent police interrogation had ended. The stage was set for *Miranda*.

Indeed, *Spano* signaled that something like *Miranda* was in the cards. Chief Justice Warren's opening sentence in *Spano* was, "This is another in the long line of cases presenting the question whether a confession was properly admitted into evidence under the Fourteenth Amendment."[77] The "long line of cases" locution suggests that the Court had tired of deciding these issues on a case-by-case basis. The second sentence in *Spano* suggested the *Miranda* compromise that would follow seven years later: "As in all such cases, we are forced to resolve a conflict between two fundamental interests of society; its interest in prompt and efficient law enforcement, and its interest in preventing the rights of its individual members from being abridged by unconstitutional methods of law enforcement." An opinion that created rights that could be easily waived would (and did) address both concerns.

To be sure, Justices Jackson and Frankfurter tried to stem the *Ashcraft* tide. In his majority opinion in *Stein v. New York*, Jackson included the following two sentences: "Interrogation is not inherently coercive, as is physical violence. Interrogation does have social value in solving crime, as physical force does not."[78] In 1961, Justice Frankfurter, who also dissented in *Ashcraft*, tried one last time to wrest the analytical structure away from the one Black had created. Throughout a "long and brilliant career" Frankfurter "returned to the confession problem with obsessive regularity. The story of his ultimate, utterly abject and deeply personal failure to make sense of the area poignantly embodies all of the difficulties" in the voluntariness inquiry.[79]

Given the task of writing the Court's opinion in *Culombe v. Connecticut*, another murder case, Justice Frankfurter insisted that the proper inquiry was whether the pressure of the interrogation acted to overbear the will of the suspect.[80] One can almost hear him saying, "Forget the *Ashcraft* nonsense about inherent coercion. Overbearing the will is what matters." An old New Dealer, Frankfurter recognized the difficulty of making that determination—assuming that custodial interrogation is inherently coercive is an easier task—and he wrote a lengthy, scholarly opinion that sought to create a jurisprudential framework within which the suspect's internal psychological state could be inferred from "external, 'phenomenological' occurrences and events."[81]

But Frankfurter's effort to avoid the easy logic of *Ashcraft* and *Spano* was doomed to failure. In Seidman's words, the opinion "grapples with the problem in all its intricacy" and "explicates the full complexity of the problem."[82] Yet "it is riven with contradictions from beginning to end and leaves the effort to justify and systematize the Court's role in shambles." Only Justice Stewart joined Frankfurter's opinion that announced the judgment of the Court. What could have been a majority opinion for six justices wound up being an opinion for two. Moreover, it took Frankfurter thirty-four pages to apply his framework to the facts before the Court—nineteen pages to describe the "phenomenological" facts and events, and fifteen pages to infer the suspect's psychological state and then decide that he had not confessed voluntarily.[83]

Chief Justice Warren, who agreed that the confessions were inadmissible, refused to join Frankfurter's opinion because it "has not been the custom of the Court . . . to write lengthy and abstract dissertations" when deciding cases.[84] The irony here is rich; five years later Warren would write the "convoluted, repetitious, and seemingly interminable" *Miranda* opinion.[85] Justices Douglas, Black, and Brennan also agreed that the confessions were inadmissible and also refused to join Frankfurter's opinion.[86] Perhaps even more devastating to Frankfurter's attempt to bring clarity to the confessions problem, Justices Harlan, Clark, and Whittaker *accepted* his analytical structure and reached precisely the opposite conclusion—that the confession was voluntary. Seidman describes Frankfurter's failure: "The Justices who concurred on an analytical framework for resolving the problem disagreed on the result . . . while the Justices who concurred on the result disagreed on the analytic framework producing that result. In short, the *Culombe* opinion was a total disaster."[87] It was the opinion of "an old man at the very end of his long and brilliant career."[88]

By 1964, the Court's confessions doctrine was truly "in shambles."[89] Two lines of cases existed. One line, featuring *Chambers* and *Ashcraft*, asked only whether compulsion was applied to the suspect. Though a crude, imperfect inquiry, it is at least a coherent quest. Unfortunately, it will almost always lead to the exclusion of the confession. Cases where, in Jackson's words, "a guilty person gives himself up to the law and becomes his own accuser" are rare indeed.[90] When the Court faced really blameworthy defendants, like Lisenba, the Court returned to the *Brown* question of whether compulsion *produced* the confession. In the ordinary run-of-the-mill case, excluding *Brown*, the second question is crude, imperfect, and unanswerable. Did Lisenba confess because of the fifty-eight hours of grueling interrogation over two sessions or because his accomplice had accused him of being the mastermind and he wanted to tell his side of the story? No one could ever know. In Welsh White's understated words: "The premises that undergirded the [due process confessions] test . . . were never clear."[91]

So much for the common law voluntariness norm. It had been undone by twentieth-century skepticism about whether or when humans act freely. What the Court needed was a rule, not a soft norm. As Bradley observed, "The Court, excluding evidence case by case resulting from illegal police practices, was simultaneously aware both that it was not a rulemaking body and that it must be."[92] The Court had tried a rule in the 1940s and 1950s, drawn from the federal rule of procedure that required production of an arrested person before a commissioner "without unnecessary delay."[93] The Court held in 1943 that a violation of that rule required exclusion of any statements made after the unnecessary delay.[94] But this was not much of a rule—what is "unnecessary"? Moreover, the rule applied only to federal cases, and the troubling cases of the period beginning with *Brown* were all state cases. Perhaps worst of all, Congress could always (and did in 1968) change the rule.[95]

The next attempt at a rule had its origin, oddly enough, in the Sixth Amendment right to counsel.[96] In 1964, the Court suggested, ever so tentatively, a rule in *Escobedo v. Illinois* that sometimes required the presence of counsel during interrogation.[97] The Court held that, on the facts of *Escobedo*, the Sixth Amendment right to counsel had been violated. There were, however, three fatal flaws in the *Escobedo* approach as a solution to the run-of-the-mill police interrogation problem. First, Escobedo had already retained a lawyer and repeatedly asked to talk to his lawyer who was, during the three-hour interrogation, also trying to see his client.[98] These facts set the case apart from almost all routine police interrogations.

To be sure, it was possible to extend the *Escobedo* principle to run-of-the-mill interrogations. That is where *Escobedo*'s second and third flaws become critical. The text of the Sixth Amendment provides a right to counsel "[i]n all criminal prosecutions."[99] Because Escobedo was the target of the police investigation and because he had a lawyer who was trying to reach him, it was plausible, barely, to analogize what Escobedo faced to a "criminal prosecution." But the questioning of a typical suspect who is arrested on bare probable cause, and who does not have a lawyer, does not look like a criminal prosecution. It was fashionable in the twentieth century to argue that courts were free to do as they wished, and that even the clearest rule did not limit judicial discretion. Perhaps the most robust of these claims was that a court was free to ignore the constitutional language requiring the president to be at least thirty-five years old and allow a "particularly precocious thirty-four year old" to assume the office.[100]

That notion was, of course, utter hogwash, and *Escobedo*'s fate is yet one more proof that language is ultimately a limiting factor. Ludwig Wittgenstein famously remarked, "If I tell someone 'Stand roughly here'—may not this explanation work perfectly? And cannot every other one fail too?"[101] Even an activist Supreme Court like the Warren Court in the mid-1960s was not willing to interpret questioning of a suspect at the beginning of a criminal investigation as a "criminal prosecution."

The third flaw of *Escobedo* was political. The most effective solution to the interrogation problem was to require counsel for all interrogations. The American Civil Liberties Union amicus brief in *Miranda*, written by Anthony Amsterdam and Paul Mishkin, argued that only the presence of counsel could dispel the inherent compulsion of police interrogation.[102] Facing the political problem of requiring states to raise armies of lawyers, the Court could have, as Sandra Guerra Thompson points out, instead banned police interrogation.[103] As much as the Court might have wanted to move to either of those solutions, it surely sensed that the political costs would be extreme.

That left the Court with a stark choice. It could retreat to Justice Frankfurter's complex process that sought to infer internal psychological states. Or it could embrace the easy logic of *Ashcraft* as elaborated in *Spano*. Some insight into which way the Court would go can be gained from Frankfurter's opening paragraph in *Culombe*:

> Once again the Court is confronted with the painful duty of sitting in judgment on a State's conviction for murder, after a jury's verdict was found flawless by the State's highest court, in order to determine whether the defendant's confessions, decisive for the conviction, were admitted into evidence in accordance with the standards for admissibility demanded by the Due Process Clause of the Fourteenth Amendment.[104]

Painful duties are best avoided. It should have been predictable that the Court would adopt the *Ashcraft-Spano* model. And Yale Kamisar was there, in real time, to urge the Court down the *Ashcraft* road. In perhaps the most influential article ever published about police interrogation, "Equal Justice in the Gatehouses and Mansions of American Criminal Procedure," Kamisar, in 1965, embraced the analogy between the courtroom and the police interrogation room.[105] He showed how solicitous the process is when the defendant reaches the courtroom—the "mansion"—and how very different it is in the police interrogation room—the "gatehouse." If the Fifth Amendment privilege limited the way defendants could be questioned in the courtroom, why not in the police interrogation room?

> The courtroom is a splendid place where defense attorneys bellow and strut and prosecuting attorneys are hemmed in at many turns. But what happens before an accused reaches the safety and enjoys the comfort of this veritable mansion? Ah, there's the rub. Typically he must first pass through a much less pretentious edifice, a police station with bare back rooms and locked doors.[106]

Ashcraft set the stage. *Spano* expanded the definition of illegal police interrogation. *Culombe, McNabb,* and *Escobedo* were, for different reasons, unworkable "solutions" to the puzzle of when police interrogation crossed the line between constitutional and unconstitutional. Now Kamisar had given the Court the doctrinal solution. Why not take *Escobedo*'s idea that counsel could assure voluntariness and give it a new doctrinal home? Forget the due process clause. Who knew what process is due suspects at the interrogation stage anyway? The Fifth Amendment provides that no person "shall be compelled in any criminal case to be a witness against himself."[107] If police interrogation was inherently coercive, as *Ashcraft* claimed, why wouldn't the Fifth Amendment give suspects the right not to answer any question and the right to consult with counsel before deciding whether to answer?

If all of that is right, then it remained only to operationalize the principle by requiring the police to warn the suspect that he need not answer questions and, to protect his right to choose, to tell him that he can have a lawyer advise him during interrogation. Indeed, the Court had already laid the groundwork for this radical departure from a totality of the circumstances test. In *Haley v. Ohio*, in 1948, Justice Douglas's plurality opinion emphasized the need of the fifteen-year-old suspect for "counsel and support if he is not to become the victim first of fear, then of panic."[108] A young suspect "needs someone on whom to lean lest the overpowering presence of the law, as he knows it, may not crush him." He had no friend to stand at his side "as the police, working in relays, questioned him hour after hour, from midnight until dawn. No lawyer stood guard to make sure that the police went so far and no farther, to see to it that they stopped short of the point where he became the victim of coercion."

Justice Frankfurter provided the critical fifth vote to reverse Haley's conviction. While he did not join Douglas's opinion, his separate opinion even more clearly signals where the Court would turn eighteen years later in *Miranda*. The key to the case, for Frankfurter, was that

> [d]uring the course of the interrogation the boy was not advised that he was not obliged to talk, that it was his right if he chose to say not a word, nor that he was entitled to have the benefit of counsel or the help of his family. Bearing upon the safeguards of these rights, the Chief of Police admitted that while he knew that the boy "had a right to remain mute and not answer any questions" he did not know that it was the duty of the police to apprise him of that fact.[109]

In *Gallegos v. Colorado*, decided only four years before *Miranda*, the Court expanded the *Haley* notion of counsel and support.[110] The Court had begun to talk about whether suspects are the equal of their police interrogators:

[A] 14-year-old boy, no matter how sophisticated, is unlikely to have any conception of what will confront him when he is made accessible only to the police. That is to say, we deal with a person who is not equal to the police in knowledge and understanding of the consequences of the questions and answers being recorded and who is unable to know how to protest his own interests or how to get the benefits of his constitutional rights.[111]

To be sure, Gallegos was only fourteen years old. But all that remained after *Gallegos* was to find a basis to conclude that adult suspects were not much better off than juveniles, and then we would have all the ingredients for the *Miranda* stew. We would have *Escobedo* without the embarrassing textual problem that the Sixth Amendment created. Moreover, if the right to counsel is conceptualized as a mechanism to protect the right not to answer questions, *it can be waived.* The expected political costs of creating a waivable right to counsel were not as high as for the ACLU position or for a flat ban on interrogation. Now we have what turns out to be a consummate compromise—*Miranda v. Arizona.*[112]

B. *Miranda* Changes the World of Interrogation

Lacking real-world data, the *Miranda* Court drew its description of police interrogation strategies from the Inbau-Reid manual first published in 1942 and still in print.[113] The Inbau-Reid manual treats police as the "good guys" trying to get the truth from unwilling suspects, but the *Miranda* Court turned the tables and treated police as the deviant player in the interrogation room. Sullen, unwilling suspects in the Inbau-Reid manual become vulnerable, frightened lost souls who are too easily tricked or bullied. It is a remarkable change from *Lisenba*, Wigmore, and hundreds of state cases from the early part of the twentieth century. Forget Lisenba, whose wife's murder the Court described in grisly detail. Now we have the police as the deviant actor, unfairly trading on the weaknesses of suspects. Justice John Marshall Harlan II accused the Court of painting a "generally black picture of police conduct"[114] and of "portray[ing] the evils of normal police questioning in terms which I think are exaggerated."[115]

A threshold goal of the interrogator is to be alone with the subject "to prevent distraction and to deprive him of any outside support."[116] The interrogator's "confidence in his guilt undermines his will to resist." In the hands of a skilled interrogator, the subject "merely confirms the preconceived story the police seek to have him describe. Patience and persistence, at times relentless questioning, are employed." The subject, described in Inbau-Reid as the "quarry" of the interrogator, must be "manuever[ed] . . . into a position from which the desired objective may be attained." If necessary, "the police may resort to deceptive stratagems such as giving false legal advice. It is important to keep the subject off balance, for example, by trading on his insecurity about himself or his surroundings. The police then persuade, trick, or cajole him out of exercising his constitutional rights."

Modern police interrogation, the Court tells us, is "psychologically rather than physically oriented."[117]

> To highlight the isolation and unfamiliar surroundings, the manuals instruct the police to display an air of confidence in the suspect's guilt and from outward appearance to maintain only an interest in confirming certain details. The guilt of the subject is to be posited as a fact. The interrogator should direct his comments toward the reasons why the subject committed the act, rather than court failure by asking the subject whether he did it. Like other men, perhaps the subject has had a bad family life, had an unhappy childhood, had too much to drink, had an unrequited desire for women. The officers are instructed to minimize the moral seriousness of the offense, to cast blame on the victim or on society. These tactics are designed to put the subject in a psychological state where his story is but an elaboration of what the police purport to know already—that he is guilty. Explanations to the contrary are dismissed and discouraged.[118]

The interrogator "must rely on an oppressive atmosphere of dogged persistence. He must interrogate steadily and without relent, leaving the subject no prospect of surcease. He must dominate his subject and overwhelm him with his inexorable will to obtain the truth."[119] To solve a serious crime, the officer should be prepared to interrogate "for days, with the required intervals for food and sleep . . . to avoid a charge of duress that can be technically substantiated," but "with no respite from the atmosphere of domination."

Custodial interrogation, the Court concluded, thus "exacts a heavy toll on individual liberty and trades on the weakness of individuals."[120] The critical fact about custodial interrogation is that its purpose is

> to subjugate the individual to the will of his examiner. This atmosphere carries its own badge of intimidation. To be sure, this is not physical intimidation, but it is equally destructive of human dignity. The current practice of incommunicado interrogation is at odds with one of our Nation's most cherished principles—that the individual may not be compelled to incriminate himself. Unless adequate protective devices are employed to dispel the compulsion inherent in custodial surroundings,

no statement obtained from the defendant can truly be the product of his free choice.[121]

To help combat the inherently compelling atmosphere of custodial police interrogation, the Court gave Escobedo's right to counsel a new "home" in the Fifth Amendment. Counsel will "assure that the individual's right to choose between silence and speech remains unfettered throughout the interrogation process. A once-stated warning, delivered by those who will conduct the interrogation, cannot itself suffice to that end among those who most require knowledge of their rights."[122] Thus, the Court concluded: "the need for counsel to protect the Fifth Amendment privilege comprehends not merely a right to consult with counsel prior to questioning, but also to have counsel present during any questioning if the defendant so desires."[123]

The recharacterization of police interrogation, that began in *Chambers* and *Ashcraft*, is now complete. Suspects must be encouraged to make "free choices," and police attempts to undermine those free choices are seen as, at best, unfortunate and, at worst, deviant. The bare back-rooms of the third degree are to be replaced with orderly interrogation and a lawyer at the side of the accused to advise whether and when to answer police questions, and to defeat police strategies designed to force him to forsake his "free and rational choice."[124] The *Miranda* dissents, naturally, objected to the majority's characterization of police interrogation. Justice Harlan, for example, wrote: "Society has always paid a stiff price for law and order, and peaceful interrogation is not one of the dark moments of the law."[125]

It seems unlikely that, when he sat down to write the majority opinion in *Miranda*, Chief Justice Earl Warren anticipated the intensity of the reaction that greeted the decision. But he had been a California prosecutor, attorney general, and governor, and he was probably not surprised by the forceful opposition from the four dissenters.[126] Justice Frankfurter was no longer on the Court, but his role as defender of the "overbear the will test" was filled by Justices Harlan, Clark, Stewart, and White. During the Court's conference on *Miranda*, Justice Harlan said that Warren's approach would "repudiate all of our precedents and history."[127] Justices Stewart and White noted that compulsion means coercion, which "is not present here."[128]

Facing this kind of criticism, Warren strove mightily to make the holding appear connected with the past and the present. He drew on the law in Ceylon, India, England, and Scotland to show that *Miranda* was not out of step with the world.[129] We hazard a guess that *Miranda* is the only time the Court has relied on the law in Ceylon, now Sri Lanka. Justice Harlan's dissent blew pretty big holes in the majority's reliance on foreign law, showing how the relevant institutions in those countries differed greatly from those in the United States.[130]

Warren relied on *Bram v. United States* to show that *Miranda* was not out of step with the past.[131] *Bram* held that the admissibility of confessions in federal court was determined by the Fifth Amendment privilege against compelled self-incrimination, the same doctrinal move underlying *Miranda*. As Justice Harlan noted, however, *Bram* was the only case standing for that proposition; all of the Court's other confession cases were based on due process or common law, both of which made voluntariness the touchstone.[132] Moreover, *Bram* by implication had rejected the *Miranda* solution. If lack of warnings was sufficient to make the confession inadmissible, there would have been no need to consider, as *Bram* did rather at length, the facts of the questioning before concluding that the answer was involuntary. More significant, one year before *Bram*, the Court in *Wilson v. United States* squarely held that the lack of warnings did not render a confession inadmissible,[133] and *Bram* cited and quoted from *Wilson* with approval.[134] Thus, except for *Bram*'s reliance on the Fifth Amendment as an analytical structure, it supported the *Miranda* dissents rather than the majority. The Court never admitted that *Wilson* had rejected its holding and never attempted to square *Miranda* with eighty years of precedent. Citing *Wilson* and a later case, however, Justice Harlan pointed out in dissent that "the right to warnings [had] been explicitly rebuffed in this Court many years ago."[135]

Another attempt to connect with the past was Warren's recitation of the seventeenth-century Star Chamber controversy involving the "Levellers," a group that included the brave John Lilburn. Here is Warren's version:

> We sometimes forget how long it has taken to establish the privilege against self-incrimination, the sources from which it came and the fervor with which it was defended. Its roots go back into ancient times. Perhaps the critical historical event shedding light on its origins and evolution was the trial of one John Lilburn, a vocal anti-Stuart Leveller, who was made to take the Star Chamber Oath in 1637. The oath would have bound him to answer to all questions posed to him on any subject. The Trial of John Lilburn and John Wharton, 3 How. St. Tr. 1315 (1637). He resisted the oath and declaimed the proceedings, stating:
>
> "Another fundamental right I then contended for, was, that no man's conscience ought to be racked by oaths imposed, to answer to questions concerning himself in matters criminal, or pretended to be so."
>
> On account of the Lilburn Trial, Parliament abolished the inquisitorial Court of Star Chamber.... We cannot depart from this noble heritage.[136]

The difficulty with the Lilburn history is that it had nothing, nothing at all, to do with interrogations in criminal cases. The Lilburn controversy was over the power of the Star Chamber to compel an oath to answer questions, usually in cases against political opponents of the monarch. The Star Chamber, however, was not a common law court that tried criminal cases. Created by the monarchs in the fourteenth century, the Star Chamber had more power than common law courts, which lacked the authority even to compel a defendant to testify at trial.

As we saw in chapter 3, the common law of confessions during the Lilburn period admitted out-of-court confessions made by the accused *without exception* and without concern about compulsion or voluntariness.[137] The earliest common law skepticism about involuntary confessions came a half-century after the Lilburn-Star Chamber controversy. Thus, the Court's lofty rhetoric about Lilburn is not only beside the point but actually proves the thesis of the dissenters (though they too seemed unaware of the relevant history). With the solitary exception of *Bram,* the privilege against compelled self-incrimination had for three centuries been completely separate from the law of confessions.[138] Lilburn's case had consequences, of course—it led Parliament to abolish the Star Chamber—but its connection to the common law of voluntariness is, in our view, nonexistent.

It is surprising that the *Miranda* Court did not follow the historical trail that *Bram* partly illuminated in its detailed examination of eighteenth and nineteenth century confessions cases. After all, the Court could not rely on *Bram*'s holding, which implicitly rejected *Miranda*'s holding, and the Court had to ignore *Wilson,* which explicitly rejected a warnings requirement. But, as we saw in chapters 3 and 4, the historical trail leads to a pretty remarkable world that connects with *Miranda* much more securely than the authorities that the Court provided. The *Miranda* Court ignored the English Indictable Offenses Act of 1848 that required magistrates to warn the accused before questioning him.[139] That act would have supported a claim that the default position in Anglo-American law for over a century was the very procedure that *Miranda* required. The outlier or deviation, the argument goes, was the period from roughly 1880–1960 when police were sometimes willing to do almost anything to get a confession. That period could have been dismissed as a product of police desperation when faced with organized crime, Prohibition, the Great Depression, and rising crime rates.

C. Reactions to *Miranda*

Anyone who has watched police shows on television—for example, the apparently endless iterations of *Law and Order*—has heard the *Miranda* warnings so many times that the words "you have a right to remain silent" probably sound as inevitable and morally neutral as gravity or the sun rising in the east. But *Miranda* caused intense controversy. In 1966, the FBI index crime rate was in the midst of a decades-long sharp ascent.[140] The 1965 riots in Watts and the harsh response unnerved the nation. Riots erupted in Newark in 1967 and would consume many American cities after Martin Luther King, Jr. was murdered in Memphis in April 1968. The Vietnam War was increasingly killing and wounding our young men, and the draft was intensely unpopular. Hippies, marijuana, LSD, the Beatles, and the Rolling Stones were disruptive influences on American youth. The American public was resentful and in a sour mood.

If the Court thought it would appease critics by permitting waiver of the newly created rights to silence and to counsel, it was mistaken; the initial tidal wave of criticism assumed that few suspects would waive, and the political costs turned out to be very high indeed. The *Miranda* dissents foreshadowed the firestorm that would greet *Miranda*. Concluding that the Court "goes too far on too little," Justice Tom Clark rose to defend the police from the majority's attack:

> Nor can I join in the Court's criticism of the present practices of police and investigatory agencies as to custodial interrogation. The materials it refers to as "police manuals" are, as I read them, merely writings in this field by professors and some police officers. Not one is shown by the record here to be the official manual of any police department, much less in universal use in crime detection. Moreover, the examples of police brutality mentioned by the Court are rare exceptions to the thousands of cases that appear every year in the law reports. The police agencies—all the way from municipal and state forces to the federal bureaus—are responsible for law enforcement and public safety in this country. I am proud of their efforts, which in my view are not fairly characterized by the Court's opinion.[141]

Even the patrician Justice Harlan could not resist a claim that *Miranda* portended grave harm: "I believe the decision of the Court represents poor constitutional law and entails harmful consequences for the country at large."[142] But the most hostile criticism was in Justice White's dessent:

> In some unknown number of cases the Court's rule will return a killer, a rapist or other criminal to the streets and to the environment which produced him, to repeat his crime whenever it pleases him. As a consequence, there will not be a gain, but a loss, in human dignity. The real concern is not the unfortunate consequences of this new decision on the criminal law as an abstract, disembodied series of authoritative proscriptions, but the impact on those who rely on the public authority

for protection and who without it can only engage in violent self-help with guns, knives and the help of their neighbors similarly inclined. There is, of course, a saving factor: the next victims are uncertain, unnamed and unrepresented in this case.[143]

In sum, in the fall of 1966, the police felt outgunned and abandoned by the Supreme Court. When *Miranda* was announced, "In every part of the country and in all ranks, police complained bitterly at what they considered this heaviest of reprimands from the Supreme Court so far."[144] Police chiefs in Boston, Philadelphia, Cleveland, and Los Angeles condemned *Miranda* as a shield for the guilty, and the police chief of Los Angeles went so far as to predict that *Miranda* "would effectively end the use of confessions in convicting criminals."[145]

Congress sought political gain by attacking *Miranda* while debating the Omnibus Crime Control and Safe Streets Act of 1968. Arkansas Senator John McClellan said that "if this effort to deal with these erroneous Court decisions is defeated, every gangster and overlord of the underworld; every syndicate chief, racketeer, captain, lieutenant, sergeant, private, punk, and hoodlum in organized crime; every murderer, rapist, robber, burglar, arsonist, thief, and conman will have cause to rejoice and celebrate."[146] President Johnson signed the act into law, requiring federal judges to admit "voluntarily given" confessions.

Both Republican Richard Nixon and Independent George Wallace sought to use the Warren Court as a campaign issue in 1968 against Democrat Hubert Humphrey. Wallace said that the Supreme Court was a "sorry, lousy, no-account outfit."[147] Murderers and rapists are "just laughin'" while the police are crying for help." If a criminal "knocks you over the head," he will be "out of jail before you're out of the hospital and the policeman who arrested him will be on trial. . . . But some psychologist says, 'well he's not to blame, society's to blame. His father didn't take him to see the Pittsburgh Pirates when he was a little boy.'"[148] Wallace "promise[d] his audience, wildly cheering by now: 'If we were President today . . . you wouldn't get stabbed or raped in the shadow of the White House, even if we had to call out 30,000 troops and equip them with two-foot-long bayonets and station them every few feet apart.'"[149]

Richard Nixon's strategy was to "appear as a 'more respectable alternative'" to Wallace, "countering his rhetoric 'with a velvet-glove version of the mailed fist.'"[150] Although there were many contentious issues in the 1968 campaign (Vietnam, welfare, inflation, taxes, President Johnson's War on Poverty, Social Security), "the issue that stood out, its theme in every speech at every airport and on every makeshift stage, the one that was remembered most vividly years later, was [Nixon's] appeal for 'law and order.'" Focusing specifically on *Miranda*, Nixon said in Ohio two weeks before the election:

I was in Philadelphia the other day. I found that a cab driver who had been cruelly murdered and robbed, and the man who murdered and robbed him had confessed the crime, was set free because of a Supreme Court decision. An old woman, who had been brutally robbed and then murdered—the man who confessed the crime was set free because of a Supreme Court decision. . . . And an old man who had been robbed and clubbed to death—and the man who confessed the crime was set free in Las Vegas because of a Supreme Court decision. My friends, when that's happening in thousands of cases all over America, I say this. Some of our courts have gone too far in their decisions weakening the peace forces as against the criminal forces in the United States of America. And we're going to change that.[151]

Just as telling as the attacks on the Court by Wallace and Nixon was Hubert Humphrey's failure to defend the Court. Only one position was presented to the American voter in 1968: The Court had gone too far in the direction of protecting criminals; the criminal forces were gaining the upper hand over the peace forces; something had to be done to right the ship. As Fred Graham put it:

Where its predecessors had been bold, *Miranda* was to be brazen— *Gideon v. Wainwright*[152] had created a constitutional right to counsel in felony cases at a time when all but five states already provided it; *Mapp v. Ohio*[153] had extended the exclusionary rule to illegal searches after roughly one-half of the states had adopted the same rule; *Miranda* was to impose limits on police interrogation that no state had even approached prior to the *Escobedo* decision.[154]

Nixon carried Ohio by 90,000 votes and defeated Humphrey at the national level by only 500,000 votes.[155] It seems likely that the "law and order" attack on *Miranda* was part of the reason for Nixon's victory.

Why deviance shifted from suspected rapists, robbers, and murderers to the police for the *Miranda* majority is not entirely clear. Gerald Caplan noted that *Escobedo* "shows sympathy for Danny Escobedo because he was the underdog. One detects what Thurman Arnold referred to as 'the humanitarian notion that the underdog is always entitled to a chance.'"[156] Caplan continued:

Perhaps the impulse to allow even the unquestionably guilty some prospect of escaping detection or conviction is universal. Wigmore referred to this impulse as the "instinct of giving the game fair play." Pound characterized it as "the sporting theory" of justice, and Bentham derisively labeled it "the fox hunter's reason." Under this view, fairness is given that special definition that sportsmen reserve for their games. Bentham elaborated on his analogy to the fox hunt: "The fox is to have a fair chance for his life: he must have . . . leave to run a certain length of way, for the express purpose of giving him a chance for escape." Fairness, so defined, dictates that neither side should have an undue advantage; the police and the criminal should be on roughly equal footing and the rules of the game should be drawn to avoid favoring one side or the other. . . . The state was sovereign, but so was the individual. The individual possessed the "sovereign right . . . to meet the state on terms as equal as their respective strength would permit . . . strength against strength, resource against resource, argument against argument."[157]

Caplan is correct that the Court's attitude toward police and suspects had changed dramatically by the time we get to *Escobedo* and *Miranda*. He offers two theories for the radical change, both limited to the 1960s. First, "*Miranda* seems most understandable as an exaggerated response to the times rather than as an enunciation of a natural right mined at last from the Constitution. *Miranda* was a child of the racially troubled 1960's and our tragic legacy of slavery."[158] A related point was the 1960s understanding of the causes of crime:

[I]t was popular to see the criminal as a type of victim; he was caught in the role assigned to persons in his circumstances, a member of the underclass. One spoke not of volition but of status or condition. The idea of individual guilt and remorse for wrongful deeds was out of fashion. The causal factors of criminality were thought to lie outside the individual, in the deeper, corrupt foundations of the society—the so-called 'root causes.'[159]

Accurate as far as it goes, Caplan's account ignores the historic relationship between the law of interrogation and larger cultural forces that define deviance and shape the legal reaction to perceived threats to social order. Far from evolving in a more or less straight line to the shining hill of *Miranda*, the history of law regulating interrogation is contingent and always in flux. Indeed, Anglo-American law since the seventeenth century has shifted dramatically about once a century. If we narrow the historical focus to the last two centuries, the claim is that, once the storm of the early twentieth century had passed, *Miranda* merely reconnected with the Hawkins-Leach dictum that ruled the confessions world for over a century.

To be sure, the reconnection is largely a matter of rhetoric. In chapter 8, we will consider how *Miranda* evolved into the doctrine that Chief Justice Rehnquist was able to embrace (if somewhat tepidly) for seven members of the Court in 2000. In chapter 9, we address whether *Miranda* succeeded, which requires us to

"Are You All Right?"

Figure 7.1 Copyright, The Commercial Appeal, 1966

identify what the Court's goals probably were. We will conclude that *Miranda* fails in some fundamental ways, that it was largely rhetoric from the beginning, and that the parsimonious application of *Miranda* by later Courts made it emptier still of substantive content. Rhetoric is important, as it affirms our values, but *Miranda* on the ground appears to offer far less protection than the Hawkins-Leach dictum did in the late eighteenth and early nineteenth centuries. Our ultimate conclusion, reached in chapter 9, is that courts view the current law of interrogation as the best of both worlds. American law affirms our commitment to fair play and level playing fields by giving suspects the key to the interrogation room, but when they hand the key back and incriminate themselves, courts are eager to receive those confessions.

CHAPTER 8

Miranda Changes the Confessions World

At ten A.M. on June 13, 1966, Washington, D.C. was experiencing cool weather: It was only 68 degrees. [1] But inside the Supreme Court building, emotions ran hot as Chief Justice Warren read his entire sixty-one-page opinion for the five-justice majority in *Miranda v. Arizona*. "At times the emotion in his voice equaled that of the dissenters and bespoke the deep division in the Court over the new doctrine."[2] The dissenters read their opinions, too. "Justice Harlan, his face flushed and his voice occasionally faltering with emotion, denounced the decision as 'dangerous experimentation' at a time of a 'high crime rate that is a matter of growing concern.'"

Our goal in this chapter is to describe the evolution of the *Miranda* doctrine from its beginning on that cool June day in 1966. One way to conceptualize this evolution is to focus on *Miranda*'s rhetorical embrace of the Hawkins-Leach dictum. Indeed, *Miranda* is mostly rhetoric—its narrow holding is that the defendants in the four cases before the Court had been compelled to answer questions by the inherent coercion of police interrogation. But, as we will see, different fact patterns would arise, and it was easy for less sympathetic Courts to modify *Miranda*'s analytical structure pretty much as they pleased. The journey here, which should be familiar by now, begins with *Miranda*'s view that suspects will be "deluded instruments of their own conviction" unless they receive warnings from the authorities and make a robust choice to waive those rights. Over the decades, however, the Court gradually modified the Hawkins-Leach view of suspects by assuming that the warnings solved any problem of inherent compulsion. Waiver is now almost automatic.

Upon reflection, one should not be surprised that the Court narrowed *Miranda*'s doctrine from what its expansive dicta suggested to what it is today. As Donald Dripps explained, the Court needed a "wide" rule that would apply to almost all interrogations because its previous attempts to offer guidance on a case-by-case basis had largely failed.[3] A wide rule requires a fully theorized opinion with a deep justification. But deep justifications tend to be "intensely controversial. Rarely will a deep justification persuade a majority, and over time deep justifications that do win majority support are likely to lose it."[4] Sometimes the loss of majority support leads to a wide rule being overruled.[5] Sometimes, the wide rule continues to be accepted, but majorities for future applications are put together on a case-by-case basis and the application of the rule begins to look arbitrary.[6]

Craig Bradley has made a similar argument, concluding that the "major ideological" shift entailed by *Miranda* required a "full-blown" opinion that, over time, was "reinterpreted" and "restated" until the later decisions served not to explain but to obfuscate the original robust doctrine.[7] "This is an inevitable process, only partly explained by the fact that a subsequent Court may not like the earlier decision." Obfuscation, inconsistency, and arbitrariness are good descriptions of the current *Miranda* doctrine. The Court has never offered much of an explanation for reshaping and restating the *Miranda* doctrine.

A. *Miranda*'s Search for a Deep Justification

We begin with two examples of rights that have deep justifications. The right to a jury trial comes with a built-in deep justification because the Sixth Amendment text can be interpreted only one way: Defendants have the right to an impartial jury "in all criminal prosecutions."[8] While there have been disputes at the margin—what counts as "impartial" and how many jurors constitute a "jury"[9]—there has never been a challenge to the idea that a criminal defendant has a right to be tried by a jury.

The Sixth Amendment right to counsel offers a more complex example. The right "to have the Assistance of Counsel for his defence"[10] means, at a minimum, that the State cannot forbid a defendant from having a lawyer argue his or her case. English law at the framing did not permit a lawyer to argue cases for felony defendants;[11] the Framers' intent to establish a different regime in the United States could not be clearer. The right of defendants to appear through counsel thus has a deep justification going back to the Framers. The only issues to arise in modern times have been at the margin. Did a judge deny the right to counsel when he forbade the defendant from consulting with his lawyer during an overnight recess? Did a judge deny the right to counsel when he refused to allow a defendant to waive a conflict of interest that the lawyer would have if he represented the defendant? (The answer to these fact-sensitive questions was, respectively, "yes" and "no."[12])

There is another dimension of the right to counsel—the positive right of indigent defendants to demand that the State provide counsel. That right almost certainly does not trace its roots to the Framers. The best historical evidence indicates that the only purpose of the Sixth Amendment right to counsel was to avoid the common law rule that lawyers could not appear for felony defendants in court.[13] But the positive right to demand counsel acquired a deep justification in 1963 in the unanimous decision in *Gideon v. Wainwright*:

> [R]eason and reflection require us to recognize that in our adversary system of criminal justice, any person haled into court, who is too poor to hire a lawyer, cannot be assured a fair trial unless counsel is provided for him. This seems to us to be an obvious truth. . . . That government hires lawyers to prosecute and defendants who have the money hire lawyers to defend are the strongest indications of the widespread belief that lawyers in criminal courts are necessities, not luxuries. . . . From the very beginning, our state and national constitutions and laws have laid great emphasis on procedural and substantive safeguards designed to assure fair trials before impartial tribunals in which every defendant stands equal before the law. This noble ideal cannot be realized if the poor man charged with crime has to face his accusers without a lawyer to assist him.[14]

In 1963, one could comfortably imagine a world in which a suspect faced police interrogators without counsel and without being told of the right to remain silent. Indeed, aside from FBI interrogations, that *was* the world in which we lived.[15] One could not, however, comfortably imagine a world in which a felony defendant had to oppose a prosecutor in a courtroom. Nothing about that picture fit the 1963 image of how an adversarial justice system should function. By 1963, all but five states in the Union required appointed counsel in indigent felony cases[16]—evidence that *Gideon* tapped into a deep justification. When the Court faced the counsel issue, there were no dissents from the lofty rhetoric just quoted.

When the Court faced the interrogation issue, it attempted lofty rhetoric but delivered the new rule by a 5–4 majority over anguished dissents and without any support in state law. Unlike *Gideon*, the *Miranda* opinion offers no single deep justification. Instead, the Court employed a scattershot approach. Part I of *Miranda* attempts to show, by reference to police interrogation manuals, that police routinely take advantage of suspects by tricking, cajoling, and pressuring them into answering questions. Then in Part II, the Court seeks the kind of lofty rhetoric it achieved three years earlier in *Gideon*, by abstracting from the privilege against self-incrimination a general limit on government power:

> Thus we may view the historical development of the privilege as one which groped for the proper scope of governmental power over the citizen. As a "noble principle often transcends its origins," the privilege has come rightfully to be recognized in part as an individual's substantive

right, a "right to a private enclave where he may lead a private life. That right is the hallmark of our democracy."[17]

To the *Miranda* majority, the "private enclave" created by the privilege protects the dignitary and autonomy interests that Americans have against the government when it investigates crime:

> All these policies point to one overriding thought: the constitutional foundation underlying the privilege is the respect a government—state or federal—must accord to the dignity and integrity of its citizens. To maintain a "fair state-individual balance," to require the government "to shoulder the entire load," to respect the inviolability of the human personality, our accusatory system of criminal justice demands that the government seeking to punish an individual produce the evidence against him by its own independent labors, rather than by the cruel, simple expedient of compelling it from his own mouth.[18]

However successful one finds this rhetorical flourish, the *Miranda* Court's final analytical move is much less powerful than *Gideon's*. The *Gideon* Court moved from the rhetorical summit of a defenseless man facing his accusers and a legally trained prosecutor, to a remedy befitting the rhetoric. All defendants charged with a felony must be provided counsel. Period.

But *Miranda's* remedy did not fit its deep justification or even its rationale. After using the police interrogation manuals to "prove" that custodial interrogation is inherently coercive, and thus inimical to the values of autonomy and free choice that the Court found in the Fifth Amendment privilege, the Court concluded that "the right to have counsel present at the interrogation is indispensable to the protection of the Fifth Amendment privilege under the system we delineate today."[19] The Court goes on for pages about how the presence of counsel will protect the values it found inherent in the privilege, thus establishing the right of indigent suspects to have counsel appointed free of charge.

So far, so good. But after this sound and fury about counsel in the interrogation room, the Court quietly *gives it all away*: "An express statement that the individual is willing to make a statement and does not want an attorney followed closely by a statement could constitute a waiver."[20] *Miranda* in effect creates a procedural minefield for police and then politely provides a map of where the mines are buried. In Dripps's words, "The *Miranda* Court's waiver doctrine is plainly at odds with the rest of the opinion."[21] Rights supported by deep justifications, like the right to a jury trial and the right to counsel at trial, cannot be so easily waived. Making a deep justification for *Miranda* even less likely, the Court admitted that the procedural minefield is not even required by the Fifth Amendment privilege. In a famous paragraph that expressly disavows any attempt at a deep justification, the Court left open the possibility that its minefield is only a placeholder for a better solution:

> It is impossible for us to foresee the potential alternatives for protecting the privilege which might be devised by Congress or the States in the exercise of their creative rule-making capacities. Therefore we cannot say that the Constitution necessarily requires adherence to any particular solution for the inherent compulsions of the interrogation process as it is presently conducted. Our decision in no way creates a constitutional straitjacket which will handicap sound efforts at reform, nor is it intended to have this effect. We encourage Congress and the States to continue their laudable search for increasingly effective ways of protecting the rights of the individual while promoting efficient enforcement of our criminal laws.[22]

But a procedural mechanism that is merely a placeholder for a legislature solution, by definition, lacks the kind of deep justification that undergirds *Gideon* or the right to trial by jury.

A major difficulty with *Miranda*'s attempt to use the Fifth Amendment privilege as a deep justification for requiring warnings and waiver is that police questioning looks very different from the other contexts in which the privilege applies. A witness summoned before a grand jury or a congressional committee has days or weeks of notice and time to plan a strategy about testifying. If a witness refuses to answer, the government can overcome that resistance with an offer of use immunity, which protects the witness from having her testimony used in a criminal case against her.[23] If the witness still refuses to answer—as Susan McDougal did when questioned about Bill and Hillary Clinton's Whitewater real estate deal—she can be imprisoned for contempt.[24]

Little about police interrogation looks like what we just described. Suspects typically have no notice that they will face police interrogation and thus no time to prepare for the questioning. Police have no formal authority to compel answers; they cannot ask a court to find a suspect in contempt. And police cannot overcome an assertion of the privilege with an offer of use immunity. A consequence of the lack of police authority to compel answers is that suspects have the power to resist the interrogator. They can say nothing and pay no formal price. There is no reason, then, to disagree with the Court in *Bram* and *Miranda* that suspects have what amounts to a privilege not to answer police questions. But when the Court sought to formalize the exercise of the privilege in the alien landscape of the police interrogation room, it risked major discontinuities. And it got them—delivered by the hands of future Courts unfriendly to *Miranda*, to be sure, but in the views of Bradley and Dripps inevitable in any event.[25]

Even at the time it was handed down, *Miranda* was not the great victory that it might seem on first reading. It was less than *Escobedo v. Illinois*[26] seemed to promise, and certainly less than the ACLU requested in its amicus brief. *Escobedo* found a Sixth Amendment counsel violation in the police interrogation on somewhat unusual facts: Escobedo had already retained a lawyer and repeatedly asked to talk to his lawyer who was, during the three-hour interrogation, trying to see his client. The Court said that "[t]he 'guiding hand of counsel' was essential" because police interrogation interrogation "was the 'stage when legal aid and advice' were most critical."[27] If *Escobedo* were extended to typical police interrogation, as the ACLU requested, then police would either have to provide a lawyer during routine interrogations or show a *Johnson v. Zerbst* knowing and intelligent waiver of counsel.

Given the promise of *Escobedo*, Corinna Barrett Lain concludes that *Miranda* "was a comparatively weak decision," one that does not deserve the claim that it was robustly counter-majoritarian.[28] Seidman claims that *Miranda* is "best characterized as a retreat from the promise of liberal individualism brilliantly camouflaged under the cover of bold advance."[29] To Seidman, what *Miranda* added to the right to counsel cases and the robust form of the voluntariness principle "was a mechanism by which the defendant could give up these rights." Laurence Benner agrees: "The *Miranda* retreat therefore transformed the debate about self-incrimination into a debate about waiver."[30] In a similar vein, Lain comments that "the Court's ruling did nothing whatsoever to prevent the coercion police used to make suspects talk from translating to the waiver context."[31] If this is the best way to view *Miranda*, it was not, as we argued in chapter 7, a compromise. It was a full-out retreat.

Whether *Miranda* was a compromise or a brilliant retreat under cover of an attack, we agree with Bradley and Dripps that it was unstable from the beginning. Given the lack of a deep justification and given the Court's refusal to tie the warnings and waiver regime tightly to the Fifth Amendment privilege, it was inevitable that the path of future decisions would be to ease the admission of incriminating statements. For example, it remained for later, more conservative Courts to determine how easy it was going to be to prove waiver. And, as we will see, waiver became very easy to prove. The expansive dicta in *Miranda* requiring an express waiver of the right to counsel became, well, dicta to be discarded.

Miranda's lack of a deep justification showed up in other ways as well. Despite the Court's best efforts to ground the decision on a "fair state-individual balance," later Courts limited *Miranda* to its custodial interrogation context. Later Courts were not moved by arguments that coercive environments existed outside the custodial interrogation matrix. In *Rhode Island v. Innis*, for example, the state court had found that Innis was subjected to "subtle coercion" and thus was being interrogated in violation of *Miranda*.[32] The Court rejected the premise that "subtle coercion" was the equivalent of interrogation. Defendants must show that they are subject to custodial interrogation before *Miranda* applies, coercion or no coercion. In *Oregon v. Mathiason*, the Court, in a per curiam opinion, held that because Mathiason could not show that he was in custody, he could not show a *Miranda* violation even if he were subjected to coercive interrogation.[33] The foundation for the *Miranda* holding—that custodial interrogation was inherently coercive—was now being used as its ceiling.

In sum, the Court has not adequately explained the underlying theory of the *Miranda* doctrine. Indeed, *Miranda*'s protection is sometimes broader than that offered by the Fifth Amendment on which *Miranda* is based. The Court often expresses the breadth of the protection by saying that *Miranda* is prophylactic— a doctrine developed to protect the privilege by excluding some confessions that are not compelled.[34] Yet the protection is narrower as well. The Court has found greater protection in the "pristine" Fifth Amendment privilege than in *Miranda*'s prophylactic protection.[35] A violation of the "pristine" privilege sometimes has greater evidentiary consequences than a "mere" violation of *Miranda*.

We will offer alternative explanations of the Court's *Miranda* doctrine, each of which we believe is more satisfying than the Court's easy assumption that *Miranda* is just different from the Fifth Amendment privilege. But we wish to be clear: We offer the alternative explanations not to reject the Court's characterization of *Miranda* as different from the privilege. Rather, we simply want to dig deeper than the Court to explain why *Miranda* is broader, but shallower, than the privilege from which it sprang.

The explanations we offer are about *Miranda* and not the Fifth Amendment privilege. Our book is about interrogation law. What the Fifth Amendment contributes to interrogation law is *Miranda*. As the Court has observed, the protection against involuntary confessions that exists alongside *Miranda* has "retained a due process" focus even after the Court incorporated the privilege into the Fourteenth Amendment.[36] Thus, it is fair to say that, as far as the law of police interrogation in the United States is concerned, there is *Miranda* and there is the due process prohibition of involuntary confessions.

In chapter 7, we claimed that *Miranda* represented a return to the long-standing Anglo-American view that confessions should be viewed with a healthy dose of skepticism. By 1966, the stresses and strains that produced the third degree in American law had moderated. The Depression had ended, the Second World War was won, the 1950s were a calm decade, organized crime was no longer on the ascendancy, America had become the world-dominant military and economic power, and the Vietnam War had yet to drain our self-confidence. The Court felt free to implement a version of the Hawkins-Leach dictum.

Yet that claim does not foreclose the cynical view that *Miranda* was a full-scale retreat from the promise of the Court's right to counsel cases. Whatever else the *Miranda* Court might have intended, there is no gainsaying that the Court intended to ease the burden of judges in deciding confessions cases. The Court had known, at least since Justice Frankfurter failed to articulate a workable test in *Culombe v. Connecticut* in 1962, that the voluntariness test left both trial and appellate judges without much guidance.[37] As the *Miranda* doctrine developed, it eased the judicial burden without a significant effect on the confessions rate.[38] As we will see in more detail in the next chapter, rights were waived easily and often. The admission of confessions became soothingly routine. The political costs the Court paid for *Miranda* turned out to be excessive. Police and prosecutors should have been thanking the Court. We turn now to the issue of how *Miranda* operates on the ground.

B. Did *Miranda* Succeed?

The success or failure of *Miranda* turns on how its goal is defined. If the goal was to make it easier to show that suspects consented to the interrogation, and thus gave "voluntary" statements, then, yes, it succeeded admirably in the large sub-universe of cases—roughly 80%—where suspects waive their rights.[39] *Miranda* waivers created, in Seidman's words, "a world where we need no longer be concerned about official coercion because defendants have definitionally consented to their treatment. When things go wrong, then, it is hardly 'our' fault."[40]

If the goal is defined as avoiding or mitigating compulsion, one must ask whether the goal was to dispel compulsion from the *entire interrogation* or only to ensure that the suspect gives a non-compelled waiver of his right to remain silent. Most of the *Miranda* opinion suggests that the goal was to cleanse the entire interrogation of compulsion—as unrealistic as that sounds to modern ears. The Court said that the "privilege is fulfilled only when the person is guaranteed the right 'to remain silent unless he chooses to speak in the unfettered exercise of his own will.'"[41] Warnings were necessary, the Court wrote, because "[u]nless adequate protective devices are employed to dispel the compulsion inherent in custodial surroundings, no statement obtained from the defendant can truly be the product of his free choice."[42]

One would think that dispelling compulsion would reduce the rate at which suspects answer police questions. This assumes, of course, that suspects calibrate their interests the way that judges or academics predict. The rational course of action for a guilty suspect, who is told that he need not talk to police and that he can confer with a lawyer, is to ask for a lawyer and say nothing else. We will revisit the assumption that suspects engage in rational behavior later in the chapter, but for now we indulge it. The *Miranda* dissents predicted that suspects would take the rational course and refuse to talk to police. We saw Justice White's heated prose earlier. Justice Harlan concluded: "There can be little doubt that the Court's new code would markedly decrease the number of confessions."[43]

What counts as a marked decrease in the number of confessions is open to question. Indeed, the extent to which *Miranda* has reduced the confessions rate has been the subject of rather fierce debate,[44] but all agree that suspects waive their rights and speak to the police in roughly 80% of custodial interrogations. It should not surprise one that suspects often waive their rights. If the *Miranda* Court was correct that custodial interrogation is inherently compelling, the goal of a noncompelling *process* of interrogation was unattainable. It could be achieved only when the suspect invoked the right to counsel, and the interrogation proceeded with counsel at the suspect's side. Indeed, there are passages in the opinion that suggest the Court had this model in mind: "[T]he need for counsel to protect the Fifth Amendment privilege comprehends not merely a right to consult with counsel prior to questioning, but also to have counsel present during any questioning if the defendant so desires."[45]

But the Court drew back from the widest rules—requiring counsel or banning custodial interrogation—and compromised on a rule that permitted suspects to waive the right to silence and to counsel. However many suspects invoke their rights, some will not. For those suspects, in *Miranda*'s own words: "A once-stated warning, delivered by those who will conduct the interrogation, cannot itself suffice" to "assure that the individual's right to choose between silence and speech remains unfettered throughout the interrogation process."[46] The Court, in effect, conceded that when suspects waive, police coercion will taint the subsequent questioning.

Achieving a noncompelling interrogation process in all cases was thus doomed from the beginning once the *Miranda* Court chose to permit waiver. But it is possible to ensure that the *waiver decision* is not the product of compulsion. Later Courts have focused on this goal, and both Donald Dripps and Larry Rosenthal argue that it has been achieved. To Dripps, *Miranda* created a "special waiver rule applicable in the unique context of custodial interrogation."[47] He draws an analogy to how the privilege is exercised before a legislative committee or grand jury. Compared to witnesses who appear before those bodies, the "suspect in custody is under a different and more intense kind of pressure to speak rather than stand silent. He is given the *Miranda* warning to place him in a position to claim the privilege that is roughly equivalent to the position of the witness before the grand jury."[48] But "once the warning has been given, the traditional waiver rule is re-instated."[49] The suspect must invoke the *Miranda* rights to secure the protection of the Fifth Amendment privilege. Otherwise, he has waived the privilege.

Rosenthal's view is similar:

> The *Miranda* warnings ensure that the suspect knows that he need not
> participate in interrogation and is being asked to surrender that right.
> For purposes of the Fifth Amendment, no more is required to obtain a
> valid waiver, at least under the settled principles of waiver law that
> *Miranda* applied. As we have seen, a waiver is valid as long as a suspect
> intentionally relinquishes a known right, and the *Miranda* warnings
> ensure that a suspect knows that he has a right to remain silent and is
> facing a decision whether to relinquish his right when he is asked to
> waive. Thus, while *Miranda* does not eliminate the compulsion inherent
> in custodial interrogation, it instead produces a valid waiver of the right
> to be free from that compulsion.[50]

Dripps and Rosenthal are right that long-recognized principles of waiver focus
on the moment of waiver and not what comes next. So, for example, a defendant
waives the privilege in the courtroom by taking the witness stand, and the prosecutor is permitted to pursue a vigorous cross-examination that will cause enor-
mous pressure to answer. A reading of *Miranda* that focuses on non-compelled
waivers rather than non-compelled *responses* to police questions could explain
both the high waiver rate and the high rate of incriminating responses. The waiver
rate is high because the warnings succeed in momentarily dispelling the coercive
atmosphere of the police interrogation, which induces waivers. The rate of incriminating responses is high because the post-waiver interrogation atmosphere
remains coercive. Of course, it is also possible that the warnings do *not* dispel the
inherent coercion, even for a moment, and that all, or most, waivers are compelled. We will return to that possibility later in the chapter.

In a similar vein, George Thomas has argued that *Miranda* doctrine today
requires only notice of the right not to answer questions and the right to consult
with counsel.[51] Thomas identified two ways to understand *Miranda*'s connection
to the Constitution.[52] First, there might be a "strong force" connection to the
Fifth Amendment privilege. So understood, *Miranda* creates an irrebuttable presumption of compulsion if a confession is taken during custodial interrogation
without a valid waiver of the rights that *Miranda* found implicit in the privilege.
The obvious problem with this interpretation is that later Courts did not understand *Miranda* that way. For more than thirty years, the Court decided case after
case that separated *Miranda* from the strong-force connection to the Fifth
Amendment.

The second understanding, which Thomas calls the "weak force" connection,
is that *Miranda* creates a presumption of compulsion that can be rebutted.[53]
While this explains all of the Court's cases seeking to create separation between

Miranda and the Fifth Amendment privilege, what it lacks is an account of *when* or *why* the presumption should be rebutted. The Court has proceeded in an ad hoc basis without an overarching theory. Thomas's theory is that the Court has, since 1971, seen *Miranda's* function as providing suspects with sufficient notice of the right to remain silent and the right to counsel. This can best be viewed as the Court creating a due process notice requirement within the Fifth Amendment privilege. If a debtor who is behind in her payments must be given due process notice before her stereo can be seized,[54] the Fifth Amendment privilege must require due process notice before the State deprives a suspect of her right not to answer questions posed by state actors.

The debtor can, of course, waive her right to contest the seizure of her property by not showing up at the hearing.[55] The suspect in the police interrogation room can similarly waive *Miranda* by listening to the warnings and talking to the police. Waiver can be found even in a case, *North Carolina v. Butler*, where the suspect refuses to sign the waiver form and states, "I will talk to you but I am not signing any form."[56] While finding waiver there is entirely consistent with due process notice theory, it would diminish the Fifth Amendment privilege to compare what Butler did with deciding to take the witness stand and testify.

Also consistent with *Miranda*-as-notice is *Davis v. United States*.[57] The issue in *Davis* was the effect of a suspect's ambiguous reference to counsel. *Miranda* clearly stated its preference for defense counsel to help ameliorate the inherent compulsion of police interrogation: "If, however, [the suspect] indicates *in any manner* and at any stage of the process that he wishes to consult with an attorney before speaking there can be no questioning."[58] A later case, *Edwards v. Arizona*, made clear that police may not interrogate after a request for counsel unless the suspect reinitiates discussion about the investigation.[59] But what does it mean to "request counsel"? Did it include, as *Miranda* said, indicating "in any manner" that the suspect "wishes to consult with an attorney"?

On the facts of *Davis*, the suspect waived his *Miranda* rights both orally and in writing and answered questions for over an hour. At that point he said, "Maybe I should talk to a lawyer."[60] The Court split 5–4 on the question of whether the interrogators were constitutionally required to clarify what the suspect meant. The majority of five held that an ambiguous "request" for counsel was not an invocation of counsel and, more important, that it created no duty on the part of the interrogators to ask clarifying questions.[61] The majority did not refer to the "in any manner" language from *Miranda* and thus did not have to explain how its holding squared with *Miranda's* intent.

Justice Souter, concurring in the judgment, did quote the "in any manner" language as well as *Miranda's* language that its goal was "to assure that *the individual's right to choose* between speech and silence remains unfettered throughout the interrogation process."[62] This, of course, assumes that *Miranda* intended that the response to police questions, as well as waiver, be non-compelled. The majority's response to Souter is instructive: "[T]he primary protection afforded suspects subject to custodial interrogation is the *Miranda* warnings themselves."[63] The key point in time has become, as Dripps, Rosenthal, and Thomas have argued, the moment of giving the warnings and obtaining a waiver.

To be sure, the *Davis* Court then said that "full comprehension of the rights to remain silent and request an attorney [is] sufficient to dispel whatever coercion is inherent in the interrogation process."[64] But this nod toward *Miranda* as ameliorating inherent coercion throughout the process is difficult to square with the *Davis* rule that police need not even repeat the warnings when a suspect appears to be stumbling toward a request for a lawyer. If one looks at what the Court did in *Davis*, it fits with the idea that waiver is easily proved because the critical part of *Miranda*'s protection is the content of the warnings.

That *Davis* was about notice and not about dispelling inherent coercion was made plain in 2010. In *Berghuis v. Thompkins*, the police read the *Miranda* rights to a murder suspect and had him read the last one aloud—one not required by *Miranda*—that he had "the right to decide at any time before or during questioning" to assert the right to remain silent or the right to counsel.[65] Thompkins declined to sign the form indicating that he understood his rights and never gave an explicit waiver. After sitting virtually silent through constant interrogation for almost three hours, he eventually answered a police question and admitted killing the victim.[66] The Court held that "a suspect who has received and understood the *Miranda* warnings, and has not invoked his *Miranda* rights, waives the right to remain silent by making an uncoerced statement to the police."[67]

Thus, *Miranda* doctrine as understood today does not even require an express waiver, despite the language in *Miranda* that it would take an "express statement that the individual is willing to make a statement to waive the right to silence.[68] Like almost everything in the *Miranda* opinion, the "express statement" language was dicta. As Bradley has noted, to reject dicta from *Miranda* raises questions about the scope of the principle of stare decisis.[69] Normally, a court is bound only by the narrow holding of its precedents. Thus, a court facing a due process challenge to the voluntariness of a confession would attempt to square the facts of the interrogation and the characteristics of the suspect as closely as possible to earlier cases. That was one of the Court's frustrations with the voluntariness doctrine. The richness of the "totality of the circumstances" approach made it difficult to find a binding precedent. *Miranda* opted for the "wide rule" alternative that was legislative in scope. Once later Courts began to pick the dicta away from the holding, however, not much was left of the wide rule.

Berghuis did more to undermine *Miranda*'s wide waiver rule than make plain that no express waiver is required. The record contained "conflicting evidence about whether Thompkins" indicated that he understood his rights.[70] But that did not stop the majority from holding that there "was more than enough evidence in the record to conclude that Thompkins understood his *Miranda* rights."[71] This surfeit of evidence was based on giving him a written copy of the warnings, determining that he "could read and understand English," giving him "time to read the warnings," and providing the fifth warning that he could decide at any time to use his right to silence or to a lawyer. There is no way to know whether the fifth warning is critical to the holding in *Berghuis* until another case comes along. If it turns out not to be critical, then *Berghuis* in effect holds that an English speaker who hears the warnings can be presumed to understand them.

Not much is left of the "heavy burden" that *Miranda* put on "the government to demonstrate that the defendant knowingly and intelligently waived his privilege against self-incrimination and his right to retained or appointed counsel."[72] The burden can perhaps be satisfied when an English speaker hears the warnings and talks to the police. *Berghuis* relied on language from *Davis* that "the primary protection afforded suspects subject[ed] to custodial interrogation is the *Miranda* warnings themselves."[73] Notice was given and notice is all that *Miranda* now requires.

Viewing *Miranda* as requiring a form of due process notice, rather than ameliorating the pressure of police interrogation, explains all of the cases separating *Miranda* from the Fifth Amendment privilege. The prosecution in *Harris v. New York* used a statement taken in violation of *Miranda* to impeach a defendant who told an inconsistent story in court.[74] Harris was decided in 1971 when the *Miranda* majority had presumably shrunk to four. Gone were Chief Justice Warren and Justice Fortas, who formed part of the majority, and Justice Clark who dissented. Their replacements, Chief Justice Burger, Justice Powell, and Justice Marshall could be expected to split two to one against *Miranda*, with Marshall the likely supporter.

The Court could have overruled *Miranda*, but that would have left it open to the criticism that the Court is a super-legislature, and that when membership changes, the law changes. As Geoffrey Stone put it, a "direct overruling" of *Miranda* would have seemed "unattractive, for such action would inescapably raise strong doubts about the integrity and the stability of the judicial process."[75] Thus, the Court did what it would do many times over the next forty years—distinguish *Miranda*. Acknowledging language in *Miranda* that the prosecution could not use *for any purpose* statements taken without warnings and waiver, the Court in *Harris* held that this language was dicta and thus did not bind the Court.[76]

Once that dicta had been neutralized, it was difficult to defend the right of witnesses to perjure themselves. The Court characterized the issue as whether the "shield provided by *Miranda*" could be "perverted into a license to use perjury by way of a defense, free from the risk of confrontation with prior inconsistent utterances."[77] Stating the issue that way made the Court's holding predictable: Statements taken in violation of *Miranda* can be used to impeach.

But *Harris* is limited to *Miranda* violations. *New Jersey v. Portash* later held that a statement compelled by threat of contempt of court cannot be used for impeachment.[78] The Court distinguished *Harris* this way: "[A] defendant's compelled statements, as opposed to statements taken in violation of *Miranda*, may not be put to any testimonial use whatsoever against him in a criminal trial."[79]

Portash and *Harris* settled the question of whether statements taken in violation of *Miranda* are compelled under the Fifth Amendment: They are not. But *Harris* and *Portash* settled this question differently than the Court's dicta in *Miranda* "settled" it. *Miranda* sought to connect its holding securely to the Fifth Amendment privilege, but this dicta was ultimately rejected by later Courts. "Wide rule" dicta weighs less in the stare decisis balance than narrow holdings. *Harris* and *Portash* are narrow holdings. They trump *Miranda*'s strong-force dicta.

New York v. Quarles also made clear that *Miranda* is different from the Fifth Amendment privilege.[80] *Quarles* held that, given reason to believe that the suspect had hidden a gun in a grocery store, the officer could ask about the location of the gun without giving *Miranda* warnings. *Quarles* is the only case where the Court permitted the introduction of statements taken without notice. The Court performed a cost-benefit balance to conclude that the threat to public safety outweighed the benefit of a rule designed to protect the Fifth Amendment privilege.[81] What is missing in a strong-force understanding of *Miranda* is an account of *why* the privilege should not apply during an exigency. As Justice O'Connor said in dissent, "since there is nothing about an exigency that makes custodial interrogation any less compelling, a principled application of *Miranda* requires that respondent's statement be suppressed."[82]

Dripps argues that a single question asked in a grocery store is not "secret stationhouse questioning under the complete control of the police" and thus did not constitute the "evil of custodial interrogation" that *Miranda* sought to ameliorate.[83] Perhaps. But *Quarles* is equally well explained if *Miranda* is understood to require due process notice that the suspect does not have to answer questions. If this is the right way to understand *Miranda*, O'Connor's dissent misses the point. The majority's balance might be wrong, but the attack that the Court is ignoring Fifth Amendment compulsion goes nowhere. *Miranda* is about notice, not ameliorating compulsion, and due process is sufficiently flexible to permit different procedures depending on the cost to the party charged with the responsibility of providing notice. The Court requires actual notice to known or reasonably ascertainable creditors of an estate, for example, but notice by publication suffices for all other creditors.[84] The Court in *Quarles* concluded that the cost of providing notice to suspects in situations where public safety is threatened is too high to bear. This is a stark due process form of analysis.

Michael Mannheimer argues that the Court "inappropriately" used a cost-benefit balance in *Quarles*.[85] If *Miranda* had a strong-force connection to the privilege, we would agree. But the Court has chosen the weak-force understanding. Whether appropriate or not, it is the state of *Miranda* doctrine today. Mannheimer's "unified theory" of testimonial evidence explains *Quarles*, *Harris*, and other oddball Fifth Amendment cases (as well as Sixth Amendment confrontation clause cases) by insisting that the privilege protects only statements made in contemplation of their use in court for the truth of the matter asserted. A statement that the "gun is over there" does not qualify, nor does impeaching Harris by using his statements to show that his testimony should not be believed.[86] As much as we like Mannheimer's "unified theory," it does not capture what the Court often says it is doing in the Fifth Amendment arena; moreover, his theory forces him to call for *Portash* to be overruled.

A due process understanding of *Miranda* explains not only the outcomes of the Court's *Miranda* cases but also the analysis that the Court uses. Consider the cases deciding whether a violation taints other evidence discovered by means of the violation. In *Oregon v. Elstad*, the police took a single incriminating statement while in the suspect's house, without warnings, and then back at the police station gave warnings and took a fuller statement.[87] If *Miranda* were a strong-force application of the privilege, the second statement would be inadmissible unless the prosecution could meet the difficult burden of showing that the taint of the earlier violation had somehow become attenuated.[88] But since *Miranda* is a weak-force application of the privilege, all it requires is notice. The only statements introduced were given after Elstad received what the Court held to be adequate notice of his *Miranda* rights, and they were admissible.[89]

In a later *Elstad*-type case, *Missouri v. Seibert*, the Court splintered badly over what constituted adequate notice, but all agreed that notice was the issue.[90] The police used the initial confession, taken in violation of *Miranda*, to encourage Seibert to confess minutes after giving warnings and obtaining a "waiver."[91] The police then "resumed the questioning with 'Ok we've been talking for a little while about what happened on Wednesday the twelfth, haven't we?' and confronted her with her prewarning statements" that were highly incriminating.[92]

The *Seibert* plurality put the notice issue this way: "These circumstances must be seen as challenging the comprehensibility and efficacy of the *Miranda* warnings to the point that a reasonable person in the suspect's shoes would not have understood them to convey a message that she retained a choice about continuing to talk."[93] For Kennedy, concurring in the judgment, the police conduct "undermines the *Miranda* warning and obscures its meaning."[94] To the dissent, the issue was whether the second statement was voluntary, but this depends, in large part, on whether Seibert understood that she had a choice not to answer questions.[95]

Our due process theory of *Miranda* explains the Court's weak-force under-standing of *Miranda*. When there is a threat to the public safety, no notice is necessary. In all other cases, statements are admissible if the suspect who faces custodial interrogation received adequate notice of his or her *Miranda* rights. Notice is adequate if the warnings are fairly communicated to the suspect. It does not matter if the suspect knows the crime for which the police intend to interrogate him[96] or if the suspect hedges his waiver by saying that he would not sign a statement until his lawyer arrived.[97] If notice was given by reading the warnings, and was not undermined as in *Seibert*, the weak-force privilege of *Miranda* is satisfied.

Moreover, notice can be adequate even if the warnings deviate from those the Court suggested in *Miranda*. In *Duckworth v. Egan*, the Court held the notice adequate even though the warnings said that if the suspect wanted a lawyer to be appointed, he could not get one until he appeared in court.[98] "The inquiry is simply whether the warnings reasonably "conve[y] to [a suspect] his rights as required by *Miranda*."[99] Because the warnings made plain that the suspect could end questioning until he had talked to a lawyer, the Court held that they were adequate.[100] In 2010, the Court reiterated the *Duckworth* principle, noting: "Although the warnings were not the *clearest possible* formulation of *Miranda*'s right-to-counsel advisement, they were sufficiently comprehensive and compre-hensible when given a commonsense reading."[101]

In her 2010 dissent in *Berghuis v. Thompkins*, Justice Sotomayor said that "*Miranda* and our subsequent cases are premised on the idea that custodial inter-rogation is inherently coercive. Requiring proof of a course of conduct beyond the inculpatory statements themselves is critical to ensuring that those state-ments are voluntary admissions and not the dubious product of an overborne will."[102] With all due respect to Justice Sotomayor, she is right about *Miranda* but wrong about "subsequent cases." As we have shown in this chapter, the subse-quent cases rejected *Miranda*'s wide rule dicta about cleansing the entire interro-gation of compulsion in favor of a narrow rule that asks only if the suspect is given sufficient notice of his rights. *Berghuis* and some of the other cases reject-ing a strong-force reading of *Miranda* were decided 5–4, and we suppose that the Court could yet return to a strong-force understanding of the relationship between *Miranda* and the Fifth Amendment privilege.[103] But to do that would require overruling several cases and thus seems unlikely.

Whatever the intent of the *Miranda* Court, later Courts separated *Miranda* from the Fifth Amendment privilege. The Court has created a framework within which a suspect can decide whether to talk to the police. Dripps and Rosenthal argue that *Miranda* is no more, and no less, than an application of standard waiver principles: "*Miranda* warnings provide the ingredients for a valid waiver of Fifth Amendment rights; in this sense as well, *Miranda* worked no innovation, but merely applied settled law."[104] We have argued that the Court's current view of the privilege requires only that suspects receive adequate notice of Fifth Amendment rights.[105]

Of course, even if the reader accepts that *Miranda* has only a weak-force connection to the privilege, and even if the reader accepts that waiver is the only point at which courts should worry about compulsion, Rosenthal might be wrong that the warnings are sufficient to dispel the inherent coercion of police interrogation long enough to produce a valid waiver. Dripps might be wrong that *Miranda* warnings place suspects facing custodial interrogation "in a position to claim the privilege that is roughly equivalent to the position of the witness before the grand jury."[106] And Thomas and Leo might be wrong that the warnings constitute sufficient notice of the right to remain silent. Laurence Benner might be right that later Courts retreated from *Miranda* by "reducing the concept of waiver to a formalistic ritual."[107] We will turn to *Miranda* problems and partial solutions in the next chapter.

So far we have presented the *Miranda* Court's likely understanding of its creation—that its function was to preserve free choice not only at the moment of waiver but also during the interrogation that followed. We also presented two alternative understandings that explain the Court's subsequent doctrine— *Miranda* as notice and *Miranda* as applying standard waiver rules. In explaining and critiquing these theories, we indulged the conventional assumption that rational suspects who are guilty and who are given a serious waiver moment, without trickery or pressure, would quite often do what is in their long-term best interests and say nothing other than "I want a lawyer."

That approximately 80% of suspects waive *Miranda* and incriminate themselves challenges this conventional wisdom, thus requiring an additional assumption that either the warnings are inadequate or are routinely undermined by police interrogation tactics. But what if the whole premise on which the warnings are based were false? What if suspects really do want to talk to police? This is a third alternative explanation of the *Miranda* world of today. Because it rejects the rationalist premise of the explanations so far, we devote a separate section to it.

C. Hierarchy of Preferences

Why do humans do things that they know might hurt them? The answer must lie in the ordering of preferences. Take, for example, the government-mandated warning labels on cigarette packs. As Patrick Malone wryly concluded, "Next to the warning label on cigarette packs, *Miranda* is the most widely ignored piece of official advice in our society."[108] Malone's humor makes a serious point: The beneficiaries of social campaigns to improve life through information often seem incapable of acting on that information.

Assume that a cigarette smoker reads the warnings and believes them. She knows that if she keeps smoking she will likely die sooner than if she stops smoking. But the preference for a cigarette when she is 16 or 26 or 36 or 46 or 56 can outweigh in her mind the risk of a horrible death from cancer, hopefully in the distant future. Those who wish to change preferences fail to take into account that preferences for current relief or pleasure are often of a higher order than the preference to avoid the future effect of a particular decision. What else explains that 56,000 Americans were infected with HIV in 2008, mostly from unprotected sex?[109] This hierarchy of preferences is a basic component of human nature.

Criminologists have long argued that those who commit crimes are less likely than non-criminals to defer gratification.[110] They tend to have a "weakened sense" of the future. As Jim Morrison of the Doors put it in a song: "Well, I woke up this morning and I got myself a beer. The future's uncertain and the end is always near."[111] And in his case, of course, the end *was* near. He died the year after that song was released on an album.[112]

Seidman argues that preferences about talking to the police are "not individual, autonomous, and pre-existing. Instead, they are socially constructed in the course of the very transaction that the court is asked to review."[113] Thus, "the problem with custodial interrogation is not that it might represent a doomed effort to restructure preferences, but that it risked succeeding in such re-structuring" with the effect that most suspects want to talk to police.

Based on his observations of homicide detectives in Baltimore, David Simon concluded that they " like to imagine a small, open window at the top of the long wall in the large interrogation room. More to the point, they like to imagine their suspects imagining a small, open window at the top of the long wall."[114] This window offers an "escape hatch," an Out that every suspect seeks. Every suspect who talks must imagine "himself parrying questions with the right combination of alibi and excuse; every last one sees himself coming up with the right words, then crawling out the window to go home and sleep in his own bed."[115] The dominant preference is not to be trapped in the interrogation room with the police. Every decision the suspect makes is drenched with hope that he can find a way out of the room.

> The effect of the illusion is profound, distorting as it does the natural hostility between hunter and hunted, transforming it until it resembles a relationship more symbiotic than adversarial. That is the lie, and when the roles are perfectly performed, deceit surpasses itself, becoming manipulation on a grand scale and ultimately an act of betrayal. Because

what occurs in an interrogation room is indeed little more than a carefully staged drama, a choreographed performance that allows a detective and his suspect to find common ground where none exists.[116]

Police interrogation produces a constellation of powerful forces that might defy any judicial attempt to persuade suspects to resist the interrogators. The conventional wisdom is that *Miranda* warnings have had little or no effect on the rate at which suspects talk to police because of a failure in the way the warnings are constructed or delivered or because police have found deceptive and manipulative ways of persuading suspects to waive their rights. But perhaps the interaction between the suspect and the police will produce roughly the same rate of cooperation regardless of what the warnings say or how they are delivered.

These overlapping, shifting preferences complement each other in subtle and fast-changing ways, producing countless complex interactions that resemble a quantum state in physics. To explain how these forces produce a choice may be beyond the current understanding of human psychology. But part of the outline of this "choice mechanics" seems clear enough. It would never assume that any preference is stable, though some might prove to be. It would assume that a rational actor might choose a perceived benefit because of a momentary desire even though a longer view would clearly show that the "benefit" was illusory. It would factor in the idiosyncrasies of each of our unique human experiences. Norman Bates, the main character in *Psycho*, would have a different set of preferences that would interact differently when police suggest that he killed his mother than would, say, a person raised in an orphanage. The person raised in the orphanage who had a happy experience would have a different set of preferences from the person who had an unhappy experience.

The decision of whether or how to interact with the police is potentially affected by one's sex; education; history of drug and alcohol use; childhood experiences; attitude toward authority and experiences with authority figures (parents, police, teachers, nuns); feelings of belonging or obligation to relevant communities (school, peer group, church, gang, work group); whether one has a job, what kind of job, and how successful one is at that job; the time of day or night; how much sleep one had the night before; how much coffee one had or needs; whether one just had or needs sex (booze, pills, narcotics, cigarettes, whatever); whether and how many times one has experienced police interrogation and what one feels about the outcome(s); how long ago one ate, what food, and how much. And so on ad infinitum.

We know that most suspects cannot resist the effect of powerful preference-creating forces created by police interrogation as it occurs today, and this might be true even when the police play it "straight" and refrain from using deceptive strategies. If our rough description of the hierarchy of preferences is more or less right, the due process "overbear the will" voluntariness test was, and continues to be, incoherent. When the suspect speaks to police, that act represents his will at the moment. But Aristotle, Wigmore, Kamisar, and the New Deal Supreme Court knew that.

The contribution of pulling back the curtain on the hierarchy of preferences is to show that *Miranda* was probably destined to make little difference in the interrogation room, even if the Court had found a wide rule with a stable deep justification. The set of variables that interact in staggeringly complex ways to produce the choice to talk or not to talk to police is so immense and personal to each suspect that the warnings become a mere blip on the radar screen. Any added variable, to be sure, can move some suspects toward the decision not to talk, and there is no reason to doubt that *Miranda* sometimes does that. But one can also tell a plausible story in which the warnings move some suspects to decide to talk as a way of making themselves appear innocent. We have no way to know the size of either group.

One fact is clear: Suspects waive their *Miranda* rights in roughly 80% of interrogations. Whether this is because of the hierarchy of preferences or because of the undermining (by police and later Courts) of the waiver moment or some other factor, it is nonetheless the confessions world in which we currently live. As one police lieutenant put it in 1986, *Miranda* "doesn't, frankly, interfere much with confessions, surprisingly enough. . . . It's human nature, once you start answering questions, to keep answering questions. . . . Well, he's already talked to me for fifteen minutes. He'll say yes, he'll keep talking."[117] Or as a prosecutor said, "The *Miranda* issue, is perhaps substantially insignificant. There's a reason for that. The smarter the police are and the way they conduct themselves, the more likely it is that the *Miranda* problem would never appear on the prosecutor's desk."

D. *Miranda* Today

For many years, *Miranda* has enjoyed universal acceptance, if not love, from the players in the criminal justice system. The police have learned that, whatever the reason, giving warnings does not seem to make suspects less likely to talk to them. Suspects talk to police because at the moment it seems like the most beneficial course to take. Prosecutors rarely lose a motion to suppress a confession. Defense lawyers make motions to suppress but don't really expect to win them. Judges can decide *Miranda* issues much more easily than issues raised by the old voluntariness test.

The United States Supreme Court, after decades of reining in *Miranda*, had an epiphany in 2000. In *Dickerson v. United States*, the Court concluded that

Miranda has "become embedded in routine police practice to the point where the warnings have become part of our national culture."[118] In the same paragraph, the Court took credit for subsequent cases that "have reduced the impact of the *Miranda* rule on legitimate law enforcement while reaffirming the decision's core ruling that unwarned statements may not be used as evidence in the prosecution's case in chief." Everyone seems happy.

But there is a dark side to the *Miranda* "success" story, and that story is what happens as interrogations proceed. The *Miranda* Court anticipated waivers,[119] though probably not as frequently as is the case. But to the extent the *Miranda* majority thought about postwaiver interrogation, the justices could have hoped that the *Ashcraft-Chambers-Spano* due process test would influence courts. While the Court's due process cases had apparently failed to cause lower courts to value fairness and suspect autonomy as much as the FDR New Deal Court did, the message in *Miranda* was that courts needed to pay more attention to how suspects were treated by interrogators. That attention could have translated into lower courts embracing something approaching the Court's view of how due process limits interrogation.

It did not happen. As we will see in the next chapter, lower courts continued to apply a minimalist due process test, and now the Supreme Court no longer sets a high rhetorical bar that might be used to win close cases. In effect, *Miranda* has rolled back the due process clock to something like *Lisenba*. As Craig Bradley puts it, *Miranda* is "a rug under which concerns about the fairness and reliability of confessions can be swept."[120] The next chapter considers the *Miranda* "rug" and other problems that plague the current law of interrogation.

But the history is clear: The law of interrogation has once again wrenched itself from the Hawkins-Leach world into a Wigmore rationalist world.

CHAPTER 9

Miranda Today

The nature of our project changes in this chapter. The earlier chapters described how and why interrogation law developed the way it did. In chapter 8, for example, we offered theories that, we hope, explain the current state of the *Miranda* doctrine better than the Supreme Court's on-again, off-again characterization of *Miranda* as prophylactic. But in the final two chapters, we will both describe the current law governing interrogation and offer a normative vision of how it can be improved.

We also narrow our scope in this chapter to interrogation problems connected to *Miranda*. A theme of this book is that something akin to *Miranda* has been the default position in Anglo-American law since Blackstone's eighth edition in 1778. The Hawkins-Leach dictum that appeared in 1787 neatly captures *Miranda*'s key premise—that official interrogation is inherently coercive. For more than a century, English and American courts applied a version of this dictum. Moreover, we discovered an 1828 New York statutory approach, probably influenced by John Graham's 1823 monograph, that required warnings remarkably like *Miranda* would require in 1966.

In chapter 8 we focused on *Miranda*; the Court's big gun in the attempt to cleanse compulsion from the police interrogation room. To keep the narrative relatively clean and relatively short, we keep the focus on *Miranda* in this chapter. *Miranda* was a once-in-a-century attempt to solve the problem of compelled confessions and deserves its own treatment.

As we sought to show in chapter 8, *Miranda* changed the interrogation world in ways that were dramatic and profound, but ultimately superficial. Imagine telling Wigmore that the Court would require police to warn suspects they had a right not to answer questions and a right to counsel, and then require police to respect their decision to remain silent or to invoke counsel. We also showed in chapter 8 that subsequent Courts rendered the *Miranda* regime less potent by making the critical moment that of waiver. Warnings make waiver almost always valid, and suspects waive their rights in roughly 80% of interrogations.

A. *Miranda* Waiver Problems

1. ROUTINE CASES

Even if one accepts the Court's modification of *Miranda* into a weak-force waiver doctrine, it might still fail to achieve the goal of reducing the level of inherent compulsion at the moment of waiver. There are several ways in which *Miranda* might fail as a weak-force waiver doctrine in routine cases.

First, the warnings themselves might not be comprehensible. One of the best studies on comprehensibility was published by Morgan Cloud and co-authors in 2002.[1] The researchers compared subjects who were mentally retarded or bor-derline mentally retarded—the average IQ was 55.5[2]—with subjects who suf-fered no mental retardation. The researchers found that the nondisabled subjects exhibited a high degree of comprehension of the rights entailed by the warnings, ranging from 83% to 90% using four broad measures.[3] To be sure, this finding likely overstates the comprehension of the typical nondisabled suspect. Sus-pects under arrest and facing police interrogation are surely more stressed and would be less likely to think clearly than participants in a lab experiment. But the Cloud study nonetheless suggests that not much of the 80% waiver rate can be attributed to incomprehensibility of the warnings. Intuitively, being told that "you have a right to remain silent" seems easily comprehended even if the sus-pect is under intense stress.

Beyond lack of comprehension, warnings might fail in other ways. Police sometimes undermine the warnings. Charles Weisselberg, Barry Feld, Welsh White, and Richard Leo have, in different venues, made a powerful argument that police often use "softening up" techniques that drain the warnings of their effectiveness.[4] These techniques include suggesting the value of talking to police and minimizing the importance of warnings by blending them with booking questions or a nonthreatening conversation. Perhaps the most effective strategy is to tell the suspect that he will not be able to tell his side of the story until the bureaucratic ritual is satisfied.

Based on the research and observations of others, and his own examination of interrogation-training materials in California, Weisselberg sums up the evidence as follows:

> We do not today have a clean separation between administration of *Miranda* warnings and the use of interrogation tactics, at least not in the way the *Miranda* Court envisioned. Observational studies and my review of training materials provide significant evidence that the warnings and waiver regime has moved at least partway into the interrogation process, contrary to the "time out" from the pressures of interrogation the Court imagined. Officers may use pre-*Miranda*

conversation to build rapport, which is important to obtaining a *Miranda* waiver and—eventually—a statement. Officers may also downplay the significance of the warning or portray it as a bureaucratic step to be satisfied before a conversation may occur. There is also evidence that police often describe some of the evidence against suspects before seeking waivers. A few cases have approved extreme versions of this tactic.[5]

And there are two doctrinal wrinkles that potentially drain the warnings of their ability to negate the inherent compulsion of police interrogation. One is whether courts police the waiver and invocation "boundaries" to keep those moments from becoming tainted by compulsion. Though the law on this point was in flux until 2010, *Berghuis v. Thompkins* made clear that the Supreme Court does not expect much in terms of boundary patrolling.[6] Indeed, in removing the last residue of the "heavy burden" waiver language from Miranda doctrine, *Thompkins* is perhaps the most significant *Miranda* case yet decided. As we noted in the last chapter, police carefully read Thompkins his rights, which included "the right to decide at any time before or during questioning to use your right to remain silent and your right to talk with a lawyer while you are being questioned."[7] After almost three hours of questioning during which Thompkins said nearly nothing, the interrogator found his weak spot. He asked if he believed in God and if he prayed to God.[8] When Thompkins answered yes to both, tears welled up in his eyes, and the officer asked: "Do you pray to God to forgive you for shooting that boy down?" Thompkins answered, "Yes."

Thompkins made two arguments. One was that his lengthy silence had somehow invoked his right to remain silent. The Court rejected that argument with relative ease—though the dissent found it "counterintuitive[]" that a suspect had to talk to invoke the right to remain silent.[9] But if silence can invoke *Miranda*, how would courts draw the line when silence matured into an invocation? Three hours? Two? One? Would it matter if, as Thompkins did, the suspect responded to two or three questions that did not relate to the investigation? What if the questions were about the investigation?

That *Thompkins* lost on this issue is thus not surprising. The statement of the rule was, however, significant. "The Court has not yet stated whether an invocation of the right to remain silent can be ambiguous or equivocal, but there is no principled reason to adopt different standards for determining when an accused has invoked the *Miranda* right to remain silent and the *Miranda* right to counsel at issue in *Davis*."[10] An unambiguous invocation standard is easier for courts to apply because it "results in an objective inquiry that 'avoid[s] difficulties of proof and . . . provide[s] guidance to officers' on how to proceed in the face of ambiguity."[11]

But we are left with the nagging doubt that substantial compulsion will often attend interrogations in which police ignore attempted invocations of the right to silence that are less than crystal clear. In *United States v. Banks*, for example, a detective read the suspect his *Miranda* rights in the back of the squad car and asked him if he understood them.[12] He said that he did. The officer then read a waiver form and asked if he was willing to waive his rights. He responded: "Get the f—out of my face. I don't have nothing to say. I refuse to sign [the waiver form]."[13] The federal magistrate held that this was not a clear assertion of his right to remain silent but was, instead, "the statement of somebody who is angry about what is happening to them, which makes a certain amount of sense under these circumstances."[14] Why it was not both an angry response *and* an invocation is not clear to us, but the Seventh Circuit affirmed. Presumably, *Thompkins* validates the outcome in *Banks*. Neither "I don't have nothing to say" nor "I refuse to sign" the waiver form is an explicit invocation of the right to remain silent, though writing that makes us wonder what happened to the spirit of *Miranda*.

On the way to the federal building, the detective told the suspect that his co-conspirators referred to him behind his back as "Big Dumbo."[15] At the federal building, he was given *Miranda* warnings again but was not presented a waiver form or asked whether he wished to waive his rights. During the subsequent interrogation, police played a tape of Banks's co-conspirators making fun of him, and he made incriminating statements. Was this waiver? That question returns us to *Thompkins*.

Thompkins's second *Miranda* argument was that the State had failed to sustain its burden of demonstrating waiver. Implicit in this argument was that, at a minimum, the State must show an express waiver that is distinct from the act of answering questions. This argument follows from *Miranda* itself: "An express statement that the individual is willing to make a statement and does not want an attorney followed closely by a statement could constitute a waiver. But a valid waiver will not be presumed simply from the silence of the accused after warnings are given or simply from the fact that a confession was in fact eventually obtained."[16] The *Thompkins* Court acknowledged: "Some language in *Miranda* could be read to indicate that waivers are difficult to establish absent an explicit written waiver or a formal, express oral statement"[17] and then proceeded to rewrite that part of *Miranda*. The rule now is: "Where the prosecution shows that a *Miranda* warning was given and that it was understood by the accused, an accused's uncoerced statement establishes an implied waiver of the right to remain silent."[18]

Return to *Banks*. Because the suspect admitted that he understood his *Miranda* rights and because his statement appeared uncoerced, the suspect waived *Miranda* even though he made no express waiver. His earlier statements about having nothing to say probably fail the *Thompkins* "unambiguous" test for invocation. *Thompkins* changed, perhaps clarified, a lot about how *Miranda* is understood.

Does a *Miranda* world with *Thompkins* boundaries permit too much compulsion at the critical points of waiver and putative invocation? That, of course, is a normative question. But imagine what might have been going through the mind of the suspect in *Banks*. He had told the officer, about as clearly as possible, to leave him alone, that he had nothing to say, and that he was not going to sign a waiver. He is then told by the detective that his co-conspirators are making fun of him. When next given warnings, he is not asked to sign a waiver. Nor does he give an express waiver before the detective plays a tape of his co-conspirators making fun of him and then begins to interrogate him. The suspect might have changed his mind about answering police questions. Or he might have resigned himself to having to submit to police questioning.

It seems inevitable that some suspects will react with resignation to a detective's refusal to take seriously the "I won't talk to you" signal. This was the point that Justice Souter made in his separate opinion in *Davis*—where the Court required an unambiguous request for counsel before it counted as invocation. In an opinion joined by three other justices, Souter wrote:

> When a suspect understands his (expressed) wishes to have been ignored (and by hypothesis, he has said something that an objective listener could "reasonably," although not necessarily, take to be a request), in contravention of the "rights" just read to him by his interrogator, he may well see further objection as futile and confession (true or not) as the only way to end his interrogation.[19]

It thus seems to us that the *Thompkins* boundaries will not always suffice to negate the inherent compulsion of police interrogation at the waiver point. The number of cases of boundary failure is yet unknown. One effect of *Thompkins* is to avoid what would otherwise be a rich irony. If courts were left to puzzle whether to credit ambiguous requests for counsel or to remain silent, they would be back in the game of trying to infer the suspect's will. By requiring unambiguous signals, the Court has greatly reduced the "mind-reading" required of courts, at a unquantified cost in compulsion.

And there is another doctrine that permits police to avoid the serious waiver moment that the *Miranda* Court contemplated, even on a weak-force understanding of *Miranda*. The narrow statement of the holding in *Miranda* is limited to custodial interrogation. Thus, if courts conclude that what the police did is not interrogation, or that the suspect was not in custody, then there is no need for even a softened-up waiver. In *Oregon v. Mathiason*, for example, the Court held that a parolee was not in custody even though he was questioned in a police interrogation room and had been told, falsely, that his fingerprints were found at the scene of the crime.[20] The key to the per curiam opinion was that the police told him he was not under arrest and, in fact, allowed him to leave when the interrogation was over.[21]

As Justice Marshall pointed out in his dissent, however, the "coercive elements" acting on Mathiason were "pervasive" even if he was not technically in custody.[22] Marshall pointed the way to an evolving *Miranda* doctrine that would count coercive pressure without regard to custody, based on substance over form: "[F]aithfulness to *Miranda*" required the Court to consider whether the particular police conduct had the "coercive aspects" of custodial interrogation rather than creating bright-line categories that would be exempted from *Miranda*.[23] But Marshall's argument was based on the strong-force understanding of *Miranda*, which by the time of *Mathiason* in 1977 no longer commanded a majority.

The custody-interrogation boundary thus permits courts to ignore what would otherwise be an invocation. In *Burket v. Angelone*, the murder suspect agreed to come to the station "to help with the investigation."[24] During the "interview," police lied and told him that a hair sample matching his had been found in the victims' residence.[25] He then admitted being in their house on the day they were killed and, two minutes later, said "I'm gonna need a lawyer." Police responded by telling him that he was not under arrest and was free to leave at any time. "Burket continued to talk with the detectives" and incriminated himself. The Fourth Circuit held that because he was not in custody, he had no Fifth Amendment right to counsel.[26] Despite a clear statement that he wanted counsel, Burket lost his motion to suppress, his subsequent appeals, and his petition for a writ of habeas corpus.[27]

George Thomas analyzed 211 *Miranda* cases he drew at random from Westlaw in 2002.[28] There is a selection bias in choosing cases from Westlaw because almost all—94%—of the cases were appellate cases.[29] But the bias should be in the direction of finding *more* claims of *Miranda* violations than actually occur because most cases without plausible arguments will not reach trial or, if they do, will not be appealed. In the Westlaw data set, no warnings were given in 60 of the 211 cases, but statements were suppressed in only 10 of them.[30] Thus, in over 80% of the no-warning cases, lower courts read Supreme Court doctrine as permitting police not to give warnings.

Another artifact of the weak-force understanding of *Miranda* appears in Thomas's Westlaw survey in the way the courts described the involuntariness claims—both of the waiver and of the subsequent statement. The claims in almost all cases lacked details that might prove involuntariness and had an almost pro forma quality to them. "The typical claim was that the waiver or confession was involuntary or that the police used trickery or deception, with few underlying details as to what constituted the coercion or the trickery."[31]

Reading these cases, one gets the impression that the lawyers often made an involuntariness claim as a "Hail Mary" pass or to protect against a claim of ineffective assistance. This reading is borne out by an American Bar Association report, "Criminal Justice in Crisis," published in 1986.[32] Defense lawyers surveyed reported that "[v]ery rarely" did they win a *Miranda* suppression motion. One assistant public defender said that he "[s]eldom, if ever" had a motion to suppress granted. "The difference between zero and none, lately. . . . And I don't really have the complaint, today, about *Miranda* not being given as often, near as often as I did years ago. But I don't see the courts throwing out *Miranda* cases." It thus appears that defense lawyers perceive the chance of winning a suppression motion as nil when police give the warnings. This could either be because police are at least formally playing by *Miranda*'s rules or because lawyers are cynical about the willingness of courts to exclude confessions—or both, of course.

As *Thompkins* makes plain, the evolution of *Miranda* has happened on the watch of Courts that construed *Miranda* narrowly even as a waiver or notice doctrine. Thus, if Thomas is right that *Miranda* is about giving notice, or if Dripps and Rosenthal are right that *Miranda* represents merely the standard application of waiver law, the reader would be entitled to conclude that *Miranda* is less than a robust success. One could not, however, conclude that *Miranda* has been a complete failure. In Thomas's 2002 study, suspects invoked *Miranda* 14% of the time and did not challenge the validity of the waiver in another 40% of the cases.[33]

One could conclude, using these data, that *Miranda* "worked" half the time. Invocation is an act that demonstrates that the inherent compulsion of the police-dominated atmosphere has been ameliorated. A suspect who tells police he will not answer questions or wants a lawyer is directly challenging the police authority to conduct the interrogation as they please. An unchallenged waiver should also count as a success for the weak-force *Miranda* theory. If the defendant felt he was tricked or compelled, presumably he would have challenged the State's claim that he waived his rights.

Whatever the failures of *Miranda* as ensuring notice or a valid waiver, failure is magnified when the suspect lacks the full capacity to process information. Though lack of capacity exists in other contexts (intoxication, lack of language facility), the most vexing contexts are when suspects are young or suffer from mental retardation. We turn now to those contexts.

2. LACK OF CAPACITY

Part of our argument in this book is that the Court inadvertently lost most of the value in the voluntariness test that *Miranda* sought to supplement. One largely lost value is the due process focus on the characteristics of the suspect, which is almost always muted or nonexistent in *Miranda* cases. As noted in the last section, Morgan Cloud and co-authors conducted an empirical study of mentally retarded subjects who were asked the meaning of the *Miranda* warnings. Only 31% of the subjects indicated an understanding of the right to counsel, which was the highest level of rights' comprehension.[34] To take another example from the Cloud study, the subjects were asked whether two sentences—"You do not have to make a statement and have the right to remain silent," and "You do not have to say anything about what you did"—have the same meaning.

> [T]he control group gave the correct answer 91 percent of the time. In stark contrast, the retarded subjects were correct only 10 percent of the time. Similarly, only 20 percent of the disabled subjects answered correctly the question, "Do you have to tell the police what happened?" compared to 96 percent of the controls. Random guessing would have yielded 50 percent correct. Only 31 percent of the disabled gave correct answers when asked, "Do you have to answer the police if they ask you any questions? " [—]far lower than the 50 percent from random guessing and the 82 percent correct score obtained by the control group.[35]

The authors concluded that their empirical research showed that "retarded people simply do not understand their *Miranda* rights. They do not understand the words comprising the warnings. They do not understand the rights themselves. They do not understand the legal context in which the rights arise. *Miranda* fails to protect the rights of mentally retarded people."[36] Moreover, the study's findings "suggest that people who are not classified as retarded, but who have low IQs, also may not understand the warnings." The study continued:

> Both our theoretical and empirical analyses lead to the conclusion that the language of the relevant constitutional doctrines is meaningless as it has been employed with mentally retarded suspects. The words of the *Miranda* warnings themselves are "meaningless" to mentally retarded suspects, who simply do not understand them. The words used to define the waiver test are "meaningless" in a different sense: they are applied to mentally retarded suspects in ways that contradict the very meaning of the words by which the standard is defined. Disabled suspects' waivers of the rights described in the *Miranda* warnings are "voluntary, knowing, and intelligent" only if we are willing to manipulate and distort the very meaning of these terms. Finally, the words of these confessions may themselves be meaningless. The cognitive and social weaknesses experienced by mentally retarded people ensure that some of their confessions will be false. When subjected to the pressures

of custodial interrogation, mentally retarded people are more likely than others to confess to crimes they did not commit.[37]

In *Miller v. State*, the trial judge found as a matter of state law that Miller was "a mentally retarded individual"[38] and thus not eligible for the death penalty. Yet the trial judge and the Indiana Supreme Court not only found his *Miranda* waiver voluntary but also voluntary beyond a reasonable doubt—the standard in Indiana.[39] The court fell into a familiar trap when it noted in connection with the waiver analysis: "There is no allegation or indication that police knew that he was mentally retarded."[40] What difference could that possibly make in whether the suspect understood the rights he was "waiving"? Either he understood the warnings well enough to waive his rights or he did not. The officer's misconduct is relevant in civil rights claims for damages but not, we think, on the waiver or voluntariness questions.

One might have expected the state courts in *Miller* to inquire into the level of mental disability and discuss whether a suspect who functioned at that level could validly waive *Miranda*. The trial judge found that Miller's IQ was "approximately 70 to 75 *or below*,"[41] and 70 is typically used as the borderline measure of mental retardation.[42] As we will see shortly, the United States Supreme Court under the old due process test took pains to account for a suspect's mental limitations. What makes *Miller* even odder is that the interrogation does not appear to comport with *Miranda*, at least the pre-*Thompkins* version, even if the suspect had not been retarded. When Miller heard that his name was mentioned on television in connection with the rape and murder of a seventy-one-year-old woman, Miller "voluntarily went to the police station to 'get it cleared up.'"[43] He arrived at 5:30 P.M. and was placed in an interview room that locked automatically from the outside. He waited there, alone, for two hours.

A detective joined Miller in the locked interrogation room and began to gather "background and preliminary information."[44] At some point during this questioning, the detective "considered the defendant to be a suspect and orally informed the defendant of his rights." The court mentions no evidence of waiver. During the next six hours, the detective's "questioning became more focused and included confronting the defendant" with assertions that he was guilty. The detective showed Miller a police report that falsely characterized the death as accidental. He also lied about the evidence against Miller. He told Miller that witnesses had seen him in the hallway outside the victim's office, which was untrue. He showed Miller a fingerprint card and computer printout that proved Miller's fingerprints were found in the victim's office; no fingerprint match had yet been made. Shortly before 1:00 A.M., after six hours of intense questioning, Miller admitted involvement in the victim's death.

At that point, the detective left Miller alone for forty-five minutes.[45] When he returned, he told Miller that he was under arrest and that he wanted to put the rest of the interrogation on tape. At this point, after six hours of interrogation, after Miller admitted being in the victim's office when she fell and died, the detective went over the *Miranda* warnings thoroughly, pausing after each right to ask him if he understood the right.[46] As to each right, Miller acknowledged that he understood. In response to the detective's concluding question: "What does it mean to you when I tell you your rights?" he responded, "It means that if I didn't want to, you know, say anything, that I can talk to an attorney or I could, you know, come on with (inaudible) you know, to get this cleared up."

This is a powerful piece of evidence that, at the moment of the second set of warnings, Miller more or less understood his rights. Moreover, Miller invoked his right to counsel after making incriminating statements in the second phase of the interrogation.[47] The state supreme court seemed to assume that invocation entailed understanding not only the right to counsel at that moment but also the right to counsel and to remain silent for the six hours the police relentlessly questioned him before the second set of warnings. But this is, to say the least, a contestable proposition.

To compare *Miller* with pre-*Miranda* cases is both instructive and sad. In *Fikes v. Alabama*, the Court suppressed a confession made by a black man who was "uneducated" and "of low mentality, if not mentally ill."[48] The only coercive factor was interrogation over several days in isolation.[49] Miller was interrogated for over six hours in a locked interrogation room. Unlike *Fikes*, there was no need to speculate about whether Miller was mentally incapacitated. He was legally determined to be mentally retarded. We will return to *Fikes* later in the chapter, when we show the desirable flexibility of the due process test that the Court relied on before it decided *Miranda*. For now, it suffices to say that Miller would have won a due process claim if decided by the 1957 Supreme Court.

Indeed, when the Court was presented evidence in 1960 that a suspect had been diagnosed as mentally ill, it unanimously reversed his conviction even though he was questioned for only five or six hours.[50] The striking aspect of *Blackburn v. Alabama* is that almost all of the opinion is about the suspect's mental capacity; very little is said about the interrogation. No one disputed the sheriff's claim that Blackburn was not "threatened . . . . in any way." Nor was there evidence that the police lied to him about evidence that "proved" his guilt. Miller's problem, it seems, was being judged by *Miranda* 2002 standards rather than the Supreme Court's 1950s due process standards.

A similar capacity issue arises with juveniles. Here, too, the Court has also largely abandoned the protections of the pre-*Miranda* due process cases. In *Haley v. Ohio*, five members of the 1948 Court said that advising a fifteen-year-old of his right to remain silent was not enough to make his confession voluntary.[51]

The plurality rejected the proposition that "a boy of fifteen, without aid of counsel, would have a full appreciation of that advice" and would know that he had "a freedom of choice." Justice Frankfurter's separate opinion stressed that the juvenile had no "appreciation of his rights" and that "the means of asserting them were effectively withheld from him by the police."[52] To be sure, the interrogation was five hours in length and began at midnight,[53] so what is remarkable is not the finding of involuntariness but that the plurality did not "give any weight to recitals which merely formalize constitutional requirements."[54]

Gallegos v. Colorado was decided four years before *Miranda* reordered the interrogation universe.[55] Over a spirited dissent, the Court held that the use of a confession given by a suspect who was fourteen years old violated due process, even though there was "no evidence of prolonged questioning."[56] Indeed, "the basic ingredients of the confession came tumbling out as soon as he was arrested."[57] While the Court cited instances of police misconduct,[58] the most significant factor was Haley's age.

> [A] 14-year-old boy, no matter how sophisticated, is unlikely to have any conception of what will confront him when he is made accessible only to the police. That is to say, we deal with a person who is not equal to the police in knowledge and understanding of the consequences of the questions and answers being recorded and who is unable to know how to protest his own interests or how to get the benefits of his constitutional rights.[59]

And then, in the next paragraph: "A lawyer or an adult relative or friend could have given the petitioner the protection which his own immaturity could not. Adult advice would have put him on a less unequal footing with his interrogators."

The concern with the special vulnerabilities of juveniles continued in the 1967 seminal decision of *In re Gault*, where the Court said: "With respect to juveniles, both common observation and expert opinion emphasize that the 'distrust of confessions made in certain situations' to which Dean Wigmore referred. . . . is imperative in the case of children from an early age through adolescence."[60] The special concern present in *Haley, Gallegos,* and *Gault* would end in 1979 in a 5–4 *Miranda* decision, *Fare v. Michael C.*[61] Sixteen years old, Michael C. responded to the *Miranda* warnings by asking to speak to his probation officer.[62] The police refused the request but repeated that he did not have to talk to them without an attorney present unless he wanted to.[63] He agreed to talk.

The California Supreme Court held that the request to talk to the probation officer was an indication that Michael C. did not want to talk to police without help.[64] The state court had written in an earlier case that it was "fatuous" to assume that a minor who faces custodial interrogation "will be in a position to call an attorney for assistance."[65] Thus, courts should recognize that the "call for help from the only person to whom he normally looks" for help—his parents in the earlier case—should be taken as an invocation of the right to remain silent. The *Michael C.* state court extended that holding to a request to talk to a probation officer.[66]

The Supreme Court reversed, insisting that the only invocations that would produce assistance or require the police to stop questioning were the ones set out in *Miranda*—a request for counsel or an assertion of the right to remain silent.[67] Michael C. did neither and thus there was no invocation. One can quibble with the Court on this point, preferring the state court's more common-sense view, but the real failure of *Michael C.* is what happened next. To say that the juvenile did not invoke *Miranda* is not to say that he waived *Miranda*. Despite *Haley's* admonition that formulaic warnings will not assure a voluntary confession when the suspect is fifteen, *Michael C.* treated a sixteen year old as an adult without even acknowledging *Haley*. How did the Court know that Michael C. had waived his *Miranda* rights? Because there was "no indication that he was of insufficient intelligence to understand the rights he was waiving, or what the consequences of that waiver would be. He was not worn down by improper interrogation tactics or lengthy questioning or by trickery or deceit."[68] But this, of course, is the same standard applied to adults.

We agree with Kenneth King that the standard used to evaluate whether a juvenile has waived *Miranda* has been "taken directly from adult *Miranda* jurisprudence and incorporated without modification."[69] Courts thus hold "that a juvenile's individual character or maturity is irrelevant to the voluntariness analysis and that the use of psychological ploys, which play on a child's vulnerability and susceptibility to pressure, are unobjectionable." In sum, "courts have forgotten that children are different from adults and require extra protection." How could the Court in *Michael C.* believe that a sixteen year old, who has been denied a chance to speak with his probation officer, possessed an adult's ability to refuse to talk to police officers? If police are authority figures to adults, imagine how they appeared to Michael C. after they had denied his request for help.

To be sure, the attitude toward juvenile crime has changed dramatically in the last four decades. *In re Gault* was decided in 1967, just as the attitude had begun to shift from juvenile offenders as children who needed the help of adults to juvenile offenders as dangerous and largely beyond help. These attitudes are necessarily reflected in judicial approaches to the law of interrogation, precisely as our deviance thesis predicts. But some applications of adult standards seem bizarre to us.

Incredibly, the application of adult waiver standards to juveniles has extended to those as young as eleven. We offer three examples. Suspecting that

Christopher W. had set a fire at a church, a police officer took him into custody and "after reciting *Miranda* rights, interrogated him."[70] After about an hour of unsuccessful interrogation, the officer produced a New Testament and asked Christopher if he believed in God, and if he knew that church was God's home. When the eleven-year-old answered yes, the officer asked him if he could place his hand on the Bible, look the officer in the eye, and say he had not been in the church that burned. At that point, Christopher confessed.

The opinion is a page and one-half, with no dissent *and no mention of waiver*. When the suspect is eleven years old, a court perhaps should hold that waiver is impossible as a matter of law. If waiver is theoretically possible, it should be the critical issue. The South Carolina Court of Appeals seemed to assume that merely answering questions was sufficient to show that an eleven year old understood and waived his *Miranda* rights. The state court contented itself with noting that "his testimony shows he is intelligent, quick, and articulate. Furthermore, Christopher, who has had several experiences with the police, testified he understood his right to remain silent and the meaning of his statement."[71] The court's facile assumption, that an intelligent eleven year old is the best judge of whether he understands his right to remain silent and whether he is able to act on that knowledge, is stunning.

In *Matthews v. State*, police interrogated a thirteen year old who was a murder suspect.[72] Here is how the court described the waiver:

> Detective Knowles stated that, because of appellant's age, he employed a different procedure when he advised her of her rights. Although, when questioning an adult, Detective Knowles would normally explain the *Miranda* rights one time only, because of appellant's age he went through the *Miranda* rights twice. He stated that appellant verbally and physically indicated that she understood the rights, and that he was convinced she understood the waiver when she signed it. . . . Detective Knowles further stated that appellant appeared to be alert and oriented, that her demeanor was very cool and calm, and that her speech was clear and forthright.[73]

The Arkansas Court of Appeals rejected the waiver argument in a single paragraph, which concludes: "Although appellant's age is a factor to consider in determining the voluntariness of her waiver, our review of the totality of the circumstances has not convinced us that the trial court's ruling on the issue of waiver was clearly erroneous."[74] At least the Arkansas court, unlike the South Carolina court, recognized that waiver is the critical issue when a very young suspect is interrogated. But we are not persuaded that a valid waiver is proven by reading the warnings twice to a "cool and calm" thirteen year old. In our view, it adds nothing for the officer to make the self-serving statement that he believed that she understood her rights.

The *Matthews* court relied on an Arkansas case holding that a twelve year old who read at a fourth-grade level waived his *Miranda* rights.[75] An "educational examiner," apparently the only expert witness in the earlier case, testified that the boy lacked the "intellectual development . . . to perceive the implications and consequences of signing [the] form after having it read to him." So what did the Arkansas court rely on? The juvenile and his mother, who was present, "agreed that his statement was not coerced," and the juvenile was "calm and attentive" during the three and one-half hour interrogation with no break.[76] But a suspect's demeanor and the absence of coercion are both irrelevant to a juvenile's capacity to understand and waive *Miranda*. The issue should be capacity, not whether his will was overborne or how he appeared.

In re M.D. involved a thirteen year old suspected of vandalism.[77] His "waiver" was secured after he was taken to the sheriff's office where

> Deputy Perry read him his *Miranda* rights. Deputy Perry explained to appellant that he had the right to an attorney, and had him read over a *Miranda* waiver. Deputy Perry testified that appellant (1) then signed the waiver "free [sic] and willingly," (2) showed remorse after writing his confession, and (3) never asked questions about the waiver. Appellant never asked for an attorney or his parents.[78]

One might have expected the court at least to concede that this is thin waiver gruel when the suspect is thirteen. The officer read the rights to him, told him he had a right to a lawyer, and then had him read the waiver form. That the officer believed the waiver valid, that the juvenile showed remorse after confessing, and that he never asked questions about the waiver or requested help are completely beside the point in analyzing waiver. But the Ohio Court of Appeals was satisfied. The court cited these facts and added two other irrelevant facts: that one of the officers was "comfortable appellant understood what a *Miranda* warning was" and that "there is nothing in the record to suggest he was of insufficient intelligence based upon his age or that he was mentally impaired and was unable to understand his *Miranda* rights."[79] The court thus held that a thirteen year old, of ordinary intelligence for that age, can understand, and act on, his *Miranda* rights without any attempt to explain the complex, underlying concepts.

Even when a juvenile suspect wins, it feels like a loss. Wesley was "an educationally impaired youth of low average intelligence" and eleven years old when interrogated.[80] The officer noted that "Wesley was 'slow,' fidgety, and had trouble paying attention." When Wesley's attention wandered, "the officer would try to 'get him back to my attention.'" The court-appointed psychologist found "that

Wesley was 'very immature' and had reading abilities of the second grade, fourth month." He also testified during the suppression hearing that "in his opinion, it was beyond the cognitive abilities of most eleven-year-old children to make a free and unconstrained choice about whether to speak to a police officer"—a position we very much embrace—"and that Wesley's impairments rendered it substantially more difficult for him to decide whether or not to confess."

The officer interrogated Wesley for almost two hours. He testified it was a "constant struggle to keep Wesley focused on him and his questions."[81] Yet the trial judge admitted the confession, and the New Hampshire Supreme Court retreated to a laundry list of factors to hold that the confession was involuntary: "The repeated and prolonged questioning of eleven-year-old Wesley, despite his continued denial of any involvement in the fire, coupled with the absence of any supportive adult during the interview, lead us to conclude that Wesley's will was overborne."[82] But the court appears to rely largely on the New Hampshire rule that the State had to prove voluntariness "beyond a reasonable doubt," noting that the evidence presented to the trial court is perhaps "sufficient to support a finding by a preponderance of the evidence" in favor of admitting the confession.[83] The federal standard is preponderance of the evidence.[84] If most states followed that standard, then Wesley's confession might have been admissible despite his age and reading level!

We would have written a different opinion, holding that an eleven year old who has the reading ability of a seven year old cannot waive *Miranda*, by any standard of proof, and thus cannot be interrogated. *That* is the message we want to send the police. To be sure, Wesley apparently committed the serious crime of trying to burn down his house. But if the authorities cannot prove it without his confession, we would be happy to allow civil commitment to proceed rather than a delinquency adjudication.

The net effect of these cases is to put the burden of proof on very young suspects to demonstrate they are of "insufficient intelligence" or "mentally impaired," rather than putting the burden of proving waiver on the State. Most courts effectively put the burden of disproving waiver on adult defendants. While this is a retreat from language in *Miranda*, it can be justified because the Court has morphed *Miranda* into a notice case. But how can courts believe that eleven and twelve year olds are effectively put on notice by rights that many adults cannot comprehend?

Thomas Grisso's study found that 63% of juveniles and 37% of adults received a "zero" credit on one or more items in terms of comprehending the terms in the warnings.[85] When the issue was understanding the significance of the rights, 45% of juveniles, compared with 15% of adults, received zero credit for understanding the right to counsel. "The most common confusion about this warning statement concerned the time and place an attorney could be consulted, 'interrogation' often being misconstrued as an adjudication hearing."

Though most juveniles understood that they did not have to talk to police, 55% "believed that they would have to explain their criminal involvement in court if questioned by a judge."[86] The ability to comprehend and understand the warnings varied, as one would expect, by age. Grisso concluded that "juveniles younger than fifteen years of age failed to meet both the absolute and relative (adult norm) standards for comprehension."[87] The "vast majority of these juveniles misunderstood at least one of the four standard *Miranda* statements, and compared with adults, demonstrated significantly poorer comprehension of the nature and significance of the *Miranda* rights."

Barry Feld examined tapes of interrogations of juveniles by the St. Paul police department, limited to those who were sixteen and seventeen years old.[88] His conclusions are consistent with Grisso's field research. Feld found, "Sixteen- and seventeen-year old juveniles exhibit relatively adult-like competence in the interrogation room . . . [and] do appear to understand the contents of the *Miranda* warnings."[89] Indeed, "about the same proportions of [sixteen- and seventeen-year old] juveniles as adults appear able to exercise their rights both prior to and during the course of questioning." The significance of Grisso's and Feld's findings is to support the *Haley* Court's intuition that "a boy of fifteen, without aid of counsel," would not "have a full appreciation of" the right to remain silent.[90] The Court was also right to reject the confession of the fourteen-year-old suspect in *Gallegos* and, we believe, the state courts that found valid waivers from children aged eleven, twelve, and thirteen are wrong as a matter of law.

Grisso and Feld support the *Fare v. Michael C.* Court's assumption that a juvenile who is sixteen years old is capable of waiving *Miranda*. These studies do not, however, support the Court's easy assumption that Michael C. *did* waive his rights. There is, of course, no magic age when a juvenile suddenly becomes capable of waiving *Miranda* rights. What is needed is a more searching inquiry into the juvenile's capacity, much like the Court did in the due process cases that preceded *Miranda*. Certainly, more is required than merely finding that a juvenile was of average intelligence. The findings of Grisso and Feld manifestly reject as absurd cases applying the *Michael C.* analytical framework to suspects who are eleven, twelve, and thirteen.

We do not mean to suggest that all courts treat young suspects as having adult capacity to waive *Miranda* and make voluntary confessions. A counterexample is a case arising out of the murders of nine people, including six Buddhist monks, in a temple near Phoenix in 1991.[91] Investigators initially arrested and interrogated four individuals from Tucson. After relentless questioning, all made incriminating statements. They later recanted their confessions, and the authorities ultimately agreed that the confessions were false. A lawsuit against the Maricopa County Sheriff's office was settled in 1994 for $2.8 million.

Authorities later focused on Johnathan Doody, seventeen years old, who was interrogated from nine at night until ten the next morning.[92] The interrogator's "recitation of *Miranda*'s basic warnings consume twelve pages of transcript, largely a byproduct of the detective's continuous usage of qualifying language." In an en banc ruling, the Ninth Circuit concluded that the *Miranda* warnings, as given, "negated the intended effect of the *Miranda* warning."[93] The court also held that Doody's confession was involuntary.[94] The Supreme Court vacated the Ninth Circuit's judgment and remanded for reconsideration of the *Miranda* holding in light of *Florida v. Powell*[95] but, presumably, the judgment about voluntariness will stand. Whether it stands, the opinion strikes the right tone and asks the right questions about how juveniles might perceive a relentless police interrogation.

The Ninth Circuit began its due process voluntariness analysis by quoting Justice Frankfurter's opinion in the 1949 case of *Watts v. Indiana*:

> When a suspect speaks because he is overborne, it is immaterial whether he has been subjected to a physical or a mental ordeal. Eventual yielding to questioning under such circumstances is plainly the product of the suction process of interrogation and therefore the reverse of voluntary. We would have to shut our minds to the plain significance of what here transpired to deny that this was a calculated endeavor to secure a confession through the pressure of unrelenting interrogation. The very relentlessness of such interrogation implies that it is better for the prisoner to answer than to persist in the refusal of disclosure which is his constitutional right.[96]

The Ninth Circuit noted that the United States Supreme Court "has consistently reminded us that 'admissions and confessions of juveniles require special caution.'"[97] But the most recent Supreme Court citation that the majority offers is the 1967 case of *In re Gault*. Indeed, most of the Supreme Court quotes came from the 1940s, the 1950s, and the early 1960s—the heyday of the due process test. Naturally, the Ninth Circuit focused on *Gallegos* and *Haley*, cases that essentially held that suspects who were fourteen and fifteen simply were not capable of understanding the consequences of cooperating with police during intense interrogation.

To be sure, Doody was seventeen, not fourteen. Thus, critical to the majority's analysis were the aspects of the nearly thirteen-hour interrogation that were designed to sap Doody's will to resist: (1) He was an "unsophisticated teenager";[98] (2) he was not offered a break during the first nine hours of the interrogation;[99] (3) he was not a "native of this country"; (4) he was interrogated by "tag-teams of two, three and four detectives" whose tone ranged from "pleading" to "scolding to sarcastic to demeaning to demanding" to "downright chilling";[100] (5) almost thirteen hours of interrogation took place overnight, making him "sleep-deprived";[101] and (6) immediately before he confessed, the detectives told him "that he *had* to answer their questions."[102] While it might not be as relevant as the factors just mentioned, the court also noted, "By the end of the interrogation, Doody was sobbing almost hysterically."[103] Moreover, "this same task force questioned four adult men and, undoubtedly using the same tactics, procured what the State concedes were false confessions from all four."[104] If "the will of four adult men was overborne to the extent that they confessed to murders they did not commit," why wouldn't "the will of this young teen" be "similarly overborne"?

Luckily for Doody, the police taped the interrogation—seventeen audiotapes in all.[105] It seems unlikely that Doody would have won, even in the liberal Ninth Circuit, if all the defense had was his recollection and the testimony of the interrogators. "The audiotapes of Doody's interrogation are dispositive in this case, as we are not consigned to an evaluation of a cold record, or limited to reliance on the detectives' testimony."[106] Instead, the court heard "an extraordinarily lengthy interrogation of a sleep-deprived and unresponsive juvenile under relentless questioning for nearly thirteen hours by a tag team of detectives, without the presence of an attorney, and without the protections of proper *Miranda* warnings." The tapes "reveal a picture that bears no resemblance to the avuncular scene painted by the Arizona Court of Appeals."[107] Nor was the *Doody* majority impressed with the evidence of maturity on which the state courts relied—his "participation in ROTC, his not-yet-completed high school studies, his work as a grocery store bagger, his ability to speak English as a second language and his lack of mental disability."[108]

The Ninth Circuit adopted an approach to analyzing the coercive factors that is very different from that used by the Arizona Court of Appeals and by most courts today. *Doody* acknowledged the cumulative effect of the various factors rather than analyzing each factor in isolation. As we will see in more detail in the next section, the Ninth Circuit's approach is the one the Supreme Court used before *Miranda*.

Three of the eleven judges who comprised the en banc panel in *Doody* found the thirteen-hour interrogation to comport with due process—or at least close enough that the deference owed by federal courts when reviewing final state court decisions should have carried the day.[109] Whatever the right result when applying a deferential standard of review, we believe that the trial court and state court of appeals reached the wrong result when they found that neither *Miranda* nor the due process clause was violated by the interrogation that Doody faced.

And we turn, now, to due process claims more generally.

B. Emptying Due Process of Meaning

As Leo put it in 2008, "The *Miranda* warning and waiver ritual. . . . . makes almost no difference in American police interrogation because virtually all suspects waive (or are legally constructed to have waived) their *Miranda* rights, and almost no confession is ever excluded from evidence at trial because of a *Miranda* violation."[110] For the large universe of suspects who waive their rights, the *Miranda* "revolution" did not protect them from police interrogation. Instead, *Miranda* has effectively deprived those suspects of the voluntariness flourish that the FDR Court created from the due process clause. Thus, odd though it may sound, and as totally weird as it would have sounded to the nine members of the *Miranda* Court, a case can be made that suspects as a whole are worse off now when they get to court than before *Miranda* was decided.

A harder question is whether suspects are also worse off in the police interrogation room. At one level, the answer is likely "no." As Leo has observed, *Miranda* has almost certainly contributed to a "civilizing" of police interrogation practices.[111] The third degree was on its way out when *Miranda* was decided but, according to interrogation manuals, police interrogators still seemed to treat suspects as prey. By the 1980s, the "training manuals taught police a kinder and gentler way to interrogate while still creating the opportunity to overbear the will of suspects." Precisely how much *Miranda* contributed to this "civilizing" of police is impossible to know. But being trained to tell your adversary that he need not cooperate with you and that you must accept his decision not to talk or to consult with counsel must, over time, contribute to that "kinder and gentler" police interrogation. Whether that is a benefit to suspects is a difficult call. Confessing after having one's will worn down in a kindly way seems just as detrimental to suspects, if more pleasant, as earlier interrogation methods.

In chapter 7 we surveyed some of the key voluntariness cases as the Court made its way, in fits and starts, toward *Miranda*. The focus showed how the cases built toward *Miranda*. In this chapter, we want to show how the due process doctrine can be understood on its own terms and without regard to the path to *Miranda*. We begin that task in this subsection by showing one of the chief virtues of the voluntariness test—its flexibility. We offer two examples.

In *Fikes v. Alabama*, a black man was arrested as a suspect in a series of burglaries and rapes.[112] In examining whether the interrogation violated the due process clause, the Court stressed: "It is, of course, highly material to the question before this Court to ascertain petitioner's character and background."[113] The Court continued:

> He is a Negro, 27 years old in 1953, who started school at age eight and left at 16 while still in the third grade. There was testimony by three

psychiatrists at the trial, in connection with a pleaded defense of insanity, to the effect that petitioner is a schizophrenic and highly suggestible. His mother testified that he had always been "thick-headed." Petitioner worked in a gas station in his home town of Marion, some 30 miles from Selma. So far as appears, his only prior involvement with the law was a conviction for burglary of a store in November 1949; he was released on parole in January 1951.

Fikes was interrogated repeatedly for about ten days, but there was no evidence of coercion or physical abuse.[114] Yet focusing on his "low mentality," his "isolation," and the failure to take him before a magistrate as required under state law, the Court held that the "totality of the circumstances that preceded the confessions in this case goes beyond the allowable limits. The use of the confessions secured in this setting was a denial of due process."[115] The flexibility and indeterminacy of the pre-*Miranda* due process test is on full display in *Fikes*.

A virtue of *Miranda* from an efficiency perspective is that it treats all suspects alike. Anyone, even someone who is mentally disabled or eleven years old, is presumed able to understand that "you have the right to remain silent" means one does not have to answer police questions. It is, we have tried to point out, a highly contestable assumption and turns out to be a vice from the perspective of justice or fairness. The due process "voluntariness" test, on the other hand, was horribly inefficient because it is based on a "complex of values" and "the role played by each in any situation varies according to the particular circumstances of the case."[116] In *Haley v. Ohio*, where the suspect was fifteen, the Court noted, "Mature men possibly might stand the ordeal from midnight to 5 a.m. But we cannot believe that a lad of tender years is a match for the police in such a contest. He needs counsel and support if he is not to become the victim first of fear, then of panic."[117] Voluntariness is flexible enough to permit a court to find the confessions of Fikes and Haley a violation of due process even if the interrogation would not have violated the due process rights of white businessmen like Lisenba or Ashcraft.

So when 1966 dawned, the Court's voluntariness doctrine was supple and fact-sensitive. But the very flexibility that was the virtue of the Court's voluntariness test *in the hands of the Supreme Court* permitted lower courts to admit confessions pretty much whenever the judge thought it made sense. Trial and state appellate courts, after all, had found no reason to suppress the confessions of Haley, Gallegos, and Fikes, along with eight other state cases that the Court reversed in the period 1957 to 1963—an average of more than one a year.[118] One reason to decide *Miranda* as if it were a statute regulating interrogation was to get the Court (and the lower courts) out of the business of reviewing thousands of voluntariness claims. It worked, though probably not in the way the Court imagined. The

Miranda opinion contemplates a world where lawyers guide suspects through the minefield of police interrogation, where uncooperative suspects insist on their right to remain silent, or where contrite suspects volunteer a confession.

Instead, most suspects waive *Miranda* and courts accept acts of waiver as strongly presumptive of voluntariness, both of the waiver itself and of statements made following waiver. In the Court's words, only "rare" cases permit "a colorable argument that a self-incriminating statement was 'compelled' despite the fact that the law enforcement authorities adhered to the dictates of *Miranda*."[119] An empirical study of all lower court *Miranda* cases in 1999 and 2000 bears out how "rare" these cases are. Welsh White found only nine cases that held the postwaiver confession involuntary, and four of those were based on state constitutional law.[120]

It is possible that *Miranda* has made the due process voluntariness test even less protective than it was prior to 1966. Courts sometimes use the warnings "offensively" to sanitize the interrogation that follows by relying on the fact that warnings were given repeatedly. Proving waiver sometimes has the effect of eliding or suppressing the question of whether the subsequent statements are voluntary. In the garden-variety case, these developments make sense as a starting place. If there is doubt about whether the suspect answered police questions voluntarily, the repeated warning that he need not answer should weigh in favor of voluntariness. And if the statement follows relatively quickly after waiver, this, too, is evidence of voluntariness. In many cases, however, courts allow the warnings to carry more weight in the voluntariness calculus than we think justified.

1. *MIRANDA* WAIVERS USED "OFFENSIVELY"

In his analysis of *Chavez v. State*, Alfredo Garcia provides a dramatic example of the "offensive" use of *Miranda*.[121] Detectives in three shifts interrogated Chavez for thirty hours with minimal breaks.[122] After thirty hours, he was allowed to sleep for six hours—on the floor of the police interview room. He was then interrogated for another twelve hours. Twice during the marathon interrogation, a polygraph examiner told him that he had failed the polygraph test.[123] The Florida Supreme Court in a per curiam opinion, with not a single dissenting justice, held that Chavez's interrogation produced a voluntary confession.[124]

What is more disappointing than the outcome is the court's analysis. As for a *Miranda* waiver, Chavez's initials on a Spanish-language rights form apparently provided all the evidence the court needed to conclude that he had "knowingly" waived *Miranda*.[125] As for voluntariness of his statements, what follows is the state supreme court's analysis of whether Chavez's confession was voluntary:

> Although Chavez was questioned over the course of several days, he was
> provided with food, drink, and cigarettes (as requested) at appropriate

times, and permitted to have frequent breaks. His interrogation was also interspersed with time away from the police facilities for visits to various properties, a six-hour rest period (where Chavez was offered a blanket and a pillow), and times when he was left alone for quiet reflection. He was repeatedly given Miranda warnings, in Spanish, and indicated each time that he fully understood them. Consequently, the trial court did not err in denying Chavez's motion to suppress on this ground. [126]

Notice how courts manipulate facts to get the result they want. The hours spent on the floor between interrogations were a *rest period*. The court never mentions that he had to sleep on the floor—this comes from Garcia's study of the trial record[127]—but the court seems to think it important that he was offered a blanket and a pillow, as if this somehow reduced the pressure of the interrogation. The police twice took him to the scene of the crime while questioning him about where he hid the body. The court viewed these trips a *respite*: "time away from the police facilities for visits to various properties," as if being brought to the scene of the crime while being interrogated was a pleasure trip. What was the most important indicator of voluntariness? "He was repeatedly given *Miranda* warnings, in Spanish, and indicated each time that he fully understood them."

As Garcia concluded, "Rather than assisting the suspect, what *Miranda* wrought for Chavez was an argument that a seventy-five hour interrogation which resulted in various incriminating statements was voluntary and thus constitutional."[128] Garcia then asks us to

> [i]magine for a moment a world without *Miranda*. Without the waivers, would the prosecution and the trial court have found it more difficult to establish that Chavez's incriminating statements were "voluntarily" given? Does not the case seem redolent of *Ashcraft v. Tennessee*, where the Court held that a thirty-six hour continuous interrogation of the suspect was "inherently coercive" and not voluntary? . . . Quite simply, what the officers had in *Chavez* that the officers in *Ashcraft* lacked was the great *Miranda* warnings to sanitize a clearly involuntary confession.

Garcia is correct that the *Ashcraft* Court would have decided in Chavez's favor. But what he misses is that the Tennessee Supreme Court, with one dissenting justice, had ruled against Ashcraft.[129] Reading *Lisenba* to "concede[] to each state the right to determine the question of the admissibility of confessions to itself, subject only to the overpowering requirement . . . of fair play," the state court thought *Ashcraft* insufficiently noteworthy even to publish the opinion.[130]

It was only by virtue of the United States Supreme Court granting certiorari that Ashcraft won his involuntariness claim.

The FDR-flavored Court that decided Ashcraft's case was probably uniquely positioned to shift the emphasis from whether the suspect's will was overborne—*Lisenba*— to whether unacceptable pressures were placed on him—*Chambers* and *Ashcraft*. It is not as clear to us as it is to Garcia and Welsh White[131] that the due process voluntariness analysis applied today by lower courts is meaningfully different than it was pre-*Miranda*. To be sure, courts today sometimes rhetorically rely on the warnings to "sanitize" a high-pressure interrogation. The Eleventh Circuit, for example, rejected the defendant's involuntariness argument in *Morgan v. Zant* as "without merit," without even disclosing the length of the interrogation, because the officers testified "that Morgan received numerous *Miranda* warnings prior to making any statement, and that he willingly confessed, these warnings notwithstanding."[132]

Giving *Miranda* warnings is, of course, relevant to voluntariness. Chavez and Morgan could have ended the interrogation at any point by simply invoking their rights. Repeated warnings reminded them that they did not have to talk. And lower courts did not need *Miranda* warnings to find admissible confessions made in cases against Fikes, Blackburn, Ashcraft, White, Haley, Gallegos, Spano, Chambers and other defendants. Thus, it appears that not much has changed in due process voluntariness in the lower courts.

2. *MIRANDA* WAIVERS ELIDING THE VOLUNTARINESS INQUIRY

Judges elide the issue of voluntariness of statements with the waiver question for two sensible reasons. Judging from judicial opinions, defense lawyers do not distinguish the question very often. And the two questions *are* governed by the same standard of voluntariness. Moreover, the Court in 1984 said that *Miranda*'s safeguards are intended "as much as possible to free courts from the task of scrutinizing individual cases to try to determine, after the fact, whether particular confessions were voluntary."[133] As the New Hampshire Supreme Court recently put it: "While compliance with *Miranda* does not conclusively establish the voluntariness of a later confession, it is one factor that a trial court can consider."[134]

But courts sometimes confuse waiver and voluntariness. In *State v. Reliford*, the Tennessee Court of Criminal Appeals introduced the suppression issue by saying that the "trial court determined that the defendant signed the advice of rights form and that he freely and voluntarily talked to the police officers."[135] This sounds like the court saw the issue as the voluntariness of the confession. The next sentence is, "The trial court's determination at the suppression hearing that a confession was voluntary is presumptively correct on appeal." The issue now clearly seems the voluntariness of the confession. Two sentences later, the court wrote, "When determining whether an accused has voluntarily, knowingly, and intelligently waived his *Miranda* rights, this court must consider the totality of the circumstances which existed when the accused waived these rights." Now the focus is on waiver.

When resolving the issue in favor of the State, the court kept the emphasis on waiver: "The trial court accredited the testimony of the sergeant and determined that the defendant knowingly and voluntarily signed the waiver of rights form." Of course, it is possible that the trial court expressly resolved both the waiver and voluntariness issue. If so, the appellate court opinion obscures that clarity.

As long as courts can move back and forth effortlessly between the waiver question and the voluntariness question, they can obscure and avoid most due process issues.

3. APPLYING MINIMALIST DUE PROCESS STANDARDS

One way to find a confession admissible is to put a heavy burden on defendants to demonstrate significant coercion before finding a due process violation. To make the defendant's task even more difficult, courts often examine each objectionable technique in isolation and then ask whether it is, by itself, coercive. Lower courts rarely do what the Court did in the 1940s to the 1960s, which is to look at the "totality of the circumstances." To be sure, courts sometimes say that is what they are doing. But the proof is in the method by which the totality is analyzed.

For example, in *State v. Harris*, the suspect was handcuffed and taken to the police station where he was placed in a 10 foot by 10 foot interview room and "shackled to the floor."[136] Except for bathroom breaks, he remained shackled to the floor for seven hours and was interrogated for two and one-half hours. The officers suggested to him that witnesses had seen him at the scene of the shooting, that witnesses had picked his photo out of a photo array, and that there was blood on his coat.[137] All of these incriminating facts were false. Although eyewitnesses had picked photos of *other men* from the array, the officers did not mention that inconvenient fact. Attempting to provide exculpatory evidence, Harris asked to use the phone to call an alibi witness.[138] The police refused the request. As for *Miranda*, the court stated that the warnings were given and he "agreed to talk" to the police.[139]

Harris, unlike *Chavez*, does not rely on the *Miranda* waiver in resolving the due process inquiry. Instead, the court looked at each potentially coercive fact in isolation and placed the burden on Harris to show that it rendered his confession involuntary: "Harris fails to cite any case law establishing that a nearly 7-hour detention is too long. Likewise he has not pointed to any case law to support his proposition that his confession was involuntary because he was restrained by shackles."[140] Recall that eight hours of questioning plus the "false friend" technique caused Spano's will to be "overborne by official pressure, fatigue and sympathy falsely aroused."[141] If the same Court had been writing the *Harris* opinion, it would have gone something like this: "Shackled to the floor for seven hours, led to believe by police lies that his case was hopeless, facing interrogators whose purpose was to break his will, denied the opportunity to speak to the outside world, Harris saw no choice but to confess. Moreover, police who intentionally mislead a suspect about evidence of guilt are acting in a way that is inconsistent with due process. In sum, he was 'subjected to pressures to which, under our accusatorial system, an accused should not be subjected.'[142] The confession must be suppressed." But the Kansas Supreme Court unanimously held Harris's confession voluntary and thus admissible.

In *State v. Jackson*, Raleigh police told Jackson "that they wanted to talk with him as a possible witness" in a murder case.[143] Though not under arrest, he accompanied police to the Investigative Division where he "was fully advised of his *Miranda* rights and waived those rights in writing." The North Carolina Supreme Court remarked, "He never requested an attorney." He was "interviewed" for almost three hours and agreed to return the next day "for further interviews and to take a polygraph test." The detectives also asked for the shoes and pants he had worn the day of the homicide. He gave them shoes and pants but not the ones he had worn that day.

The next day, he again waived *Miranda* in writing and took a polygraph.[144] The state court tells us, again, that he "did not request an attorney at any time." He was "interviewed" for four hours after the polygraph. A detective told him that there was blood on his shoes and pants, though Jackson, of course, knew that could not be the victim's blood because he gave the police the wrong clothes. When the "interview" was over, police told Jackson "that they would get back in touch with him later."

About twelve days later, police approached Jackson on the street and told him that they "wanted to talk with him about the murder."[145] He was not arrested and, the state court assured the reader, "voluntarily got into the car with Officer Williams and went to the police station." By now, the routine should be familiar: Jackson "was again advised of all of his *Miranda* rights, waived those rights in writing, and consented to be questioned by the officers without the presence of an attorney." Police "told the defendant he was not under arrest and that he was not in custody. He was not handcuffed and the interview room door was not locked."

The "interview" lasted four and one-half hours, during which police lied again about the evidence.[146] The detective showed him a knife with a bloody fingerprint that the police said was Jackson's. He told Jackson that his fingerprints were also found in the victim's apartment and that an eyewitness could identify him leaving the victim's apartment with that knife. The state court conceded that "[t]hese statements were not true." The detective told Jackson that the maximum penalty for first degree murder was the death penalty. But the state court assured the reader that "defendant was not threatened that if he did not cooperate he would get the death penalty." At some point, one of the officers said that if he pleaded not guilty "that the other officers would probably go into court and testify that defendant was a black man, killing and raping white women."[147]

Just before midnight, one of the detectives

"...went over the evidence again with the defendant, stating that the police had a murder weapon, they had defendant's fingerprints and the defendant's fingerprints at the scene, that they were on a knife sharpener and on a wooden post on the decedent's front porch, and that they had a witness who saw the defendant coming out the door carrying a knife. These statements were not true. At that point the defendant responded that he did it.[148]

The state supreme court held, 4–3, that Jackson's confession was voluntary. The key facts, in the court's view, that support a finding of voluntariness were: (1) He "was never in custody or under arrest before he confessed"; (2) an officer told him "on the day he confessed that he was free to go at any time"; (3) " he was not restrained, not touched, threatened, or intimidated"; (4) "he was taken where he wanted to go after the first two sessions with the officers"; (5) "he walked to the police station one day"; (6) "there was at least a week between the second and third interviews"; (7) Jackson "had an extensive criminal history and had previous experience with interrogation"; (8) "Jackson was repeatedly given proper *Miranda* instructions although he was not in custody"; (9) Jackson "was not questioned for undue periods of time, and no promises or threats were made to him"; (10) Jackson "made misrepresentations to the officers and was aware to some extent that the officers were not truthful with him."[149]

This list is less impressive than its length might suggest. Facts (1), (2), (3), (4), (5), and (8) simply restate the same theme: Jackson was not physically restrained and had been repeatedly given warnings. Presumably, the court is inviting the reader to infer that Jackson was not in custody and thus no *Miranda* violation was even possible. In addition, if Jackson believed he was free to leave, it would weaken his coercion argument. The time between interviews, (6), seems irrelevant to us. That he had prior experience with interrogation is relevant but not, in our view, particularly weighty. As for his knowledge that the police had lied to him about blood on his pants and shoes, we believe that should be added to the coercion side of the balance, as we will explain shortly. Thus, almost the entire "work" in the court's voluntariness calculation is done by the lack of custody and fact (9) that he "was not questioned for undue periods of time, and no promises or threats were made to him."

But the lack of promises or threats is contestable. The dissent added some facts that the majority conveniently left out: The police told Jackson that "no one could help him after he was placed in the gas chamber"; that "if his girlfriend was bearing his child he would not be the one to raise it if he were convicted"; "that if there were extenuating circumstances, defendant should 'bring [them] to light' or otherwise risk suffering the death penalty"; that Jackson "might avoid the death penalty by playing on the jurors' emotions at trial"; that "if he told the truth 'it would certainly come out in court that he cooperated.'"[150]

Then there was the "promise" that if he pleaded not guilty, the other officers would go to court and testify that he was a "black man, killing and raping white women." No threats? No promises? One should keep in mind the context—Jackson was a black man in North Carolina; the victim was a white woman; and North Carolina has a history of racial violence. North Carolina was, of course, a slave state that joined the Confederacy. It saw the first protest in the nation against white-only lunch counters, at the F.W. Woolworth lunch counter in Greensboro in 1960. The protests prompted deadly white backlash.[151] About eighteen months before police "interviewed" Jackson, marchers in a "Death to the Klan" rally in Greensboro were gunned down by group of Ku Klux Klansmen and members of the American Nazi Party.[152] Five marchers were killed. Greensboro is eighty miles from Raleigh.

An all-white state jury acquitted the Klansmen and Nazis six months before Jackson confessed to the murder in Raleigh. When Jackson was repeatedly questioned by the Raleigh police, his world included the history of slavery and segregation, the deaths in Greensboro, and the acquittals of the Klansmen and Nazis who killed the marchers. The police aggravated Jackson's vulnerability by telling him that he faced the gas chamber, they knew he was lying to them, and they would testify in court about his vicious murder and rape of white women. Jackson would have known the effect on the jury of the murder and rape accusation. For shameful decade after shameful decade, black men charged with raping white women had been lynched—guilty or not—a fact that Jackson surely knew.

Moreover, he faced what appeared to be overwhelming evidence against him, constructed out of police lies. The majority seemed to believe that his knowledge of the police lying about some evidence might lead him to think that they were lying about other evidence. But the opposite inference is, to us, more likely. A black man charged with raping and murdering a white woman in North Carolina in 1981 could very easily believe that the police would fabricate whatever evidence it took to send him to the gas chamber. We prefer the dissent's reading of Jackson's interrogation: "Absent torture or other physical abuse, it would be difficult to conceive of interrogation tactics more likely to produce an untruthful, unreliable confession than the ones utilized in this case."[153]

Many scholars believe that the problems we have surveyed here are the result of later Courts and lower courts failing to apply *Miranda*'s principles as robustly as the Warren Court intended. But we must not forget Seidman's powerful critique from the last chapter. Perhaps *Miranda* was, from the beginning, a compromise, and a retreat from a world in which lawyers attended all interrogations. Perhaps *Miranda* all along was meant to support the status quo where police interrogated mostly guilty suspects and usually obtained a confession. Indeed, according to Seidman, *Miranda* works better to maintain the status quo than the voluntariness test. "The imagery of consent and equality, so powerfully and simply invoked by Chief Justice Warren's rhetoric, dominates popular culture in a way that the old confusing, complex, and contradictory law of . . . voluntariness never could."[154] In sum, *Miranda* has "led us into a trap" and the "escape route from our present predicament is not nearly so well marked" as it was before *Miranda*.[155]

C. What Hath *Miranda* Wrought?

No one knows how many suspects are moved to stay silent because of the warnings. Nor do we know how many suspects might talk because of the warnings. They are, after all, an official indication that the police believe the suspect is guilty, and they thus invite a response if the suspect is to maintain that he is innocent. We do know that roughly 80% of suspects waive their rights and speak to the police. After waiver, they face the inherent compulsion that *Miranda* condemned. We agree with Bradley that *Miranda* "has surely not wiped out confessions that due to factors like physical coercion, psychological ploys, mental incapacity, and fatigue are not sufficiently 'voluntary' to be considered either fair or reliable."[156]

We would partly agree with Garcia that "*Miranda* has produced paradoxes that the Warren Court would have never imagined—circumstances in which the 'old' voluntariness approach affords more protection to criminal suspects than the putative safeguards outlined in the decision."[157] Garcia's paradoxes are there as long as the old due process approach is that of the Supreme Court of the 1940s, 1950s, and 1960s. Given the repeated need to reverse state courts that found confessions voluntary on gruesome facts, it strikes us as unlikely that lower courts were embracing the Supreme Court's robust due process approach. But, at a minimum, defendants today are deprived of the lofty rhetoric of the FDR Supreme Court. The *Ashcraft-Spano* due process protection seems as far as a distant star.

Sandy Thompson despairs that "there is truly nothing left of *Miranda*. . . . The *Miranda* chapter has effectively come to a close."[158] Garcia would have the Court overrule *Miranda*. But we do not despair as much as Thompson or Garcia for three reasons. First, *Dickerson v. United States* affirmed *Miranda* in 2000,[159] thus effectively closing the door on overruling it, at least for many years (Garcia wrote two years before *Dickerson* was decided). Second, viewing *Miranda* as due process notice makes clear its appeal: It is part of basic fairness to tell a suspect that he has a right not to answer police questions, and that part of the *Miranda* chapter continues to resonate. Third, we hope our solutions presented in chapter 10 will move courts, at least partly, back to the Supreme Court's robust due process voluntariness doctrine that existed before it was eclipsed by the glare of *Miranda*.

CHAPTER 10

Interrogation Law

THE FUTURE?

Our book, so far, has sketched a dialectic between the Hawkins-Leach dictum and a rationalist view of interrogation law. In the twentieth century alone, the law shifted abruptly toward Wigmore's rationalist pole, then back to *Miranda*'s version of the Hawkins-Leach dictum and, finally, back to a more rationalist view as the Court narrowed *Miranda*'s robust dicta. Going forward, we think the rationalist view will prevail, at least in the intermediate term.

We believe that the future of the law governing interrogation will be a dualistic one: one set of rules for "ordinary" police interrogation and quite a different set governing the interrogation of those viewed as sources of information rather than as potential criminal defendants. We begin with ordinary police interrogation, by which we mean interrogation intended to produce statements that can be used against the suspect in a criminal trial.

A. Treating *Miranda*'s Trouble Spots

In chapters 8 and 9, we highlighted some of *Miranda*'s trouble spots. One is that it is unclear how effectively the warnings provide adequate notice of the rights waived if suspects talk to police. Another is that courts tend to treat a *Miranda* waiver as a near-conclusive presumption that all subsequent statements are uncoerced.[1] A third trouble spot is that some suspects lack the capacity to waive *Miranda*, most notably juveniles and the mentally impaired.

A fourth trouble spot, which we did not mention in chapter 9, is that interrogators sometimes construct the confession;, a phenomenon that Richard Leo has exposed based on observing thousands of police interrogations.[2] From this wealth of data about police interrogation, Leo concludes that one goal of detectives is to construct a narrative that shows the suspect's confession as "authentic, compelling, and self-corroborating."[3] Interrogators seek a coherent and believable story line with a statement of the suspect's motives and explanations, knowledge of intimate details of the crime, and expressions of emotion that "humanize the admission, seemingly rendering it the natural product of lived experience."[4]

The narrative should be capable of persuading the key parties in the criminal justice system as the case goes forward: the prosecutor, the judge, the jury, and the court of appeals. When the narrative makes sense as a story, it will cue listeners to interpret other evidence as consistent with the narrative. To create this convincing narrative, police sometimes supply missing information to the suspect. The threat to innocent suspects is obvious. An innocent suspect who finally succumbs to police pressure and concedes that he must have done it, even though he cannot remember how, can be "helped" to create the narrative of how he did it by police eager to have a story that they can "sell" to prosecutors, judges, and juries.

Larry Rosenthal takes the position that what appears to Leo and Thomas as constructing a confession is really nothing more, or less, than police confronting a suspect with evidence of his guilt.[5] But in this, as in much else in life, the truth is complex. It is one kind of interrogation tactic to confront a silent suspect with evidence that his DNA or fingerprints were found at the scene, whether true or false. What the police did to Michael Crowe is a different kind of interrogation. He was fourteen years old, in police custody, and under suspicion of murdering his sister. As Leo described it, the police "shattered Crowe's confidence in his memory" and eventually convinced him to agree with them that the reason he did not remember the crime was the rage that had caused him to kill his sister:[6] "The only way I even know I did this is because she's dead and because the evidence says that I did."[7] Crowe was exonerated by a conclusive DNA match with the real killer.[8]

The incidence of false confessions is unknown, but the Innocence Project data suggest that it is far from trivial. False confessions are the third leading cause of wrongful convictions.[9] There is a harm beyond the false confession concern. To the extent that the confession does not really "belong" to the suspect and to the extent it was constructed by the police, it undermines the fact-finding function of the criminal process. Suspects in large numbers likely plead guilty to more serious offenses, or receive longer sentences, than might otherwise have been the case had the suspect's halting, incomplete, inconsistent story been the one that the system accepted as his "confession." Though the false-conviction literature concentrates on defendants who are wholly innocent, defendants who are convicted of greater offenses than they committed are also falsely convicted.

These trouble spots can be ameliorated, though not completely solved, with one simple solution: recording the relevant contact between the police and the suspect. We realize that recording is hardly a new recommendation. Perhaps one hundred other writers are on record recommending some form of recording.[10] Nonetheless, we believe that the future of ordinary police interrogation is intimately connected with recording. As we saw in *Doody*, an accurate recording of an interrogation permits courts to put themselves in the position of the suspect and make a more informed decision about waiver and voluntariness.

We envision a world in which technology allows almost the entire encounter between a suspect and the police to be easily recorded—from arrest to the end of interrogation. Motion-sensitive recording devices could be placed in all police cruisers and even attached to the officers themselves. David Harris reports that police departments are already experimenting with "body-worn video" devices that attach to the officer's ear and that record all that she sees.[11]

Rooms in a police station could be equipped with motion-sensitive recording devices. This would solve the problem of police "tuning up" the suspect prior to, or during stops in, the recording. Many have argued that if police knew they were being recorded, they would be less likely to undermine *Miranda* and less likely to engage in coercive interrogation techniques. Indeed, because police cannot know precisely where a judge will draw the coercion line, the incentive will be for the officer to stop considerably short of that line. As we saw in *Doody* in the last chapter, however, police will sometimes come close to, or go over, the line, even when they know the recorder is running. The beauty of recording is that it matters not a bit whether it encourages police to put less, or more, pressure on suspects. Whatever transpires between the police and the suspect will be there for the defense lawyer, the prosecutor, the judge, the jury, and the world to see.

The recordings might reveal a police interrogation world where police routinely take advantage—by coercion, trickery, and deception—of confused suspects who do not appear to make choices that we would accept as truly theirs. If so, judges would suppress more confessions than they do today. Prosecutors might offer more favorable plea bargains to avoid the risk of having confessions suppressed. Legislatures might, the past notwithstanding, be shamed into enacting specific restrictions on interrogation that would ease the pressure on suspects.

Richard Leo in 2008 set out some potential rule-like restrictions on interrogations, prohibiting some types of police deception, threats, and promises, and limiting the length of interrogations. Leo would also forbid interrogation in the absence of probable cause.[12] The late Welsh White made a set of similar recommendations in 2001.[13] When reviewing White's book, Andrew Taslitz fearlessly predicted that it is "likely over time to have a significant practical impact" because its focus on protecting innocence is "more likely to move policymakers to action in a law-and-order world than are pleas to respect the rights of the guilty."[14] So far the legislative cannons have been silent.

We will largely avoid prescriptive rules in this chapter, in part because police can find their way around almost any set of rules. Moreover, we are skeptical about legislative willingness to inhibit the ability of police to obtain confessions (which mostly come from guilty suspects). Whether the political will can ever be found to restrict police interrogators is unknown, but at least the legislatures in jurisdictions that record interrogations would make that decision knowing the reality of what police interrogation looks like.

It is possible that the recordings will reveal a police interrogation world where suspect and interrogator circle each other like a mongoose and a cobra. In this world, *Miranda* is merely a piece of furniture that can be easily moved aside, but the suspects who respond to the police might seem to be making genuine, if ill-advised, choices to talk to the police. Judges who refuse to suppress confessions in that world would be making wise decisions. And legislatures could safely continue to leave the regulation of police interrogation in the hands of the courts. Even in this world, of course, there will be some cases that show the kind of pressure and deception that should cause a judge to suppress a confession. Moreover, judges (and juries) who watch the entire interrogation can better sort out the difference between confronting a suspect with evidence of guilt and constructing a confession from a suspect who appears genuinely not to remember the crime. The beauty of recording is that the full picture is there for the judge and jury to see, warts and all.

Larry Rosenthal pointed out that if juries were squeamish about police interrogation tactics, many confessions from guilty suspects would be suppressed.[15] The "cost" of this development, should it occur, would be to increase the number of years that guilty defendants are on the street. We imagine, however, that this cost would be quite low. First, when police engage in the kind of tactics associated with false confessions—lengthy, relentless questioning that includes lies about evidence of guilt; fabricating evidence of guilt; promising lenient treatment in exchange for a confession; and helping the suspect construct a confession when she does not appear to remember the details—we think the confession ought to be rejected even if, in some cases, the defendant is guilty. The risk of eliciting false confessions is just too high when police use these tactics. Second, juries who see the ordinary tricks of police interrogation will not, we think, be inclined to punish police by ignoring what appears to be a genuine confession of guilt. Third, if the police tactics are in a gray area between truly overpowering and routine interrogation, the prosecutor can sweeten the plea offer. Because the odds of conviction still favor the State, in most cases even a discounted deal will probably be roughly commensurate with the culpability of the defendant.

Another potential cost of a universal recording requirement is the drain on judicial time in viewing the tapes and lengthier suppression hearings as the defense lawyer attacks police tactics. But the recording requirement imposed by the Minnesota Supreme Court in *State v. Scales* seems to have worked.[16] *Scales* was decided in 1994, but we searched in vain for a case, article, or news story even alluding to problems in implementation. Brad Colbert, a Minnesota public defender, informed us that when a defendant challenges his confession, the trial judge views the recording prior to the hearing.[17] If the judge admits the confession, and the defendant wishes to challenge it before the jury, the recording is played in court while the jury follows along with a transcript.

A recording requirement might create other costs, such as an increase in habeas petitions and an increase in claims of ineffective assistance of counsel. Prisoners whiling away time would, after all, be motivated to view the recording, and they are likely to see possible *Miranda*, right to counsel, and due process violations that they could not have reconstructed from memory. But these costs, to us, pale in comparison with the advantages that a full picture of interrogation provides the defense, the prosecution, and the judge. How can knowing the truth about police interrogation be bad for justice?

We will now discuss some specific problems that *Miranda* has either failed to remedy or, perhaps, has made worse.

1. THE UNRELIABILITY PROBLEM

Leo is right that "[t]here is no worse error in American criminal justice than the wrongful prosecution, conviction, and incarceration of an innocent person, especially in capital cases."[18] And Dan Medwed is right that "American criminal law is undergoing a transformation due to the increasing centrality of issues related to actual innocence in courtrooms, classrooms, and newsrooms."[19] Thus, additional safeguards will be needed, and should, up to a point, be politically possible, no matter which world of interrogation emerges from the recordings. The defendant will, of course, have the right to have the judge and jury view the electronic recording and draw their own conclusion. If the police are seen blatantly constructing a confession from a suspect who has made a halting, confused admission, a judge could easily suppress it as involuntary or a jury could reject it as unreliable. Sufficient threats, trickery, and deception coupled with promises of favor should lead a judge or jury to reject a confession.

At a minimum, defendants should have the right to have a jury rule on whether the confession is reliable. The Supreme Court agrees. In *Crane v. Kentucky*, the defendant, who was sixteen at the time, testified that "he had been badgered into making a false confession."[20] The police denied using coercion or "sweating," and the trial judge admitted the confession. The case came to the United States Supreme Court on the narrow question of whether Crane had the right to argue to the jury that his confession was unreliable. The trial court held, and the state supreme court affirmed, that once the trial judge found the confession voluntary, the defendant could not offer evidence of involuntariness, although he could offer "any competent evidence relating to authenticity, reliability or credibility of the confession."[21] One judge dissented, arguing that evidence of coercion is obviously related to reliability and thus should be admitted under the majority's own statement of the rule.[22]

A unanimous Supreme Court agreed with the dissent in the state court:

> The holding below rests on the apparent assumption that evidence bearing on the voluntariness of a confession and evidence bearing on its credibility fall in conceptually distinct and mutually exclusive categories. Once a confession has been found voluntary, the Supreme Court of Kentucky believed, the evidence that supported that finding may not be presented to the jury for any other purpose. This analysis finds no support in our cases, is premised on a misconception about the role of confessions in a criminal trial, and, under the circumstances of this case, contributed to an evidentiary ruling that deprived petitioner of his fundamental constitutional right to a fair opportunity to present a defense.[23]

The issue of reliability thus ultimately belongs to the jury. But defendants who seek to prove the falsity of their confessions face the obvious hurdle of persuading a jury that what was said voluntarily (according to the trial judge) was in fact not true. Given the human desire to avoid pain, why would anyone who is innocent make incriminating statements? Since we know that this phenomenon occurs, though we do not know the frequency, it makes sense to permit defendants who claim that they falsely confessed to present expert witnesses who could explain to jurors how it is possible for the innocent to confess and under what conditions it is most likely to occur.

In addition, a cautionary jury instruction should be available if the defendant requests it. Here's one version: "The defendant has claimed that his confession, though legally voluntary, is in fact false. I instruct you that cases exist in which DNA evidence has proven that a legally voluntary confession turned out to be false." Many false confessions tend to be halting, evasive, and indirect. Letting the jury see the interrogation, with an instruction that alerts them to the possibility that the confession might be false, should permit the jury to make a fair decision about how much weight to give the confession. Indeed, the truth or falsity of incriminating statements is not a binary proposition, as English cases first held in the eighteenth century. A jury might believe that some of the admissions are true but give them so little weight that the prosecution fails to prove guilt beyond a reasonable doubt.

In sum, recording is particularly helpful in ameliorating the unreliability problem. Recording will also be beneficial, though perhaps less so, in remedying the lack of capacity problem.

2. THE CAPACITY PROBLEM

Part of our argument in this book is that the Court inadvertently lost most of the value in the voluntariness test that *Miranda* sought to supplement. We have seen that waiver creates an almost irrebuttable presumption that any subsequent statements are made voluntarily. We saw that even mental disabilities are largely ignored on the voluntariness issue when a suspect waives *Miranda*, unlike the Court's earlier approach in its due process cases. By lack of capacity, we include the capacity to waive the legalistic rights that *Miranda* created as well as the capacity, if waiver is held valid, to make a voluntary confession. The two capacities are obviously linked, but suspects could have the capacity to understand the warnings but not the capacity to make a voluntary choice about confessing given the pressure brought to bear by interrogators.

As noted in the last chapter, Morgan Cloud and co-authors conducted an empirical study of mentally retarded subjects who are asked the meaning of the *Miranda* warnings.[24] The question that sought to uncover an understanding of the right to remain silent had the control group giving the correct answer 86% of the time while the mentally retarded subjects were correct only 10% of the time.[25] Across the board, the retarded subjects recorded understanding rates far below those of the control group.

To what extent will recording the interrogation prove beneficial to suspects who lack the capacity to waive *Miranda* or to make a voluntary choice about confessing? It is difficult to know until studies have been conducted, but, at a minimum, recording will allow the judge and jury to gauge for themselves whether the suspect *appeared* to have the capacity to waive *Miranda* or to make a choice about confessing. We would be surprised if a judge or jury would find a waiver valid after watching the face of an eleven year old as an officer gives the warnings in a rote fashion. And we hope that most judges and juries would find the admission involuntary after the eleven year old was interrogated for an hour and then asked to put his hand on the Bible and swear that he had nothing to do with burning a church. But, again, the beauty of recording is that it gives the judge, and then the jury, maximum information. We would feel better about a ruling against an eleven-year-old suspect if the judge and the jury watched the recording of the warnings, the waiver, and the subsequent interrogation.

We expect that "waivers" will often be rejected if mentally impaired suspects manifest their disabilities. Those who have learned to mask their disabilities will have a more difficult time persuading the judge and jury that they lacked the capacity to waive. But they will still be in a superior position to defendants who have to make arguments based on testimony of what the participants recalled from the interrogation process. Thus, while recording will not solve the capacity problem, it should substantially ameliorate it.

3. IMPROVING THE DUE PROCESS VOLUNTARINESS TEST

We are not optimistic that courts will apply a due process test with much enthusiasm after determining that a *Miranda* waiver was valid. But to the extent courts still talk about due process rights that exist independently of *Miranda*, and they ought to, they should at least use better terminology than "voluntariness." We showed in chapter 4 that voluntariness, understood as "overbear the will" is incoherent. However suspects come to decide to talk to police, even if after torture, their will was not literally overborne. Faced with talk or X, they made a choice to talk rather than X. All conscious utterances are, and must be, willed actions.

The FDR Court's shift to whether compulsion was applied—in cases like *Ashcraft* and *Chambers*—is a coherent, if difficult, inquiry. One way to get past the difficulty of determining whether the police applied compulsion is to draw on Alan Wertheimer's argument that what underlies the notion of voluntariness in confessions law is a normative theory about whether the forced choice is a reasonable one.[26] Perhaps because courts and legal scholars have wrestled, unsuccessfully, with the Fourth Amendment question of what searches and seizures are reasonable, we prefer a somewhat different locution—whether the choice is one that society views as morally permissible. For instance, when a robber gives a bank teller a choice between "your money or your life," society does not accept that as morally permissible. Focusing more narrowly on police interrogation, the moral choice theory asks, in the choice between talk or X, whether X is something that society believes police ought to be able to force on suspects. We do not, for example, want police to put suspects in the position of choosing between confessing or suffering extreme physical pain. That, of course, is *Brown v. Mississippi*. During the heyday of the Hawkins-Leach dictum, many English courts held it improper to give a suspect a choice between being silent or telling the truth. Today, that choice would not be considered improper.

We believe that all due process voluntariness cases can be usefully viewed through the lens of whether the choice the suspect faced was one that society permits the police to force on a suspect. But we should be clear. This is neither, at bottom, an original idea nor one that it is self-executing or precise. The roots go back at least as far as Yale Kamisar in 1963 and include versions by Albert Alschuler in 1997 and Mark Godsey in 2005. In 1963, Kamisar unmasked the "voluntariness" test as having "obscured" the "real reasons for excluding confessions."[27] He urged that courts "scrap the 'voluntariness' terminology altogether" and replace it with a test that focused on whether the interrogation entailed "forbidden police methods."[28] Kamisar offers examples of forbidden police methods—e.g., preventing a suspect from having contact with his lawyer or purposely keeping a suspect who has been unlawfully arrested from being brought before a magistrate[29]—but the only definition of "forbidden police methods" he gives is "offensive or deliberate and systematic police misconduct."[30]

Albert Alschuler in 1997 also rejected confessions tests based on free will: "[E]fforts to assess whether confessions were the product of free will were always misguided—incoherent in concept, unadministerable in practice, and incompatible with our general understanding of the Bill of Rights as a body of restraints on improper governmental conduct."[31] To Alschuler, most of the talk about free will is the kind of talk one does "when one is in a funk, drunk, in France, or at a university."[32] Instead, Alschuler proposes to ask whether the police conduct is offensive.[33] Like Kamisar, Alschuler offers examples but no definition. His examples include interrogations that are too long or police fabricating evidence and misrepresenting the strength of the case against the suspect, especially when also promising leniency.[34]

Mark Godsey in 2005 proposed replacing voluntariness with a test that focuses on whether the police threatened the suspect with what he calls an "objective penalty."[35] Conceding that "[d]efining the concept of an objective penalty is not an easy task,"[36] Godsey provides some rough guidance. Courts would begin with the baseline that the suspect is entitled to expect, which should be drawn from "reasonable law enforcement practices, customs, norms and societal expectations."[37] If the police threaten to move the suspect below that baseline, then he has suffered an objective penalty, and his statements in response to the threat are inadmissible. For example, if the police tell a suspect they will arrest her husband if she does not confess, this is a threat to move the suspect below the baseline she is entitled to expect *if the police lack probable cause to arrest her husband.*[38] If the police do have grounds to arrest her husband, then Godsey would treat a statement about not arresting him if she confesses as an offer rather than a threat and would find it permissible.

Our moral choice theory is similar to these approaches in that all require explicitly moral judgments about police conduct. It must be offensive and systematic police misconduct, an objective penalty, or a choice that society is not prepared to have police force on a suspect. We acknowledge that our approach lacks precision. How does a court decide what choices society is prepared to have police force on suspects? But this problem plagues the other morality-based approaches, though Godsey's baseline approach probably comes closest to precision. However imprecise, all of the normative theories are preferable to the "overbear the will" test. An imprecise test that at least asks the right question is better than an incoherent inquiry that is also imprecise.

One way to "surround" the vagueness problem of our moral choice inquiry is to recognize, as Larry Rosenthal suggested to us, that there is a subcategory of cases that are relatively easy to resolve—where the police make a threat other than the threat to convict the suspect after a fair trial.[39] This first-stage inquiry, which we call the "external threat" inquiry, can be traced to Justice Harlan's opinion for the Court in *McGautha v. California*.[40] The issue there was whether the privilege against self-incrimination was offended when the State put a defendant to the choice of testifying on the issue of punishment and having the jury consider that testimony on guilt, or not testifying at all. Because the "threat" was merely an increased risk of conviction, it was not external to the attempt to fairly convict him and thus constitutionally permissible.[41]

The "external threat" inquiry explains most of the Court's due process voluntariness cases. In *Payne v. Arkansas*, the police chief told Payne that there were thirty or forty people outside the jail who wanted to get him, and that if he would "tell him the truth" the chief "would probably keep them from coming in."[42] The Court found it "obvious from the totality of this course of conduct, and particularly the culminating threat of mob violence, that the confession was coerced and did not constitute an 'expression of free choice.'"[43] How much easier to hold that Payne confessed when faced with mob violence—a threat that had nothing to do with convicting him after a fair trial.

In *Lynum v. Illinois*, one of the arresting officers told Lynum that she "could get 10 years and the children could be taken away, and after [she] got out they would be taken away and strangers would have them."[44] If she cooperated, on the other hand, the officer "would see they weren't [taken away]; and he would recommend leniency and I had better do what they told me if I wanted to see my kids again." Lynum's children were three and four years old; their father was dead.

Justice Stewart, writing for a unanimous Court, invoked the voluntariness mantra: "We have said that the question in each case is whether the defendant's will was overborne at the time he confessed."[45] The Court held that it was "clear" that Lynum's will was overborne and her confession "not voluntary." But it is only a bizarre use of the word "will" that allows a court to claim that she didn't will her confession. Of course she did. She decided she would rather receive the promised benefits of confessing—leniency and keeping her children—than face the penalties that the police threatened. How much easier is a case like *Lynum* if a court instead asked whether she confessed after the police made a threat external to the case against her.

In *Rogers v. Richmond*, the assistant chief of police told the suspect that he was going to bring his wife in for questioning unless he confessed—by Rogers's account, the chief said "that he would be 'less than a man' if he failed to confess and thereby caused her to be taken into custody."[46] Rogers testified that "his wife suffered from arthritis, and [that] he confessed to spare her being transported to the scene of the interrogation." In *Rogers*, the Court came close to an external threat theory of voluntariness. Confessions are induced by "constitutionally impermissible methods," the Court said, when a suspect is "subjected to pressures to which, under our accusatorial system, an accused should not be subjected."[47] Assuming that the police lacked probable cause to arrest Rogers's wife, they made a threat that is external to the case against him and should be held impermissible.

Similarly, *Spano* can be understood as a mild external threat case. Though the Court discussed the length of time he was questioned—his statement was finally taken at 4:05 a.m. —and the refusal to provide access to counsel,[48] the fact that seemed most worrisome to the Court was the "false friend" ploy. The detectives had Spano's police friend claim that his job was in jeopardy because Spano had called him after killing the victim.[49] The friend "played this part of a worried father, harried by his superiors, in not one, but four different acts, the final one lasting an hour." Though the threat is mild, it is external to the case against Spano.

As we understand Larry Rosenthal's argument, he would limit the category of "involuntary" confessions to those induced by external threats, but we think that there is a residual category in which police methods, even without an external threat, become so oppressive that they fall outside the choices that society is willing to force on suspects. To begin with an extreme hypothetical, consider the murder suspect who is questioned for seventy-two hours, nonstop, without being permitted to eat or sleep. At the seventy-two-hour mark, the district attorney offers to reduce the charge to assault with a six-month suspended sentence in exchange for a confession. We think it pellucid that this interrogation violates due process. If this is right, then the due process question in the absence of external threats is simply a question of degree, and interrogations with less pressure are candidates for this residual category.

A good example of the residual category is *Blackburn v. Alabama*.[50] The Court described the defendant as a twenty-four-year-old black man with a "lengthy" history of mental illness, who "had been discharged" from the armed forces in 1944 "as permanently disabled by a psychosis."[51] The robbery occurred during Blackburn's "unauthorized absence" from a Veterans Hospital mental ward. The Veterans Administration diagnosis was "100% 'incompetent'" and "'schizophrenic reaction, paranoid type.'"[52]

On the issue of police tactics, the Court stressed "the eight- to nine-hour sustained interrogation in a tiny room which was upon occasion literally filled with police officers; the absence of Blackburn's friends, relatives, or legal counsel; [and] the composition of the confession by the Deputy Sheriff rather than by Blackburn."[53] The Court conceded that the confession might have been made "during a period of complete mental competence."[54] But "the chances of the confession's having been the product of a rational intellect and a free will" were "remote" and thus the interrogation a denial of due process.

Along the way, Chief Justice Warren's opinion tried to identify the values served by the voluntariness doctrine. The Court started with "the likelihood that the confession is untrue" and "the preservation of the individual's freedom of will."[55] But the Court assured the reader that neither of those values is "the sole interest at stake." The Court quoted *Spano* "that in the end life and liberty can be as much endangered from illegal methods used to convict those thought to be criminals as from the actual criminals themselves."[56] The Court concluded that "a complex of values underlies the stricture against use by the state of confessions which, by way of convenient shorthand, this Court terms involuntary, and the role played by each in any situation varies according to the particular circumstances of the case." This is pretty close to acknowledging that "voluntariness" is really a stand-in for values that have nothing to do with the exercise of will. We think the real issue is the moral permissibility of the choice created by the police—in Blackburn's case, the choice of a suspect with severe mental illness to confess or face interrogation for eight or nine hours, with no end in sight, in a "tiny room" sometimes "filled with police officers."

We now apply our moral choice test to some of the other cases discussed in the last chapter. Unlike the majority in *State v. Jackson*,[57] we believe that a true totality of the circumstances test, taking into account the racial context, would conclude that the police threatened Jackson with the death penalty. This is an example of a threat that is internal to the case but that, when considered with the racial context and the repeated lies about evidence against him, suggests he was "subjected to pressures to which, under our accusatorial system, an accused should not be subjected."[58]

In *Miller v. State*, where the defendant was found as a matter of state law to be mentally retarded, our moral choice theory suggests suppressing his confession.[59] We think that lying to a mentally disabled suspect to make the case look hopeless weighs more heavily against admission than if the suspect is not disabled. The impaired suspect is less able to appreciate his options and more likely to confess falsely. Thus, the choice Miller faced between confessing and continuing an interrogation that falsely demonstrated an overwhelming case against him is not a choice, we hope, that society is prepared to accept.

We do not claim that all voluntariness questions are easy to resolve under our moral choice analysis. Hard cases, such as *State v. Harris*, remain hard cases.[60] He was shackled to the floor, the police fabricated much evidence against him, and they kept from him the exculpatory evidence that someone else was identified at a lineup. Still, he was only questioned for two and one-half hours and, as far as the court's opinion reveals, police made no threats or promises. However a court would rule under our moral choice theory, we believe that the right question to ask is some variation of whether Harris was "subjected to pressures to which, under our accusatorial system, an accused should not be subjected."

We turn now to interrogation in search of information rather than convictions, usually directed at suspected terrorists.

B. Interrogation Law: When the Goal is Obtaining Information

Our focus in chapters 2 through 9 was the interrogation of those suspected of ordinary crimes. As chapter 1 noted, however, the 9/11 mass murder of Americans opened a new chapter in methods of interrogation. To be sure, according to some accounts, the CIA has been using extreme interrogation methods for decades,[61] but the chapter that opened after 9/11 brought these methods more fully to light. We know that coercive interrogation methods, such as water-boarding, have been used against suspected terrorists. In addition, allegations arose that terrorism suspects were sent to other nations by a process called "extraordinary rendition." The purpose of extraordinary rendition is to allow intelligence agencies in other nations to use interrogation methods, including torture, that American law prohibits.

That the United States has engaged in the process of extraordinary rendition, although never admitted, is supported by substantial evidence.[62] As the result of one well-known allegation of extraordinary rendition, Maher Arar, a dual Syrian and Canadian citizen, brought a federal lawsuit that accused senior United States officials of sending him to Syria to be tortured.[63] In 2007, "Democratic and Republican lawmakers urged the Bush administration to apologize to Mr. Arar."[64]

A June 2006 report of the Council of Europe concluded that several member nations wrongfully colluded with the CIA in its rendition activities, sometimes by turning a "blind eye."[65] Multiple sources indicate that the CIA utilizes secret detention centers, or "black sites," and various types of airplane transfer sites on European soil, both of which facilitate rendition.[66] According to the European Parliament, the CIA has conducted "at least 1,245 flights" to accomplish these renditions.[67] An Italian court in November 2009 convicted twenty-three Americans of kidnapping a Muslim cleric from the streets of Milan in 2003.[68] The cleric claimed that the kidnapping was part of a plot to render him to Egypt for interrogation and torture. Those convicted included the CIA base chief in Milan at the time of the kidnapping, an air force colonel, and twenty-one CIA operatives. All were tried in abstentia, and it is unlikely that any will serve time in an Italian prison.

Whatever the extent of the extraordinary rendition and the use of coercion by U.S. intelligence agents, a little-noticed Supreme Court case from 2003 has surprising implications for interrogation of suspected terrorists. At least some of the suspected terrorists have been and will be tried in civilian court. This will give them the chance to move to suppress their statements as involuntary under the Fifth Amendment due process clause or as compelled under federal evidence law.[69]

Whether *Miranda* would apply to these former "enemy combatants" is a more difficult question. The Fifth Amendment privilege applies by its terms to "any person."[70] But even if "any person" includes enemy combatants who have no connection with the United States, the Court in *Quarles* made plain that *Miranda* is a procedural safeguard that can be withheld when questions are "reasonably prompted by a concern for the public safety."[71] Interrogators seeking information about future attacks might fit within a *Quarles* exception. To be sure, the public safety concern in *Quarles* was more imminent—locating a gun thought to be hidden in a store—than concerns that arise in the interrogation of suspected terrorists. But the scope and scale of the threat to public safety posed by terrorists suggests that a *Quarles*-type exception be made to *Miranda*.

In the wake of the failed attempt to detonate a bomb in Times Square in 2010, Attorney General Eric Holder called for legislation to dispense with *Miranda* warnings when interrogating suspected terrorists—in his words, to make the law "relevant to our time and the threat that we now face."[72] While awaiting legislation, the FBI set out guidelines for when agents can dispense with warnings in an "unsigned, internal memorandum."[73] Unsurprisingly, the guidelines broaden the *Quarles* exception to fit the terrorism context: "In light of the magnitude and complexity of the threat often posed by terrorist organizations, particularly international terrorist organizations, and the nature of their attacks, the circumstances surrounding an arrest of an operational terrorist may warrant significantly more extensive public safety interrogation without Miranda warnings than would be permissible in an ordinary criminal case."

One little-noticed issue remains. There are two groups of suspected terrorists for whom the suppression right has little relevance. The first, and obvious, group includes those against whom the authorities have enough evidence to convict without their statements. Presumably, if the government decides to try Khalid Sheikh Mohammed in civilian court, his case fits in this category. If not, there will be political hell to pay. Going forward, and facing the prospect of civilian trials for some of the terrorist suspects, future interrogators will have incentives either to comply with constitutional standards or amass sufficient evidence to convict that is independent of the confession evidence.

Those whom the government never intends to bring to trial make up a second group, which includes low-level suspects who might be released back to their countries once the interrogators have learned what they know. At the other end of the spectrum, there are probably higher level suspects who might be kept indefinitely if releasing them is simply too dangerous to contemplate; the great Apache chief Geronimo was a federal prisoner until his death twenty-two years after he surrendered.[74] For those who will never face trial, are there constraints on interrogators' attempts to coerce information? One constraint, of course, is that interrogators will not always know ex ante which suspects fit into the category that will never face trial, which will create an incentive for interrogators to avoid easily proven coercion.

But the question remains whether any remedy other than suppression might be available. Answers lurk in a 2003 case, *Chavez v. Martinez*.[75] The issue was whether Martinez could sue, under 42 U.S.C. § 1983, the police officer who conducted a highly coercive interrogation of him. To bring suit under § 1983, a litigant must allege a violation of the United States Constitution or a federal statute. One might assume that a coercive interrogation violates the United States Constitution, but that assumption turns out to be superficial and at least partly wrong.

Investigating a police shooting, Chavez questioned the victim, Martinez, in the emergency room while he was receiving treatment. There can be little doubt that the questioning was coercive.

> Martinez "had been shot in the face, both eyes were injured; he was screaming in pain, and coming in and out of consciousness while being repeatedly questioned about details of the encounter with the police." His blinding facial wounds made it impossible for him visually to distinguish the interrogating officer from the attending medical personnel. The officer made no effort to dispel the perception that medical treatment was being withheld until Martinez answered the questions put to him. There was no attempt through *Miranda* warnings or other assurances to advise the suspect that his cooperation should be voluntary. Martinez begged the officer to desist and provide treatment for his wounds, but the questioning persisted despite these pleas and despite Martinez's unequivocal refusal to answer questions.[76]

Though this description appears in a dissenting opinion, none of the opinions denied that Martinez was subjected to coercion.

If Martinez had been prosecuted, his statements would have been suppressed. No threat to public safety justified dispensing with warnings, and the questioning in the emergency room thus violated *Miranda*. Moreover, the due process doctrine that began in *Brown v. Mississippi* and evolved into *Spano v. New York* would also lead to suppression on the grounds that his statements were coerced. Because he was not prosecuted, however, the police conduct became an issue only when Martinez sued Chavez in a civil action for violating his constitutional right to be free from coercive questioning.

Thomas's opinion for a plurality of four justices noted that the language of the Fifth Amendment privilege forbids compelling a person "*in any criminal case*" to be "a *witness* against himself."[77] As Thomas put it, "We fail to see how, based on the text of the Fifth Amendment, Martinez can allege a violation of this right, since Martinez was never prosecuted for a crime, let alone compelled to be a witness against himself in a criminal case." On that issue, Justice Souter and Justice Breyer, in a separate opinion, essentially agreed with the plurality, concluding that the claim for civil damages by Martinez was outside the "Fifth Amendment's core."[78]

Alan Dershowitz concludes that in the wake of *Chavez*: "If the objective of the interrogation is to produce intelligence information rather than evidence... you may have no constitutional rights at all."[79] But we believe that Souter left that door ajar when he concluded that Martinez cannot "make the 'powerful showing,' subject to a realistic assessment of costs and risks, necessary to expand protection of the privilege against compelled self-incrimination to the point of the civil liability he asks us to recognize here."[80] To Souter, the suppression remedy that Martinez would have if prosecuted criminally was a sufficient remedy unless Martinez could show the suppression remedy "has been systemically defective."[81]

If a litigant could show a regime of coercive interrogation designed merely to secure information, rather than convictions, the suppression remedy would have a deterrent effect close to zero and thus be "systemically defective." Our hypothetical terrorist litigant who will never be tried could show what Martinez could not—a "limiting principle" that would keep tort liability from attaching to every interrogation that produces an involuntary statement.[82] Instead, only suspected terrorists could seek tort damages for coercive interrogation, which is hopefully a very small number of cases. That kind of limiting principle might attract five votes in favor of permitting detainees to bring suit as long as they could show that they are cut off from a suppression remedy.[83]

To be sure, two of those five theoretical votes belong to justices who are no longer on the Court,[84] leaving the issue up in the air. Complicating matters is the Obama administration's goal to try some of the Guantánamo Bay detainees in civilian court.[85] That group would have access to a suppression remedy, which leaves them outside the category of those who can only avail themselves of a civil remedy. The first detainee to be tried civilly, however, was acquitted on 279 of 280 charges, creating doubt about how many detainees will face a civilian trial.[86]

Terrorist suspects have an alternative argument. As the plurality pointed out, rejecting the privilege does not mean "that police torture or other abuse that results in a confession is permissible so long as the statements are not used at trial."[87] It simply means that the appropriate constitutional provision is the due process clause. This is a stronger argument because it does not suffer the textual problems of the privilege argument. One can imagine an account of due process of law that forbids coercive questioning qua questioning. And, indeed, the Court unanimously agreed that the due process clause prohibits certain State methods of interrogation. The dispute is over what those methods are.

The proper standard to measure whether Chavez violated Martinez's constitutional rights is what the Court calls substantive due process. How substantive due process differs from procedural due process in the context of regulating police conduct is far from clear. The use of substantive due process to deter police misconduct arose at a time when the Court had yet to require states to suppress evidence found in violation of the Fourth Amendment prohibition of unreasonable searches and seizures. The Court thus turned to substantive due process to remedy and deter egregious police misconduct.

In the seminal case of *Rochin v. California,* officers broke into Rochin's bedroom and tried to prevent him from swallowing capsules suspected to be morphine.[88] When he managed to swallow the capsules, police took him to a hospital where his stomach was "pumped" and he vomited two morphine capsules. In 1949, California did not require the exclusionary rule under state law, and the federal rule was not then available in state court. Rochin thus claimed that the state conduct violated due process of law.

Offended by the conduct of the officers, yet wary of creating a broad right that would wreck havoc in state justice systems, the *Rochin* Court crafted the substantive due process right to be very narrow indeed. Here is the key passage:

> This is conduct that shocks the conscience. Illegally breaking into the privacy of the petitioner, the struggle to open his mouth and remove what was there, the forcible extraction of his stomach's contents—this course of proceeding by agents of government to obtain evidence is bound to offend even hardened sensibilities. They are methods too close to the rack and the screw to permit of constitutional differentiation.[89]

One might plausibly ask why *Rochin* is still relevant after *Mapp v. Ohio*'s holding in 1961 that courts must suppress evidence, like that obtained from Rochin, if the search or seizure was unreasonable.[90] The answer to that question can be found by implication in *Chavez.* At least six members of the *Chavez* Court seemed to accept the underlying premise that "ordinary" due process standards, developed in cases like *Ashcraft* and *Spano,* apply when the issue is whether to suppress a confession in a criminal prosecution but do not govern the due process issue in a *civil* trial.[91] Why a heightened standard should apply in civil cases is never explained but, presumably, the Court wishes to protect police officers and municipalities from an avalanche of civil suits.

Thus, for six members of the Court, Martinez could rely only on the *Rochin* shock-the-conscience test. The plurality found their conscience not shocked and would have reversed the Ninth Circuit's holding that Martinez had shown a constitutional violation. But five members of the Court joined Part II of Justice Souter's opinion, which left "the scope and merits" of any due process claim to be decided on remand.[92] The Ninth Circuit, however, did not address the scope and merits of Martinez's claim when it sent the case to the district court for trial, and the Supreme Court denied certiorari when the case came back for a second look.[93] *Chavez* thus stands for the proposition that the due process clause forbids police interrogation methods that go too far, even when the confession is not offered into evidence, but it is unclear how far is too far.

In a later case, the Ninth Circuit held that improper promises and threats directed to a developmentally delayed child did not shock the conscience: "While these allegations might be relevant to the question of whether [the child's] confession was in fact voluntary and therefore admissible, an issue the juvenile court resolved in [his] favor, they fall below what is required to state a claim under the Fourteenth Amendment."[94] This is an explicit recognition of the difference between procedural due process and substantive due process in interrogation cases. Noting that the *Chavez* plurality and Justice Kennedy's separate opinion spoke of "police torture and other abuse" and "torture or its close equivalents," the Ninth Circuit concluded that the standard for showing a substantive due process violation "is quite demanding."[95]

Thus, the state of the law today regarding coercive interrogation of suspected terrorists is far from clear. If "shock the conscience" becomes the standard for civil liability, as seems likely, it would give interrogators of suspected terrorists a lot of leeway in the methods they could use without fear of liability. Whether it would permit water-boarding seems doubtful, but it might allow a range of methods that would violate the *Ashcraft-Spano* due process test. These might include cramped confinement, stress positions, sleep deprivation, nudity, and dietary manipulation.

To be sure, if the government routinely tries terrorism suspects in federal criminal court, that might alter the calculations of interrogators going forward. Concern over loss of the use of evidence in future criminal trials might induce interrogators to stick close to the *Spano* due process line. This is obviously a story that is in play. But it strikes us that if interrogators thought a future Khalid Sheikh Mohammed had information about pending terror attacks on the United States, the overriding motivation would be to obtain the information now and let the criminal case, years in the future, take care of itself, as well as any potential civil liability that might result from a court's shocked conscience.

Thus, it seems likely that the future of American confessions law will be a dualistic world—one set of rules governing police interrogation, where obtaining admissible evidence is the goal; and a shadowy, more permissive set of rules governing interrogation, where the goal is information and not admissible evidence. While the second category will be disproportionately populated by suspected terrorists, it would not be limited to that group. One can imagine a case in which it is more important to locate the victim than to prosecute the person being questioned. Imagine that police question someone who knows where a kidnap victim is being held but was not an accomplice to the kidnapping. If the person with the information does not want to tell the police—perhaps he is deathly afraid of the kidnapper—police might want to coerce the location of the victim. But these will be rare cases. The largest number will be suspected terrorists.

The shadowy, more permissive set of rules that apply mostly to the interrogation of suspected terrorists, spawned by *Chavez*, is no accident. As John Parry noted, "Concerns about terrorism, unstated in the [*Chavez*] opinions but on display in the briefs, feed the uncertainty of the middle and strengthen the hand of the justices who would narrow the privilege and limit the scope of substantive due process."[96] And a more permissive set of limitations might not be a bad thing. Again quoting Parry: "One could also argue in favor of the post-*Chavez* status quo by emphasizing the need to free law enforcement officials from microscopic review of their actions because greater legal regulation and particularly damages liability would cause, and perhaps already causes, overdeterrence."[97] Parry rejects this argument, concluding that we now live in a world of underdeterrence. In his view, U.S. agents conduct too much coercive interrogation and courts should move toward a more optimal level of deterrence.[98]

Dershowitz hopes that *Chavez* is not "the last word on this issue. . . . The privilege against self-incrimination should be construed to impose restrictions on at least *some* means of coercion, even if the resulting information is never used against a defendant at a criminal trial."[99] He urges "citizens, legislatures, judges, and scholars" to develop a jurisprudence that will appropriately constrain governmental actors even when acting to prevent terrorism.

C. What a Long, Strange Trip It's Been

In England in 1721, the only concern about out-of-court confessions, other than in treason cases, was whether the confession was offered against the one who confessed. By 1787, the law was obsessed with the risk that a confession might make a suspect "the deluded instrument of his own conviction."[100] In 1821, a New York lawyer argued that without a four-part warning of the right to remain silent and to consult with counsel, the pretrial examination by a magistrate was "a mere nullity—*void in law*—*void in conscience*, and cannot be read in evidence against the prisoner on his trial."[101] Seven years later, the New York legislature enacted the first requirement in Anglo-American law that the accused be warned of his right "to refuse to answer any question" that the magistrate puts to him and be given time "to send for and advise with counsel."[102] In 1881, the New York legislature strengthened the rights of the accused when appearing before a magistrate.[103]

But by 1881, the questioning of suspects in much of the United States had been largely turned over to police, and the emergence of handguns, large cities, and organized crime made policing dangerous and difficult. The Whig Party, which had long favored the individual over the State, disappeared into the Republican Party, which emphasized national unity to oppose slavery and maintain the Union.[104] The strife leading up to the Civil War, and the war itself, underscored the need to protect the collective. The war helped create a culture of deviance, crime, and violence that persisted for decades. Part of the response by police, at times, was the third degree directed at suspects "known" by police to be guilty.

This, too, would pass. News accounts of the third degree had turned generally negative by the time the Wickersham Commission exposed the third degree on a much larger scale than the newspaper coverage had achieved. Condemned by the commission, the third degree disappeared in favor of relentless questioning and psychological pressure as a means of securing confessions from those "known" to be guilty. In 2011, the website that offers training in the Inbau-Reid method claimed to have trained over 500,000 investigators "in the art of interviewing and interrogation."[105]

In 1966, about a quarter-century after Fred Inbau first published a manual for police interrogators,[106] *Miranda* attempted to develop a procedural mechanism to ensure that suspects were freely giving up their right not to answer police questions. Thus, in a sense, we returned to the days of the Hawkins-Leach dictum, John Graham's 1821 argument, and the New York statutes of 1828. The success of the *Miranda* method of protecting the Fifth Amendment privilege is open to debate. At least at the superficial level of suspects knowing that they can remain slient, *Miranda* appears to be largely a success. Indeed, one of *Miranda*'s critics on the Court, Chief Justice Rehnquist, concluded in 2000 that "*Miranda* has become embedded in routine police practice to the point where the warnings have become part of our national culture."[107] Moreover, "our subsequent cases have reduced the impact of the *Miranda* rule on legitimate law enforcement while reaffirming the decision's core ruling that unwarned statements may not be used as evidence in the prosecution's case in chief."

Rehnquist's comment hints at the failure of *Miranda* to prevent suspects from being "a deluded instrument of their own conviction." What has been achieved, as the law of interrogation lurched back toward the Hawkins-Leach dictum, is a rhetorical flourish that aligns quite closely with English law of the late eighteenth century. But the reality on the ground is far different. Suspects are generally put on notice that they do not have to answer questions, but the vast majority does answer, and most of them become instruments of their own conviction. But perhaps that is a good development. Perhaps having the law inform suspects that they are equals of the police and can control their interrogation—without suspects taking advantage of the offer very often—is a net positive for society as long as the innocent are not ensnared.

The law governing the interrogation of suspected terrorists is almost as shadowy as terrorism. The doctrines developed to regulate ordinary police interrogation work less well, or not at all, to regulate the interrogation of terrorists. The chief aim of a military, FBI, or CIA interrogator is to obtain evidence for the sake of foiling plots to attack the United States. Thus, they care little, or not at all, whether the evidence will be admissible years later in a criminal proceeding. The doctrine of substantive due process provides some, as yet unknown, limit by making actors liable civilly if they go too far in their interrogation methods.

In some ways, the dualistic American law of confessions has returned to England of the sixteenth and late eighteenth centuries. The law of ordinary police interrogation is, superficially at least, that of the Hawkins dictum written by Leach for the 1787 edition. The law governing interrogation of terrorists looks a little like the "protections" granted those suspected of treason in the days before Henry VIII died and Parliament enacted the Treason Act of 1547. The rack and the screw were available to be used against those suspected of trying to overthrow the monarch. On President Obama's watch, the most abusive interrogation methods used from 2001 to 2008 are probably no longer employed. But there is no law in place, either from the Supreme Court or Congress, that parallels the Treason Act and requires that confessions taken from suspected terrorists in this country be given "willingly" and "without violence."[108] There is, to be sure, an odd statute that criminalizes torture when committed outside the United States.[109] But even as to acts outside the United States, "torture" is a more restrictive category than conduct that causes unwilled confessions.

As our theory predicts, confessions law tracks, in at least a rough way, the national feeling of security or insecurity. International law did not prevent the Bush administration from using coercive interrogation techniques, perhaps even torture, against suspected terrorists because our fear level was very high after 9/11. Candidate Barack Obama promised that he would close the detention facility at Guantánamo Bay and try the detainees in civilian courts. As this book neared publication in 2012, neither campaign pledge had been achieved. Neutral principles of law work during "placid and tranquil times" but not when a nation considers itself in extremis.[110]

That the Court continued to embrace *Miranda* while the country looked the other way when suspected terrorists were harshly interrogated tells us that the country feels relatively secure from the threat of ordinary criminals but not, at least until 2008, from acts of terror. When the level of security versus insecurity changes in significant ways, the law of confessions will change again.

NOTES

Chapter 1

1. "Cook's Confession," *Times* (London), June 11, 1832.
2. David Johnston & Thom Shanker, "The Reach of War: Detainees; Pentagon Approved Intense Interrogation Techniques for September 11 Suspect at Guantanamo," *New York Times*, May 21, 2004.
3. Mark Mazzetti, "Threats and Responses: The Intelligence Agency; Questions Raised About Bush's Primary Claims in Defense of Secret Detection System," *New York Times*, September 8, 2006.
4. Jay S. Bybee, Assistant Attorney General, U.S. Department of Justice, Office of Legal Counsel, *Memorandum for John Rizzo, Acting General Counsel of the Central Intelligence Agency, Interrogation of al Qaeda Operative*, August 1, 2002, 2.
5. Id. at 14.
6. Id. at 3–4.
7. GTMO, Counterterroism Division (CTD), Inspection Special Inquiry, 09/02/2004, Case ID # 297-HQ-A1327669-A, Responses, 10, available at http://foia.fbi.gov (last visited March 17, 2011).
8. In 1998, the United Kingdom enacted a human rights act. See Human Rights Act 1998, c. 42, available at http://www.legislation.gov.uk/ukpga/1998/42/contents (last visited October 4, 2010).
9. John Henry Wigmore, *A Treatise on the System of Evidence in Trials at Common Law* (Boston: Little, Brown, 1904), vol. 1, § 865, p. 994.
10. Id. at vol. 1, p. 998.
11. Editorial, "Torturers' Manifesto," *New York Times*, April 19, 2009.
12. See William J. Haynes, "Enemy Combatants," Council on Foreign Relations, December 12, 2002, available at http://www.cfr.org/international-law/enemy-combatants/p.5312 (last visited February 12, 2011). The Bush administration's use, or creation, of "enemy combatants" has been subjected to withering criticism. See, e.g, Peter Jan Honigsberg, "Chasing 'Enemy Combatants' and Circumventing International Law: A License for Sanctioned Abuse," *UCLA J. International L. & Foreign Affairs*, 12 (2007): 4 (concluding that the term was "designed to circumvent the Geneva Conventions and international human rights laws").
13. See Felix Cohen, "Transcendental Nonsense and the Functional Approach," *Colum. L. Rev.* 35 (1935): 809–49; Karl Llewellyn, "A Realistic Jurisprudence—The Next Step," *Colum. L. Rev.* 30 (1930): 431–65.
14. See Haynes, "Enemy Combatants," 1.

15. Transcript, *60 Minutes*, air date September 20, 2002.
16. Alan Harding, *A Social History of English Law* (Harmondsworth, UK: Penguin, 1966), 267.
17. Louis Michael Seidman, "*Brown* and *Miranda*," *Calif. L. Rev.* 80 (1992): 719–22.
18. Louis Michael Seidman, "Rubashov's Question: Self-Incrimination and the Problem of Coerced Preferences," *Yale J. L. & Humanities* 2 (1990): 167.
19. Quoted in Gregory Fehlings, "Storm on the Constitution: The First Deportation Law," *Tulsa J. Comp. & Int'l. L.* 10 (2002): 67.
20. Ch. 66, 1 Stat. 577 (1798).
21. David McCullough, *John Adams* (New York: Simon & Schuster, 2001), 544.
22. 384 U.S. 436, 458–61 (1966).
23. Randall Mikkelsen, "U.S. Attorney General Eric Holder ruled out the use of 'waterboarding' as an interrogation technique for terrorism suspects on Monday, calling it a form of torture that the Obama administration could never condone," Reuters, March 2, 2009, available at http://www.reuters.com/article/2009/03/02/us-usa-security-waterboarding-id USTRE5213OE20090302?feedType=RSS&feedName=topNews (last visited March 17, 2011).
24. John T. Parry, "Torture Nation, Torture Law," *Geo. L. J.* 97 (2009): 1003.
25. John H. Langbein, *Torture and the Law of Proof: Europe and England in the Ancien Regime* (Chicago: University of Chicago Press, 2006) (1976), 14.
26. *Ames Spencer*, The Proceedings of the Old Bailey, January 14, 1686: t16860114-4, available at http://www.oldbaileyonline.org/browse.jsp?ref=t16860114-4 (last visited March 17, 2011).
27. William Hawkins, *A Treatise of the Pleas of the Crown; or, A System of the Principal Matters Relating to that Subject, Digested under Proper Heads*, ed. Thomas Leach (Dublin: London: Eliz. Lynch, 6th ed., 1788), vol. 2, 604 (emphasis added). The London sixth edition was published in 1787.
28. See chapter 3 section D.; chapter 4 section B. 7.
29. See, e.g., *Regina v. Drew*, 8 Car. & P. 140, 173 Eng. Rep. 433, 433 (1837).
30. Office of Legal Policy, "Report to the Attorney General on the Law of Pretrial Interrogation," *U. Mich. J. L. Reform* 22 (1988–1989): 564.
31. Joseph Perez, *The Spanish Inquisition* (New Haven, CT: Yale University Press, 2005), 26–57 & 146–48.
32. Exec. Order No. 13491, January 22, 2009, 74 F.R. 4893.
33. Mike Hepworth & Bryan S. Turner, *Confession: Studies in Deviance and Religion* (London: Routledge & Kegan Paul, 1982), 19.
34. Deidre Blanchfield, "Public Executions in Nineteenth Century England," available at University of Michigan-Dearborn, http://www.umd.umich.edu/casl/hum/eng/classes/434/geweb/PUBLICEX.htm (last visited July 20, 2008).
35. "Execution of John Any Bird Bell for Murder," *Times* (London), August 2, 1831.
36. "Execution of Patch," *Times* (London), April 9, 1806.
37. "Execution of Hussey for the Murders at Greenwich," *Times* (London), August 4, 1818.
38. "Hussey's Confession," *Times* (London), August 10, 1818., id., September 3, 1818.
39. "Hussey's Confession," *Times* (London), August 22, 1818.
40. "Charles Hussey," *Times* (London), September 3, 1818.
41. "Parricide, Execution of Chennel and Chalcraft for the Murder of Chennel's Family," *Times* (London), August 15, 1818.
42. Perez, *The Spanish Inquisition*, 26–57.
43. See, e.g., Matthew 27: 11–12; Luke 23: 3.
44. David T. Johnson, *The Japanese Way of Justice: Prosecuting Crime in Japan* (New York: Oxford University Press, 2002), 23. It seems likely that the crime rates in Japan have increased since 1991, and we know that crime rates in New York City have fallen, but as the example in the text took place in 1993, the 1991 rates are an apt comparison.
45. Id. at 257.

46. Id.
47. Id. at 258.
48. Seidman, "Rubashov's Question," 167.
49. 314 U.S. 214 (1941).
50. Id. at 229–31.
51. Id. at 231–32.
52. Id. at 233–34.
53. See Yale Kamisar, "Equal Justice in the Gatehouses and Mansions of American Criminal Procedure: From Powell to Gideon, from Escobedo to . . .," in *Criminal Justice in Our Time*, ed. A. E. Dick Howard (Charlottesville: University Press of Virginia, 1965), 80.
54. Gerald M. Caplan, "Questioning *Miranda*," *Vand. L. Rev.* 38 (1985): 1442.
55. Honigsberg, "Chasing Enemy Combatants," 4. The 1944 case is *Korematsu v. United States*, 323 U.S. 214 (1944).
56. Morgan Cloud, "Quakers, Slaves and the Founders: Profiling to Save the Nation," *Miss. L. J.* 73 (2003): 374.
57. Id. at 370 & 374–90.
58. Congressional Resolution (August 25, 1777), reprinted in Thomas Gilpin, *Exiles in Virginia* (Philadelphia: 1848), app. at 259.
59. Cloud, "Quakers, Slaves and the Founders," 374.
60. Id. at 389.

Chapter 2

1. Adolf Friedrich Rudorff, *Römische Rechtsgeschichte* (Leipzig: Verlag von Bernhard Tauchnitz, 1859), § 133, p. 445–46 (translation provided by Paul Axel-Lute, Deputy Director and Collection Development Librarian, Rutgers University School of Law, Newark).
2. Titus Livy, *The War With Hannibal*, Books XXI–XXX of *The History of Rome from its Foundation* (New York: Penguin Classics, 1965), 391.
3. A. H. M. Jones, *The Criminal Courts of the Roman Republic and Principate* (Totowa, NJ: Rowman & Littlefield, 1972), 114–15.
4. Hepworth & Turner, *Studies in Deviance*, 2.
5. Barry Nicholas, *An Introduction to Roman Law* (Oxford: Clarendon Press, 1962), 69.
6. *Digest of Justinian*, ed. Theodore Mommsen, trans. Allen Watson (Philadelphia: University of Pennsylvania Press, 1985), bk. 48, c. 18, n.1 (Ulpian).
7. Id. [bracket appears in translation].
8. Id. at n.22 & n.23.
9. Jones, *Criminal Courts of the Roman Republic*, 116.
10. Id.
11. James. L. Strachan-Davidson, *Problems of the Roman Criminal Law* (Oxford: Clarendon Press, 1969), vol. 2, 205, 209.
12. For a more detailed account of the ordeal and the Fourth Lateran Council, see George C. Thomas III, *The Supreme Court on Trial: How the American Justice System Sacrifices Innocent Defendants* (Ann Arbor: University of Michigan Press, 2008), 62–86.
13. John H. Langbein, "Torture and Plea Bargaining," *U. Chi. L. Rev.* 46 (1978): 4.
14. Langbein, *Torture and the Law of Proof*, 7.
15. Langbein, "Torture and Plea Bargaining," 5.
16. Sir Frederick Pollock & Frederick William Maitland, *The History of English Law Before the Time of Edward I* (Cambridge: Cambridge University Press, 2nd ed., 1899), vol. 2, 579. For a contemporaneous example, see Assize Clarendon, c. 12 (1166), available at the Internet Medieval Source Book, http://www.fordham.edu/halsall/sbook1n.html (last visited February 17, 2011).
17. Robert Bartlett, *Trial by Fire and Water: The Medieval Judicial Ordeal* (Oxford: Clarendon Press, 1986), 26.

18. Id. at 4–7.
19. R.C. Van Caenegem, ed., *English Lawsuits From William I to Richard I* (London: Selden Society, 1990), vol. 1, 122 (case 150).
20. Bartlett, *Trial by Fire and Water*, 64. See also William Blackstone, *Commentaries on the Laws of England* (London: University of Chicago Press, 1979), vol. 1 *340.
21. Bartlett, *Trial by Fire and Water*, 111.
22. Doris M. Stanton, *English Justice between the Norman Conquest and the Great Charter, 1066–1215* (Philadelphia: The American Philosophy Scholar, 1964), 29.
23. Id. at 26.
24. Robert Bartlett, *England Under the Norman and Angevin Kings* (Oxford: Clarendon Press, 2000), 283 (quoting from the *Anglo-Saxon Chronicle*, a contemporary historical account compiled by English monks).
25. Id. (quoting from the *Anglo-Saxon Chronicle*).
26. For a description of how Henry secured the throne, see Thomas, *The Supreme Court on Trial*, 73–74.
27. W. L. Warren, *Henry II* (Berkeley, Ca.: University of California Press, 1973), 64–77.
28. Id. at 53–64.
29. Assize Clarendon, c.1 (1166).
30. Id. at c.2. Henry II presumably chose the water ordeal over the ordeal by fire because the former was more difficult to game. A common form of the water ordeal cast the accused into a pit of water. If he floated, it meant that he was not telling the truth. Doris Stenton marshaled evidence that the water ordeal was more efficacious than William II found the order by fire. In the years just after the Assize of Clarendon, Stenton noted "the digging and blessing of ordeal pits, and lists of men from most shires who 'perished in the judgment of water.'" *Doris M. Stenton*, English Justice Between the Norman Conquest and the Great Charter, 1066–1215 (Philadelphia: American Philosophical Society, 1964), 71.
31. Langbein, "Torture and Plea Bargaining," 4.
32. Assize Clarendon, c.13 (1166).
33. Steven Muhlberger, Medieval England, "Wessex Conquers England," The Orb, available at http://www.the-orb.net/textbooks/muhlberger/wessex.html (last visited February 12, 2011).
34. Charles E. Odegaard, "Legalis Homo," *Speculum* 15 (1940): 191.
35. *Crane v. Kentucky*, 476 U.S. 683 (1986). See also Ellen Barry, "Rape Suspect Says She Was Fooled Into Confessing," *New York Times*, June 12, 2007.
36. As a theoretical matter, of course, the defendant benefits from a presumption of innocence and the requirement that the State prove guilt beyond a reasonable doubt. In most cases, however, if the defendant does nothing to defend, he will be convicted.
37. David J. Seipp, "Legal History: The Year Books, Medieval English Legal History, An Index and Paraphrase of Printed Year Book Reports, 1268–1535" (Seipp's Abridgement), BU School of Law, available at http://www.bu.edu/law/faculty/scholarship/yearbooks/ (last visited February 13, 2011).
38. Mike Ashley, *The Mammoth Book of British Kings & Queens* (New York: Carroll & Graf, 1998), 589 & 591–94.
39. Bartlett, *England Under the Norman and Angevin Kings*, 191.
40. Year Books, Edward I, 1295, Folio Number RS 543–45, Seipp Number 1295.023rs, Seipp trans., available at http://www.bu.edu/phpbin/lawyearbooks/display.php?id=1171 (last visited February 13, 2011). I quote from a translation of the full case report, kindly supplied to us by Dr. Paul Brand, All Souls College, Oxford, adapted from a translation by Dr. Henry Summerson, also of All Souls College, copy available from George Thomas.
41. *Butler's Case*, Year Books, Edward I, 1295, Folio Number RS 543–45, Seipp Number 1295.023rs.
42. Anthony Babington, *The English Bastille: A History of Newgate Gaol and Prison Conditions in Britain 1188–1902* (New York: St. Martin's Press, 1971), 14.
43. Id. at 21.

44. *Butler's Case*, Year Books, Edward I, 1295, Folio Number RS 543–45, Seipp Number 1295.023rs.
45. Philip Ziegler, *The Black Death* (New York: Harper & Row, 1969), 17.
46. Year Books, Edward III, 1348, Folio Number 101a, Seipp Number 1348.279ass, Seipp trans., available at http://www.bu.edu/phpbin/lawyearbooks/display.php?id=11820 (last visited February 11, 2011).
47. Id.
48. E-mail from David J. Seipp to Paul Axel-Lute, Deputy Director and Collection Development Librarian, Rutgers University Library for the Center for Law & Justice, October 20, 2006.
49. Ziegler, *Black Death*, 15.
50. Id. at 17.
51. For information about being an "approver," see Henry of Bracton, *On the Laws and Customs of England*, George Woodbine, ed.; Samuel Thorne, trans., vol. 2, 346 available at Harvard law Library, http://hlsl5.law.harvard.edu/bracton/Unframed/English/v2/346.htm (last visited February 15, 2011).
52. Id. For information about the compilation of Bracton's treatise, see id. "About the Work," available at http://hlsl5.law.harvard.edu/bracton//index.htm (last visited February 15, 2011).
53. Year Books, Henry IV, 1411, Folio Number 28-C.L.J. 105, Seipp Number 1411.103clj, Seipp trans., available at http://www.bu.edu/phpbin/lawyearbooks/display.php?id=16311 (last visited February 13, 2011).
54. See, e.g., Year Books, Henry VI, 1440, Folio Number 47b, Seipp Number 1440.121, Seipp trans., available at http://www.bu.edu/phpbin/lawyearbooks/display.php?id=17962 (defendant, after arraignment in open court, "confessed the treason and became appellor (approver))" (last visited February 13, 2011).
55. Year Books, Edward III, 1345, Folio Number RS 175–77, Seipp Number 1345.119rs, Seipp trans., available at http://www.bu.edu/phpbin/lawyearbooks/display.php?id=10835 (last visited February 13, 2011).
56. Id.
57. *Herrera v. Collins*, 506 U.S. 390, 427–28 (1993) (Scalia, J., concurring). See also Daniel S. Medwed, "The Zeal Deal: Prosecutorial Resistance to Post-Conviction Claims of Innocence," *B.U. L. Rev.* 84 (2004): 129 (noting that prosecutors faced with irrefutable evidence of innocence sometimes continue to avoid having the conviction vacated).
58. See, e.g., Year Books, Henry IV, 1406, Folio Number 3a, Seipp Number 1406.104, Seipp trans., available at http://www.bu.edu/phpbin/lawyearbooks/display.php?id=15873 (last visited February 13, 2011).
59. Matthew Hale, *The History of the Pleas of the Crown* (London: E. and R. Nutt and R. Gosling, 1736), vol. 2, 319.
60. See, e.g., T. B. Howell and T. J. Howell, *General Index to the Collection of State Trials* (London: Longman, Rees, Orme, Brown & Green et al., 1828), 223, available in HeinOnLine, World Trials, Complete Collection of State Trials and Proceedings for High Treason and Other Crimes and Misdemeanors (by implication).
61. J. H. Baker, ed., *Reports of Cases by John Caryll* (London: Selden Society, 1999), vol. 1, 111–12 (*Marsshe v. Archer*, King's Bench, 1492).
62. Year Books, Edward II, 1313, Folio Number 43 SS 114–15, Seipp Number 1313.062ss, Seipp trans., available at http://www.bu.edu/phpbin/lawyearbooks/display.php?id=3341 (last visited February 13, 2011).
63. Year Books, Edward III, 1353, Folio Number 137b, Seipp Number 1353.165ass, Seipp trans., available at http://www.bu.edu/phpbin/lawyearbooks/display.php?id=12538 (last visited February 13, 2011).
64. See, e.g., Year Books, Richard, 1484, Folio Number 12b–13a, Seipp Number 1484.031, Seipp trans., available at http://www.bu.edu/phpbin/lawyearbooks/display.php?id=21097 (last visited February 13, 2011).

65. If the defendant could not read, it was conclusively presumed that he was not a cleric, and he was hanged. See Year Books, Henry IV, 1406, Folio Number 3a, Seipp Number 1406.104, Seipp trans., available at http://www.bu.edu/phpbin/lawyearbooks/display.php?id=15873 (last visited February 13, 2011).

66. See, e.g., Year Books, Henry VI, 1440, Folio Number 47b, Seipp Number 1440.121, Seipp trans., available at http://www.bu.edu/phpbin/lawyearbooks/display.php?id=17962 (last visited February 13, 2011).

67. *Reports of Cases by John Caryll*, vol. 1, 111 (*Marsshe v. Archer*, 1492).

68. Langbein, *Torture and the Law of Proof*, 71.

69. Id. at 73–77.

70. Year Books, Henry IV, 1399, Folio Number 1a, Seipp Number 1399.001, Seipp trans., available at http://www.bu.edu/phpbin/lawyearbooks/display.php?id=15418 (last visited February 13, 2011).

71. See sources cited id., under "Editing Notes."

72. Raleigh Trevelyan, *Sir Walter Raleigh* (New York: Henry Holt, 2002), 387. Raleigh was not executed for fifteen years, and then was "merely" beheaded, but our point is that English justice countenanced pretty gruesome punishments.

73. Edward Raymond Turner, *The Privy Council of England in the Seventeenth and Eighteenth Centuries, 1603–1784* (Baltimore: Johns Hopkins Press, 1927), 55.

74. Langbein, *Torture and the Law of Proof*, 73.

75. Id. at 82.

76. We ignore the ineffectual Edward VI, who ruled for six years, and Queen Jane, who ruled for only nine days, giving way to Mary I. Ashley, *British Kings & Queens*, 636–38.

77. Id. at 640.

78. Langbein, *Torture and the Law of Proof*, 82.

79. Id. See also id., 94–123 (Table of Warrants).

80. Id. at 82.

81. Blackstone's *Commentaries*, vol 4, *321.

82. Langbein, *Torture and the Law of Proof*, 90 & 137.

83. Id. at 137–38.

84. Id. at 139.

85. 1 Ed. VI, c. 12, s. 22 (1547) (spelling modernized).

86. Staundford, *Les Plees del Coron* (1557), 142–43 (translation in Wigmore, *Treatise on the System of Evidence*, 1904 ed., vol. 1, § 818, p. 922).

87. Leonard W. Levy, *Origins of the Fifth Amendment* (Chicago: Ivan R. Dee, 1968) (1999).

88. Id. at 42.

89. Turner, *The Privy Council*, 38.

90. Jeremy Bentham, *Rationale of Judicial Evidence* (London: Hunt and Clarke, 1827), vol. 5, 244.

91. See Act for [the Regulating] the Privie Councell and for taking away the Court commonly called the Star Chamber, Statutes of the Realm, 16 Charles I, c. 10 (1641).

92. Ancient Charters relating to the First Settlement of Virginia, Articles, Instructions and Orders set down and established by us, twentieth day of November, [1606], 70.

93. Virginia General Assembly, Act I, 1662, available in William Waller Hening, *The Statutes at Large; being a Collection of all the Laws of Virginia from the First Session of the Legislature, in the Year 1619* (New-York: R. & W. & G. Bartow, 1823), vol. 1, 181.

94. William Hudson, "A Treatise of the Court of Star Chamber," in *Collectanea Juridica* (London: E. and R. Brooke, Bell-Yard, Temple-Bar, 1792), 127. The approximate date derives from page 1 of Hudson's treatise, which recounts that the son of William Hudson gave a hand-written copy of the treatise to Chief Jusice Finch after Hudson's death in 1635.

95. Edward Coke, *The Third Part of the Institutes of the Laws of England* (London: W. Clarke and Sons, 1807), vol. 3, 217, cap. 101.

96. See, e.g., Edward Coke, *The Fourth Part of the Institutes of the Laws of England* (London: E. and R. Brooke, Bell-Yard, near Temple Bar, 1797), vol. 4, 177–78, cap. 31 (noting that a man "convicted by verdict or confession, &c. is not bailable, because it appeareth that he is guilty").
97. Coke, *Fourth Part of the Institutes*, 25, cap. 2.
98. Samuel Rawson Gardiner, *What Gunpowder Plot Was* (London: Longmans, Green, 1897), 27.
99. Id. at 26.
100. Id. at 28.
101. 7 Wm. III c.3 (1695), British History Online, available at, http://www.british-history.ac.uk/report.aspx?compid=46810 (last visited February 15, 2011).
102. Lawrence Herman, "The Unexplored Relationship Between the Privilege Against Compulsory Self-Incrimination and the Involuntary Confession Rule (Part I)," *Ohio St. L.J.* 53 (1992): 128.
103. *Proceedings against Edward Duke of Somerset, for High Treason and Felony, at Winchester*, 1 How. St. Tr. 515, 517 (1551).
104. *The Trial of Thomas Howard duke of Norfolk, before the Lords at Westminister, for High Treason*, 1 How. St. Tr. 957, 978 (1571).
105. *The Trial of Sir Christopher Blunt, Sir Charles Davers, Sir John Davis, Sir Gilly Merrick, and Henry Cuffe, at Westminster, for High Treason*, 1 How. St. Tr. 1409 (1600).
106. See id., *A fuller account of the Trial of Sir Christopher Blunt, Sir Charles Davers, Sir John Davis, Sir Gilly Merrick, and Henry Cuffe*, at 1419. Attorney General Coke was present at the trial but the evidence was offered by Yelverton, the queen's serjeant. Id.
107. *The Trial of Sir Walter Raleigh, knight at Winchester, for High Treason*, 2 How. St. Tr. 1, 22 (1603).
108. William Hawkins, *A Treatise of the Pleas of the Crown; or, A System of the Principal Matters relating to that Subject, digested under proper Heads* (London: Eliz. Nutt, 1721), vol. 2, 429.
109. *Trial of Sir Walter Raleigh*, 26.
110. George Thomas develops this point in more detail in Thomas, *Supreme Court on Trial*, 86–90.
111. *Trial of Sir Walter Raleigh*, 29.
112. John H. Langbein, "The Origins of Public Prosecution at Common Law," *The American Journal of Legal History* 17 (1973): 314.
113. One of the arguments the Anti-Federalists made against ratifying the United States Constitution was its failure to require a local jury. The Anti-Federalists insisted on a right to trial by jury in the vicinage, or local community, because "a jury of the peers would, from their local situation, have an opportunity to form a judgment of the *character* of the person charged with the crime, and also to judge the *credibility* of the witnesses." See Neil H. Cogan, ed., *The Complete Bill of Rights* (New York: Oxford University Press, 1997), 419 (quoting one of the Framers). To be sure, by 1788, the argument for self-informing juries was weak, and the Anti-Federalists essentially lost the point. The compromise, reflected in the Sixth Amendment, requires juries drawn from the district in which the crime occurred. See U. S. Const. amend. VI. As no state had more than one district at the time, and today the average state has only two districts, this is a far cry from a requirement of a truly local jury.
114. 1 & 2 Phil. & Mary. c. 13 (1554–55) (bail); 2 & 3 Phil. & Mar. c. 10 (1554–55) (committal).
115. John H. Langbein, *The Origins of the Adversary Criminal Trial* (Oxford: Oxford University Press, 2003), 43.
116. Id. at 44.
117. Id. at 41, n.156, relying on Thomas Smith, *De Republica* 113 and *The Clerk of Assize* 14 (London 1660) & Langbein, *Origins of the Adversary Criminal Trial*, . at 42.
118. Herman, "The Unexplored Relationship (Part I)," 128.

Chapter 3

1. *New World Encyclopedia*, s.v. "Great Fire of London," available at http://www.newworlden-cyclopedia.org/entry/Great_Fire_of_London (last visited February 16, 2011).
2. Id.
3. Id.
4. The information about the construction and structure of the Old Bailey was drawn from "History of The Old Bailey Courthouse: London's Central Criminal Court," 1673–1834, available at http://www.oldbaileyonline.org/static/The-old-bailey.jsp (last visited February 21, 2010). All 100,000 of the Old Bailey cases are available on that website as well. It is an invaluable resource.
5. Id.
6. Langbein, *Origins of the Adversary Criminal Trial*, 220.
7. J. M. Beattie, *Crime and the Courts in England, 1660–1800* (Princeton, NJ; Princeton University Press, 1986), 365.
8. *Unnamed Defendant*, The Proceedings of the Old Bailey, July 11, 1677, available at http://www.oldbaileyonline.org/browse.jsp?id=t16770711-11&div=t16770711-11 (last visited February 21, 2011).
9. *Unnamed Defendant*, The Proceedings of the Old Bailey, September 6, 1677, available at http://www.oldbaileyonline.org/browse.jsp?ref=t16770906-1 (last visited February 20, 2011).
10. *Ames Spencer*, The Proceedings of the Old Bailey, January 14, 1686, available at http://www.oldbaileyonline.org/browse.jsp?ref=t16860114-4 (last visited February 20, 2011).
11. *Ann Smith and Ann Simmons*, The Proceedings of the Old Bailey, December 5, 1688, available at http://www.oldbaileyonline.org/browse.jsp?ref=t16881205-16 (last visited February 20, 2011). The modern definitions of theft crimes had yet to solidify. "Theft" was often described as "robbery."
12. *William Mosely*, The Proceedings of the Old Bailey, December 5, 1688, available at http://www.oldbaileyonline.org/browse.jsp?ref=t16881205-7 (last visited February 20, 2011).
13. *Matthew Davis*, The Proceedings of the Old Bailey, July 11, 1694, available at http://www.oldbaileyonline.org/browse.jsp?ref=t16940711-26 (last visited February 20, 2011).
14. *Elizabeth Yalden*, The Proceedings of the Old Bailey, December 3, 1695, available at http://www.oldbaileyonline.org/browse.jsp?ref=t16951203-8 (last visited February 20, 1999).
15. *Edward Clements*, The Proceedings of the Old Bailey, January 11, 1712, available at http://www.oldbaileyonline.org/browse.jsp?ref=t17120111-20 (last visited February 20, 2011).
16. Hawkins, *Treatise of the Pleas of the Crown*, 1721 edition, vol. 2, 429.
17. Id., vol. 2, at 333.
18. Year Books, Edward III, 1348, Folio Number 101a, Seipp Number 1348.279ass, Seipp trans., available at http://www.bu.edu/phpbin/lawyearbooks/display.php?id=11820 (last visited February 11, 2011).
19. See 1 & 2 Phil. & Mar. c. 13 (1554) (examination prior to bail decision); 2 & 3 Phil. & Mar. c. 10 (1555) (examination prior to committal where bail denied).
20. Hale, *History of the Pleas of the Crown*, vol. 2, 284.
21. Id., title page.
22. Id., vol. 2, at 61, n. (f).
23. Id., vol. 2, at 96, n. (i).
24. Larry Herman concludes that the passage about taking confessions without "menace" or "undue terror" was "undoubtedly added" by Emlyn because it does not appear in the 1682 edition of Hale's *History of the Pleas of the Crown*, which he had seen, or for that matter the 1678 edition, which we have seen. Herman, "Unexplored Relationship," 148 & n.262. But the lack of mention in the earlier Hale editions is ambiguous because they were just fragmentary pieces of the entire manuscript. The 1678 edition, for example is only 238 pages that are small with very large margins. The 1682 edition is roughly the same length. The 1736 edition, on the other hand, contains 1122 pages of generous size and narrow

margins. The earlier editions thus omitted most—probably close to 90%—of Hale's original manuscript.

25. A general rule that out-of-court confessions are admissible is, for example, inconsistent with the interpretation of Coke and others that the Treason Act of 1547 applied to out-of-court confessions and thus required them to be made willingly and without violence. But Hawkins finds this dissonance "remedied" by 7 W. 3. 3. See Hawkins, *Treatise of the Pleas of the Crown*, 1721 ed., vol. 2, 429. As we saw in chapter 2, this 1695 statute required testimony of witnesses in open court and thus made clear that it did not require out-of-court confessions to be made willingly and without violence.

26. Hale, *History of the Pleas of the Crown*, vol. 2, 284–85.

27. *The Trial of Sir Christopher Blunt* et al., 1 How. St. Tr. at 1419.

28. *Ann Smith and Ann Simmons*, The Proceedings of the Old Bailey, December 5, 1688, available at http://www.oldbaileyonline.org/browse.jsp?ref=t16881205-16 (last visited February 20, 2011).

29. By 1738, juries in the Old Bailey deliberated in open court without retiring to a separate room. Beattie, *Crime and the Courts in England*, 396. But Beattie claims that this practice was not followed in the Old Bailey in the seventeenth century, leaving inference as the best explanation for the reporter's description of why the jury acquitted in *Smith and Simmons*.

30. *Tobias Isaacs, Rachael Isaacs*, The Proceedings of the Old Bailey, July 9, 1740, available at http://www.oldbaileyonline.org/browse.jsp?ref=t17400709-34 (last visited February 20, 2011).

31. *The Trial of Charles White, for the Murder of Sir John Dineley Goodere*, 17 How. St. Tr. 1079, 1085 (1741).

32. J. M. Beattie, *Crime and the Courts in England*, 365 (pre-1740 rule); Langbein, *Origins of the Adversary Criminal Trial*, 221–22 (unsettled era).

33. *Richard Hill*, The Proceedings of the Old Bailey, July 14, 1742, available at http://www.oldbaileyonline.org/browse.jsp?ref=t17420714-8 (last visited February 20, 2011) (acquittal).

34. Id.

35. Richard Burn, *The Justice of the Peace, and Parish Officer* (London: Henry Lintot, 1755), vol. 1, 296.

36. Hawkins, *Treatise of the Pleas of the Crown*, 3rd. ed., 1739, vol. 2, 429.

37. Hale, *History of the Pleas of the Crown*, vol. 1, 585.

38. Id., vol. 2, 284.

39. Burn, *Justice of the Peace*, vol. 2, 429 (emphasis added).

40. Sir Geoffrey Gilbert, *The Law of Evidence* (London: Henry Lintot, Law Printer to the King, 1756), 139.

41. Id. at 140.

42. Langbein, *Origins of the Adversary Criminal Trial*, 221.

43. Michael Foster, *A Report of Some Proceedings . . . and Other Crown Cases to Which Are Added Discourses upon a Few Branches of the Crown Law* (Oxford: Clarendon Press, 1762), 243.

44. Langbein, *Origins of the Adversary Criminal Trial*, 221–22.

45. *Benjamin March*, The Proceedings of the Old Bailey, February 22, 1764, available at http://www.oldbaileyonline.org/browse.jsp?ref=t17640222-25 (last visited February 20, 2011).

46. Langbein, *Origins of the Adversary Criminal Trial*, 222.

47. Id. at 222, n.189.

48. *Lawrence Balfe and Edward Kirk*, The Proceedings of the Old Bailey, January 12, 1769, available at http://www.oldbaileyonline.org/browse.jsp?ref=t17690112-22 (last visited February 20, 2011).

49. Hawkins, *Treatise of the Pleas of the Crown*, 6th ed., 1787, vol. 2, 604 (emphasis added).

50. Blackstone's *Commentaries*, 8th ed., 1778, vol. 4, 357.

51. *Rex v. Thompson*, 1 Leach 291, 168 Eng. Rep. 248 (K.B. 1783).

52. Id., 168 Eng. Rep. at 249, n. (a).

53. Hawkins, *Treatise of the Pleas of the Crown*, 6th ed., 1787, vol. 2, 604.

54. 1 Leach 262, 168 Eng. Rep. 234, 235 (1783).
55. Thomas Leach, *Cases in Crown Law, Determined by the Twelve Judges, by the Court of King's Bench, and by Commissioners of Oyer and Terminer and General Gaol Delivery* (London: T. Whieldon, 1789), 248.
56. Langbein, *Torture and the Law of Proof*, 62–64.
57. Wigmore, *Treatise on the System of Evidence*, 1904 ed., vol. 1, § 865, p. 996.
58. Langbein, *Origins of the Adversary Criminal Trial*, 230.
59. Id. at 233.
60. John Locke, *Two Treatises of Government and A Letter Concerning Toleration* (New Haven, CT: Yale University Press, 2003), second treatise, 102 (first published, 1690).
61. Id. at 106.
62. Thomas Hobbes, *Leviathan* (London: Penguin Books, 1981), 268–69 (first published, 1651).
63. Alan Harding, *A Social History of English Law* (Harmondsworth, UK: Penguin, 1966), 267.
64. Boyd Hilton, *A Mad, Bad, and Dangerous People? England 1783–1846* (Oxford: Clarendon Press, 2006), 1–2.
65. The Proceedings of the Old Bailey, London's Central Criminal Court, 1674 to 1913, London, 1760–1815, "Population," available at http://www.oldbaileyonline.org/static/London-lifelate18th.jsp#population (last visited March 12, 2011).
66. E. G. Dowdell, *A Hundred Years of Quarter Sessions: The Government of Middlesex from 1660–1760* (Cambridge: Cambridge University Press, 1932), 24.
67. Henry Fielding, *An Enquiry into the Causes of the late Increase of Robbers &c* (London: A. Millar, 1751).
68. J. M. Beattie, "Sir John Fielding and Public Justice: The Bow Street Magistrates' Court, 1754–1780," *L. & Hist. Rev.* 25 (2007): 61.
69. Id.
70. Id.
71. John Fielding, *Extracts from such of the Penal Laws as Particularly relate to the Peace and Good Order of the Metropolis* (London: H. Woodfall & W. Strahan, 1768), 7.
72. Id.; Beattie, "Sir John Fielding," 77.
73. John Fielding, *Extracts*, 7.
74. Beattie, "Sir John Fielding," 76.
75. William Augustus Miles, *A Letter to Sir John Fielding, Knt., occasioned by His extraordinary Request to Mr. Garrick for the Suppression of the Beggar's Opera* (London: J. Bell, 1773), 19.
76. Id. at 19–20.
77. Id. at 20–21.
78. Beattie, *Crime and the Courts in England*, 137; J. J. Tobias, *Crime and Industrial Society in the 19th Century* (New York: Schocken Books, 1967), 41.
79. M. Dorothy George, *Life in London in the XVIIIth Century* (New York: A.A. Knopf, 1925), 10 (quoting John Feltham, *Picture of London* (London: Phillips, 1802), 276).
80. Id. at 321.
81. Frank O'Gorman, *The Long Eighteenth Century* (London: Hodder Arnold, 1997), 105. One reader asked why Parliament increased capital crimes when the violent crime rate was declining. A similar phenomenon occurred in the United States, where we have much better data. The number of violent crimes fell by more than 50 percent in the past three decades—from 4.1 million in 1981 to 1.5 million in 2009—and yet the prison population is up almost four-fold over the same period. Compare U.S. Department of Justice, Office of Justice Programs, Bureau of Justice Statistics, "Key Facts at a Glance, Four Measures of Serious Violent Crime, Total Violent Crime," available at http://bjs.ojp.usdoj.gov/content/glance/tables/4meastab.cfm (last visited March 18, 2011); and "Key Facts at a Glance, Correctional Populations Number of persons under correctional supervision," available at http://bjs.ojp.usdoj.gov/content/glance/tables/corr2tab.cfm (last visited March 18, 2011). Perhaps falling crime rates increase the public appetite for yet lower rates.

82. J. J. Tobias, *Urban Crime in Victorian England* (New York: Schocken Books, 1972), 200.
83. "Durham Assizes," *Times* (London), August 6, 1818.
84. O'Gorman, *The Long Eighteenth Century*, at 105.
85. Id.
86. *Regina v. Baldry*, 2 Den. 430, 169 Eng. Rep. 568, 574 (1852).
87. Hawkins, *A Treatise of the Pleas of the Crown*, 6th ed., 1787, vol. 2, 604, n.2.
88. See *United States v. Patane*, 542 U.S. 630 (2004) (holding that physical evidence is none-theless admissible despite being found by virtue of a violation of *Miranda*).
89. Dowdell, *A Hundred Years of Quarter Sessions*, 16.
90. 1 & 2 Phil. & Mar. c. 13 (1554) (bail) ("shall put in writing" and "shall certifie [sic] at the next generall [sic] Gaol Deliverye"); 2 & 3 Phil. & Mar. c. 10 (1555) (committal) ("shall put in writing").
91. "Denbighshire Great Sessions," *Times* (London), August 21, 1819.
92. "Mansion House—Late Robbery at Grantham," *Times* (London), August 25, 1815.
93. "Police," *Times* (London), August 29, 1816.
94. Hilton, *A Mad, Bad, and Dangerous People*, 320.
95. Untitled, *Times* (London), November 23, 1802.
96. "Picking Pockets," *Times* (London), October 29, 1807. The case is also reported in the re-cords of the Old Bailey. See *Ann Williams*, theft, Proceedings of the Old Bailey, October 28, 1807, available at http://www.oldbaileyonline.org/browse.jsp?ref=t18071028-5 (last visited February 20, 2011). She was acquitted.
97. "Bow Street," *Times* (London), February 18, 1831.
98. "Bow Street," *Times* (London), June 8, 1833.
99. John Impey, *The Practice of the Office of Sheriff and Undersheriff; Also, the Practice of the Office of Coroner* (London: W. Clarke and Sons, 3rd. ed., 1812), 428.
100. Id at 432. See also 1 & 2 Phil. & Mar. c. 13 (1554).
101. Impey, *Practice of the Office of Sheriff*, 429.
102. "Providential Discovery of a Most Barbarous Murder," *Times* (London), January 23, 1830.
103. Id.
104. Bruce P. Smith, *Miranda's Prehistory* (unpublished paper), 18–22 (draft) (paper in Thom-as's possession, provided on September 13, 2009).
105. *Robert Davidson*, theft, Proceedings of the Old Bailey, November 30, 1796, available at http://www.oldbaileyonline.org/browse.jsp?ref=t17961130-61 (last visited February 20, 2011).
106. William Dickinson, *A Practical Exposition of the Law Relative to the Office and Duties of a Justice of the Peace* (London: Reed and Hunter, 1813), vol. 1, 457.
107. "Trim Assizes," *Times* (London), July 28, 1815.
108. *Rex v. J. Harris, W. Evans, and J. Butler*, 1 Mood. 339, 168 Eng. Rep. 1295 (1832).
109. *Regina v. Arnold*, 8 Car. & P. 621, 622, 173 Eng. Rep. 645, 645 (1838).
110. "Horrid Murderer," *Times* (London), November 27, 1817.
111. *Rex v. Pountney and Another*, 7 Car. & P. 302, 173 Eng. Rep. 134 (1836).
112. *Regina v. Kerr*, 8 Car. & P. 176, 173 Eng. Rep. 449, 451 (1837).
113. *Regina v. Morton*, 2 M. & Rob. 514, 174 Eng. Rep. 367 (1843).
114. *Regina v. Baldry*, 2 Den. 430, 169 Eng. Rep. 568 (1852).
115. J. Chitty, *A Practical Treatise on the Criminal Law* (London: A. J. Valpy, 1816), vol. 1, 85.
116. Holt 597, 171 Eng. Rep. 353 (1817).
117. Wigmore, *Treatise on the System of Evidence*, 1904 ed., vol. 1, § 848, p. 969.
118. 2 Leach 553, 168 Eng. Rep. 379 (1791).
119. Id., 168 Eng. Rep. at 380 & 383.
120. Edward Foss, Preface, *A Biographical Dictionary of the Judges of England from the Conquest to the Present Time* (Boston: Little Brown, 1870), ix.
121. Langbein, *Origins of the Adversary Criminal Trial*, 212.
122. Id. at 213.

123. Ry. & Mood. 432, 171 Eng. Rep. 1073, 1074 (1826).
124. 8 Car. & P. 140, 141, 173 Eng. Rep. 433, 433 (1837).
125. 1 Car. & K. 248, 174 Eng. Rep. 796 (1843).
126. 1 Criminal Law Cases 108 (1844). See *also Regina v. Farley*, 1 Cox C. C. 76, (1844); *Regina v. Morton*, 2 Mood. & R. 514, 174 Eng. Rep. 367 (1843). (1843).
127. Wigmore, *Treatise on the System of Evidence*, 1904 ed., vol. 1, § 865, p. 905.
128. *Rex v. Kingston*, 4 Car. & P. 387, 172 Eng. Rep. 752 (1830).
129. *Regina v. Taylor*, 8 Car. & P. 732, 173 Eng. Rep. 694 (1839).
130. "Glocestershire Assizes," *Times* (London), September 9, 1818.
131. 5 Car. & P. 536, 172 Eng. Rep. 1087 (1833).
132. *Richard Hill*, theft, Proceedings of the Old Bailey, July 14, 1742, available at http://www.oldbaileyonline.org/browse.jsp?id=t17420714-8-defend71&div=t17420714-8#highlight (last visited February 20, 2011).
133. *Regina v. Boswell, Joseph Wilkes, James Wilks, and Giles*, Car. & M. 584, 174 Eng. Rep. 645, 646.(1841).
134. Id., 174 Eng. Rep., 647.
135. *Rex v. Spencer and Another*, 7 Car. & P. 775, 173 Eng. Rep. 338, 339 (1837).
136. *Rex v. Thomas and Others*, 6 Car. & P. 353, 172 Eng. Rep. 1273 (1834). In the other case, *Rex v. Enoch and Pulley*, 5 Car. & P. 539, 172 Eng. Rep. 1089 (1833), the inducement was made by a female assigned to keep the suspect from harming herself while the constable "went to the inquest."
137. *Ann Williams*, theft, Proceedings of the Old Bailey, October 28, 1807, available at http://www.oldbaileyonline.org/browse.jsp?ref=t18071028-5 (last visited February 20, 2011).
138. *Rex v. Row, Russ & Ry.* 153, 168 Eng. Rep. 733, 734 (1809).
139. 1 Mood. 453, 168 Eng. Rep. 1341, 1341 (1835).
140. Id., 168 Eng. Rep. at 1342.
141. *Rex v. Clewes*, 4 Car. & P. 221, 172 Eng. Rep. 678, 680 (1830).
142. Id., 168 Eng. Rep. at 679.
143. Id., 168 Eng. Rep. at 680.
144. *Rex v. Gilham*, 1 Mood. 186, 168 Eng. Rep. 1235, 1235 (1828).
145. Id., 168 Eng. Rep. at 1236.
146. Id., 168 Eng. Rep. at 1237.
147. Id.
148. Id., 168 Eng. Rep. at 1242.
149. Id.
150. *Regina v. Sleeman*, Dears 248, 169 Eng. Rep. 714, 715 (1853).
151. 1 Leach 262, 168 Eng. Rep. 264 (1783).
152. See 168 Eng. Rep. at 235, n. (a) 2. This note was added to the *Warickshall* opinion by the reporter in the same way that editors added cites to later cases and to Hale, Hawkins, and Blackstone.
153. Id., 168 Eng. Rep. at 235.
154. *Rex v. Green and Others*, 5 Car. & P. 312, 172 Eng. Rep. 990 (1832).
155. *Rex v. Court*, 7 Car. & P. 487, 173 Eng. Rep. 216 (1836).
156. *Rex v. Richards*, 5 Car. & P. 318, 172 Eng. Rep. 993 (1832).
157. *Rex v. Lloyd*, 6 Car. & P. 393, 172 Eng. Rep. 1291 (1834).
158. *Regina v. Wilkinson*, 8 Car. & P. 663, 175 Eng. Rep. 663, 664 (1838).
159. See *Rex v. Spilsbury, Ferrall, and Others*, 7 Car. & P. 186, 173 Eng. Rep. 82, 83 (1835); *Rex v. Harris*, 1 Mood. 339, 168 Eng. Rep. 1295, 1296 (1832).
160. *Spilsbury*, 173 Eng. Rep. at 83.
161. 11 & 12 Vict., c. 42, para. XVIII (1848), available at http://www.legislation.gov.uk/ukpga/Vict/11-12/42/contents/enacted (last visited March 3, 2011).
162. See generally Wesley MacNeil Oliver, "Magistrates' Examinations, Police Interrogations, and *Miranda*-Like Warnings in the Nineteenth Century," *Tulane L. Rev.* 81 (2007): 777–828.

163. Smith, *Miranda's* Prehistory, 60–61 (draft).
164. 3 Car. & K. 331, 175 Eng. Rep. 576, 577 (1850).
165. Id., 175 Eng. Rep. at 577–78.
166. *R. v. Kimber*, 3 Cox Crim. Cases 223, 224 (1849).
167. *Sansome* cited *Regina v. Bond*, 1 Den. 517, 169 Eng. Rep. 353 (1849). *Sansome*, 175 Eng. Rep., 578.
168. Id., 175 Eng. Rep. at 577.
169. Id., 175 Eng. Rep. at 578.

Chapter 4

1. Massachusetts Body of Liberties (1641), c. 45, available at http://history.hanover.edu/texts/masslib.html (last visited March 19, 2011).
2. Claudia Durst Johnson, *Daily Life in Colonial New England* (Westport, CT: Greenwood Press, 2002), 27. See also George Francis Dow, *Every Day Life in the Massachusetts Bay Colony* (Mineola, NY: Dover Publications, 1988), 153 (noting a 1629 journal entry that a "notorious wicked fellow" who boasted of his wickedness "fell sick of ye [small] pocks and dyed").
3. Langbein, *Torture and the Law of Proof*, 71.
4. Richard Weisman, *Witchcraft, Magic, and Religion in 17th-Century Massachusetts* (Amherst: University of Massachusetts Press, 1984): 155. Proctor's son did not confess, but Proctor claimed that two other boys confessed following similar treatment.
5. Lawrence M. Friedman, *A History of American Law* (New York: Simon & Schuster, 2nd ed. 1985), 71.
6. Weisman, *Witchcraft, Magic, and Religion*, 155 & 156.
7. Id. at 152.
8. *State v. Hobbs & Strong*, 1803 WL 184 (Vt.) (italics in original), at *1.
9. George C. Thomas III, "Colonial Criminal Law and Procedure: The Royal Colony of New Jersey 1749–57," *New York University Journal of Law & Liberty* 1 (2005): 694 (five pretrial examinations) & 673 (forty-nine trials in sample).
10. Julius Goebel & T. Raymond Naughton, *Law Enforcement in Colonial New York, A Study in Criminal Procedure (1664–1776)* (reprinted, Montclair, NJ: Patterson Smith, 1970), 134.
11. See Alexis de Toqueville, *Democracy in America*, trans. Henry Reeve (New York: Bantam Books, 2000) (reprint of 1835 edition), 618.
12. Id. at 61–62.
13. See The Proceedings of the Old Bailey, "A Population History of London, 1760–1815," available at http://www.oldbaileyonline.org/static/Population-history-of-london.jsp#a1760–1815 (last visited January 7, 2011).
14. U.S. Bureau of the Census, "Population of the 46 Urban Places: 1810," tbl. 4, available at http://www.census.gov/population/www/documentation/twps0027/tab04.txt (last visited January 7, 2011).
15. United States Dec. Independence (1776).
16. United States Const., Preamble.
17. See U.S. Const. amends. I–IX.
18. Matthew Hale, *The History of the Pleas of the Crown* (Philadelphia: 1st American edition, 1847).
19. William Blackstone, *Commentaries on the Laws of England* (San Francisco: Bancroft-Whitney, 1916).
20. Id., vol. 2, at 2594–595.
21. Act of February 11, 1777, Ch. 5, § 1, 1776–77 Pa. Laws 18.
22. Ohio Laws, Chapter I, § 1, 1804; Virginia Laws, Chapter III, § I, 1776.
23. U.S. Const. art. III. sect. 3.
24. Some states explicitly followed the Marian statutes. See William Schley, *A Digest of the English Statutes of Force in the State of Georgia* (1826), 212; William Kilty, *A Report of All Such*

English Statutes as existed at the time of the first emigration of the people of Maryland, and which by experience have been found applicable to their local and other circumstances ... (1811), 234; *State v. Grove*, 1 N.C. 63 (1794) (prisoner discharged because examination not committed to writing within two days as required by 2 & 3 Phil.& M. c.10, held not repealed by Laws of 1715, c.1); Horace Binney, *Reports of Cases Adjudged in the Supreme Court of Pennsylvania*, v. 3 (1811), App.: The Report of the Judges of the Supreme Court of the Commonwealth of Pennsylvania ... (December 19 & 20, 1808), 621. Other states enacted statutes that tracked the Marian statutes quite closely. See L. Moreau Lislet, *A General Digest of the Acts of the Legislature of Louisiana passed from the year 1804 to 1827* (1828), 630–32: Act of .January 23, 1805; William Paterson, *Laws of the State of New Jersey* (New Brunswick, NJ: printed by Abraham Blauvelt, 1800), 129–30 (Act of November 22, 1794); Laws of the State of New York, Act of January 30, 1787, ch. 8, 1787.

25. Leonard MacNally, Rules of Evidence on Pleas of the Crown Illustrated from Printed and Manuscript Trials and Cases (Philadelphia: P. Byrne, 1804), 37.

26. Thomas Cooper, *Statutes at Large of South Carolina*, No. 112 & No. 113, (1712), 409; John Fauchereaud Grimké, *The South Carolina Justice of Peace* (New-York: T. & J. Swords, 3rd ed., 1810), 165, para. 3 & para. 6 (citing the Marian acts as authority for principle that the justice of the peace shall take the examination of the person bailed or committed).

27. See *A Collection of All Such Acts of the General Assembly of Virginia of a Public and Permanent Nature, As Are Now In Force* (Richmond: printed by Augustine Davis, 1794), chap. CXLVII, 302 (repealing all acts of Parliament) (December 27, 1792); id. at chap. LXXIV, 109–13 ("An Act directing the Method of proceeding against free Persons charged with certain Crimes. . . .") (November 13, 1792).

28. Rhodom A. Green & John W. Lumpkin, *The Georgia Justice* (Milledgeville, GA: P. L. & B. H. Robinson, 1835), 160.

29. *State v. Collins*, 2 Del. Cas. 181 (1803).

30. John C. B. Davis, *The Massachusetts Justice* (Worcester, MA: Warren Lazell, 1847), 242; William Waller Hening, *The New Virginia Justice* (Richmond: J. & G. Cochran, 1820), 200–201; Henry Hitchcock, *The Alabama Justice of the Peace* (Cahawba, AL: William B. Allen, 1822), 98–99; Mordecai McKinney, *The Pennsylvania Justice of the Peace* (Harrisburg, PA: E. Guyer, 1839), 60; and William Smith, *The Justice of the Peace* (New York: J.F. Handley, 1841), 424.

31. McKinney, *Pennsylvania Justice of the Peace*, 60.

32. Act of January 30, 1787, ch. 8, New York Laws, 354.

33. William Dickinson, *A Practical Exposition of the Law Relative to the Office and Duties of a Justice of the Peace* (London: Reed and Hunter, 1813), vol. 1, 457.

34. John A. Dunlap, *The New York Justice; or a Digest of the Law Relative to Justices of the Peace in the State of New-York* (New York: Isaac Riley, 1815), 100.

35. *Conductor Generalis* (Albany, NY: E. F. Backus, 1819), 93.

36. Simon Greenleaf, *A Treatise on the Law of Evidence* (Boston: Little Brown, 1842), vol. 1, § 225, p. 262 (emphasis in original).

37. See Revised Statutes of Arkansas c. 45, § 33 (1838); Revised Statutes of Missouri, art. II, § 15 (1835); Revised Statutes of New York, vol. 2, part IV, Ch. II, § 15 (1829).

38. Greenleaf, *Treatise on the Law of Evidence*, vol. 1, § 224, p. 261 n.2.

39. *Commonwealth v. Dillon*, 4 U.S. 116, 116 (Pa. 1792).

40. Id.

41. Id. at 118.

42. *State v. Baynard*, 1 Del. Cas. 662 (Del. Oyer & Terminer 1794), *3.

43. *State v. Doherty*, 2 Tenn. 80 (1806), *6.

44. 2 N.C. 482 (N.C. Super. L. & Eq. 1797), *1.

45. 2 N.C. 455 (1797).

46. Confessions "are ever liable to be obtained by artifice, false hopes, promises of favour, or menaces; seldom remembered accurately, or reported with due precision." Blackstone's *Commentaries*, 8th ed., 1778, vol. 4, * 357.

47. *Charles Hope's Case*, 1 N.Y. City-Hall Recorder 159, 159 (1816).

48. Hale, *History of the Pleas of the Crown*, vol. 2, 290.

49. Wigmore, *Treatise on the System of Evidence*, 1904 ed., vol. 3, § 2070, p. 2778.

50. David A. Moran, "In Defense of the Corpus Delicti Rule," *Ohio St. L. J.* 64 (2003): 829.

51. Richard A. Leo, Steven A. Drizin, Peter J. Neufeld, Bradley R. Hall, & Amy Vater, "Bringing Reliability Back In: False Confessions and Legal Safeguards in the Twenty-First Century," *Wis. L. Rev.* (2006): 502–3.

52. *Charles Hope's Case.*

53. *State v. Aaron, slave of L. Solomon*, 4 NJ L. 231, *7 (N.J. 1818).

54. Id. at *6 & *8.

55. Id. at *7 (emphasis in original).

56. Moran, "In Defense of the Corpus Delicti Rule," 834–35.

57. *Commonwealth v. Drake*, 15 Mass. 161 (1818).

58. *State v. Negro Absolom*, 2 Del. Cas. 32 (Del. Quar. Sess. 1808), *1.

59. *State v. Phelps*, 11 Vt. 116 (1839), 5 (Westlaw version) (quoting Thomas Starkie, *A Practical Treatise on the Law of Evidence and Digest of Proofs in Civil and Criminal Proceedings* (London: J. & W. T. Clarke, 1824), vol. 2, 49 (emphasis in original)).

60. *State v. Fields & Webber*, 7 Tenn. 140 (Tenn. Err. & App. 1823), *2.

61. *State v. Bostick*, 4 Del. 563 (Del. O. & T. 1845), *2.

62. Id.

63. Id. at *3 (Justice Harrington, dissenting) (emphasis in original).

64. A remarkable sixteen editions were published, the first in 1842, the last in 1899. See Simon Greenleaf, *A Treatise on the Law of Evidence*, 16th ed., Revised, Enlarged, and Annotated by John Henry Wigmore (Boston: Little Brown, 1899),; Greenleaf, 1842 edition.

65. Greenleaf, *Treatise on the Law of Evidence*, 1842 edition, vol. 1, § 214, p. 247–48 (emphasis in original).

66. See Thomas, *Supreme Court on Trial*, 15–30, Susan Bandes, "Loyalty to One's Convictions: The Prosecutor and Tunnel Vision," *Howard L. J.* 49 (2006): 475–94.

67. Greenleaf, *Treatise on the Law of Evidence*, 1842 edition, vol. 1, § 215, p. 250 (emphasis in original).

68. Id., vol. 1, 266 (emphasis in original).

69. Revised Statutes of New York, vol. 2, part IV, chap. II, § 15, (1829) (date of passage December 10, 1828).

70. Dickinson, 1813, vol. 1, 457; J. Chitty, (1816), vol. 1, 85.

71. Revised Statutes of New York, vol. 2, part IV, chap. II, § 15.

72. Revised Statutes of Arkansas, c. 45, § 33 (1838); The Revised Statutes of Missouri, art. III, § 15 (1835).

73. Oliver, "Magistrate's Examinations."

74. Id. at 793–95.

75. *People v. Bodine*, 1 Edm. Sel. Cas. 36 (N.Y. Sup. Ct. 1845), *19.

76. Id. at *18.

77. 8 Car. & P. 621, 173 Eng. Rep. 645 (1838).

78. *Bodine*, 1 Sel. Cas. 36, *19.

79. Id. at *18 (emphasis added).

80. Holt 597, 171 Eng. Rep. 353 (1817).

81. *Harris*, 1 Car. & K. 248, 174 Eng. Rep. 796 (1843); *Drew*, 8 Car. & P. 140, 173 Eng. Rep. 433 (1837). See Dickinson, 1813, vol. 1, 457 (noting "excessive mildness" of English law on confessions).

82. Coke, *Third Part of the Institutes of the Laws of England*, 137.

83. Langbein, *Origins of the Adversary Criminal Trial*, 272.

84. *The Report of Hiram Maxwell's Case* (New York: Gould & Banks, 1823), available at Heinonline, World Trials, 42 (statement of Thomas Emmet).

85. H. W. Howard Knott, "John Andrew Graham," *Dictionary of American Biography* (New York: Scriber's Sons, 1931), vol. 7, 478.

86. *People v. Foot*, 1 Wheeler 70, 71 (1822).

87. John A. Graham, *Speeches, Delivered at the City-Hall of the City of New-York in the Courts of Oyer and Terminer, Common Pleas, and General Sessions of the Peace* (New York: George Forman, 2nd ed., 1812); Norman Mailer, *Advertisements for Myself* (New York: Putnam's, 1959).

88. Graham, *Speeches, Delivered at the City-Hall of the City of New-York*, 48, *People v. Sebray Bogert*.

89. Id. at 57, *People v. Williams*.

90. Id. at 60.

91. Id. (emphasis in original).

92. Id. at 70, *People v. Davis* (emphasis in original).

93. Id. at 71.

94. Id. at 33, *People v. James Bluet*.

95. Id. at 34.

96. *Report of Hiram Maxwell's Case*, 2.

97. *People v. Maxwell*, 1 Wheeler 163, 165 (1823).

98. Constitution of New York, 1777, National Humanities Institute website, available at http://www.nhinet.org/ccs/docs/ny-1777.htm (last visited March 3, 2011). Thomas Davies thinks that a right against compelled self-incrimination might be implicit in a prohibition of the creation of courts that proceed other than "according to the course of the common law." E-mail from Davies to George Thomas, March 5, 2008.

99. See Laws of the State of New York, Tenth Session, c. 1 (1787), available at http://www.courts.state.ny.us/history/pdf/Library/New%20York%20Bill%20of%20Rights.pdf (last visited March 3,2011).

100. The Second Constitution of New York, 1821, Art. VII, § 7 (original "wit-ness" modernized to "witness"), available at http://www.nycourts.gov/history/constitutions/1821_constitution.htm (last visited March 3, 2011).

101. *Report of Hiram Maxwell's Case*, 10.

102. Id. at 15 (emphasis in original).

103. Id. at 16.

104. Id. at 20 (emphasis in original).

105. Id. at 21.

106. Id. at 22–23 (emphasis in original).

107. Id. at 11–12.

108. Id. at 12–13 (emphasis in original).

109. Id. at 23–24.

110. *People v. Maxwell*, 1 Wheeler 163, 166 (New York Criminal Recorder 1823).

111. *Report of Hiram Maxwell's Case*, viii.

112. Id. at vii.

113. See id. at 25 (Adams); id. at 27 (Jefferson); id. at 28 (John Jay, former governor); id. at 30 (Morgan Lewis, former governor); id. at 32 (De Witt Clinton, former governor); id. at 35 (Jackson); id. at 37 (Marshall).

114. Id. at 25–26.

115. Id. at 37 (italics removed).

116. Id. at vii (emphasis in original).

117. Id. at 66–67.

118. Id. at 41.

119. Id. at 42.

120. Id. at 50 (David B. Ogden, Esq. "eminent Counsellor and Advocate at the American Bar").

121. Id. at 44–45.

122. Id. at 45 (emphasis in original).

123. Id. at 48.

124. Id. at 47.

125. Id. at 46.

126. Laws of the State of New-York, Thirty-Sixth Session, 1813, vol. 2, chap. civ., II.

127. Compare *Report of Hiram Maxwell's Case*, 13, with Revised Statutes of New York, vol. 2, part IV, chap. II, §§ 14 & 15 (1829).

128. George C. Edwards, *A Treatise on the Powers and Duties of Justices of the Peace and Town Officers in the State of New-York under the Revised Statutes with Practical Forms* (Bath, NY: Printed by David Rumsey, 1830), 207–9 (discussion of procedure) & 209 ("certain cases").

129. Id. at 206–9.

130. James F. Richardson, *The New York Police: Colonial Times to 1901* (New York: Oxford University Press, 1970), 16.

131. Id. at 17 (constables) & 19 (watchmen).

132. Id. at 21.

133. Id. at 15.

134. Id. at 19.

135. Id. at 17 (1800) & 29 (1832).

136. Id. at 24.

137. Id. at 28–29.

138. Raymond L. Cohn, "Immigration to the United States," tbl. 1, EH.Net, available at http://eh.net/encyclopedia/article/cohn.immigration.us (last visited March 5, 2011).

139. Richardson, *New York Police*, 32 (1845) & 19 (1800).

140. Id. at 51.

141. Oliver, "Magistrate's Examinations," 805.

142. Id. at 810–11.

143. See, e.g., "Report of Joint Committee on Police Matters in the city and county of New-York, and county of Kings, No. 97," in Senate, March 4, 1856 (committee charge was legislation "for the suppression and punishment of crime, and the better protection of persons charged with crime").

144. "Report of Select Committee on Code of Criminal Procedure, No. 150," in Assembly, March 2, 1855.

145. Id. at § 449 n., at p.15.

146. "Superintendent Walling: His Trial Before the Police Board," *New York Times*, March 13, 1875.

147. "Report of the Select Committee Appointed by the Assembly of 1875 to Investigate the Causes of the Increase of Crime in the City of New York," Rep. No. 106 (1876), 69.

148. Revised Statutes of New York, vol. 2, part IV, chap. II, § 15, p. 708 (1829).

149. "Report of the Select Committee Appointed by the Assembly of 1875 to Investigate the Causes of the Increase of Crime," 69.

150. New York L. 1881, ch.442.

151. *Report of Hiram Maxwell's Case*, 59 (David Graham, Esq., "eminent Counsellor and Advocate at the New-York Bar").

152. See, e.g., *People v. Rogers*, 18 N.Y. 9 (1858), *14 (citing with approval *Commonwealth v. Mosler*, 4 Pa. 264 (1846), holding that a caution was not necessary to admit a confession made to a constable). See also *Ward v. People*, 3 Hill. 395 (N.Y. Sup. Ct. 1842).

153. Friedman, *History of American Law*, 2nd ed., 578.

154. "Clubbing a Minor Offense," *New York Times*, October 3, 1894.

155. Wigmore, *Treatise on the System of Evidence*, 1904 ed., vol. 1, § 865, p. 994.

156. See John H. Wigmore, "Nemo Tenetur Seipsum Prodere," *Harv. L. Rev.* 5 (1891–92): 72 n.1 (citing Jeremy Bentham, *Rationale of Judicial Evidence* (London: Hunt and Clarke, 1827), vol. 5, book 9, c. 3 & c. 4.

157. Wigmore, *Treatise on the System of Evidence*, 1904 ed., vol. 1, § 823, p. 934–35.

158. Jeremy Bentham, *Rationale of Judicial Evidence* (London: Hunt and Clarke, 1827), vol. 5, 208.

159. Id. at 240.

160. Id. at 221.

161. Wigmore, *Treatise on the System of Evidence*, 1904 ed., vol. 1, § 865, p. 995.

162. Id. at § 820, p. 927.
163. Id. Wigmore gives no citation for the case involving a glass of gin, but we found a reference to it in Henry H. Joy, *On the Admissibility of Confessions and Challenges to Jurors in Criminal Cases in England and Ireland* (Dublin: Andrew Milliken, 1842), 17 (*Rex v. Sexton* (1822)).
164. Wigmore, *Treatise on the System of Evidence*, 1904 ed., vol. 1, § 822, p. 931.
165. Langbein, *Origins of the Adversary Criminal Trial*, 233.
166. Wigmore, *Treatise on the System of Evidence*, 1904 ed., vol. 1, § 824, p. 937 (emphasis in original).
167. Id. at § 831, p. 945.
168. Id. at § 824, p. 936.
169. Alan Wertheimer, *Coercion* (Princeton, NJ: Princeton University Press, 1987), 6–7. For Aristotle's treatment, which did not of course involve a bank robbery, see Aristotle, *Nichomachean Ethics*, book 3, part 1, 1110a 1–22.
170. Wertheimer, *Coercion*, 6 n. 4 (emphasis added).
171. Id. at 170–75.
172. Wigmore, *Treatise on the System of Evidence*, 1904 ed., vol. 1, § 865, p. 995.
173. 168 U.S. 532 (1897).
174. 110 U.S. 574, 584 (1884).
175. Id. at 585.
176. Id. at 584.
177. Id. at 585.
178. *Sparf v. United States*, 156 U.S. 51, 55 (1895).
179. *Pierce v. United States*, 160 U.S. 355, 357 (1896).
180. 162 U.S. 613 (1896).
181. See id., 16 S.Ct. 896 (statement of facts).
182. 162 U.S. at 624.
183. Four justices dissented in *Sparf* but not on the issue of whether the confession made while in irons was admissible.
184. Wigmore, *Treatise on the System of Evidence*, 1904 ed., vol. 1, § 2266, p. 3131.
185. Herman, "Unexplored Relationship (Part II)," *Ohio St. L.J.* 497 (1992): 531–32.
186. Id. at 530. See, e.g., *Perovich v. United States*, 205 U.S. 86, 91 (1907) (phrasing the issue as whether the statements were "induced by duress, intimidation, or other improper influences"). The privilege was resurrected in *Malloy v. Hogan*, 378 U.S. 1 (1964) (holding that it applied to the states via the due process clause) and, of course, in *Miranda*, which explicitly relied on *Bram*.
187. A new theory appeared in 1943, the so-called *McNabb-Mallory* rule. See *Mallory v. United States*, 354 U.S. 449 (1957); *McNabb v. United States*, 318 U.S. 332 (1943). This rule, which did not involve any inquiry into voluntariness, instead depended on whether officers made an arrested person available for arraignment "without unnecessary delay" as required by federal rules of procedure. If not, statements were suppressed as the fruit of the violation of the rule.
188. *Bram*, 168 U. S., 561–62.
189. Id. at 539.
190. Id. at 542–43 (ellipsis in original).
191. Wigmore, *Treatise on the System of Evidence*, 1904 ed., vol. 1, § 832, p. 947 n.1.
192. *People v. McCullough*, 45 N.W. 515, 517 (Mich. 1890).
193. Id. (emphasis added).
194. *People v. Dunnigan*, 128 N.W. 180, 181 (Mich. 1910).
195. *People v. Barric*, 49 Cal. 342, 345 (1874).
196. *People v. Thompson*, 84 Cal. 598, 605 (1890).
197. *People v. Siemsen*, 153 Cal. 387, 392 (1908).
198. Id.
199. Id. at 394.
200. *Rafe v. State*, 20 Ga. 60 (1856), *6.

201. William B. McCash, "Thomas Cobb and the Codification of Georgia Law," *Georgia Historical Quarterly* 62 (1978): 9.

202. Bond Almand, "The Preparation and Adoption of the Code of 1863," *Ga. B. J.* 14 (1951): 167 (emphasis in original).

203. Id.

204. William Hawkins, *A Treatise of the Pleas of the Crown; or, A System of the Principal Matters Relating to that Subject, Digested under Proper Heads,* ed. John Curwood (London: Printed for B. Sweet; R. Phenny; A. Maxwell, and R. Stevens and Sons; Lincoln's Inn; Law Booksellers and Publishers; and J. Cumming, Dublin, 8th ed., 1824), vol. 2, 595.

205. 11 Ga. 225 (1852).

206. Id. at *8 (emphasis in original).

207. *Berry v. State,* 10 Ga. 511, at *6 (1851).

208. 55 Ga. 591 (1876).

209. Id. at *3.

210. Id. at *4 (observation embedded in the chief justice's opinion for the court; no separate opinions were issued).

211. Id.

212. 15 S.E. 10 (Ga. 1891) (facts stated in syllabus "by the Court").

213. Id. at *10.

214. *Miller v. State,* 21 S.E. 128, 129 (Ga. 1894).

215. Id.

216. *Dixon v. State,* 39 S.E. 846 (Ga. 1901) (facts stated in syllabus "by the Court").

217. *Smith v. State,* 54 S. E. 190, 190 (Ga. 1906).

218. 92 S.E. 309, 311 (Ga. App. 1917).

219. Id. at 312.

220. Id.

221. Id.

222. *Morris v. State,* 125 S.E. 508 (Ga. App. 1924) (facts stated in syllabus "by the Court").

223. Id. at 508, *Wilson,* 92 S.E. at 314.

224. John Henry Wigmore, *A Treatise on the Anglo-American System of Evidence in Trials at Common Law* (Boston: Little Brown, 1923), vol. 2, § 833, pp. 159–60 nn.2–5.

Chapter 5

1. Harding, *Social History of English Law,* 384 (quoting an 1834 statute).

2. Hilton, *A Mad, Bad, and Dangerous People?* 7 (food supplies), 23 (debtor's prisons), 14 (blight).

3. Clive Emsley, "Crime and the Victorians," in BBC's *British History, Victorians* (2001), available at http://www.bbc.co.uk/history/british/victorians/crime_01.shtml (last visited March 23, 2011).

4. Tobias, *Urban Crime in Victorian England,* 41.

5. Id.

6. Id at 218, tbl. I.

7. The Proceedings of the Old Bailey, "A Population History of London, The Demography of Urban Growth, 1815–1860," available at http://www.oldbaileyonline.org/static/Population-history-of-london.jsp#a1815–1860 (last visited February 17, 2011).

8. Id.

9. Charles Dickens, *Oliver Twist,* introduction and notes by Jill Muller (New York: Barnes & Noble Classics, 2003), x.

10. Tobias, *Urban Crime,* 128.

11. Id. at 145.

12. 11 & 12 Vict., c. 42, para. XVIII (1848), available at http://www.legislation.gov.uk/ukpga/Vict/11-12/42/contents/enacted (last visited March 3, 2011).

13. 2 Den. 430, 169 Eng. Rep. 568, 570 (1852).
14. Id., 169 Eng. Rep. at 568.
15. Id., 169 Eng. Rep. at 569 (no citation given to *Russell*).
16. Id., 169 Eng. Rep. at 573.
17. 2 M. & Rob. 514, 174 Eng. Rep. 367 (1843).
18. See *The Queen v. Harris*, 1 Cox C. C. 106 (South Wales Circuit, 1844).
19. *Baldry*, 169 Eng. Rep., 574.
20. Id.
21. Id at 228.
22. Id. at 575.
23. Id.
24. Wigmore, *Treatise on the System of Evidence*, vol. 1, 1904 ed., § 837, p. 953.
25. 168 U.S. 532 (1897).
26. *Regina v. Moore*, 2 Den. 522, 169 Eng. Rep. 608 (1852).
27. Id., 169 Eng. Rep. at 609.
28. Id., 169 Eng. Rep. at 610.
29. 2 F. & F. 833, 175 Eng. Rep. 1308, 1308 (1862).
30. *Regina v. Reason*, 12 Cox C. C. 228 (1872).
31. Id. at 228
32. Id. at 229.
33. Id. Five years earlier, Wigmore had revised Greenleaf's treatise to suggest that the real test was whether the threat or promise was "likely" to have caused the suspect to tell "an untruth." See Greenleaf, *A Treatise on the Law of Evidence*, 16th ed., 1899, § 219, p. 354.
34. *Reason*, 12 Cox C. C., 229.
35. 15 Cox C. C. 656 (1885).
36. Id. at 657.
37. Id. at Note.
38. Wigmore, *Treatise on the System of Evidence*, vol. 1, 1904 ed., § 820, p. 927.
39. Id., vol. 1, 1904 ed., § 847, p. 966 n.6 (discussing *Rex v. Gibney*, Jebb Cr. C. 15 (1822)).
40. See id., vol. 1, 1904 ed., § 847, p. 966 n.7 (discussing several Irish cases).
41. 15 Ir. C. L. 60, 70 & 80 (1864).
42. Wigmore, *Treatise on the System of Evidence*, vol. 1, 1904 ed., § 847, p. 966.
43. *Johnston*, 15 Ir. C. L., 87. See also id. (opinion of Judge O'Brien). Judge Deasy appears to embrace the same theory when he agrees with the law as the defendant stated it about the effect of custody. Id. at 71.
44. Id. at 85.
45. Id. at 84.
46. Id. at 76.
47. 14 Cox C. C. 607, 608 (1881).
48. Id.
49. Id. at 609.
50. 18 Cox C. C. 717, 718 (1898).
51. William Blackstone, *Commentaries on the Laws of England*, additional notes by George Sharswood (Philadelphia: J. P. Lippincott, 1898), vol. 2, 356.
52. Id. at n.16.
53. Leslie Stephen, *The Life of Sir James Fitzjames Stephen* (London: Smith, Elder, & Co., 1895), 271.
54. The Indian Evidence Act (London: Macmillan, 1872) § 24, p. 163.
55. Id. at § 26, p. 163.
56. Id. at § 27, p. 163 & § 28, pp. 163–64.
57. Id. at § 29, p. 164.
58. Henry Raymond Fink, *The Indian Evidence Act* (Calcutta: Wyman, 1872), 2 (speech delivered by James Fitzjames Stephen: "On the occasion of presenting to the Supreme Council

of India, the report of the Select Committee on the Bill to define and amend the Laws of Evidence").

59. Gordon S. Wood, *The Radicalism of the American Revolution* (New York: Vintage Books, 1991), 95.

60. Id.

61. *Elmore v. State*, 137 So. 185, 186 (Ala. 1931).

62. See, e.g., Greenleaf, *Treatise on the Law of Evidence*, 16th ed., 1899, § 219, p. 354 (after stating the Hawkins-Leach "hope or fear" dictum, Wigmore sets out in brackets his "probably not true" test as the "foundation" of the confessions rule).

63. *Commonwealth v. Preece*, 5 N.E. 494, 495 (Mass. 1885).

64. *Maull v. State*, 11 So. 218, 218 (Ala. 1891).

65. Wigmore, *Treatise on the System of Evidence*, vol. 1, 1904 ed., § 832, pp. 947–48 n.3.

66. We searched for "fair risk" in the same sentence with "false" and "confession." See *Black v. State*, 630 So.2d 609 (Fla. App. Dist. 1993); *Williams v. State*, 281 Ark. 91 (1983); *State v. Mullin*, 249 Iowa 10 (1957); *State v. Green*, 273 P. 381 (Or. 1929); *State v. Sherman*, 35 Mont. 512 (1907); *State v. Doyle*, 146 La. 973 (1920); *Cooper v. State*, 237 P. 865, 867 (Okla. Crim. 1925); *Palakiko v. Territory of Hawaii*, 188 F.2d 54 (1951); *United States v. Gorayska*, 482 F.Supp. 576, S.D.N.Y., 1979; *Bradford v. Johnson*, 354 F.Supp. 1331, E.D.Mich., July 14, 1972; *Stephenson v. Boles*, 221 F.Supp. 411, N.D.W.Va., September 05, 1963; *United States v. Price*, 1962 WL 4604, 32 C.M.R. 812, AFBR (1962); *United States v. McKay*, 1958 WL 3365, 26 C.M.R. 307, 9 USCMA 527, CMA (1958).

67. *State v. Sherman*, 90 P. 981 (Mont. 1907).

68. Id. at 983.

69. *State v. Green*, 273 P. 381, 385 (Or. 1929).

70. To be sure, the court held the confession inadmissible, id., on very odd facts. The defendant, who claimed to be innocent, agreed to confess as part of what he thought was a scheme to "buy his way" out of the charge. Id. at 383–84.

71. *Pollack v. State*, 253 N.W. 560, 567 (Wis. 1934).

72. Id. at 566.

73. Id.

74. Id. at 567.

75. *People v. Castree*, 143 N. E. 112, 122 (Ill. 1924).

76. *People v. Fox*, 150 N. E. 347, 348–49 (Ill. 1926).

77. *Brown v. United States*, 13 F.2d 298, 299 (D.C. Cir. 1926).

78. *State v. Kerns*, 198 N.W. 698, 701 (N.D. 1924).

79. *Commonwealth v. Green*, 20 N. E. 2d 417, 420 (Mass. 1939).

80. *Commonwealth v. Hipple*, 33 A. 2d 353, 355–56 (Penn. 1939).

81. 260 P. 138 (Mont. 1927).

82. Id. at 144.

83. Id. at 145.

84. Id.

85. Wigmore, *Treatise on the System of Evidence*, 1923 ed., vol. 2, § 832, pp. 157– 159 n.3.

86. *Arizona v. Fulminante*, 499 U.S. 279, 285 (1991).

Chapter 6

1. Jerome Frank, *Courts on Trial* (Princeton, NJ: Princeton University Press, 1949), 100.

2. See *State v. Fields & Webber*, 7 Tenn. 140 (Tenn. Err. & App. 1823), * 2.

3. Friedman, *History of American Law*, 2nd ed., 338.

4. In 1860, Atlanta's population was 9,954. See Campbell Gibson, "Population of the 100 Largest Cities and Other Urban Places in the United States: 1790–1990," available at http://www.census.gov/population/www/documentation/twps0027/tab09.txt (last visited January 27, 2011). The Georgia statute is discussed in chapter 4.

5. See *Wilson v. State*, 92 S.E. 209 (Ga. App. 1917), discussed in chapter 4.

6. Demographia, "Greater London, Inner London & Outer London, Population & Density History," available at http://www.demographia.com/dm-lon31.htm (last visited January 27, 2011).

7. Colin Holmes, *John Bull's Island: Immigration and British Society 1871–1971* (London: Macmillan, 1988), 276 (comparing immigration into the two countries from 1871–1971).

8. Raymond L. Cohn, "Immigration to the United States," tbl. 1, EH.Net, available at http://eh.net/encyclopedia/article/cohn.immigration.us (last visited January 27, 2011).

9. Holmes, *John Bull's Island*, 30 (England and Wales); U.S. Department of Commerce, Bureau of the Census, Historical Statistics of the United States, 1789–1945, Series B 279–303, Country of Birth of the Foreign-Born Population (Census); 1850–1940.

10. "That Rebel Geography," *New York Times*, December 8, 1889.

11. Drew Gilpin Faust, *This Republic of Suffering: Death and the American Civil War* (New York: Alfred A. Knopf, 2008), 3.

12. Id. at 41.

13. Id. at xi.

14. Id. at 58.

15. Id. at 69.

16. Id. at 60.

17. Theodore Brantner Wilson, *The Black Codes of the South* (University: University of Alabama Press, 1965), 170–73 (lists laws of fourteen states).

18. Id. at 69.

19. A. W. Ward, G. W. Prothero, Stanley Leathes, *The Cambridge Modern History* (Cambridge: Cambridge University Press, 1903), vol. 7, 641.

20. Cong. Globe, 39th Cong., 1st Sess. 1838 (April 7, 1866) (Representative Sidney Clarke, R-KS) (commenting on the need for the Civil Rights Bill).

21. Id. at 2082 (April 21, 1866) (Representative Sidney Perham, R-MA).

22. "All About a Rebel Flag: A Violent Controversy Progressing in a Jersey Town," *New York Times*, July 14, 1890.

23. "The Navy at Fort Fisher: Brooklyn Children See the Stars and Bars," *New York Times*, May 19, 1894.

24. "Statues to the Rebel Dead," *New York Times*, February 21, 1881 (from the *Boston Traveler*).

25. See Alan Cromartie, *The Constitutionalist Revolution, An Essay on the History of England, 1450–1642* (Cambridge: Cambridge University Press, 2006), 234–274.

26. Friedman, *History of American Law*, 2nd ed., 589 n.44.

27. Id. at 589.

28. James Goodman, *Stories of Scottsboro* (New York: Vintage Books, 1995), 15.

29. *The Western Mirror* (Cambridge City, Indiana), February 1, 1866.

30. *New York Times*, November 17, 1900.

31. *New York Times*, December 17, 1900.

32. *New York Times*, February 26, 1901.

33. *New York Times*, June 1, 1901.

34. *New York Times*, June 20, 1901.

35. *New York Times*, December 18, 1900.

36. *New York Times*, July 9, 1901.

37. *New York Times*, March 3, 1901.

38. *New York Times*, August 2, 1901.

39. *New York Times*, August 23, 1901.

40. Friedman, *History of American Law*, 2nd ed., 665.

41. "Man Shot Five Times; Wounding of Janitor by a Tenant in Dispute Over 25 Cents Excites a Mob of Italians," *New York Times*, May 13, 1901.

42. "Mrs. Nation Begins Her Crusade Anew," *New York Times*, January 22, 1901.

43. "Mrs. Nation Horsewhipped," *New York Times*, January 25, 1901.

44. "Mob Threatens Mrs. Nation," *New York Times,* January 27, 1901.
45. "More Kansas Saloons Fall Under the Axe," *New York Times,* January 31, 1901.
46. "Saloon Raiders Kill Woman," *New York Times,* February 20, 1901.
47. "White House Shut to Carrie Nation," *New York Times,* January 31, 1907.
48. "Negro Dies at the Stake: Florida Mob Pours Oil on Him and Applies a Match," *New York Times,* May 29, 1901.
49. "Negro Dies at the Stake: Fred Alexander Dragged from Leavenworth Jail by a Mob," *New York Times,* January 15, 1901.
50. "Lynchers May Go Scot Free," *New York Times,* January 17, 1901.
51. "Prayer Precedes a Lynching," *New York Times,* March 3, 1901.
52. "Jury Fails to Agree; Mob Hangs Negro," *New York Times,* March 18, 1901.53.
53. "Supreme Court Justices Denounce 'Third Degree,'" *New York Times,* July 20, 1902.
54. *New York Times,* January 26, 1908.
55. FBI, "A Brief History of the FBI, Lawless Years: 1921–1933," available at http://www.fbi.gov/about-us/history/brief-history (last visited February 8, 2011).
56. Marilynn Johnson, *Street Justice: A History of Police Violence in New York City* (Boston: Beacon Press, 2003), 122.
57. "Third Degree in Police Parlance," *New York Times,* October 6, 1901.
58. See, e.g., *Charles Hope's Case,* 1 N. Y. City-Hall Recorder 159 (1816) ("police magistrates"); *Report of Hiram Maxwell's Case,* Heinonline, World Trials, 2, 1823 (examination of suspect had been "taken in the Police Office").
59. Wigmore, *Treatise on the System of Evidence,* 1923 ed., vol. 2., § 851, pp. 196–97.
60. Carolyn B. Ramsey, "In the Sweat Box: A Historical Perspective on the Detention of Material Witnesses," *Ohio St. J. Crim. L.* 681 (2009).
61. Id. at 695 (changed capitalization).
62. Richard A. Leo, *Police Interrogation and American Justice* (Cambridge, MA: Harvard University Press, 2008), 41–79.
63. Named for its chair, former attorney general George Wickersham, the commission was appointed by President Hoover in 1929 and issued fourteen reports, including one on the administration of justice, in 1931. Id. at 44–45 & n.2.
64. "Seeks Death After Sweat," *Chicago Daily Tribune,* August 10, 1907 (noting that an "anti-sweating bill . . . came up before the last legislature and was tabled in the senate"); Ky. Rev. Stat. § 422.110 (enacted 1912; see Charles T. McCormick, "Some Problems and Developments in the Admissibility of Confessions," *Texas L. Rev.* 24 (1946): 254).
65. *Congressional Record,* 61st Cong., 2d Sess. Report No. 597 (April 26, 1910); *Congressional Record,* 62d Cong., 1st Sess, Report No. 128 (August 4, 1911).
66. *People v. Loper,* 159 Cal. 6, 14 (1910).
67. "Women Launch Police Inquiry," *Los Angeles Times,* May 6, 1927.
68. "Legalize It or Abolish It," Saturday Evening Post, March 6, 1926.
69. "Third Degree in Police Parlance," *New York Times,* October 6, 1901.
70. "The Third Degree," *Los Angeles Times,* March 13, 1926 (referring to the March 6, 1926 *Saturday Evening Post* story).
71. U.S. Department of Justice, National Institute of Justice, Office of Justice Programs, *Crime and Justice Atlas 2000,* "United States Murder Rate, 1900–1998," available at http://www.jrsa.org/programs/Crime_Atlas_2000.pdf (last visited February 1, 2011).
72. See, e.g., "Hope to Wipe Out Black Hand," *New York Times,* June 13, 1909 (Ohio, Pennsylvania, West Virginia, Indiana, Illinois); "Blew Up the Banana King," *New York Times,* January 19, 1908 (Maryland); "Blackmail for Merchant," *New York Times,* October 28, 1910 (Toronto); "Black Hand's Foe Warned," *New York Times,* May 3, 1909 (Louisiana). "Blackhander, Who Demanded $35,000, Caught in a Trap by Asa G. Candler," *Atlanta Constitution,* April 7, 1909.
73. "Attack on Priest, 'Black Hand's' Enemy," *New York Times,* September 20, 1904.
74. "'Black Hand' after Baker," *New York Times,* December 12, 1904.

75. "'Black Hand' in Murder," *New York Times*, August 29, 1904.
76. "Store Wrecked by Bomb," *New York Times*, November 26, 1907; "Black Hand Plants Bomb," id., July 17, 1907.
77. "Woman and Girl Torn by a Bomb," *New York Times*, June 4, 1907.
78. "Big Bomb Wrecks 5-Story Tenement," *New York Times*, December 22, 1907.
79. "Must Stop Outrages by the Black Hand," *New York Times*, January 26, 1908.
80. "Is 'the Black Hand' a Myth or a Terrible Reality?" *New York Times*, March 3, 1907.
81. "Must Stop Outrages by the Black Hand," *New York Times*, January 26, 1908.
82. *New York Times*, July 25, 1908.
83. "Is the Black Hand a Myth or a Terrible Reality?" *New York Times*, March 3, 1907.
84. "Unveil Petrosino Monument," *New York Times*, March 14, 1910.
85. "Senator Pierantoni Talks of Black Hand," *New York Times*, September 14, 1910.
86. FBI, "Organized Crime, Italian Organized Crime—Overview," available at http://www.fbi.gov/hq/cid/orgcrime/lcnindex.htm (last visited January 29, 2011).
87. "Petrosino's Slayer Working as a Miner," *New York Times*, January 9, 1910.
88. "Unveil Petrosino Monument," *New York Times*, March 14, 1910.
89. Report of the Select Committee Appointed by the Assembly of 1875 to Investigate the Causes of the Increase of Crime, 1875," 7.
90. "Third Degree in Police Parlance," *New York Times*, October 6, 1901.
91. "The Ashburn Murder," *New York Times*, July 21, 1868.
92. "The Ashburn Murder," *New York Times*, September 12, 1868.
93. "The Ashburn Murder Case," *Atlanta Constitution*, September 13, 1868.
94. "Third Degree in Police Parlance," *New York Times*, October 6, 1901.
95. "To Abolish the Third Degree," *New York Times*, July 6, 1902.
96. "Suspect Tells Third Degree," *Los Angeles Times*, March 25, 1932.
97. "Officers Hang Alleged Bandit," *Los Angeles Times*, April 23, 1915.
98. "Boys Tell Torture Tale," *Los Angeles Times*, November 26, 1924.
99. See, e.g., "Inquisition Method Hit By Speaker," *Los Angeles Times*, January 27, 1929.
100. "Third Degree Made a Science," *Los Angeles Times*, December 17, 1910.
101. "Garrison Sues Police Heads," *Los Angeles Times*, August 14, 1931.
102. Campbell Gibson, "Population Density of the 100 Largest Cities and Other Urban Places in the United States: 1790 to 1990," Population Division, U.S. Bureau of the Census, available at http://www.census.gov/population/www/documentation/twps0027/tab15.txt (last visited February 1, 2011.
103. "In Behalf of the Rack," *New York Times*, May 19, 1877.
104. "She Shot a Chinaman," *Chicago Daily Tribune*, November 13, 1888.
105. "Chicago Thieves Identified," *New York Times*, July 15, 1896.
106. *Chicago Daily Tribune*, July 14, 1896.
107. "Holdup Men Kill One More Victim," *Chicago Daily Tribune*, January 6, 1908.
108. "Accused of Ten Murders," *New York Times*, July 26, 1895.
109. "Suit Case Mystery Solved by Confession," *New York Times*, November 3, 1905.
110. "Thieves Used Ether to Stupefy Victims," *New York Times*, June 22, 1907.
111. "Forced to Confess by 'Third Degree,'" *Atlanta Constitution*, December 17, 1910.
112. October 15, 1890.
113. "Torturing a Prisoner," *Chicago Daily Tribune*, August 15, 1902.
114. Sidney Lens, *The Forging of the American Empire* (London: Pluto Press, 2003), 188–89.
115. "Torturing a Prisoner," *Chicago Daily Tribune*, August 15, 1902.
116. "The Police Inquisition," *New York Times*, July 6, 1897. Nack's first name and suggestions of her middle-class status can be found at "Mrs. Nack's Story Told," *New York Times*, November 11, 1897.
117. We point out that this is yet another example of a news story being told with a point of view about the morality of the conduct being described.
118. "Mrs. Nack's Story Told," *New York Times*, November 11, 1897.

119. "Woman Principal Rebuked," *New York Times*, April 20, 1902.
120. "Supreme Court Justices Denounce 'Third Degree,'" *New York Times*, July 20, 1902. Supreme Court justices in New York in 1902 were either trial judges or intermediate appellate judges. The highest court in New York is the Court of Appeals.
121. "Black Hand Now in Staffeldt Murder," *New York Times*, July 3, 1907. "Black Hand" referred to the signer of three letters sent to the family of the murder victim.
122. "'Third Degree'" Put Under Ban," *Atlanta Constitution*, July 4, 1907.
123. Letter, "Torture to Force Confession," *New York Times*, June 24, 1909.
124. "Tortured by 'Third Degree' into Confessing Murder," *Atlanta Constitution*, April 8, 1910.
125. "'The Third Degree,'" *New York Times*, April 17, 1910.
126. "Judge Scores 'Third Degree,'" *Los Angeles Times*, December 4, 1910.
127. "'Third Degree Condemned," *Los Angeles Times*, December 10, 1910.
128. "Third-Degree Methods Fail," *Los Angeles Times*, March 9, 1917.
129. "Police Methods Assailed," *Los Angeles Times*, May 30, 1925 (quoting from appellate opinion).
130. "New Ban on Third Degree," *Los Angeles Times*, December 20, 1928.
131. "Seeks Death After Sweat," *Chicago Daily Tribune*, August 10, 1907.
132. "Accuses Police of 'Third Degree'; Victim Innocent," *Chicago Daily Tribune*, January 30, 1913.
133. "Backs Story of Haas Beating," *Chicago Daily Tribune*, February 4, 1913.
134. "Accuses Police of 'Third Degree'; Victim Innocent," *Chicago Daily Tribune*, January 30, 1913.
135. "Backs Story of Haas Beating," *Chicago Daily Tribune*, February 4, 1913. See also "Alderman Fights Police Tortures," *Chicago Daily Tribune*, February 2, 1913.
136. "Sweated Four Days; Sues Hoyne," *Chicago Daily Tribune*, August 2, 1913.
137. "Is the 'Third Degree' Justified?" *Atlanta Constitution*, July 5, 1909.
138. "After 'Third Degree' He Killed Himself," *Atlanta Constitution*, May 20, 1910.
139. "Probing the 'Third Degree,'" *Atlanta Constitution*, May 15, 1910.
140. "Lowden Vetoes 52 Measures As Assembly Ends," *Chicago Daily Tribune*, June 30, 1917.
141. "'Third Degree' Talked into Senate Discard," *Chicago Daily Tribune*, May 14, 1923.
142. *People v. Rogers*, 303 Ill. 578, 589–91 (1922). The state constitution then in effect provided that one supreme court judge be elected from each of seven districts. See Ill. Const. Art. VI, § 6 (1870).
143. See Senate Bill 33, Illinois 53d General Assembly, 1923.
144. *Dodig v. State*, 31 Ohio C.D. 507, 1908 WL 598 (Ohio Cir.), at *2.
145. Edward Marshall, "About Criminals," *Atlanta Constitution*, September 29, 1894.
146. See "Measuring Worth: Six Ways to Compute the Relative Value of a U.S. Dollar, 1774 to Present," available at http://www.measuringworth.com/ppowerus/ (using 1875 as beginning year) (last visited February 11, 2011).
147. Marshall, "About Criminals."
148. At least two websites claim, without citation, that Byrnes made his fortune because he was corrupt. See, e.g., "Thomas F. Byrnes," Wikipedia, available at http://en.wikipedia.org/wiki/Thomas_F._Byrnes (last visited February 11, 2011). One site claims that when Teddy Roosevelt became president of the Board of Police Commissioners in 1895, he fired Byrnes for "selective enforcement." See "Historical Timeline in Investigation," available at http://www.criminology.fsu.edu/faculty/nute/history.html (last visited February 11, 2011).
149. Marshall, "About Criminals."
150. "U.S. Bar Committee Decries 'Third Degree,'" *Chicago Daily Tribune*, August 16, 1913. The headline is profoundly misleading. We wondered if the editor of the newspaper was, in effect, endorsing the minority report.
151. "New York Officials Deny Being Brutal," *New York Times*, August 11, 1931.
152. See *Monroe v. Pape*, 365 U.S. 167 (1961) (reaffirming settled law that municipalities could not be sued under federal law).

153. "Sweated Four Days; Sues Hoyne," *Chicago Daily Tribune*, August 2, 1913.
154. "Hoyne et al. Sued by Arrest Victim," *Chicago Daily Tribune*, July 31, 1913.
155. "Officers Hang Alleged Bandit," *Los Angeles Times*, April 23, 1915.
156. "Bar Association Shows Interest in Hoyne Aids," *Chicago Daily Tribune*, November 17, 1918.
157. "Quiz of Alleged Third Degree in Office of Hoyne," *Chicago Daily Tribune*, November 30, 1918.
158. "Hoyne Friction? 4 Aids Out; One Sweitzer Friend," *Chicago Daily Tribune*, May 4, 1919.
159. "Convict Detective For 'Third Degree,'" *New York Times*, February 10, 1920.
160. "Wants Rowan Off Force," *New York Times*, March 7, 1920.
161. "Warrants for Four Cops on 'Third Degree' Charge," *Chicago Daily Tribune*, April 21, 1921.
162. "Prisoner Charges Brutality By Police," *New York Times*, September 18, 1929.
163. "'Fourth Degree' Effective," *New York Times*, August 21, 1929.
164. "Arkansas Judge Bans Use of 'Torture Chair,'" *Atlanta Constitution*, November 23, 1929.
165. Leo, *Police Interrogation*, 79.
166. Paul G. Kauper, "Judicial Examination of the Accused—A Remedy for the Third Degree," *Mich. L. Rev.* 30 (1932): 1224–55.
167. "Inventor Tells the Truth About His Lie Detector," *Chicago Daily Tribune*, September 13, 1932.
168. Gardner Bradford, "A Machine That Makes Criminals Confess!" *Los Angeles Times*, May 7, 1933.
169. W. R. Kidd, *Police Interrogation* (New York: R. V. Basuino, 1940), 68.
170. Id. at v.
171. Leo, *Police Interrogation*, 79.
172. Id. at 79–80 (quoting Gene Carte & Elaine Carte, *Police Reform in the United States: The Era of August Vollmer, 1905–1932* (Berkeley: University of California Press, 1975), 57).
173. Carte & Carte, *Police Reform in the United States*.
174. Leo, *Police Interrogation*, 80.
175. Kidd, *Police Interrogation*, 46–47.
176. Id. at 47.
177. Id. at 49.
178. Crime and Justice Atlas, 2000, *Historical Data*, United States Index Crime Rate, 1933–1998 (showing a gradual decline from 1933 to about 1940), available at http://www.jrsainfo.org/programs/Historical.pdf (last visited February 10, 2011).
179. Susan Bandes, "Tracing the Pattern of No Pattern: Stories of Police Brutality," *Loyola L. A. L. Rev.* 34 (2001): 1275–1341; Susan Bandes, "The Patterns of Injustice: Police Brutality in the Courts," *Buff. L. Rev.* 47 (1999): 665–80.
180. Bandes, "Patterns of Injustice," 1276–77 ("suffocation with a typewriter cover," "hanging by handcuffs for hours, a cattle prod to the testicles, and Russian roulette with a gun in the suspect's mouth").
181. Jodi Rudoren, "Inquiry Finds Police Abuse, but Says Law Bars Trials," *New York Times*, July 20, 2006.
182. Monica Davey, "Judge Rules Report in Chicago Should be Released," *New York Times*, May 20, 2006.
183. Emma Graves Fitzsimmons, "Decades Later, Ex-Police Commander in Chicago Goes on Trial in Abuse Cases," *New York Times*, May 27, 2010.
184. James Warren, "Burge Case Ends With a Prison Sentence and No Little Bit of Wondering," *New York Times*, January 22, 2011.
185. Bandes, "Tracing the Pattern of No Pattern," 667.

Chapter 7

1. U.S. Const. amend. XIV.
2. *Barrington v. Missouri*, 205 U.S. 483, 486 (1907).

3. Id. at 486–87 (citing *Howard v. Fleming*, 191 U.S. 126 (1903)).

4. See *Twining v. New Jersey*, 211 U.S. 78 (1908).

5. See Thomas, *Supreme Court on Trial*, 117–47; George C. Thomas III, "Criminal Trials as Morality Plays: Good and Evil," *St. Louis U. L. Rev* 55 (2011) 1405–1432; George C. Thomas III, "Bigotry, Jury Failures, and the Supreme Court's Feeble Response, *Buffalo L. Rev.* 55 (2007): 947–80.

6. See Thomas, "Bigotry, Jury Failures, and the Supreme Court's Feeble Response," 956–62 (discussing the Scottsboro cases; see, e.g., *Powell v. Alabama*, 287 U.S. 45 (1932)).

7. 297 U.S. 278 (1936).

8. 384 U.S. 436 (1966).

9. *Brown v. State*, 158 So. 339, 339 (Miss. 1935)

10. Richard C. Cortner, *A "Scottsboro" Case in Mississippi* (Oxford: University Press of Mississippi, 1986), 11. For more details about *Brown*, see Thomas, "Bigotry, Jury Failures, and the Supreme Court's Feeble Response," 963–71.

11. Apparently surprised by the testimony about torture, the State offered hastily presented fingerprint evidence to prove that Brown was at the scene of the crime. Transcript of Record on Writ of Certiorari, *Brown v. State*, 173 Miss. 542 (No. 301), 78–96. Because the defense was not given a chance to have its own experts examine the fingerprints, and because fingerprint "science" was in its infancy, it is unclear how strong that evidence was. But the record is clear that no fingerprint evidence connected the other two defendants to the crime, and the jury convicted them, too, suggesting that the confessions were the most important evidence.

12. *Brown*, 297 U.S., 282–83 (quoting *Brown v. State*, 161 So. 465, 470 (Miss. 1935) (Griffith, J., dissenting)).

13. Id. at 284.

14. *Brown v. State*, 161 So. 465, 471 (Miss. 1935)(Griffith, J. dissenting). The United States Supreme Court included this quote from Justice Griffith's dissent. See 297 U.S., 285.

15. See *Fisher v. State*, 110 So. 361, 365 (Miss. 1926); *Whip v. State*, 109 So. 697 (Miss. 1926).

16. *Fisher*, 110 So., 365.

17. Id.

18. *Brown*, 297 U.S., 286.

19. Thomas, "Bigotry, Jury Failures, and the Supreme Court's Feeble Response," 967–70.

20. Id. at 951–55.'

21. Craig M. Bradley, *The Failure of the Criminal Procedure Revolution* (Philadelphia: University of Pennsylvania Press, 1993), 11.

22. In 1986, the United States Supreme Court made clear that a confession involuntary because of mental illness is nonetheless admissible under the federal Constitution. See *Colorado v. Connelly*, 479 U.S. 157 (1986).

23. Seidman, *"Brown* and *Miranda,"* 724.

24. 198 U.S. 45 (1905).

25. *West Coast Hotel Co. v. Parrish*, 300 U.S. 379 (1937).

26. Seidman, *"Brown* and *Miranda,"* 727.

27. Robert Weisberg, "Criminal Law, Criminology, and the Small World of Legal Scholars," *U. Colo. L. Rev.* 63 (1992): 538

28. 309 U.S. 227, 229 (1940) (quoting *Chambers v. State*, 187 So. 156, 157 (Fla. 1939)).

29. Id. at 230.

30. Id. at 231.

31. Id. at 238.

32. Id. at 239 (Justice Murphy did not participate).

33. *Brown*, 297 U.S., 280.

34. *Chambers*, 309 U.S., 237–38.

35. Id. at 241.

36. 310 U.S. 530 (1940).

37. Id. at 532.
38. Id. at 533 (quoting *Chambers,* 309 U.S., 241).
39. 309 U.S. 629 (1940).
40. *Canty v. State,* 191 So. 260, 262 (Ala. 1939).
41. 314 U.S. 219 (1941).
42. The facts in this and the next paragraph are drawn from id. at 224.
43. Id. at 229.
44. *People v. Lisenba,* 89 P. 2d 39, 96 (Cal. 1939) (Seawell, J., dissenting).
45. *Lisenba v. California,* 314 U.S., 231. The accounts differed as to why substitute counsel was not forthcoming.
46. Id. at 232.
47. Id. at 233.
48. *People v. Lisenba,* 89 P., 47 (1939) (quoting *People v. Lehew,* 287 P. 337, 339 (Cal. 1930)).
49. Id. at 47–48.
50. Id. at 54 (Seawell, J., dissenting).
51. Id. at 55 (Seawell, J., dissenting).
52. Id. at 102 (Seawell, J., dissenting).
53. *Lisenba v. California,* 314 U.S., 239.
54. Id. at 233–34.
55. 322 U.S. 143 (1944).
56. See *Miranda,* 384 U.S., 461.
57. Larry Rosenthal recently made a similar point, focusing on Justice Jackson's dissent. See Lawrence Rosenthal, "Against Orthodoxy: *Miranda* Is Not Prophylactic and the Constitution Is Not Perfect," *Chapman L. Rev.* 10 (2007): 593–94.
58. *Ashcraft,* 322 U.S., 173 (Jackson, J., dissenting).
59. Id. at 153.
60. The Court would eventually hold that a violation of the Fourth Amendment's requirement that an arrest be based on probable cause requires suppression of a subsequent confession unless the State can prove that the confession was not causally linked to the arrest or detention. See *Brown v. Illinois,* 422 U.S. 590 (1975).
61. *Ashcraft,* 322 U.S., 153.
62. Id. at 154.
63. Id.
64. Id. at 162 (Jackson, J., dissenting).
65. *Chambers,* 309 U.S., 239. The Court quoted *Zing Sung Wan v. United States,* 266 U.S. 1, 16 (1924), which was apparently the Supreme Court's first use of the "compulsion was applied" locution. But *Zing Sung Wan* was a federal case, the Constitution was not mentioned, and the Court appeared to be deciding the question as a matter of federal evidence law. So it appears that *Chambers* was the first constitutional use of the "compulsion was applied" standard.
66. *Ashcraft,* 322 U.S., 151.
67. Id. at 152.
68. Id. at 152–53.
69. Id. at 155.
70. Id. at 161 (Jackson, J., dissenting).
71. 360 U.S. 315 (1959).
72. Id. at 322.
73. Id. at 322–23.
74. Id. at 315.
75. Id. at 319.
76. Id. at 323.
77. Id. at 320–21.
78. 346 U.S. 156, 184 (1953).
79. Seidman, "*Brown* and *Miranda,*" 729–30.

80. 367 U.S. 568 (1961).
81. Id. at 603.
82. Seidman, "*Brown* and *Miranda*," 730.
83. *Culombe*, 367 U.S., 606–21 & 621–36.
84. *Culombe*, 367 U.S., 635–36 (Warren, C. J., concurring).
85. Seidman, "*Brown* and *Miranda*," 719.
86. See *Culombe*, 367 U.S., 637 (Douglas, J., concurring) (joined by Black, J.); id. at 641 (Brennan, J., concurring) (joined by Warren, C.J. and Black, J.).
87. Seidman, "*Brown* and *Miranda*," 733.
88. Id. at 730.
89. Id.
90. *Ashcraft*, 322 U.S., 161 (Jackson, J., dissenting).
91. Welsh S. White, Miranda*'s Waning Protections: Police Interrogation Practices After* Dickerson (Ann Arbor, MI: University of Michigan Press, 2001), 39.
92. Bradley, *Failure*, 13.
93. See Fed. R. Crim. Pro. 5(a).
94. *McNabb v. United States*, 318 U.S. 332 (1943). See also *Mallory v. United States*, 354 U.S. 449 (1957).
95. See 18 U.S.C. § 3501 (c).
96. U.S. Const. amend. VI.
97. 378 U.S. 478 (1964).
98. Id. at 479–83.
99. U.S. Const. amend. VI.
100. See Giradeau A. Spann, "Deconstructing the Legislative Veto," *Minn. L. Rev.* 68 (1984): 532–33.
101. Ludwig Wittgenstein, *Philosophical Investigations*, trans. G. E. M. Anscombe (Upper Saddle River, NJ: Prentice Hall, 3rd ed 1958), § 88, p. 41.
102. Donald A. Dripps, "Constitutional Theory for Criminal Procedure: *Dickerson, Miranda*, and the Continuing Quest for Broad-But-Shallow," *Wm. & Mary L. Rev.* 43 (2001): 15.
103. Sandra Guerra Thompson, "Evading *Miranda*: How *Seibert* and *Patene* Failed to 'Save' *Miranda*," *Val. U. L. Rev.* 40 (2006): 652.
104. *Culombe*, 367 U.S., 568–69.
105. Kamisar, "Equal Justice in the Gatehouses and Mansions," 19–20.
106. Id. at 19.
107. U.S. Const. amend. V.
108. 332 U.S. 596, 600 (1948).
109. Id. at 604 (Frankfurter, J., joining in reversal of judgment).
110. 370 U.S. 49 (1962).
111. Id. at 54.
112. 384 U.S. 436 (1966).
113. Fred E. Inbau, *Lie Detection and Criminal Interrogation* (Baltimore: Williams & Wilkins, 1942). The most recent version was published in 2004: Fred E. Inbau, John E. Reid, Joseph P. Buckley & Brian C. Jayne, *Criminal Interrogations and Confessions* (Sudbury, MA: Jones & Bartlett Learning, 2004). The website that offers training in the Inbau method claims that it has trained over 500,000 investigators. See John E. Reid & Associates, "Success with Reid," available at http://www.reid.com/success_reid/r_success.html, (last visited February 10, 2011).
114. *Miranda*, 384 U.S., 515 (Harlan, J., dissenting).
115. Id. at 517 (Harlan, J., dissenting).
116. Id. at 455.
117. Id. at 448.
118. Id. at 450.
119. Id. at 451.

120. Id. at 455.
121. Id. at 457–58.
122. Id. at 469.
123. Id. at 470.
124. Id. at 465.
125. Id. at 517 (Harlan, J., dissenting).
126. For an excellent summary of Warren's background and how it influenced him in writing *Miranda*, see Yale Kamisar, "How Earl Warren's Twenty-Two Years in Law Enforcement Affected His Work as Chief Justice," *Ohio St. J. Crim. L.* 3 (2005): 11–32.
127. Del Dickson, ed., *The Supreme Court in Conference (1940–1985)* (Oxford: Oxford University Press, 2001), 517.
128. Id.
129. *Miranda*, 386 U.S., 486–88.
130. Id. at 522–23 (Harlan, J., dissenting).
131. Id. at 461–62.
132. Id. at 506 & n.2 (Harlan, J., dissenting).
133. 162 U.S. 613, 623 (1896) (stating that it had been "laid down" in the common law that "if the confession was voluntary, it is sufficient, though it appear that he was not . . . warned that what he said would be used against him").
134. See *Bram*, 168 U.S. 548.
135. *Miranda*, 384 U.S., 509 (Harlan, J., dissenting). The other case was *Powers v. United States*, 223 U.S. 303 (1912) (holding that the failure to warn a defendant who testified at the preliminary hearing did not render the testimony inadmissible).
136. *Miranda*, 384 U.S., 458–60.
137. In 1547, Parliament sought to limit the use of violence to obtain confessions to treason when it forbade an indictment or conviction of treason unless the defendant "be accused by two sufficient and lawful witnesses, or shall willingly without violence confess the same." 1 Ed. VI, c. 12, s. 22 (1547) (spelling modernized). But the common law of the Lilburn period contained no similar limitation on involuntary confessions.
138. We could cite many scholars who have demonstrated the historical separation of the privilege from the common law voluntariness rule but will content ourselves with Wigmore. See Wigmore, *Treatise on the System of Evidence*, 1904 ed., vol. 1, § 823, pp. 934–35.
139. 11 & 12 Vict., c. 42, para. XVIII (1848).
140. Crime and Justice Atlas 2000, "United States Index Crime Rate, 1933–1998," 36–37, available at http://www.jrsa.org/programs/Crime_Atlas_2000.pdf (last visited March 22, 2011).
141. *Miranda*, 384 U.S., 499–500 (Clark, J., dissenting).
142. Id. at 504 (Harlan, J., dissenting).
143. Id. at 542–43 (White, J., dissenting).
144. Liva Baker, *Miranda: Crime, Law and Politics* (New York: Atheneum, 1985), 176.
145. Id.
146. 114 Cong. Rec. 14,155 (1968). For other juicy quotes from the congressional debate, see Yale Kamisar, *Cornell L. Rev.* 85 (2000): 894–907.
147. Baker, *Miranda: Crime, Law and Politics*, 243.
148. Id. at 244.
149. Id. at 243.
150. Id. at 244.
151. Id. at 248 (ellipsis in original).
152. 372 U.S. 335 (1963).
153. 367 U.S. 643 (1961).
154. Fred P. Graham, *The Self-Inflicted Wound* (New York: MacMillan, 1970), 158.
155. See "1968 Presidential General Election Results," available at http://uselectionatlas.org/RESULTS/national.php?year=1968. (last visited February 10, 2011).

156. Gerald M. Caplan, "Questioning *Miranda*," *Vand. L. Rev.* 38 (1985): 1441.

157. Id. at 1441–42.

158. Id. at 1470.

159. Id. at 1472.

Chapter 8

1. Weather History, "History for Washington, DC, Monday, June 13, 1966," Weather.Org, available at http://weather.org/ (last visited March 24, 2011).

2. Fred P. Graham, "High Court Puts New Curb on Powers of the Police to Interrogate Suspects," *New York Times*, June 14, 1966.

3. Dripps, "Constitutional Theory," 21–22.

4. Id. at 4.

5. In *Twining v. New Jersey*, 211 U.S. 78, 114 (1908), the Court refused to apply the privilege against compelled self-incrimination to the states. The opinion is largely based on history rather than a fully theorized account of the due process clause. *Twining* was overruled by *Malloy v. Hogan*, 378 U.S. 1 (1964).

6. Dripps, "Constitutional Theory," 4.

7. Craig M. Bradley, "The Uncertainty Principle in the Supreme Court," *Duke L. J.* 1986 (1986): 10–11.

8. U.S. Const. amend. VI.

9. See *Ham v. South Carolina*, 409 U.S. 524 (1970) (impartiality); *Williams v. Florida*, 399 U.S. 78 (1970) (jury size).

10. U.S. Const. amend. VI.

11. Blackstone's *Commentaries*, vol. 4, *349.

12. See *Geders v. United States*, 425 U.S. 80 (1976) (overnight recess); *Wheat v. United States*, 486 U.S. 153 (1988) (conflict of interest).

13. See, e.g., Pennsylvania Constitution, 1776, c. 1 ("right to be heard by himself and his council"); Delaware Declaration of Rights, 1776 (right "to be allowed counsel"); Concessions and Agreements of West New Jersey, 1676, c. 22 ("no Person or Persons shall be compelled to Fee any Attorney or Counciller to plead his Cause but that all Persons have free Liberty to plead his own Cause, if he please"); Massachusetts Body of Liberties, 1641 c. 26 (granting "Libertie to imploy any man" to help him "plead his . . . cause"); North Carolina Proposal to Congress, August 1, 1788 (right to "be allowed counsel in his favor); Rhode Island Proposal to Congress, May 29, 1790 (right "to be allowed counsel). See Cogan, *Complete Bill of Rights*, 401–11.

14. 372 U.S. 335, 344 (1963).

15. The FBI required warnings similar to those the Court required in *Miranda*. See *Miranda*, 384 U.S. at 483–84. But no states required any kind of warnings before interrogation. See Graham, *Self-Inflicted Wound*, 158.

16. Id.

17. *Miranda*, 384 U.S., 460.

18. Id.

19. Id. at 469.

20. Id. at 475.

21. Dripps, "Constitutional Theory," 20.

22. *Miranda*, 384 U.S., 467.

23. See *Kastigar v. United States*, 406 U.S. 441 (1972).

24. Steve Barnes, "Susan McDougal Back in Arkansas for Trial," *New York Times*, March 9, 1999. McDougal served eighteen months in federal prison when she would not answer questions put to her by a federal prosecutor before a grand jury.

25. See Bradley, "Uncertainty Principle," 10–11; Dripps, "Constitutional Theory," 4.

26. 378 U.S. 478 (1964).

27. Id. at 486 (quoting *Powell v. Alabama*, 287 U.S. 45, 69 (1932) ("guiding hand") and *Massiah v. United States*, 377 U.S. 201 (1964) ("critical stage")).
28. Corinna Barrett Lain, "Countermajoritarian Hero or Zero? Rethinking the Warren Court's Role in the Criminal Procedure Revolution," *U. Pa. L. Rev.* 152 (2004): 1409.
29. Seidman, "*Brown* and *Miranda*," 744.
30. Laurence A. Benner, "Requiem for *Miranda*: The Rehnquist Court's Voluntariness Doctrine in Historical Perspective," *Wash. U.L.Q.* 67 (1989): 161.
31. Lain, "Countermajoritarian Hero or Zero," 1409
32. 446 U.S. 291, 296 (1980).
33. 429 U.S. 492 (1977) (per curiam).
34. See, e.g., *Oregon v. Elstad*, 470 U.S. 298, 306–9 (1985).
35. See *New Jersey v. Portash*, 440 U.S. 450, 459 (1979).
36. *Colorado v. Connelly*, 479 U.S. 157, 163 (1986).
37. See chapter 7 A.
38. We acknowledge that Paul Cassell has forcefully argued that the *Miranda* regime has reduced the confessions rate and thus the conviction rate. See, e.g., Paul G. Cassell, "*Miranda*'s Social Costs: An Empirical Reassessment," *Nw. U. L. Rev.* 90 (1996): 387–499. Leo and Thomas have, in separate articles, analyzed the available data and concluded that any effect on the current confessions rate is, at best, small. See Richard A. Leo, "The Impact of *Miranda* Revisited," *J. Crim. L. & Criminology* 86 (1996): 648; George C. Thomas III, "Plain Talk About the *Miranda* Empirical Debate: A 'Steady-State' Theory of Confessions," *U.C.L.A. L. Rev.* 43 (1986): 958. See also Stephen J. Schulhofer, "*Miranda*'s Practical Effect: Substantial Benefits and Vanishingly Small Social Costs," *Nw. U. L. Rev.* 90 (1996): 562. Even though the reduction that Cassell measures is small in terms of a percentage, it would result in hundreds of thousands of lost convictions. See Paul G. Cassell & Richard Fowles, "Handcuffing the Cops? A Thirty-Year Perspective on *Miranda*'s Harmful Effects on Law Enforcement," *Stanford L. Rev.* 50 (1998): 1126. Regardless of who is right about the effect on the confessions rate, and acknowledging that a small rate decline will translate into hundreds of thousands of lost convictions, we nonetheless stand behind the claim in the text that there is no proof of a significant decline in the rate that is attributable to *Miranda*.
39. See Paul G. Cassell & Bret S. Hayman, "Police Interrogation in the 1990s: An Empirical Study of the Effects of *Miranda*," *UCLA L. Rev.* 43 (1996): 859 (waiver rate of 84%); Richard A. Leo, "Inside the Interrogation Room," *J. Crim. L. & Criminology* 86 (1996): 276 (waiver rate of 78%).
40. Seidman, "*Brown* and *Miranda*," 752.
41. *Miranda*, 384 U.S., 460 (quoting *Malloy v. Hogan*, 378 U.S. 1, 8 (1964)).
42. Id. at 458.
43. Id. at 516 (Harlan, J., dissenting).
44. See note 38 supra.
45. *Miranda*, 384 U.S., 470.
46. Id. at 469.
47. Donald Dripps, "Is *Miranda* Caselaw Really Inconsistent: A Proposed Fifth Amendment Synthesis," *Const. Commentary* 17 (2000): 23.
48. Id. at 25–26.
49. Id. at 26.
50. Rosenthal, "Against Orthodoxy," 597–98.
51. George C. Thomas III, "Separated at Birth But Siblings Nonetheless: *Miranda* and the Due Process Notice Cases," *Mich. L. Rev.* 99 (2001): 1081–1120.
52. Id. at 1088. Thomas argued in 2001 that there are three ways to understand *Miranda*'s constitutional pedigree but, for our purposes here, two of them can be combined.
53. Id.
54. See *Fuentes v. Shevin*, 407 U.S. 67 (1972).
55. Id. at 82.

56. 441 U.S. 369, 371 (1979).
57. 512 U.S. 452 (1994).
58. *Miranda*, 384 U.S., 444–45 (emphasis added).
59. 451 U.S. 477, 485 (1981).
60. *Davis*, 512 U.S., 455.
61. Id. at 462.
62. Id. at 471 & 469 (Souter, J., concurring in the judgment) (quoting *Miranda*, 384 U.S. at 469) (emphasis added by Souter)).
63. Id. at 460.
64. Id. at 460 (quoting *Moran v. Burbine*, 475 U.S. 412, 427 (1986)).
65. 130 S.Ct. 2250, 2256 (2010).
66. "He did give a few limited verbal responses, however, such as 'yeah,' 'no,' or 'I don't know.' And on occasion he communicated by nodding his head." Id. at 2256–57.
67. Id. at 2264.
68. *Miranda*, 384 U.S. at 475.
69. Bradley, "Uncertainty Principle," 35.
70. *Berghuis*, 130 S.Ct. at 2256.
71. Id. at 2262.
72. *Miranda*, 384 U.S. at 475.
73. Id. at 2263 (quoting *Davis v. United States*, 512 U.S. 452, 460 (1994)).
74. 401 U.S. 222 (1971).
75. Geoffrey Stone, "The *Miranda* Doctrine in the Burger Court," *Sup. Ct. Rev.* 1977 (1977): 99.
76. *Harris*, 401 U.S., 224.
77. Id. at 226.
78. 440 U.S. 450 (1979). The Court had reached the same conclusion a year earlier when the compulsion came not from the contempt power, as in *Portash*, but from police interrogation that rendered the suspect's statement involuntary. See *Mincey v. Arizona*, 437 U.S. 385, 398 (1978). But the analysis is more revealing in *Portash*.
79. *Portash*, 440 U.S. 450, 459.
80. 467 U.S. 649 (1984).
81. Id. at 656–58.
82. Id. at 665 (O'Connor, J., concurring in the judgment in part and dissenting in part). Justice O'Connor dissented from the Court's holding that the statement was admissible; she concurred in the judgment that the gun should be admitted, though she used a different analysis to reach that result than the Court used.
83. Dripps, "Is *Miranda* Caselaw Really Inconsistent," 42.
84. See *Tulsa Prof'l Collection Servs., Inc. v. Pope*, 485 U.S. 478 (1988).
85. Michael J. Zydney Mannheimer, "Toward a Unified Theory of Testimonial Evidence Under the Fifth and Sixth Amendments," *Temple L. Rev.* 80 (2007): 1161.
86. As Mannheimer notes, Dripps had offered this as an alternative explanation for *Harris* seven years before Mannheimer's article appeared. See id. at 1155; Dripps, "Is *Miranda* Caselaw Really Inconsistent," 34.
87. 470 U.S. 298, 301–2 (1985).
88. Id. at 305.
89. Id. at 314–15.
90. 542 U.S. 600 (2004) (plurality).
91. Id. at 604–5.
92. Id. at 605.
93. Id. at 617.
94. Id. at 618 (Kennedy, J., concurring in the judgment).
95. Id. at 624 (O'Connor, J., dissenting).
96. *Colorado v. Spring*, 479 U.S. 564 (1987).

97. *Connecticut v. Barrett*, 479 U.S. 564 (1987).
98. 492 U.S. 195 (1989).
99. Id. at 203 (quoting *California v. Prysock*, 453 U.S. 355, 361 (1981)).
100. Id. at 205.
101. *Florida v. Powell*, 559 U.S. ___, 130 S.Ct. 1195, 1206 (2010).
102. 130 S.Ct. 2250, 2272–73 (2010) (Sotomayor, J, dissenting).
103. The other 5–4 weak force cases include *Harris v. New York*, 401 U.S. 222 (1971) (impeachment); *New York v. Quarles*, 467 U.S. 649 (1984) (public safety); and *Davis v. United States*, 512 U.S. 452, 460 (1994) (what counts as an invocation of the right to counsel).
104. Rosenthal, "Against Orthodoxy," 596. See also Dripps, "Is *Miranda* Caselaw Really Inconsistent," 26.
105. "Adequate notice" includes no notice when public safety justifies the failure to provide warnings.
106. Dripps, "Is *Miranda* Caselaw Really Inconsistent," 26.
107. Benner, "Requiem," 162.
108. Patrick Malone, "'You Have the Right to Remain Silent': *Miranda* After Twenty Years," *American Scholar* 55 (1986): 368.
109. Center for Disease Control, HIV/AIDS, Basic Statistics, "HIV Incidence Estimate," available at http://www.cdc.gov/hiv/topics/surveillance/basic.htm#incidence (last visited March 23, 2011).
110. See, e.g., Franklin E. Zimring & Gordon J. Hawkins, *Deterrence: The Legal Threat in Crime Control* (Chicago: University of Chicago Press 1973), 98–101.
111. The Doors, "Roadhouse Blues," on *Morrison Hotel* (Electra Records, 1970).
112. "Obituaries," *New York Times*, July 10, 1971.
113. See Seidman, "Rubashov's Question," 174.
114. David Simon, *Homicide: A Year on the Killing Streets* (New York: Houghton, Mifflin, 1991), Ivy Books edition (New York: Ballantine Books, 1991), 209.
115. Id.
116. Id.
117. See "Criminal Justice in Crisis, A Report to the American People and the American Bar on Criminal Justice in the United States: Some Myths, Some Realities, and Some Questions for the Future, 2. Fifth Amendment—*Miranda v. Arizona*, The Police Perspective," DRC-Net Online Library of Drug Policy, available at http://www.druglibrary.org/special/king/cjic.htm (last visited March 23, 2011).
118. 530 U.S. 428, 443–44 (2000).
119. *Miranda*, 384 U.S. at 478.
120. Craig M. Bradley, "Supreme Court Review Behind the Dickerson Decision," *Trial* 36 (2000): 82.

Chapter 9

1. Morgan Cloud, George B. Shepherd, Alison Nodvin Barkoff, Justin V. Shur, "Words Without Meaning: The Constitution, Confessions, and Mentally Retarded Suspects," *U. Chi. L. Rev.* 69 (2002): 495–624.
2. Id. at 535.
3. Id. at 539, fig. 2.
4. See Leo, *Police Interrogation*, 119–64; White, *Miranda's Waning Protections*, 76–101; Barry C. Feld, "Juveniles' Competence to Exercise *Miranda* Rights: An Empirical Study of Policy and Practice," *Minn. L. Rev.* 91 (2006): 74–77; Charles D. Weisselberg, "Mourning *Miranda*," *Cal. L. Rev.* 96 (2008): 1547–63; See also Wrightsman & Pitman, *Miranda Ruling*, 148–50.
5. Weisselberg, "Mourning *Miranda*," 1562.
6. 130 S.Ct. 2250 (2010).

7. Id. at 2256.
8. Id. at 2257.
9. Id. at 2266 (Sotomayor, J., dissenting).
10. Id. at 2260.
11. Id. (quoting *Davis,* 512 U.S., 458–59).
12. 78 F.3d 1190, 1196 (7th Cir. 1996).
13. Id. at 1196 n.6.
14. Id. at 1197.
15. Id. at 1196.
16. *Miranda,* 384 U.S., 475.
17. *Berghuis,* 130 S.Ct., 2260–61.
18. Id. at 2262.
19. *Davis,* 512 U.S., 472–73 (Souter, J., concurring in the judgment).
20. 429 U.S. 492, 493 (1977) (per curiam).
21. Id. at 495.
22. Id. at 498 (Marshall, J., dissenting).
23. Id. (Marshall, J., dissenting).
24. 208 F.3d 172, 195 (4th Cir. 2000).
25. Id.
26. Id. at 197.
27. Id. at 177.
28. George C. Thomas III, "Stories About *Miranda,*" *Mich. L. Rev.* 102 (2004): 1959–2000.
29. Id. at 1962.
30. Id. at 1972, tbl. 1.
31. Id. at 1981.
32. See "Criminal Justice in Crisis," Fifth Amendment—*Miranda v. Arizona,* The Prosecutor's Perspective," available at http://www.druglibrary.org/special/king/cjic.htm (last visited March 23, 2011).
33. Thomas, "Stories About *Miranda,*" at 1974–74, tbl. 2 (14% invoked and 75 out of 186 did not challenge).
34. Cloud, et al., "Words Without Meaning," 550, fig. 7.
35. Id. at 546.
36. Id. at 590. See also White, Miranda's *Waning Protections,* 201–202.
37. Cloud, et al., "Words Without Meaning," 591.
38. 770 N.E.2d 763, 766 n.3 (Ind. 2002).
39. Id. at 767. The standard the Supreme Court requires is a mere preponderance of the evidence. See *Lego v. Twomey,* 404 U.S. 477, 478–79 (1972).
40. *Miller,* 770 N.E.2d, 769.
41. Id. at 766 n.3 (emphasis added).
42. Cloud, et al., "Words Without Meaning," 536.
43. *Miller,* 770 N.E.2d, 768.
44. Id.
45. Id.
46. Id. at 769.
47. Id.
48. 352 U.S. 191, 196 (1957).
49. Id. at 194–96.
50. *Blackburn v. Alabama,* 361 U.S. 199, 201–202 & 204 (1960).
51. 332 U.S. 596 (1948) (plurality).
52. Id. at 601 (plurality) & id. at 607 (Frankfurter, J., joining in reversal of judgment).
53. Id. at 599.
54. Id. at 601. According to Frankfurter, Haley was not advised of his rights during the interrogation. It was only after he had confessed orally did the police "read to the boy a clause

giving the conventional formula about his constitutional right to make or withhold a state-ment." Id. at 604 (Frankfurter, J., joining in reversal of judgment). But neither the plurality nor Frankfurter make the timing crucial. *Haley* is best read, we think, as a rejection of giving any weight to warnings when the suspect is fifteen.

55. 370 U.S. 49 (1962).
56. Id. at 54.
57. Id.
58. Id. at 55.
59. Id. at 54.
60. 387 U.S. 1, 48 (1967) (quoting 3 Wigmore, *A Treatise on the System of Evidence*, § 822, 3rd ed., 1940).
61. 442 U.S. 707 (1979).
62. Id. at 710.
63. Id. at 711.
64. *In re Michael C.*, 579 P.2d 7, 10 (Cal. 1978).
65. Id. at 9 (quoting *People v. Burton*, 491 P.2d 793, 798 (Cal. 1971)).
66. Id. at 10.
67. *Fare*, 442 U.S., 723–24.
68. Id. at 726–27.
69. Kenneth J. King, "Waiving Childhood Goodbye: How Juvenile Courts Fail to Protect Chil-dren From Unknowing, Unintelligent, and Involuntary Waivers of *Miranda* Rights," *Wis. L. Rev.* 2006: 470.
70. *In re Christopher W.*, 329 S.E.2d 769, 769 (S. Car. Ct. App. 1985).
71. Id. at 770.
72. 991 S.W.2d 639 (Ark. Ct. App. 1999).
73. Id. at 643.
74. Id. at 643–44.
75. *Ingram v. State*, 918 S.W.2d 724, 727–28 (Ark. Ct. App. 1996).
76. Id. at 728.
77. 2004 WL 2505161 (Ohio App. 12 Dist.).
78. Id. at *2.
79. Id. at *6.
80. *In re Wesley B.*, 145 N.H. 428, 431 (2000).
81. Id. at 431–32.
82. Id. at 432.
83. Id. at 433. To be sure, the court uses the preponderance of the evidence language to dis-cuss whether Wesley was able to understand the juvenile proceedings. But the very next sentence—"We cannot find that the State has established beyond a reasonable doubt that the confession was voluntary"—suggests that the court meant to signal that there might have been a preponderance of evidence on that issue, too.
84. *Lego v. Twomey*, 404 U.S. 477, 487–89 (1972).
85. Thomas Grisso, "Juveniles' Capacities to Waive *Miranda* Rights: An Empirical Analysis," *Cal. L. Rev.* 68 (1980): 1154.
86. Id. at 1158–59.
87. Id. at 1160.
88. Feld, "Juveniles' Competence to Exercise *Miranda* Rights," 61–62 (explaining that the study is limited to older juveniles because other delinquency hearings are closed to the public and confidential).
89. Id. at 90.
90. *Haley*, 332 U.S., 601.
91. See Gary L. Stuart, *Innocent Until Interrogated: The True Story of the Buddhist Temple Massa-cre and the Tucson Four* (Tucson: University of Arizona Press, 2010).
92. *Doody v. Schriro*, 596 F.3d 620, 623 (9th Cir. 2010).

93. Id. at 623–24.

94. Id. at 653.

95. *Ryan v. Doody*, 131 S.Ct. 456 (2010). The warnings approved in *Florida v. Powell*, 559 U.S. ___, 130 S.Ct. 1195 (2010), were nothing like the ones in *Doody*. Indeed, on remand, the Ninth Circuit affirmed its earlier rulings. See Doody v. Ryan, 649 F.3d 986 (9th Cir.), cert. denied, Ryan v. Doody, 132 S.Ct. 414 (2011).

96. *Doody*, 596 F.3d, 638 (quoting *Watts v. Indiana*, 338 U.S. 49, 53–54 (1949)).

97. Id. (quoting *In re Gault*, 387 U.S. at 45).

98. Id. at 639.

99. Id. at 641.

100. Id. at 643.

101. Id. at 642.

102. Id. at 643 (emphasis in original).

103. Id. at 645.

104. Id. at 643.

105. Id. at 644.

106. Id. at 639.

107. Id. at 644.

108. Id. at 641.

109. Id. at 662–63 (Tallman, Judge, dissenting).

110. Leo, *Police Interrogation*, 27.

111. Id. at 117.

112. 352 U.S. 191, 192–93 (1957).

113. Id. at 193.

114. Id. at 194–96 (length of interrogation) & 197 (no evidence of "brutality" or coercion).

115. Id. at 196–97.

116. *Blackburn v. Alabama*, 361 U.S. 199, 207 (1960).

117. 332 U.S. 596, 599–600 (1948). See also *Harris v. South Carolina*, 338 U.S. 68, 70 (1949) (noting that it was "relevant" that "Harris was an illiterate").

118. See *Haynes v. Washington*, 373 U.S. 503 (1963); *Lynum v. Illinois*, 372 U.S. 528 (1963); *Columbe v. Connecticut*, 367 U.S. 568 (1961); *Rogers v. Richmond*, 365 U.S. 534 (1961); *Blackburn v. Alabama*, 361 U.S. 199 (1960); *Spano v. New York*, 360 U.S. 315 (1959); *Payne v. Arkansas*, 356 U.S. 560 (1958); *Thomas v. Arizona*, 356 U.S. 390 (1958); *Fikes v. Alabama*, 352 U.S. 191 (1957).

119. *Berkemer v. McCarty*, 468 U.S. 420, 433 n.20 (1984).

120. White, Miranda's *Waning Protections*, 122, n.40.

121. Alfredo Garcia, "Is *Miranda* Dead, Was it Overruled, or is it Irrelevant?" *St. Thomas L. Rev.* 10 (1998): 499–502. See *Chavez v. State*, 832 So.2d 730 (Fla. 2002) (per curiam).

122. Garcia, "Is *Miranda* Dead," 499–502.

123. Id. at 500.

124. Three justices concurred in result only, without explaining why they did not join the majority opinion. *Chavez*, 832 So. 2d, 767.

125. Id. at 750 (initialed form) & 738 (waived).

126. Id. at 749.

127. Garcia, "Is *Miranda* Dead," 500.

128. Id. at 501. According to Garcia, the State admitted that Chavez was in custody for seventy-five hours rather than the fifty-four hours noted in the Florida Supreme Court's opinion. Compare Garcia, "Is *Miranda* Dead," 500 & n.410 with 832 So.3d, 748.

129. Transcript of Record, *Ashcraft v. Tennessee*, 357. The dissenting justice filed no opinion.

130. Id. at 356. Searches in Westlaw's Tennessee cases, KeyCite, and Shepard's Citations for "Ashcraft" do not uncover an opinion. E-mail to Paul Axel-Lute from George Thomas and from Paul Axel-Lute to George Thomas, January 26, 2011.

131. See, e.g., White, Miranda's *Waning Protections*, 120–21.

132. 743 F.2d 775, 779 (11th Cir. 1984).
133. *Berkemer v. McCarty*, 468 U.S. 420, 433 (1984).
134. *State v. Bilodeau*, 2010 WL 786217 (N.H.), *3.
135. 2010 WL 1610517 (Tenn. Crim. App.), *4.
136. 105 P.3d 1258, 1263 (Kan. 2005).
137. Id. at 1265.
138. Id. at 1264.
139. Id. at 1263.
140. Id. at 1264.
141. *Spano*, 360 U.S., 323.
142. *Rogers*, 365 U.S., 541.
143. 304 S.E.2d 134, 143 (N.C. 1983).
144. Id. at 143–44.
145. Id. at 144.
146. Id.
147. Id. at 148.
148. Id. at 144.
149. Id. at 153.
150. Id. at 161 (Exum, J., dissenting).
151. Michael Riley, "Greensboro, North Carolina: The Legacy of Segregation," *Time*, June 25, 1990, 10, available at http://www.time.com/time/magazine/article/0,9171,970458,00.html (last visited February 13, 2011).
152. "The Nation in Summary; U.S. Entering Greensboro Case," *New York Times*, March 14, 1982.
153. *Jackson*, 304 S.E. 2d, 163 (Exum, J., dissenting).
154. Seidman, "*Brown* and *Miranda*," 752.
155. Id.
156. Bradley, "Supreme Court Review Behind the Dickerson Decision," 82.
157. Garcia, "Is *Miranda* Dead," 463.
158. Thompson, "Evading *Miranda*," 683.
159. 530 U.S. 428 (2000).

Chapter 10

1. See, e.g., *Berkemer v. McCarty*, 468 U.S. 420, 433 n.20 (1984) (only "rare" cases permit "a colorable argument that a self-incriminating statement was 'compelled' despite the fact that the law enforcement authorities adhered to the dictates of *Miranda*.").
2. Mark A. Godsey, "Shining the Bright Light on Police Interrogation in America," *Ohio State J. Crim. L.* 6 (2009): 730.
3. Leo, *Police Interrogation*, 168.
4. Id. at 173.
5. E-mail, Larry Rosenthal to George Thomas, April 22, 2010.
6. Leo, *Police Interrogation*, 212.
7. Id. at 213.
8. Id.
9. See Innocence Project, "Understand the Causes," available at http://www.innocenceproject.org/understand/ (last visited March 24, 2011).
10. See *State v. Scales*, 518 N.W.2d 587 (Minn. 1994), Westlaw, Citing References. When we examined the references in 2010, over 130 articles had cited *Scales*, which is, we think, a remarkablly large number We do not know how many support recording, but it is probably the majority by far.
11. See David A. Harris, "Picture This: Body-Worn Video Devices (Head Cams) as Tools for Ensuring Fourth Amendment Compliance by Police," *Texas Tech L. Rev.* 43 (2010): 361–63.

12. Leo, *Police Interrogation*, 305–17.
13. White, Miranda's *Waning Protections*, 200–14.
14. Andrew E. Taslitz, Book Review, "*Miranda's* Waning Protections: Police Interrogation Practices After Dickerson by Welsh S. White," *Crim. Justice* 17 (2002): 59.
15. Lawrence Rosenthal, posting to CRIMPROF listserv, April 16, 2010, copy available from George Thomas.
16. 518 N.W.2d 587 (Minn. 1994).
17. E-mail from Brad Colbert to George Thomas, April 15, 2010.
18. Richard A. Leo, "False Confessions: Causes, Consequences, and Solutions," in *Wrongly Convicted: Perspectives on Failed Justice*, eds. Saundra D. Westervelt & John A. Humphrey (New Brunswick, NJ: Rutgers University Press, 2001), 47.
19. Daniel S. Medwed, "Innocentrism," *U. Ill. L. Rev.* 2008 (2008): 1549.
20. 476 U.S. 683, 685 (1986).
21. *Crane v. Commonwealth*, 690 S.W.2d 753, 755 (Ky. 1985).
22. Id. at 757 (Leibson, J., dissenting).
23. *Crane*, 476 U.S., 687.
24. Cloud, et al., "Words Without Meaning."
25. Id. at 545.
26. Wertheimer, *Coercion*, 170–75.
27. Yale Kamisar, "What Is an 'Involuntary' Confession: Some Comments on Inbau's and Reid's *Criminal Interrogation and Confessions*," *Rutgers L. Rev.* 17 (1963): 759.
28. Id. at 759 ("scrap" the "terminology") & 758 ("forbidden police methods").
29. Id. at 748.
30. Id. at 754.
31. Albert W. Alschuler, "Constraint and Confession," *Denv. U. L. Rev.* 74 (1997): 959.
32. Id. at 962.
33. Id. at 957.
34. Id. at 974–76.
35. Godsey, "Rethinking the Involuntary Confession Rule: Toward a Workable Test for Identifying Compelled Self-Incrimination," *Cal. L Rev.* 93 (2005): 515–39.
36. Id. at 518.
37. Id. at 532.
38. Id.
39. E-mail from Lawrence Rosenthal to George Thomas, April 22, 2010.
40. 402 U.S. 183 (1970). We thank Larry Rosenthal, supra note 39, for the idea to base the "external threat" on Justice Harlan's opinion for the Court in *McGautha*.
41. See *McGautha*, 402 U.S., 216–17.
42. 356 U.S. 560, 564–65 (1958).
43. Id. at 567.
44. 372 U.S. 528, 531 (1963). These facts are drawn from Lynum's testimony, but the testimony of one of the officers essentially corroborated her story. See id. at 532.
45. Id. at 534.
46. 365 U.S. 534, 536 (1961).
47. Id. at 541.
48. 360 U.S. 315, 322–23 (1959).
49. Id. at 323.
50. 361 U.S. 199 (1960).
51. Id. at 201.
52. Id.
53. Id. at 207–8.
54. Id. at 208.
55. Id. at 207.
56. Id. (quoting *Spano*, 360 U.S., 320–21).

57. 304 S.E.2d 134 (N.C. 1983).
58. *Rogers*, 365 U.S., 541.
59. 770 N.E.2d 763 (Ind. 2002)
60. 105 P.3d 1258 (Kan. 2005).
61. See, e.g., Alfred W. McCoy, *A Question of Torture: CIA Interrogation, From the Cold War to the War on Terror* (New York: Henry Holt, 2006), 64–65; Tim Weiner, "CIA Taught, Then Dropped, Mental Torture in Latin America," *New York Times*, January 29, 1997.
62. See, e.g., Jane Mayer, "Outsourcing Torture: The Secret History of America's 'Extraordinary Rendition' Program," *The New Yorker*, February 14, 2005, which reported the accounts of Maher Arar (Syrian-Canadian detainee), Dan Coleman (FBI agent), Ibn al-Sheikh al-gLibi (high-ranking Al Qaeda figure), Mohammad Zery (Egyptian asylum-seeker), Ahmed Agiza (Egyptian asylum-seeker), and Mamdouh Habib (Australian radical Muslim).
63. *Arar v. Ashcroft* et al., 585 F.3d 559 (2d Cir. 2009), en banc (affirming the dismissal of Arar's complaint because his claims were insufficiently pleaded). For a comprehensive account of Arar's ordeal, see Mayer, "Outsourcing Terror."
64. Reuters, "Rice Admits U.S. Erred in Deportation," *New York Times*, October 25, 2007.
65. Council of Europe, Committee on Legal Affairs and Human Rights, "Report: Alleged Secret Detentions and Unlawful Inter-state Transfers of Detainees Involving Council of Europe Member States," June 12, 2006, 2, available at http://assembly.coe.int/Documents/WorkingDocs/doc06/edoc10957.pdf (last visited January 31, 2011).
66. See id. at 9, 15–17; European Parliament, "CIA Activities in Europe: European Parliament Adopts Final Report Deploring Passivity from Some Member States," February 19, 2007, available at http://www.libertysecurity.org/article1354.html (last visited January 31, 2011); David Johnston, "At a Secret Interrogation, Dispute Flared Over Tactics," *New York Times*, September 10, 2006 (describing interrogation of Abu Zubaydah in a secret safe house in Thailand); David Johnston & Carl Hulse, "C.I.A. Asks Criminal Inquiry Over Secret-Prison Article," *New York Times*, November 9, 2005 (noting that the "existence of secret detention centers . . . had been previously disclosed" but describing a larger secret prison system that was a "hidden global internment network" that included "black sites" in "several democracies in Eastern Europe") (drawing from article in *The Washington Post*, September 2, 2005).
67. European Parliament Report, "CIA Activities."
68. Rachael Donadio, "Italy Convicts 23 Americans for C.I.A. Renditions," *New York Times*, November 5, 2009.
69. See, e.g., *Zing Sung Wan v. United States* , 266 U.S. 1 (1924).
70. U.S. Const. amend. V.
71. 467 U.S. 649, 656 (1984).
72. Charlie Savage, "Holder Backs a Miranda Limit for Terror Suspects," *New York Times*, May 9, 2010.
73. "F.B.I. Memorandum," *New York Times*, March 25, 2011.
74. "Old Apache Chief Geronimo Is Dead," *New York Times*, February 18, 1909 (noting that he had been prisoner of war since 1886).
75. 538 U.S. 760 (2003).
76. Id. at 798 (Kennedy, J., concurring in part and dissenting in part).
77. Id. at 766 (plurality opinion) (emphases in original).
78. Id. at 778 (Souter, J., concurring in the judgment).
79. Alan M. Dershowitz, *Is There a Right to Remain Silent?* (Oxford: Oxford University Press, 2008), xix.
80. *Chavez*, 538 U.S., 778 (Souter, J., concurring in the judgment).
81. Id. at 779 (Souter, J., concurring in the judgment).
82. Id. (Souter, J., concurring in the judgment).
83. Because the suit would be against the federal government, 42 U.S.C. § 1983 would not be available as it applies only to state actors. But the Supreme Court has created a parallel

federal constitutional tort in *Bivens v. Six Unknown Named Agents of Federal Bureau of Narcotics*, 403 U.S. 388 (1971).

84. Souter, who wrote the concurring opinion that suggested the need for a limiting principle, has retired as has Justice Stevens who joined Justice Kennedy's opinion, concurring in part and dissenting in part.

85. Charlie Savage, "Ghailani Verdict Reignites Debate Over the Proper Court for Terrorism Trials," *New York Times*, November 18, 2010.

86. Id.

87. *Chavez*, 538 U.S., 773 (plurality opinion).

88. *Rochin v. California*, 342 U.S. 165, 166 (1952).

89. Id. at 172.

90. 367 U.S. 643 (1961).

91. Justice Stevens, Justice Kennedy, and Justice Ginsburg seem to leave that question open. See John T. Parry, "Constitutional Interpretation, Coercive Interrogation, and Civil Rights Litigation After Chavez v. Martinez," *Georgia L. Rev* 39 (2005): 756.

92. *Chavez*, 538 U.S., 779–80 (opinion of the Court).

93. *Martinez v. City of Oxnard*, 337 F.3d 1091. 1091 (9th Cir. 2003) (leaving "ultimate resolution of the merits of Martinez's Fourth Amendment claim" to "resolution of contested facts"), cert. denied, *Chavez v. Martinez*, 542 U.S. 953 (2004).

94. *Stoot v. City of Everett*, 582 F.3d 910, 929 (9th Cir. 2009).

95. Id. at 928.

96. Parry, "After *Chavez*," 838.

97. Id. at 831.

98. Id.

99. Dershowitz, *Is There a Right to Remain Silent?* 175–76 (emphasis in original).

100. Hawkins, *A Treatise of the Pleas of the Crown*,6th ed., 1787, vol. 2, 604.

101. *Report of Hiram Maxwell's Case*, 13.

102. Revised Statutes of New York, volume II, §§ 13–19 (1829).

103. See the discussion of the 1881 statute in chapter 4 B. 4.

104. Paul Johnson, *A History of the American People* (New York: Harper Collins, 1999), 441–42.

105. John E. Reid & Associates, "Success with Reid," available at http://www.reid.com/ success_reid/r_success.html, (last visited February 10, 2011).

106. Fred E. Inbau, *Lie Detection and Criminal Interrogation* (Baltimore: Williams & Wilkins, 1942).

107. *Dickerson v. United States*, 530 U.S. 428, 443–44 (2000).

108. 1 Ed. VI, c. 12, § 22 (1547) (spelling modernized).

109. 18 U.S.C. § 2340A. For the definition of torture, see § 2340.

110. Cloud, "Quakers, Slaves and the Founders," 374.

BIBLIOGRAPHY

The bibliography is divided into six categories: constitutions and legislative enactments; books; articles, monographs, and book chapters; reports; newspapers; and other sources, which includes web sites. Cases are cited in the notes and are not listed here.

Constitutions, Statutes, Acts, and Rules

Arkansas, Revised Statutes, c. 45, §§ 31–38 (1838).

Delaware Declaration of Rights, 1776.

England, 11 & 12 Vict., c. 42, para. XVIII (1848).

England, 7 Wm. III c.3 (1695).

England, Act for [the Regulating] the Privie Councell and for taking away the Court commonly called the Star Chamber, Statutes of the Realm, 16 Charles I, c. 10 (1641).

England, Assize of Clarendon (1166).

Georgia Code, 1861, Pt. 3, Tit. 10, Ch. 2, Art. III. § 3716.

Human Rights Act 1998, c. 42.

Illinois Constitution, Art. VI, § 6 (1870).

Illinois, Senate Bill 33, 53d General Assembly, 1923.

Kentucky Revised Statutes §422.110 (1912).

Louisiana, *A General Digest of the Acts of the Legislature of Louisiana passed from the year 1804 to 1827* (L. Moreau Lislet, compiler, 1828).

Maryland, *A Report of All Such English Statutes as existed at the time of the first emigration of the people of Maryland, and which by experience have been found applicable to their local and other circumstances . . .* (William Kilty, compiler, 1811).

Massachusetts Body of Liberties, 1641 c. 26.

Missouri, Revised Statutes, art. II, §§ 13-17 (1835).

New Jersey, *Laws of the State* (New Brunswick, N.J.: printed by Abraham Blauvelt, William Paterson, compiler, 1800).

New Jersey, West, Concessions and Agreements of West New Jersey, 1676, c. 22.

New York, The Second Constitution of New York, 1821, Art. VII, § 7.

New York, Constitution of New York, 1777.

New York, Revised Statutes, vol. 2, part IV, chap. II (Butler & Duer revision, 1829).

New York, Thirty-Sixth Session, 1813, vol. 2, chap. civ., II.

New York, Act of Jan. 30, 1787, ch. 8, 1787.

New York, Tenth Session, c. 1 (1787).

North Carolina Proposal to Congress, August 1, 1788.

Ohio Laws, Chapter I, § 1, 1804; Virginia Laws, Chapter III, § I, 1776.

Pennsylvania Constitution, 1776, c. 1.
Pennsylvania, Act of Feb.11, 1777, Ch. 5, § 3, 1776–77 Pa. Laws 18.
Rhode Island Proposal to Congress, May 29, 1790.
South Carolina, *Statutes at Large* (Thomas Cooper, compiler, 1712).
United States Constitution, Preamble.
United States Constitution, art. III. sect. 3.
United States Constitution, amend. V.
United States Constitution, amend. VI.
United States Constitution, amends. I-IX.
United States Declaration of Independence.
United States, 18 U.S.C. § 2340A (2002).
United States, Ch. 66, 1 Stat. 577 (1798).
United States, 114 Congressional Record 14,155 (1968).
United States, Congressional Globe, 39th Cong., 1st Sess. 1838 (1866).
United States, Congressional Resolution (Aug. 25, 1777), reprinted in Thomas Gilpin, *Exiles in Virginia* (Philadelphia:1848).
United States, Exec. Order No. 13491, Jan. 22, 2009, 74 F.R. 4893.
Virginia, *The Statutes at Large; being a Collection of all the Laws of Virginia from the First Session of the Legislature, in the Year 1619* (New-York: R. & W. & G. Bartow, William Waller Hening, compiler, 1823).
Virginia, *A Collection of All Such Acts of the General Assembly of Virginia of a Public and Permanent Nature, As Are Now In Force* (Richmond: printed by Augustine Davis, 1794).
Virginia General Assembly, Act I, 1662.

Books

Aristotle, *Nichomachean Ethics*, book 3, part 1.
Ashley, Mike, *The Mammoth Book of British Kings & Queens* (New York: Carroll & Graf, 1998).
Babington, Anthony, *The English Bastille: A History of Newgate Gaol and Prison Conditions in Britain 1188–1902* (New York: St. Martin's Press, 1971).
Baker, Liva, *Miranda: Crime, Law and Politics* (New York: Atheneum, 1985).
Bartlett, Robert, *England Under the Norman and Angevin Kings* (Oxford: Clarendon Press, 2000).
Bartlett, Robert, *Trial by Fire and Water: The Medieval Judicial Ordeal* (Oxford: Clarendon Press, 1986).
Beattie, J. M., *Crime and the Courts in England, 1660–1800* (Princeton, N.J.; Princeton University Press, 1986).
Bentham, Jeremy, *Rationale of Judicial Evidence* (London: Hunt and Clarke, 1827).
Blackstone, William, *Commentaries on the Laws of England* (London: University of Chicago Press, 1979).
Blackstone, William, *Commentaries on the Laws of England* (San Francisco: Bancroft-Whitney Company, 1916).
Blackstone, William, *Commentaries on the Laws of England*, Additional Notes by George Sharswood (Philadelphia: J. P. Lippincott Company, 1898).
Bracton, *On the Laws and Customs of England* 346 (George Woodbine, ed.; Samuel Thorne, trans., 1968).
Bradley, Craig M., *The Failure of the Criminal Procedure Revolution*, (Philadelphia: University of Pennsylvania Press, 1993).
Burn, Richard, *The Justice of the Peace, and Parish Officer* (London: Henry Lintot, 1755), vol. 1.
Caryll, John, Reports of Cases (London: Selden Society, 1999), ed. J. H. Baker, vol. 1.
Carte, Gene & Elaine Carte, *Police Reform in the United States: The Era of August Vollmer, 1905–1932* (Berkeley: University of California Press, 1975).
Chitty, J., *A Practical Treatise on the Criminal Law* (London: A. J. Valpy, 1816), vol. 1.
Cogan, Neil H, ed., *The Complete Bill of Rights* (New York: Oxford University Press, 1997).

Coke, Edward, *The Fourth Part of the Institutes of the Laws of England* (London: E. and R. Brooke, Bell-Yard, near Temple Bar, 1797).

Coke, Edward, *The Third Part of the Institutes of the Laws of England* (London: W. Clarke and Sons, 1807).

Conductor Generalis (Albany, New York: E. F. Backus, 1819).

Cortner, Richard C., *A "Scottsboro" Case in Mississippi* (Oxford, Mississippi: University Press of Mississippi, 1986).

Cromartie, Alan, *The Constitutionalist Revolution, An Essay on the History of England, 1450–1642* (Cambridge: Cambridge University Press, 2006).

Davis, John C. B., *The Massachusetts Justice* (Worcester, Massachusetts: Warren Lazell, 1847).

de Toqueville, Alexis, *Democracy in America* (New York: Bantam Books, 2000) (reprint of 1835 edition).

Dershowitz, Alan M., *Is There a Right to Remain Silent?* (Oxford: Oxford University Press, 2008).

Dickens, Charles, *Oliver Twist*, Introduction and Notes by Jill Muller (New York: Barnes & Noble Classics, 2003).

Dickinson, William, *A Practical Exposition of the Law Relative to the Office and Duties of a Justice of the Peace* (London: Reed and Hunter, 1813), vol. 1.

Dickson, Del, ed, *The Supreme Court in Conference (1940-1985)* (Oxford: Oxford University Press, 2001).

Digest of Justinian (Philadelphia: University of Pennsylvania Press, 1985), ed. Theodore Mommsen, trans. Allen Watson.

Dow, George Francis, *Every Day Life in the Massachusetts Bay Colony* (Mineola, New York: Dover Publications, 1988).

Dowdell, E. G., *A Hundred Years of Quarter Sessions: The Government of Middlesex from 1660–1760* (Cambridge: Cambridge University Press, 1932).

Dunlap, John A., *The New York Justice; or a Digest of the Law Relative to Justices of the Peace in the State of New-York* (New York: Isaac Riley, 1815).

Edwards, George C., *A Treatise on the Powers and Duties of Justices of the Peace and Town Officers in the State of New-York under the Revised Statutes with Practical Forms* (Bath, New York: Printed by David Rumsey, 1830).

English Lawsuits From William I to Richard I, (London: Selden Society, 1990), ed., R.C. Van Caenegem, vol. 1.

Faust, Drew Gilpin, *This Republic of Suffering: Death and the American Civil War* (New York: Alfred A. Knopf, 2008).

Fielding, Henry, *An Enquiry into the Causes of the late Increase of Robbers* (London: A. Millar, 1751).

Fielding, John, *Extracts from such of the Penal Laws as Particularly relate to the Peace and Good Order of the Metropolis* (London: H. Woodfall & W. Strahan, 1768).

Fink, Henry Raymond, *The Indian Evidence Act* (Calcutta: Wyman & Co., 1872).

Foss, Edward, Preface, *A Biographical Dictionary of the Judges of England from the Conquest to the Present Time* (Boston: Little Brown, 1870).

Foster, Michael, *A Report of Some Proceedings . . . and Other Crown Cases to Which Are Added Discourses upon a Few Branches of the Crown Law* (Oxford: The Clarendon Press, 1762).

Frank, Jerome, *Courts on Trial* (Princeton: Princeton University Press, 1949).

Friedman, Lawrence M., *A History of American Law* (New York: Simon & Schuster, 2d ed. 1985).

Friedrich Rudorff, Adolf, *Römische Rechtsgeschichte* (Leipzig: Verlag von Bernhard Tauchnitz, 1859).

Gardiner, Samuel Rawson, *What Gunpowder Plot Was* (London: Longmans, Green, and Co., 1897).

George, M. Dorothy, *Life in London in the XVIIIth Century* (New York: A.A. Knopf, 1925).

Gilbert, Sir Geoffrey, *The Law of Evidence* (London: Henry Lintot, Law Printer to the King, 1756).

Goebel, Julius & T. Raymond Naughton, *Law Enforcement in Colonial New York, A Study in Criminal Procedure (1664–1776)* (reprinted, Montclair, N.J.: Patterson Smith, 1970).

Goodman, James, *Stories of Scottsboro* (New York: Vintage Books, 1995).

Graham, Fred P., *The Self–Inflicted Wound* (New York: MacMillan, 1970).

Graham, John A., *Speeches, Delivered at the City-Hall of the City of New-York in the Courts of Oyer and Terminer, Common Pleas, and General Sessions of the Peace* (New York: George Forman, Second Edition, 1812).

Green, Rhodom A. & John W. Lumpkin, *The Georgia Justice* (Milledgeville, Georgia: P. L. & B. H. Robinson, 1835).

Greenleaf, Simon, *A Treatise on the Law of Evidence*, 16th ed., Revised, Enlarged, and Annotated by John Henry Wigmore (Boston: Little Brown, 1899).

Greenleaf, Simon, *A Treatise on the Law of Evidence* (Boston: Charles C. Little & James Brown, 1842).

Grimké, John Fauchereaud, *The South Carolina Justice of Peace* (New-York: T. & J. Swords, Third Edition, 1810).

Hale, Matthew, *The History of the Pleas of the Crown* (Philadelphia: 1st American edition, 1847).

Hale, Matthew, *The History of the Pleas of the Crown* (London: E. and R. Nutt and R. Gosling, 1736).

Harding, Alan, *A Social History of English Law* (Harmondsworth, England: Penguin, 1966).

Hawkins, William, *A Treatise of the Pleas of the Crown; or, A System of the Principal Matters Relating to that Subject, Digested under Proper Heads* (London: Printed for B. Sweet; R. Phenny; A. Maxwell, and R. Stevens and Sons; Lincoln's Inn; Law Booksellers and Publishers; and J. Cumming, Dublin, Eighth Edition, 1824).

Hawkins, William, *A Treatise of the Pleas of the Crown; or, A System of the Principal Matters Relating to that Subject, Digested under Proper Heads* (Dublin: London: Eliz. Lynch) (Sixth Edition, 1788).

Hawkins, William, *A Treatise of the Pleas of the Crown; or, A System of the Principal Matters relating to that Subject, digested under proper Heads* (London: Eliz. Nutt, 1721), vol. 2.

Hening, William Waller, *The New Virginia Justice* (Richmond: J. & G. Cochran, 1820).

Hepworth, Mike & Bryan S. Turner, *Confession: Studies in Deviance and Religion* (London: Routledge & Kegan Paul, 1982).

Hilton, Boyd, *A Mad, Bad, and Dangerous People? England 1783-1846* (Oxford: Clarendon Press, 2006).

Hitchcock, Henry, *The Alabama Justice of the Peace* (Cahawba, Alabama: William B. Allen, 1822).

Hobbes, Thomas, *Leviathan* (London: Penguin Books, 1981) (first published, 1651).

Holmes, Colin, *John Bull's Island: Immigration and British Society 1871-1971*, (London: Macmillan, 1988).

Howell, T.B. and T.J. Howell, *General Index to the Collection of State Trials* (London: Longman, Rees, Orme, Brown & Green et al., 1828).

Hudson, William, "A Treatise of the Court of Star Chamber," in *Collectanea Juridica* (London: E. and R. Brooke, Bell-Yard, Temple-Bar, 1792).

Impey, John, *The Practice of the Office of Sheriff and Undersheriff; Also, the Practice of the Office of Coroner* (London: W. Clarke and Sons, Third Edition, 1812).

Inbau, Fred E., *Lie Detection and Criminal Interrogation* (Baltimore: The Williams & Wilkins Company, 1942).

Johnson, Claudia Durst, *Daily Life in Colonial New England* (Westport, Connecticut: Greenwood Press, 2002).

Johnson, David T., *The Japanese Way of Justice: Prosecuting Crime in Japan* (New York: Oxford University Press, 2002).

Johnson, Marilynn, *Street Justice: A History of Police Violence in New York City* (Beacon Press: Boston, 2003).

Jones, A. H. M., *The Criminal Courts of the Roman Republic and Principate* (Totowa, N. J.: Rowman and Littlefield, 1972).

Joy, Henry H., *On the Admissibility of Confessions and Challenges to Jurors in Criminal Cases in England and Ireland* (Dublin: Andrew Milliken, 1842).

Kidd, W. R., *Police Interrogation* (New York: R. V. Basuino, 1940).

Knott, H. W. Howard, "John Andrew Graham," *Dictionary of American Biography* (New York: Scriber's Sons, 1931), vol. 7.

Langbein, John H., *The Origins of the Adversary Criminal Trial* (Oxford: Oxford University Press, 2003).

Langbein, John H., *Torture and the Law of Proof: Europe and England in the Ancien Regime* (Chicago: The University of Chicago Press, 1976) (2006 edition).

Leach, Thomas, *Cases in Crown Law, Determined by the Twelve Judges, by the Court of King's Bench, and by Commissioners of Oyer and Terminer and General Gaol Delivery* (London: T. Whieldon, 1789).

Lens, Sidney, *The Forging of the American Empire* (London: Pluto Press, 2003).

Leo, Richard A., *Police Interrogation and American Justice* (Cambridge, Mass.: Harvard University Press, 2008).

Levy, Leonard W., *Origins of the Fifth Amendment* (Chicago: Ivan R. Dee, 1999) (first published in 1968).

Livy, Titus, *The War With Hannibal*, Books XXI–XXX of *The History of Rome from its Foundation* (New York: Penguin Classics, 1965).

Locke, John, *Two Treatises of Government and A Letter Concerning Toleration*, (New Haven: Yale University Press, 2003), second treatise, (first published, 1690).

Mailer, Norman, *Advertisements for Myself* (New York: Putnam's, 1959).

McCoy, Alfred W., *A Question of Torture: CIA Interrogation, From the Cold War to the War on Terror* (New York: Henry Holt and Company, 2006).

McCullough, David, *John Adams* (New York: Simon & Schuster, 2001).

McKinney, Mordecai, *The Pennsylvania Justice of the Peace* (Harrisburg, Pennsylvania: E. Guyer, 1839).

Nicholas, Barry, *An Introduction to Roman Law* (Oxford: Clarendon Press, 1962).

O'Gorman, Frank, *The Long Eighteenth Century* (London: Hodder Arnold, 1997).

Perez, Joseph, *The Spanish Inquisition* (New Haven, Connecticut: Yale University Press, 2005).

Pollock, Sir Frederick & Frederick William Maitland, *The History of English Law Before the Time of Edward I*, (Cambridge: Cambridge University Press, 2d ed., 1899).

Schley, William, *A Digest of the English Statutes of Force in the State of Georgia* (1826).

Simon, David, *Homicide, A Year on the Killing Streets* (New York: Houghton, Mifflin, 1991), Ivy Books edition (New York: Ballantine Books, 1991).

Smith, William, *The Justice of the Peace* (New York: J.F. Handley, 1841).

Stanton, Doris M., *English Justice between the Norman Conquest and the Great Charter, 1066-1215* (Philadelphia: The American Philosophy Scholar, 1964).

Starkie, Thomas, *A Practical Treatise on the Law of Evidence and Digest of Proofs in Civil and Criminal Proceedings* (London: J. & W. T. Clarke, 1824), vol. 2.

Staundford, *Les Plees del Coron* (1557).

Stephen, Leslie, *The Life of Sir James Fitzjames Stephen* (London: Smith, Elder, & Co., 1895).

Strachan-Davidson, James. L., *Problems of the Roman Criminal Law* (Oxford: Clarendon Press, 1969).

Stuart, Gary L., *Innocent Until Interrogated: The True Story of the Buddhist Temple Massacre and the Tucson Four* (Tucson, Arizona: University of Arizona Press, 2010).

Thomas III, George C., *The Supreme Court on Trial: How the American Justice System Sacrifices Innocent Defendants* (Ann Arbor, Michigan: University of Michigan Press, 2008).

Tobias, J. J., *Crime and Industrial Society in the 19th Century* (New York: Schocken Books, 1967).

Tobias, J. J., *Urban Crime in Victorian England* (New York: Schocken Books, 1972).

Trevelyan, Raleigh, *Sir Walter Raleigh* (New York: Henry Holt and Company, 2002).

Turner, Edward Raymond *The Privy Council of England in the Seventeenth and Eighteenth Centuries, 1603-1784* (Baltimore: Johns Hopkins Press, 1927).

Ward, A. W., G. W. Prothero, Stanley Leathes, *The Cambridge Modern History* (Cambridge, England: Cambridge University Press, 1903).

Warren, W. L., *Henry II* (Berkeley, Ca.: University of California Press, 1973).

Weisman, Richard, *Witchcraft, Magic, and Religion in 17th-Century Massachusetts* (Amherst, Massachusetts: The University of Massachusetts Press, 1984).

Wertheimer, Alan, *Coercion* (Princeton, N.J.: Princeton University Press, 1987).

White, Welsh S., *Miranda's Waning Protections: Police Interrogation Practices After Dickerson* (Ann Arbor, Michigan: University of Michigan Press, 2001).

Wilson, Theodore Brantner, *The Black Codes of the South* (University, Alabama: University of Alabama Press, 1965).

Wigmore, John Henry, *A Treatise on the Anglo-American System of Evidence in Trials at Common Law* (Boston: Little, Brown, and Company, 1923).

Wigmore, John Henry, *A Treatise on the System of Evidence in Trials at Common Law* (Boston: Little, Brown, and Company, 1904), vol. 1, § 865.

Wittgenstein, Ludwig, *Philosophical Investigations* (Upper Saddle River, New Jersey: Prentice Hall, 1958).

Wood, Gordon S., *The Radicalism of the American Revolution* (New York: Vintage Books, 1991).

Ziegler, Philip, *The Black Death* (New York: Harper & Row, 1969).

Zimring, Franklin E., & Gordon J. Hawkins, *Deterrence: The Legal Threat in Crime Control* (Chicago: University of Chicago Press 1973).

Articles, Monographs, and Book Chapters

Almand, Bond, "The Preparation and Adoption of the Code of 1863," *Ga. B. J* 14 (1951).

Bandes, Susan, "Tracing the Pattern of No Pattern: Stories of Police Brutality," *Loyola L. A. L. Rev.* 34 (2001).

Bandes, Susan, "The Patterns of Injustice: Police Brutality in the Courts," *Buff. L. Rev.* 47 (1999).

Beattie, J. M., "Sir John Fielding and Public Justice: The Bow Street Magistrates' Court, 1754-1780," *L. & Hist. Rev.* 25 (2007).

Benner, Laurence A., "Requiem for *Miranda*: The Rehnquist Court's Voluntariness Doctrine in Historical Perspective," *Wash. U.L.Q.* 67 (1989).

Bradley, Craig M., "Supreme Court Review Behind the Dickerson Decision," *Trial* 36 (2000).

Bradley, Craig M., "The Uncertainty Principle in the Supreme Court," *Duke L.J.* 1986 (1986).

Caplan, Gerald M., "Questioning *Miranda*," *Vand. L. Rev.* 38 (1985).

Cassell, Paul G. & Bret S. Hayman, "Police Interrogation in the 1990s: An Empirical Study of the Effects of Miranda," *UCLA L. Rev.* 43 (1996).

Cassell, Paul G. & Richard Fowles, "Handcuffing the Cops? A Thirty-Year Perspective on *Miranda's* Harmful Effects on Law Enforcement," *Stanford L. Rev.* 50 (1998).

Cassell, Paul G., "Miranda's Social Costs: An Empirical Reassessment," *Nw. U.L.Rev.* 90 (1996).

Cloud, Morgan, "Quakers, Slaves and the Founders: Profiling to Save the Nation," *Miss. L. J.* 73 (2003).

Cloud, Morgan, George B. Shepherd, Alison Nodvin Barkoff, Justin V. Shur, "Word Without Meaning: The Constitution, Confessions, and Mentally Retarded Suspects," *U. Chi. L. Rev.* 69 (2002).

Cohen, Felix, "Transcendental Nonsense and the Functional Approach," *Colum. L. Rev.* 35 (1935).

Dripps, Donald A., "Constitutional Theory for Criminal Procedure: *Dickerson, Miranda,* and the Continuing Quest for Broad-But-Shallow," *Wm. & Mary L. Rev.* 43 (2001).

Dripps, Donald, "Is *Miranda* Caselaw Really Inconsistent: A Proposed Fifth Amendment Synthesis," *Const. Commentary* 17 (2000).

Fehlings, Gregory, "Storm on the Constitution: The First Deportation Law," *Tulsa J. Comp. & Int'l. L.* 10 (2002).

Feld, Barry C., "Juveniles' Competence to Exercise *Miranda* Rights: An Empirical Study of Policy and Practice," *Minn. L. Rev.* 91 (2006).

Garcia, Alfredo, "Is *Miranda* Dead, Was it Overruled, or is it Irrelevant?," *St. Thomas L. Rev.* 10 (1998).

Godsey, Mark A., "Shining the Bright Light on Police Interrogation in America," *Ohio State J. Crim. L.* 6 (2009).

Grisso, Thomas, "Juveniles' Capacities to Waive Miranda Rights: An Empirical Analysis," *Cal. L. Rev.* 68 (1980).

Harris, David A., "Picture This: Body-Worn Video Devices (Head Cams) As Tools for Ensuring Fourth Amendment Compliance by Police", *Texas Tech L. Rev.* 43 (2010).

Herman, Lawrence, "The Unexplored Relationship Between the Privilege Against Compulsory Self-Incrimination and the Involuntary Confession Rule (Part I)," *Ohio St. L.J.* 53 (1992).

Honigsberg, Peter Jan, "Chasing "Enemy Combatants" and Circumventing International Law: A License for Sanctioned Abuse," *UCLA J. International L. & Foreign Affairs*, 12 (2007).

Kamisar, Yale, "How Earl Warren's Twenty-Two Years in Law Enforcement Affected His Work as Chief Justice," *Ohio St. J. Crim. L.* 3 (2005).

Kamisar, Yale, *Criminal Justice in Our Time*, (Charlottesville, Virginia: The University Press of Virginia, 1965), ed. A.E. Dick Howard.

Kamisar, Yale, "What Is An 'Involuntary' Confession: Some Comments on Inbau's and Reid's *Criminal Interrogation and Confessions*," *Rutgers L. Rev.* 17 (1963).

Kauper, Paul G., "Judicial Examination of the Accused—A Remedy for the Third Degree," *Mich. L. Rev.* 30 (1932).

King, Kenneth J., "Waiving Childhood Goodbye: How Juvenile Courts Fail to Protect Children From Unknowing, Unintelligent, and Involuntary Waivers of *Miranda* Rights," Wis. L. Rev. 2006 (2006).

Lain, Corinna Barrett, "Countermajoritarian Hero or Zero? Rethinking the Warren Court's Role in the Criminal Procedure Revolution," *U. Pa. L. Rev.* 152 (2004).

Langbein, John H., "The Origins of Public Prosecution at Common Law," *The American Journal of Legal History*, 17 (1973).

Langbein, John H., "Torture and Plea Bargaining," *U. Chi. L. Rev.* 46 (1978).

Leo, Richard A., Steven A. Drizin, Peter J. Neufeld, Bradley R. Hall, & Amy Vater, "Bringing Reliability Back In: False Confessions and Legal Safeguards in the Twenty-First Century," *Wis. L. Rev.* 2006 (2006).

Leo, Richard A., "False Confessions: Causes, Consequences, and Solutions," in *Wrongly Convicted: Perspectives on Failed Justice* (New Brunswick, NJ: Rutgers University Press, 2001, Saundra D. Westervelt & John A. Humphrey, eds.).

Leo, Richard A., "Inside the Interrogation Room," *J. Crim. L. & Criminology* 86 (1996).

Leo, Richard A., "The Impact of *Miranda* Revisited," *J. Crim. L. & Criminology* 86 (1996).

Llewellyn, Karl, "A Realistic Jurisprudence—The Next Step," *Colum. L. Rev.* 30 (1930).

Malone, Patrick, "'You Have the Right to Remain Silent':*Miranda* After Twenty Years," *American Scholar*, 55 (1986).

Mannheimer, Michael J. Zydney, "Toward a Unified Theory of Testimonial Evidence Under the Fifth and Sixth Amendments," *Temple L. Rev.* 80 (2007).

McCash, William B., "Thomas Cobb and the Codification of Georgia Law," *Georgia Historical Quarterly* 62 (1978).

Medwed, Daniel S., "Innocentrism," *U. Ill. L. Rev.* 2008 (2008).

Medwed, Daniel S., "The Zeal Deal: Prosecutorial Resistance to Post-Conviction Claims of Innocence," *B.U. L. Rev.* 84 (2004).

Miles, William Augustus, *A Letter to Sir John Fielding, Knt., occasioned by His extraordinary Request to Mr. Garrick for the Suppression of the Beggar's Opera* (London: J. Bell, 1773).

Moran, David A., "In Defense of the Corpus Delicti Rule," *Ohio St. L. J.* 64 (2003).

Odegaard, Charles E., "Legalis Homo," *Speculum* 15 (1940).

Oliver, Wesley MacNeil, "Magistrates' Examinations, Police Interrogations, and *Miranda*-Like Warnings in the Nineteenth Century," *Tulane L. Rev.* 81 (2007).

Parry, John T., "Torture Nation, Torture Law," *Geo. L. J.* 97 (2009).

Ramsey, Carolyn B., "In the Sweat Box: A Historical Perspective on the Detention of Material Witnesses," *Ohio St. J. Crim. L.* 6 (2009).

Rosenthal, Lawrence, "Against Orthodoxy: *Miranda* Is Not Prophylactic and the Constitution Is Not Perfect," *Chapman L. Rev.* 10 (2007).

Schulhofer, Stephen J., "Miranda's Practical Effect: Substantial Benefits and Vanishingly Small Social Costs," *Nw. U.L. Rev.* 90 (1996).

Seidman, Louis Michael, *"Brown* and *Miranda," Calif. L. Rev.* 80 (1992).

Seidman, Louis Michael, "Rubashov's Question: Self-Incrimination and the Problem of Coerced Preferences," *Yale J. L. & Humanities* 2 (1990).

Spann, Giradeau A., "Deconstructing the Legislative Veto," *Minn. L. Rev.* 68 (1984).

Stone, Geoffrey, "The Miranda Doctrine in the Burger Court," *Sup. Ct. Rev.* 1977 (1977).

Taslitz, Andrew E., Book Review, *"Miranda's* Waning Protections: Police Interrogation Practices After Dickerson by Welsh S. White," *Crim. Justice* 17 (2002).

Thomas III, George C., "Criminal Trials as Morality Plays: Good and Evil," *St. Louis U. L. Rev* 55 (2011).

Thomas III, George C., "Bigotry, Jury Failures, and the Supreme Court's Feeble Response", *Buffalo L. Rev.* 55 (2007).

Thomas III, George C., "Colonial Criminal Law and Procedure: The Royal Colony of New Jersey 1749-57," *New York University Journal of Law & Liberty* 1 (2005).

Thomas III, George C., "Stories About *Miranda," Mich. L. Rev.*, 102 (2004).

Thomas III, George C., "Separated At Birth But Siblings Nonetheless: *Miranda* And The Due Process Notice Cases," *Mich. L. Rev.* 99 (2001).

Thomas III, George C., "Plain Talk About the *Miranda* Empirical Debate: A "Steady-State" Theory of Confessions, *U.C.L.A. L. Rev.* 43 (1986).

Thompson, Sandra Guerra, "Evading *Miranda*: How *Seibert* and *Patene* Failed to "Save" *Miranda, Val. U. L. Rev.* 40 (2006).

Weisberg, Robert, "Criminal Law, Criminology, and the Small World of Legal Scholars," *U. Col. L. Rev.* 63 (1992).

Weisselberg, Charles D., "Mourning *Miranda," Cal. L. Rev.* 96 (2008).

Wigmore, John H., "Nemo Tenetur Seipsum Prodere," *Harv. L. Rev.* 5 (1891–92).

Reports

Binney, Horace, *Reports of Cases Adjudged in the Supreme Court of Pennsylvania*, v. 3 (1811).

Bybee, Jay S., Assistant Attorney General, U.S. Department of Justice, Office of Legal Counsel, *Memorandum for John Rizzo, Acting General Counsel of the Central Intelligence Agency, Interrogation of al Qaeda Operative*, August 1, 2002.

European Parliament, "CIA Activities in Europe: European Parliament Adopts Final Report Deploring Passivity from Some Member States," February 19, 2007.

New York, "Report of Select Committee on Code of Criminal Procedure, No. 150," In Assembly, Mar. 2, 1855.

New York, "Report of the Select Committee Appointed by the Assembly of 1875 to Investigate the Causes of the Increase of Crime in the City of New York," Rep. No. 106 (1876).

Office of Legal Policy, "Report to the Attorney General on the Law of Pretrial Interrogation," *U. Mich. J. L. Reform* 22 (1988–1989).

United States, Congressional Record, 62d Cong., 1st Sess, Report No. 128 (August 4, 1911).

United States, Congressional Record, 61st Cong., 2d Sess. Report No. 597 (April 26, 1910).

United States, Department of Commerce, Bureau of the Census, Historical Statistics of the United States, 1789–1945, Series B 279-303, Country of Birth of the Foreign-Born Population (Census); 1850–1940.

Newspapers

Barnes, Steve, "Susan McDougal Back in Arkansas for Trial," *The New York Times*, March 9, 1999.

Barry, Ellen, "Rape Suspect Says She Was Fooled Into Confessing," *The New York Times*, June 12, 2007.

Bradford, Gardner, "A Machine That Makes Criminals Confess," *Los Angeles Times*, May 7, 1933.

Davey, Monica, "Judge Rules Report in Chicago Should be Released," *The New York Times,* May 20, 2006.

Donadio, Rachael, "Italy Convicts 23 Americans for C.I.A. Renditions," *The New York Times,* November 5, 2009.

Fitzsimmons, Emma Graves, "Decades Later, Ex-Police Commander in Chicago Goes on Trial in Abuse Cases," *The New York Times,* May 27, 2010.

Graham, Fred P., "High Court Puts New Curb on Powers of the Police to Interrogate Suspects," *The New York Times,* June 14, 1966.

Johnston, David, "At a Secret Interrogation, Dispute Flared Over Tactics," *The New York Times,* September 10, 2006.

Johnston, David & Carl Hulse, "C.I.A. Asks Criminal Inquiry Over Secret-Prison Article," *The New York Times,* November 9, 2005.

Johnston, David & Thom Shanker, "The Reach of War: Detainees; Pentagon Approved Intense Interrogation Techniques for Sept. 11 Suspect at Guantanamo," *The New York Times,* May 21, 2004.

Marshall, Edward, "About Criminals," *The Atlanta Constitution,* September 29, 1894.

Mayer, Jane, "Outsourcing Torture: The Secret History of America's 'Extraordinary Rendition' Program," *The New Yorker,* February 14, 2005.

Mazzetti, Mark, "Threats and Responses: The Intelligence Agency; Questions Raised About Bush's Primary Claims in Defense of Secret Detection System," *The New York Times,* September 8, 2006.

Rudoren, Jodi, "Inquiry Finds Police Abuse, but Says Law Bars Trials," *The New York Times,* July 20, 2006.

Savage, Charlie, "Ghailani Verdict Reignites Debate Over the Proper Court for Terrorism Trials," *The New York Times,* November 18, 2010.

Savage, Charlie, "Holder Backs a Miranda Limit for Terror Suspects," *The New York Times,* May 9, 2010.

Warren, James, "Burge Case Ends With a Prison Sentence and No Little Bit of Wondering," *The New York Times,* January 22, 2011.

Weiner, Tim, "CIA Taught, Then Dropped, Mental Torture in Latin America," *The New York Times,* January 29, 1997.

"Accused of Ten Murders," *The New York Times,* July 26, 1895.

"Accuses Police of 'Third Degree'; Victim Innocent," *Chicago Daily Tribune,* January 30, 1913.

"After 'Third Degree' He Killed Himself," *The Atlanta Constitution,* May 20, 1910.

"Alderman Fights Police Tortures," *Chicago Daily Tribune,* February 2, 1913.

"All About a Rebel Flag: A Violent Controversy Progressing in a Jersey Town," *The New York Times,* July 14, 1890.

"Arkansas Judge Bans Use of 'Torture Chair,'" *The Atlanta Constitution,* November 23, 1929.

"Attack on Priest, "'Black Hand's' Enemy," *The New York Times,* September 20, 1904.

"Backs Story of Haas Beating," *Chicago Daily Tribune,* February 4, 1913.

"Bar Association Shows Interest in Hoyne Aids," *Chicago Daily Tribune,* November 17, 1918.

"Big Bomb Wrecks 5-Story Tenement," *The New York Times,* December 22, 1907.

"'Black Hand' after Baker," *The New York Times,* December 12, 1904.

"'Black Hand' in Murder," *The New York Times,* August 29, 1904.

"Black Hand Now in Staffeldt Murder," *The New York Times,* July 3, 1907.

"Black Hand's Foe Warned," *The New York Times,* May 3, 1909 (Louisiana).

"Blackmail for Merchant," *The New York Times,* October 28, 1910 (Toronto).

"Blew Up the Banana King," *The New York Times,* January 19, 1908 (Maryland).

"Bow Street," *The (London) Times,* February 18, 1831.

"Bow Street," *The (London) Times,* June 8, 1833.

"Boys Tell Torture Tale," *Los Angeles Times,* November 26, 1924.

"Charles Hussey," *The (London) Times,* September 3, 1818.

"Chicago Thieves Identified," *The New York Times,* July 15, 1896.

"Clubbing a Minor Offense," *The New York Times,* October 3, 1894.

"Convict Detective For 'Third Degree,'" *The New York Times*, February 10, 1920.

"Cook's Confession," *The (London) Times*, June 11, 1832.

"Denbighshire Great Sessions," *The (London) Times*, August 21, 1819.

"Execution of Hussey for the Murders at Greenwich," *The (London) Times*, August 4, 1818.

"Execution of John Amy Bird Bell for Murder," *The (London) Times*, August 2, 1831.

"Execution of Patch," *The (London) Times*, April 9, 1806.

"F.B.I. Memorandum, *The New York Times*, March 25, 2011.

"Forced to Confess by 'Third Degree,'" *The Atlanta Constitution*, December 17, 1910.

"'Fourth Degree' Effective," *The New York Times*, August 21, 1929.

"Garrison Sues Police Heads," *Los Angeles Times*, August 14, 1931.

"Glocestershire Assizes," *The (London) Times*, September 9, 1818.

"Holdup Men Kill One More Victim," *Chicago Daily Tribune*, January 6, 1908.

"Hope to Wipe Out Black Hand," *The New York Times*, June 13, 1909 (Ohio, Pennsylvania, West Virginia, Indiana, Illinois).

"Hoyne et al. Sued by Arrest Victim," *Chicago Daily Tribune*, July 31, 1913.

"Hoyne Friction? 4 Aids Out; One Sweitzer Friend," *Chicago Daily Tribune*, May 4, 1919.

"Hussey's Confession," *The (London) Times*, August 22, 1818.

"Hussey's Confession," *The (London) Times*, August 10, 1818..

"In Behalf of the Rack," *The New York Times*, May 19, 1877.

"Inquisition Method Hit By Speaker," *Los Angeles Times*, January 27, 1929.

"Inventor Tells the Truth About His Lie Detector," *Chicago Daily Tribune*, September 13, 1932.

"Is 'the Black Hand' a Myth or a Terrible Reality?," *The New York Times*, March 3, 1907.

"Is the 'Third Degree' Justified?," *The Atlanta Constitution*, July 5, 1909.

"Judge Scores 'Third Degree,'" *Los Angeles Times*, December 4, 1910.

"Jury Fails to Agree; Mob Hangs Negro," *The New York Times*, March 18, 1901.

"Lowden Vetoes 52 Measures As Assembly Ends," *Chicago Daily Tribune*, June 30, 1917.

"Lynchers May Go Scot Free," *The New York Times*, January 17, 1901.

"Man Shot Five Times; Wounding of Janitor by a Tenant in Dispute Over 25 Cents Excites a Mob of Italians," *The New York Times*, May 13, 1901.

"Mansion House—Late Robbery at Grantham," *The (London) Times*, August 25, 1815.

"Mob Threatens Mrs. Nation," *The New York Times*, January 27, 1901.

"More Kansas Saloons Fall Under the Axe," *The New York Times*, January 31, 1901.

"Mrs. Nack's Story Told," *The New York Times*, November 11, 1897.

"Mrs. Nation Begins Her Crusade Anew," *The New York Times*, January 22, 1901.

"Mrs. Nation Horsewhipped," *The New York Times*, January 25, 1901.

"Must Stop Outrages by the Black Hand," *The New York Times*, January 26, 1908.

"Negro Dies at the Stake: Florida Mob Pours Oil on Him and Applies a Match," *The New York Times*, May 29, 1901.

"Negro Dies at the Stake: Fred Alexander Dragged from Leavenworth Jail by a Mob," *The New York Times*, January 15, 1901.

"New Ban on Third Degree," *Los Angeles Times*, December 20, 1928.

"New York Officials Deny Being Brutal," *The New York Times*, August 11, 1931.

"Obituaries," *New York Times*, July 10, 1971.

"Officers Hang Alleged Bandit," *Los Angeles Times*, April 23, 1915.

"Old Apache Chief Geronimo Is Dead," *The New York Times*, February 18, 1909.

"Parricide, Execution of Channel and Chalcraft for the Murder of Channel's Family," *The (London) Times*, August 15, 1818.

"Petrosino's Slayer Working as a Miner," *The New York Times*, January 9, 1910.

"Picking Pockets," *The (London) Times*, October 29, 1807.

"Playing Poker with a Nigger," *The Western Mirror* (Cambridge City, Indiana), February 1, 1866.

"Police," *The (London) Times*, August 29, 1816.

"Police Methods Assailed," *Los Angeles Times*, May 30, 1925.

"Prayer Precedes a Lynching," *The New York Times*, March 3, 1901.

"Prisoner Charges Brutality By Police," *The New York Times*, September 18, 1929.

"Probing the 'Third Degree,'" *The Atlanta Constitution*, May 15, 1910.

"Providential Discovery of a Most Barbarous Murder," *The (London) Times*, January 23, 1830.

"Quiz of Alleged Third Degree in Office of Hoyne," *Chicago Daily Tribune*, November 30, 1918.

"Rice Admits U.S. Erred in Deportation," *The New York Times*, October 25, 2007.

"Saloon Raiders Kill Woman," *The New York Times*, February 20, 1901.

"Seeks Death After Sweat," *Chicago Daily Tribune*, August 10, 1907.

"Senator Pierantoni Talks of Black Hand," *The New York Times*, September 14, 1910.

"She Shot a Chinaman," *Chicago Daily Tribune*, November 13, 1888.

"Statues to the Rebel Dead," *The New York Times*, February 21, 1881.

"Store Wrecked by Bomb," *The New York Times*, November 26, 1907; "Black Hand Plants Bomb,"
    id., July 17, 1907.

"Suit Case Mystery Solved by Confession," *The New York Times*, November 3, 1905.

"Superintendent Walling: His Trial Before the Police Board," *New York Times*, Mar. 13, 1875.

"Supreme Court Justices Denounce 'Third Degree,'" *The New York Times*, July 20, 1902.

"Suspect Tells Third Degree," *Los Angeles Times*, March 25, 1932.

"Sweated Four Days; Sues Hoyne." *Chicago Daily Tribune*, August 2, 1913.

"That Rebel Geography," *The New York Times*, December 8, 1889.

"The Ashburn Murder Case," *The (Atlanta) Constitution*, September 13, 1868.

"The Ashburn Murder," *The New York Times*, September 12, 1868.

"The Ashburn Murder," *The New York Times*, July 21, 1868.

"The Nation in Summary; U.S. Entering Greensboro Case," *The New York Times*, March 14, 1982.

"The Navy at Fort Fisher: Brooklyn Children See the Stars and Bars," *The New York Times*, May 19, 1894.

"The Police Inquisition,"*The New York Times*, July 6, 1897.

"The Third Degree," *Los Angeles Times*, March 13, 1926.

"'The Third Degree,'" *The New York Times*, April 17, 1910.

"Thieves Used Ether to Stupefy Victims," *The New York Times*, June 22, 1907.

"Third Degree Condemned," *Los Angeles Times*, December 10, 1910.

"Third Degree in Police Parlance," *The New York Times*, October 6, 1901.

"'Third Degree' Made a Science," *Los Angeles Times*, December 17, 1910.

"Third-Degree Methods Fail," *Los Angeles Times*, March 9, 1917.

"'Third Degree' Put Under Ban," *The Atlanta Constitution, July* 4, 1907.

"'Third Degree' Talked into Senate Discard," *Chicago Daily Tribune*, May 14, 1923.

"To Abolish the Third Degree," *The New York Times*, July 6, 1902.

"Torture to Force Confession," *The New York Times*, June 24, 1909.

"Tortured by 'Third Degree' into Confessing Murder," *The Atlanta Constitution*, April 8, 1910.

"Torturers' Manifesto," *The New York Times*, April 19, 2009.

"Torturing a Prisoner," *Chicago Daily Tribune*, August 15, 1902.

"Trim Assizes," *The (London) Times*, July 28, 1815.

"U.S. Bar Committee Decries 'Third Degree,'" *Chicago Daily Tribune*, August 16, 1913.

"Unveil Petrosino Monument," *The New York Times*, March 14, 1910.

"Wants Rowan Off Force," *The New York Times*, March 7, 1920.

"Warrants for Four Cops on 'Third Degree' Charge,"*Chicago Daily Tribune*, April 21, 1921.

"White House Shut to Carrie Nation," *The New York Times*, January 31, 1907.

"Woman and Girl Torn by a Bomb," *The New York Times*, June 4, 1907.

"Woman Principal Rebuked," *The New York Times*, April 20, 1902.

"Women Launch Police Inquiry," *Los Angeles Times*, May 6, 1927.

Other Sources

"60 Minutes," transcript, air date September 20, 2002.

1968 Presidential General Election Results, available at http://uselectionatlas.org/RESULTS/
    national.php?year=1968. (last visited February 10, 2011).

Blanchfield, Deidre, "Public Executions in Nineteenth Century England," available at http://www.umd.umich.edu/casl/hum/eng/classes/434/geweb/PUBLICEX.htm (last visited July 20, 2008).

Byrnes, Thomas F., "Historical Timeline in Investigation," available at http://www.criminology.fsu.edu/faculty/nute/history.html (last visited February 11, 2011).

Byrnes, "Thomas F. Byrnes," Wikipedia, available at http://en.wikipedia.org/wiki/Thomas_F._Byrnes (last visited February 11, 2011).

Center for Disease Control, HIV/AIDS, Basic Statistics, "HIV Incidence Estimate," available at http://www.cdc.gov/hiv/topics/surveillance/basic.htm#incidence (last visited March 23, 2011).

Cohn, Raymond L., "Immigration to the United States," tbl. 1, EH.Net, available at http://eh.net/encyclopedia/article/cohn.immigration.us (last visited January 27, 2011).

Colbert, Brad, email to George Thomas, April 15, 2010, available from George Thomas.

Council of Europe, Committee on Legal Affairs and Human Rights, "Report: Alleged Secret Detentions and Unlawful Inter-state Transfers of Detainees Involving Council of Europe Member States," June 12, 2006..

Crime and Justice Atlas 2000, "United States Index Crime Rate, 1933–1998.

"Criminal Justice in Crisis, A Report to the American People and The American Bar on Criminal Justice in the United States: Some Myths, Some Realities, and Some Questions for the Future.

Doors, "Roadhouse Blues," on *Morrison Hotel* (Electra Records 1970).

Emsley, Clive, "Crime and the Victorians," in BBC's *British History, Victorians* (2001), available at http://www.bbc.co.uk/history/british/victorians/crime_01.shtml (last visited March 23, 2011).

European Parliament, "CIA Activities in Europe: European Parliament Adopts Final Report Deploring Passivity from Some Member States," February 19, 2007, available at http://www.libertysecurity.org/article1354.html (last visited January 31, 2011).

FBI, History, A Brief History of the FBI, Lawless Years: 1921–1933, available at http://www.fbi.gov/about-us/history/brief-history (last visited February 8, 2011).

FBI, "Organized Crime, Italian Organized Crime—Overview," available at http://www.fbi.gov/hq/cid/orgcrime/lcnindex.htm (last visited January 29, 2011).

Gibson, Campbell, "Population Density of the 100 Largest Cities and Other Urban Places in the United States: 1790-1990," Population Division, U.S. Bureau of the Census.

"Great Fire of London," *New World Encyclopedia.*

GTMO, Counterterroism Division (CTD), Inspection Special Inquiry, 09/02/2004, Case ID # 297-HQ-A1327669-A, Responses, 10, available at http://foia.fbi.gov (last visited March 17, 2011).

Haynes, William J., "Enemy Combatants," Council on Foreign Relations, December 12, 2002, available at http://www.cfr.org/international-law/enemy-combatants/p5312 (last visited February 12, 2011).

London, "Greater London, Inner London & Outer London, Population & Density History," available at http://www.demographia.com/dm-lon31.htm (last visited January 27, 2011).

"Measuring Worth: Six Ways to Compute the Relative Value of a U.S. Dollar, 1774 to Present," available at http://www.measuringworth.com/ppowerus/ (last visited February 11, 2011).

Mikkelsen, Randall, "U.S. Attorney General Holder," March 2, 2009, available at http://www.reuters.com/article/2009/03/02/us-usa-security-waterboarding-idUSTRE5213OE20090302?feedType=RSS&feedName=topNews (last visited March 17, 2011).

Muhlberger, Steven ,Medieval England, Wessex Conquers England, available at http://www.the-orb.net/textbooks/muhlberger/wessex.html (last visited February 12, 2011)).

Old Bailey, "A Population History of London, 1815–1860," available at http://www.oldbaileyonline.org/static/Population-history-of-london.jsp#a1815–1860 (last visited February 17, 2011).

Old Bailey, "A Population History of London, 1760–1815," available at http://www.oldbaileyonline.org/static/Population-history-of-london.jsp#a1760–1815 (last visited January 7, 2011).

Old Bailey, "History of The Old Bailey Courthouse: London's Central Criminal Court," 1673–1834, available at http://www.oldbaileyonline.org/static/The-old-bailey.jsp (last visited February 21, 2010).

Reid, John E. & Associates, "Success with Reid," available at http://www.reid.com/success_reid/r_success.html (last visited 02/10/2011).

Riley, Michael, "Greensboro, North Carolina The Legacy of Segregation," Time, June 25, 1990, at 10, available at http://www.time.com/time/magazine/article/0,9171,970458,00.html (last visited 02/13/2011).

Rosenthal. Lawrence, email to George Thomas, April 22, 2010, available from George Thomas

Rosenthal, Lawrence, posting to CRIMPROF listserv, April 16, 2010, copy available from George Thomas.

Seipp, David J., Legal History: The Year Books, Medieval English Legal History, An Index and Paraphrase of Printed Year Book Reports, 1268–1535 (Seipp's Abridgement), available at http://www.bu.edu/law/faculty/scholarship/yearbooks/. (last visited February 13, 2011).

Seipp, David J., email to Paul Axel-Lute, Deputy Director and Collection Development Librarian, Rutgers, University Library for the Center for Law & Justice, October 20, 2006.

U.S. Bureau of the Census, "Population of the 46 Urban Places: 1810," tbl. 4, available at http://www.census.gov/population/www/documentation/twps0027/tab04.txt (last visited January 7, 2011).

U.S. Department of Justice, National Institute of Justice, Office of Justice Programs, Crime and Justice Atlas 2000, "United States Murder Rate, 1900–1998," available at http://www.jrsa.org/programs/Crime_Atlas_2000.pdf (last visited February 1, 2011).

U.S. Department of Justice, Office of Justice Programs, Bureau of Justice Statistics, "Key Facts at a Glance, Four Measures of Serious Violent Crime, Total Violent Crime," available at http://bjs.ojp.usdoj.gov/content/glance/tables/4meastab.cfm (last visited March 18, 2011).

Weather History @ Weather.Org, "History for Washington, DC, Monday, June 13, 1966," available at http://weather.org/weatherorg_records_and_averages.htm (last visited March 24, 2011).

Year Books, various cases, Seipp trans., available at http://www.bu.edu/phpbin/lawyearbooks/search.php.

INDEX